PAVLOVA
PG. 181

LADIES' HOME
JOURNAL®

Recipes
2001

Ladies' Home Journal® Books
Des Moines, Iowa

Ladies' Home Journal® Books
An Imprint of Meredith® Books

LADIES' HOME JOURNAL®
Recipes 2001

Project Editor: Carrie Holcomb Mills
Contributing Project Editor: Kelly Staikopoulos
Contributing Editors: Sarah P. Basso,
    Spectrum Communication Services
Contributing Writer: Cynthia Pearson
Art Director: Richard Michels
Contributing Graphic Designer:
    Kimberly B. Zarley
Copy Chief: Terri Fredrickson
Editorial Operations Manager: Karen Schirm
Production Director: Douglas M. Johnston
Book Production Managers: Pam Kvitne,
    Marjorie J. Schenkelberg

Contributing Copy Editor: Kim Catanzarite
Proofreaders: Dan Degen, Gretchen Kauffman,
    Elizabeth Duff Popplewell
Indexer: Elizabeth Parson
Electronic Production Coordinator:
    Paula Forest
Editorial and Design Assistant: Mary Lee Gavin

MEREDITH® BOOKS
Editor in Chief: James D. Blume
Design Director: Matt Strelecki
Managing Editor: Gregory H. Kayko
Executive Food Editor: Jennifer Dorland Darling

LADIES' HOME JOURNAL®
MAGAZINE
Editor in Chief: Myrna Blyth
Managing Editor: Carolyn Noyes
Recipe Developers: Cynthia DePersio,
    Paul Piccuito
Consumer Marketing Director: Beth von Linden

MEREDITH PUBLISHING GROUP
President, Publishing Group:
    Stephen M. Lacy

MEREDITH CORPORATION
Chairman and Chief Executive Officer:
    William T. Kerr
Chairman of the Executive Committee:
    E. T. Meredith III

COVER PHOTOGRAPH:
Chocolate Nut Tart
(see recipe, page 214)
Photographer: Alan Richardson

HAM AND
CHEESE OMELET
PG. 55

All of us at Meredith® Books are dedicated to providing you with the information and ideas you need to create delicious foods. We welcome your comments and suggestions. Write to us at: Meredith® Books, Food Editorial Department, 1716 Locust St., Des Moines, IA 50309-3023.

If you would like to order additional copies of this book, call 1-800-439-4119.

SPRING LASAGNE
PG. 104

Table of Contents

SHRIMP WITH
ASPARAGUS
AND BARLEY
PG. 102

Recipes
2001

SOYFUL
SCALLOPED
POTATOES
PG. 116

Welcome back to the LHJ kitchen

MYRNA BLYTH

We're delighted to invite you inside the Ladies' Home Journal Kitchen for another year of great cooking—and eating. We create every recipe with the needs of your busy life in mind, and in this, our third annual cookbook, you'll find more than 300 recipes for quick and delicious weeknight meals, entrees that help you entertain with style and ease, holiday favorites, desserts to die for and lots more!

Each recipe is triple-tested in our kitchen so that the very first time you try a recipe, it will be worry-free. Plus, our food editors' insider tips and innovative techniques help you cook just like the pros do—with confidence and great results.

We hope you enjoy making this collection of recipes as much as we did. See you in the kitchen.

Myrna Blyth • Editor-in-Chief

Recipes
2001

classic recipes

Whether you're whipping up a homecoming dinner, hosting a brunch bash or simply making a meal to enjoy, count on these classic recipes for rave reviews. Choose from this collection of updated, enduring favorites for recipes with proven taste and appeal.

VEGETABLE
SALAD
PG. 25

heaven tickles
                    the tongue...

BANANA-NUT
BREAD
PG. 26

BUTTERFLY
COOKIES
(PALMIERS)
PG. 29

...with sensations of
sweet indulgence

DELICATE
COCONUT CAKE
PG. 31

something
savory,
something new
in gnocchi

GNOCCHI
A LA ROMAINE
PG. 15

POACHED
SALMON WITH
GREEN SAUCE
PG. 17

pissaladière

This classic French appetizer is a flaky tartlike pizza.

Prep time: 50 minutes plus rising • Baking time: 15 minutes

DOUGH:

- 1 package active dry yeast
- ½ cup warm water (105°F. to 115°F.)
- ⅛ teaspoon sugar
- ¾ cup milk
- 2 tablespoons olive oil
- 1½ teaspoons salt
- 3 to 3¼ cups all-purpose flour, divided

TOPPING:

- ¼ cup plus 2 tablespoons olive oil
- 4 cups sliced onions
- ¼ teaspoon dried thyme
- ⅛ teaspoon salt
- ⅛ teaspoon freshly ground pepper
- 2 large garlic cloves
- 2 cans (2 oz. each) flat anchovy fillets, packed in oil, drained, divided
- ½ cup freshly grated Parmesan cheese, divided
- ½ cup niçoise olives or pitted black olives
- Fresh thyme sprigs, for garnish (optional)

1. *Make dough:* Stir yeast, warm water and sugar in a large bowl and let stand 5 minutes, until bubbly. Blend milk, oil and salt into yeast mixture.

2. Gradually stir 3 cups of the flour into yeast mixture. On a lightly floured surface, knead dough 8 to 10 minutes, until smooth and elastic, gradually adding remaining ¼ cup flour as necessary.

3. Grease a large bowl. Gather dough into a ball. Place in prepared bowl, turning once. Cover and let rise in a warm, draft-free place until doubled in bulk, about 1½ hours. Shape and use immediately or punch down dough and refrigerate up to 1 hour.

4. *Make topping:* Meanwhile, heat ¼ cup of the olive oil in a large skillet over medium heat. Add onions and cook 30 minutes, until very tender, stirring frequently as the onions begin to brown. Remove from heat and add thyme, salt and pepper. Cool. Chop the garlic; add 6 of the anchovies and finely chop. Transfer to a small bowl and stir in remaining 2 tablespoons oil; set aside. Cut remaining anchovies into thin strips.

5. Adjust oven rack to middle position. Place a heavy cookie sheet on rack. Heat oven to 450°F. for 10 minutes. Remove from oven; brush sheet with oil. Let stand at room temperature 10 minutes. Meanwhile, roll dough into a 12-inch square on a lightly floured surface. Place on warm cookie sheet. Spread anchovy mixture evenly over dough. Layer with ¼ cup of the Parmesan, onions, olives, then remaining ¼ cup Parmesan. Top with anchovy strips and thyme sprigs, if desired. Bake 15 minutes, until crust is golden. Cut into squares. Makes 3 dozen.

Per appetizer: 85 calories, 4 g total fat, 1 g saturated fat, 3 mg cholesterol, 204 mg sodium, 9 g carbohydrates, 2 g protein, 29 mg calcium, 1 g fiber

onion rings

These golden rings are positively addictive!

Prep time: 15 minutes plus standing
Cooking time: 3 minutes per batch

- 1 large sweet onion (1¼ lbs.)
- ½ cup milk
- 1½ cups all-purpose flour
- Salt
- ⅛ teaspoon freshly ground pepper
- Vegetable oil, for frying

1. Slice onion into ¼-inch slices; separate slices into rings. Toss rings with milk in a large bowl. Combine flour, ¾ teaspoon salt and the pepper.

2. Heat 2 inches oil to 375°F. on a deep-fry thermometer in a heavy, large pot or deep fryer.

3. Meanwhile, drain onions, reserving milk. Dip rings, a few at a time, in flour mixture. Dip in reserved milk, then again in flour. Arrange in a single layer on a plate; let stand 30 minutes. Carefully transfer a few rings to hot oil; fry 3 minutes, until golden. Remove with tongs, allowing excess oil to drip back into pot. Transfer to a double layer of paper towels to drain. Sprinkle with additional salt. Repeat dipping and frying remaining rings, allowing oil to return to 375°F. between batches. Makes about 3 dozen rings.

Per onion ring: 40 calories, 2 g total fat, 0.5 g saturated fat, 0 mg cholesterol, 51 mg sodium, 5 g carbohydrates, 1 g protein, 8 mg calcium, 0 g fiber

fry it up

Many of our appetizers are deep fried, which requires a heavy Dutch oven or deep-fat fryer filled with 3 to 4 cups of vegetable oil. (Do not use butter or olive oil.)

Be sure to allow time to heat the oil to the proper temperature, about 375°F. If you don't have a deep-fat thermometer, drop a cube of white bread into the heated oil. If the oil is ready, bubbles will immediately appear around the bread, which will brown within 60 seconds. If the oil is not hot enough, the food will absorb too much oil and become greasy.

A good rule of thumb is to fry food in batches so the pan never gets crowded and the oil does not cool down. Turn the food constantly with a large metal slotted spoon or spatula and fry until evenly golden. Transfer the pieces to a jelly-roll pan lined with paper towels and keep them warm in a low oven (200°F.).

Deep-fried appetizers are best served immediately, while they are still piping hot and crisp.

crab cakes with two sauces

A stand-out appetizer on their own, these fabulous crab cakes are unforgettable with the addition of two tangy sauces.

Prep time: 50 minutes plus chilling
Cooking time: 4 to 6 minutes per batch

- ⅔ cup mayonnaise
- 2 large egg yolks
- 4 teaspoons dry mustard
- 2 tablespoons chopped fresh tarragon or 1 teaspoon dried tarragon
- 2 teaspoons Worcestershire sauce
- 1 teaspoon crab boil (Old Bay) seasoning

- ½ teaspoon salt
- ¼ teaspoon freshly ground pepper
- ¼ teaspoon hot red pepper sauce
- 2 pounds cooked fresh lump or jumbo crabmeat, flaked and picked over
- 2½ cups fresh bread crumbs
- 3 tablespoons vegetable oil, divided
  Creole Mustard Sauce and Celery Root Rémoulade (recipes follow)

1. Combine mayonnaise, egg yolks, mustard, tarragon, Worcestershire sauce, crab boil seasoning, salt, pepper and red pepper sauce in a large bowl. Carefully fold in crabmeat.

2. Spread bread crumbs on 2 cookie sheets. Drop crab mixture by tablespoonfuls on top of crumbs. Shape into small cakes; roll in crumbs to coat evenly. Chill 1 hour.

3. Heat 1 tablespoon of the oil in a 12-inch nonstick skillet over medium heat. Cook cakes in 3 batches 2 to 3 minutes per side, until golden, adding 1 tablespoon of the oil per batch. Transfer to paper towels to drain. *(Can be made ahead. Cool. Cover and refrigerate up to 24 hours. Reheat on cookie sheets in a 375°F. oven 15 minutes.)* Arrange crab cakes on a warm serving platter. Serve with sauces. Makes about 58 appetizers.

Per appetizer without sauce: 45 calories, 3 g total fat, 0.5 g saturated fat, 28 mg cholesterol, 108 mg sodium, 1 g carbohydrates, 3 g protein, 17 mg calcium, 0 g fiber

creole mustard sauce

This spicy sauce gets its kick from the addition of either jalapeño or red pepper sauce, whichever you have on hand. Set more of the sauce on the table when it's time to serve. Those who like things hot, hot, hot will thank you.

Total prep time: 15 minutes

- 1 cup mayonnaise
- 1 seeded and minced jalapeño chile (see tip, page 92) or 5 drops hot red pepper sauce
- ⅓ cup finely diced red bell pepper
- 2 tablespoons Dijon mustard
- 2 tablespoons chopped fresh chives

Combine mayonnaise, jalapeño, bell pepper, mustard and chives in a medium bowl. *(Can be made ahead. Cover and refrigerate up to 24 hours.)* Makes about 1½ cups.

Per tablespoon: 70 calories, 7.5 g total fat, 1 g saturated fat, 3 mg cholesterol, 57 mg sodium, 0 g carbohydrates, 0 g protein, 2 mg calcium, 0 g fiber

celery root rémoulade (EASY)

Look for small firm roots when buying celeriac, also called celery root. This brown knobby edible is the root of a special celery.

Total prep time: 10 minutes

- ½ **cup mayonnaise**
- ¼ **cup chopped fresh chives**
- 2 **tablespoons Dijon mustard**
- 2 **tablespoons fresh lemon juice**
  Pinch salt
  Pinch freshly ground pepper
- 3 **cups coarsely grated celeriac (celery root) or celery**

Combine mayonnaise, chives, mustard, lemon juice, salt and pepper in a medium bowl. Add celeriac and stir until coated. *(Can be made ahead. Cover and refrigerate up to 24 hours.)* Makes about 2 cups.

Per tablespoon: 30 calories, 3 g total fat, 0.5 g saturated fat, 1 mg cholesterol, 43 mg sodium, 2 g carbohydrates, 0 g protein, 8 mg calcium, 0 g fiber

buffalo chicken wings (EASY)

This zesty chicken appetizer may have originated in New York, but it's a favorite from coast to coast. No need for frying here; the wings are roasted to extra-crisp perfection.

Prep time: 20 minutes plus chilling • Roasting time: 1 hour

BLUE CHEESE DIP:
- ½ **cup sour cream**
- ½ **cup mayonnaise**
- 2 **ounces blue cheese, crumbled**
- 1 **green onion, thinly sliced**
- ½ **teaspoon minced garlic**
- ¼ **teaspoon salt**
- ¼ **teaspoon freshly ground pepper**
  •
- 4 **pounds chicken wings (about 18), tips trimmed**

SAUCE:
- 5 **tablespoons hot red pepper sauce**
- 2 **tablespoons butter or margarine, melted**
- 2 **teaspoons cider vinegar**
  •
- 8 **celery ribs, cut into 3-inch sticks**

1. *Make blue cheese dip:* Combine sour cream, mayonnaise, blue cheese, onion, garlic, salt and pepper in a medium bowl. Refrigerate at least 1 hour or overnight. Makes 1¼ cups.

2. Adjust oven rack to upper third of oven. Heat oven to 400°F. Cut each wing into 2 pieces at the joint. Line a roasting pan with foil; place a flat rack over foil.

3. *Make sauce:* Combine pepper sauce, butter and vinegar. Set aside 4 tablespoons of the sauce; toss remaining sauce with wing pieces in a large bowl. Arrange pieces in a single layer on rack in prepared pan.

4. Roast wing pieces 30 minutes. Turn wing pieces over, brush with 2 tablespoons reserved sauce and roast 30 minutes more, until crispy. Brush with remaining 2 tablespoons sauce; serve with blue cheese dip and celery sticks. Makes 8 servings.

Per serving: 320 calories, 29 g total fat, 8.5 g saturated fat, 89 mg cholesterol, 435 mg sodium, 3 g carbohydrates, 13 g protein, 72 mg calcium, 1 g fiber

beef: what makes the cut

Many cuts of beef are available. This guide helps you determine what's what.

CENTER CUTS from the short loin and rib section of the animal are the most tender because they are suspension muscles that receive little exercise. Because center cuts are so tender, dry heat cooking is the way to go.

CENTER-CUT PREMIUM ROASTS (rib, rib eye and tenderloin) are costly. You might want to save them for special occasions. The less pricey and leaner everyday roasts are taken from the round and bottom sirloin.

CENTER-CUT PREMIUM STEAKS include T-bone, porterhouse and rib eyes. These pricier steaks are best cooked using dry heat, as are the more affordable tender steaks, such as top sirloin. Less tender steaks (full-cut round, top round, eye round and bottom round; chuck shoulder, arm and blade; flank and skirt) are well suited to marinades.

FRONT AND REAR CUTS include chuck (chuck eye roast, pot roasts, short ribs), brisket, shank and round. Since they're taken from the front and back, they are the much-exercised muscles, and therefore less tender, requiring moist heat cooking.

POT ROASTS, cut from the chuck as opposed to the round, have more fat and flavor. Beef round roasts suited to pot roast recipes include boneless round rump roast, bottom round roast, eye round roast and round tip roast.

BEEF BRISKET is a boneless cut from the breast of the animal. Brisket comes fresh and corned. Different cuts include whole brisket, point half and point-cut brisket, flat half (also known as thick cut), flat-cut brisket and middle-cut brisket. Look for the flat half (a.k.a. first cut or thin cut) for a less fatty cut.

beef rib roast

When it comes to beef, prime rib reigns as the king of cuts. Whether you prefer the medium-rare center or crisp, browned edges, this glorious dish satisfies everyone who lives in your castle.

Prep time: 10 minutes plus standing
Roasting time: 1¾ to 2¼ hours

  1 **beef rib roast, trimmed and tied (6 ribs, about 12 lbs. total)**
  1 **teaspoon vegetable oil**
  4 **teaspoons kosher salt**
  1 **teaspoon freshly ground pepper**
AU JUS (Sauce):
  1½ **cups water**
  ¾ **cup red wine**
  ½ **teaspoon kosher salt**
  ¼ **teaspoon freshly ground pepper**

1. One hour before roasting, remove beef from refrigerator. Heat oven to 450°F. Rub ends of beef with oil; place in a roasting pan, fat side up. Sprinkle with salt and pepper. Insert an ovenproof-dial meat thermometer so tip is centered in thickest part of rib roast, not resting in fat or touching bone. (This thermometer will remain in the roast during the entire roasting time.)

2. Roast 5 minutes. Reduce oven temperature to 375°F. and roast 1¾ to 2¼ hours (9 to 12 minutes per pound), until meat thermometer registers 140°F. for medium-rare. (If you're using an instant-read meat thermometer, insert the metal shaft into the thickest part of the roast, at least 2 inches into the meat. Let stand 20 seconds.)

3. Transfer roast to a serving platter; cover and keep warm. Let stand 15 minutes before carving. (Temperature will continue to rise 5°F. to 10°F. while standing.)

4. Meanwhile, add water and wine to roasting pan. Bring to boil, scraping up browned bits from bottom; simmer 3 minutes. Skim off fat. Season au jus with salt and pepper. Strain through a sieve. Makes 1¾ cups. Serve with roast. Makes 12 servings.

Per 3 ounces beef with 2 tablespoons gravy: 240 calories, 13 g total fat, 5 g saturated fat, 78 mg cholesterol, 581 mg sodium, 0 g carbohydrates, 27 g protein, 10 mg calcium, 0 g fiber

new england boiled dinner

Use cabbage for a traditional take on this dish. For a change of pace, try Brussels sprouts.

Prep time: 20 minutes
Cooking time: 3½ hours to 4 hours 40 minutes

- 1 corned beef brisket (6 to 7 lbs.)
  Water
- 2 ounces salt pork
- 6 peppercorns
- 1 celery rib
- 1 bay leaf
- 1 large head cabbage (3 lbs.), cut into wedges, or 2 packages (10 oz. each) Brussels sprouts
- 1½ pounds small red potatoes
- 10 carrots (1½ lbs.), cut into 1½-inch pieces
- 10 small whole onions, peeled
  Mustard (optional)

1. Place brisket in a Dutch oven and add enough cold water to cover. Bring to boil over high heat; add salt pork, peppercorns, celery and bay leaf. Reduce heat to medium-low and simmer 3 to 4 hours, until meat is fork-tender.

2. Add cabbage, potatoes, carrots and onions to broth and cook 20 to 30 minutes, until tender. (If using Brussels sprouts, add to vegetables during last 15 minutes of cooking time and cook until tender-crisp.) Transfer brisket and vegetables to a large serving platter; discard broth. Remove bay leaf. Serve with mustard, if desired. Makes 8 servings.

Per serving: 785 calories, 46.5 g total fat, 13 g saturated fat, 178 mg cholesterol, 396 mg sodium, 34 g carbohydrates, 56 g protein, 134 mg calcium, 9 g fiber

hungarian stuffed cabbage rolls

In 1957, rock 'n' roll was king among kids, Dr. Spock offered sage advice to parents on the pages of LHJ and the Soviets launched Sputnik. And, in the fall of that year, LHJ took the humble hamburger on a global journey with a feature entitled "Hamburger Around the World." These Hungarian Stuffed Cabbage Rolls remain a classic. Cook them up and indulge in a dish like Mom used to make. You can use all beef if you can't find ground pork.

Prep time: 25 minutes • Cooking time: 1 hour

Water
- 1 tablespoon salt
- 8 large savoy cabbage leaves

STUFFING:
- ½ pound ground beef
- ½ pound ground pork
- 1 cup cooked long-grain rice
- 1 cup minced onions
- 1 large egg, beaten
- ½ teaspoon salt
- ¼ teaspoon dried thyme
- ⅛ teaspoon freshly ground pepper

SAUCE:
- 1 cup tomato juice
- 1 cup water
- 1 cup chopped onions
- 2 beef bouillon cubes
- 2 tablespoons chopped fresh parsley

1. Bring 4 quarts water to boil; stir in salt. Add cabbage and cook 2 minutes. Drain.

2. *Make stuffing:* Combine all ingredients in a large bowl. Divide into 8 equal portions. Wrap each portion in a cabbage leaf; tie with string.

3. *Make sauce:* Combine all ingredients in a large skillet. Add cabbage rolls; bring sauce to a simmer over medium heat. Cover and cook 1 hour, turning occasionally. Discard string. Serve rolls with sauce. Makes 4 servings.

Per serving: 465 calories, 29 g total fat, 11 g saturated fat, 142 mg cholesterol, 1,052 mg sodium, 27 g carbohydrates, 25 g protein, 102 mg calcium, 5 g fiber

veal parmigiana

The Italian word "scaloppine" translates into the cut of veal called for here—a very thin boneless slice of meat.

Prep time: 50 minutes • Baking time: 16 to 22 minutes

SAUCE:

- ¼ cup olive oil
- 6 to 7 garlic cloves, crushed through a press
- 1 can (16 oz.) tomato puree
- 2 cups canned Italian plum tomatoes
- 1 tablespoon dried basil
- 1½ teaspoons salt
- 1 teaspoon dried oregano
- ½ teaspoon freshly ground pepper
- ¼ teaspoon sugar
  Pinch crushed red pepper flakes

  •

- ⅔ cup all-purpose flour
- 1 teaspoon salt, divided
- ¼ teaspoon freshly ground pepper, divided
- 4 eggs
- 3 cups toasted fresh bread crumbs*
- 1 cup freshly grated Parmesan cheese
- ½ teaspoon paprika
- 16 veal scaloppine (about 2½ lbs.)
- 9 tablespoons olive oil, divided
- 1 pound mozzarella cheese, thinly sliced

1. *Make sauce:* Heat oil in a medium skillet over medium heat. Add garlic and cook 30 seconds, until golden. Stir in remaining sauce ingredients; cover and simmer 15 minutes. Makes about 4 cups. Set aside.

2. Meanwhile, combine flour, ½ teaspoon of the salt and ⅛ teaspoon of the pepper in a pie plate. Lightly beat eggs in a shallow bowl. Combine bread crumbs, Parmesan, remaining ½ teaspoon salt and ⅛ teaspoon pepper and the paprika in another pie plate. Coat scaloppine in flour mixture, shaking off excess; dip in egg, allowing excess to drip back into bowl, then coat with bread crumb mixture.

3. Heat oven to 350°F. Heat 3 tablespoons of the oil in a large skillet over medium-high heat. Add scaloppine, 4 at a time, and cook 2 to 3 minutes per side, until golden and almost cooked through. Repeat with remaining oil and scaloppine. Divide scaloppine between two 13×9-inch baking dishes.

Pour ¾ cup of the sauce over scaloppine in each baking dish. Top with mozzarella. Bake 15 to 20 minutes, until cheese is melted and sauce is bubbly. Turn oven to broil. Broil 1 to 2 minutes, until lightly browned. Serve with remaining sauce. Makes 8 servings.

*To toast fresh bread crumbs: Heat oven to 325°F. Process 12 slices white sandwich bread in food processor until fine crumbs. Place fresh bread crumbs on a large cookie sheet and bake 15 minutes, until golden, tossing occasionally.

Per serving:: 685 calories, 40 g total fat, 13 g saturated fat, 262 mg cholesterol, 1,420 mg sodium, 23 g carbohydrates, 55 g protein, 550 mg calcium, 2 g fiber

old-fashioned beef stew LOW FAT EASY

Cabernet Sauvignon or Merlot makes a good substitute for the Burgundy wine in this recipe.

Prep time: 25 minutes
Cooking time: 2 hours 14 minutes to 2 hours 55 minutes

- 5 slices bacon
- 1 medium onion, chopped
- 1 large garlic clove, crushed through a press
- ¼ cup all-purpose flour
- 1 teaspoon salt
- ¼ teaspoon freshly ground pepper
- 2 pounds beef top sirloin, cut into 1½-inch chunks
- 2 cups Burgundy wine
- 1 can (14½ oz.) beef broth
- 2 tablespoons chopped fresh parsley
- 3 whole cloves
  Pinch dried thyme
- 1 bay leaf
- 6 carrots, cut into 1-inch pieces (1 lb.)
- 12 small whole onions, peeled (8 oz.)
- ½ pound fresh green beans, trimmed and cut into 1-inch pieces, or 1 package (9 oz.) frozen cut green beans

1. Cook bacon in a Dutch oven over medium-high heat until crisp; remove from Dutch oven and drain on paper towels. Chop bacon; set aside. Add chopped onion and garlic to bacon drippings in

Dutch oven and cook 4 minutes, until softened; remove from pan and set aside.

2. Meanwhile, combine flour, salt and pepper. Dredge beef in flour. Add beef to same Dutch oven and cook 5 to 6 minutes, until browned on all sides. Return bacon and onion to pan; stir in wine, beef broth, parsley, cloves, thyme and bay leaf. Bring to boil. Reduce heat to medium; cover and cook 1½ to 2 hours, until meat is tender, stirring occasionally.

3. Add carrots, whole onions and fresh green beans; cover and cook 30 to 40 minutes (if using frozen green beans, add during last 5 to 10 minutes of cooking). Remove bay leaf. Makes 6 to 8 servings.

Per serving: 315 calories, 7.5 g total fat, 2.5 g saturated fat, 82 mg cholesterol, 653 mg sodium, 18 g carbohydrates, 33 g protein, 60 mg calcium, 4 g fiber

cincinnati chili EASY

Spices and chocolate mingle in this dish with spicy intrigue.

Prep time: 15 minutes • Cooking time: 3 to 3½ hours

Water
2 **pounds ground beef**
2 **medium onions, finely grated**
1 **can (16 oz.) tomato sauce**
5 **whole allspice**
5 **whole cloves**
¼ **cup chili powder**
4 **garlic cloves, minced**
2 **tablespoons vinegar**
2 **teaspoons Worcestershire sauce**
1½ **teaspoons salt**
1 **teaspoon cinnamon**
1 **teaspoon ground cumin**
½ **teaspoon ground red pepper**
½ **ounce unsweetened chocolate (½ square)**
1 **large bay leaf**

1. Place 1 quart water in a 4-quart Dutch oven and add beef, stirring until beef separates to a fine texture. Bring to slow boil over medium-high heat and boil 30 minutes.

2. Add remaining ingredients. Return mixture to boil, stirring to combine. Reduce heat to medium-

low and simmer, uncovered, 2 hours. Cover and simmer 30 minutes to 1 hour more, until chili reaches desired thickness. Cool 15 minutes, then refrigerate overnight. Skim fat off top of chili before reheating. Remove bay leaf. Makes 6 servings.

Per serving: 355 calories, 21 g total fat, 8 g saturated fat, 95 mg cholesterol, 1,086 mg sodium, 11 g carbohydrates, 31 g protein, 48 mg calcium, 4 g fiber

gnocchi à la romaine EASY

This gnocchi calls for grits instead of the usual potatoes. Pictured on page 8.

Prep time: 20 minutes plus chilling
Baking time: 25 to 30 minutes

1 **quart milk**
4 **tablespoons butter or margarine, divided**
1 **cup old-fashioned or quick-cooking grits (not instant)**
1 **teaspoon salt**
⅛ **teaspoon freshly ground pepper**
1 **cup shredded Gruyère or Swiss cheese**
3 **tablespoons freshly grated Parmesan cheese**
Chopped fresh chives (optional)

1. Heat oven to 400°F. Bring milk and 3 tablespoons of the butter to boil in a large saucepan. Gradually add grits, stirring constantly. Reduce heat to medium; cook, stirring constantly, 6 to 12 minutes, until mixture has thickened. Stir in salt and pepper. Transfer mixture to a large mixer bowl and beat on high speed 5 minutes, until creamy. Pour into a greased shallow 2-quart baking dish. Cover and refrigerate 15 minutes, until firm.

2. Uncover; invert dish onto a large cutting board and unmold. Grease same baking dish with remaining 1 tablespoon butter. Cut grits into quarters, then cut each quarter into 4 squares to form 16 slices. Arrange in rows of overlapping slices. Sprinkle top with cheeses. Bake 25 to 30 minutes, until top is lightly browned. Sprinkle with snipped chives, if desired. Makes 6 servings.

Per serving: 340 calories, 18.5 g total fat, 11 g saturated fat, 58 mg cholesterol, 652 mg sodium, 29 g carbohydrates, 14 g protein, 421 mg calcium, 0 g fiber

baked lemon pork chops

The key to this dish? Marinating the pork chops in a mixture called "brine," a solution of water, salt, sugar and seasonings, which adds moisture and flavor to the meat.

Prep time: 25 minutes plus brining
Baking time: 25 minutes

BRINE:

2	cups hot water (120°F. to 130°F.)
¼	cup salt
¼	cup firmly packed brown sugar
6	cups cold water
3	tablespoons dried thyme
	•
6	1-inch-thick lean bone-in rib or center-cut loin pork chops (about 5 lbs.)
¼	teaspoon freshly ground pepper
2	tablespoons flour
1	tablespoon olive oil
6	slices lemon
¾	cup ketchup
¾	cup water
3	tablespoons brown sugar

1. *Make brine:* Combine hot water, salt and brown sugar in a large bowl; stir 5 minutes, until salt and sugar dissolve. Stir in cold water and thyme. Let brine stand until cooled to room temperature. Pour brine into a large (2 gallon), heavy-duty resealable plastic freezer bag. Add chops, pushing them down into the brine. Seal bag, carefully pressing out air. Lay bag flat on a tray and refrigerate 24 hours, turning bag several times.

2. Remove chops from brine (discard brine). Rinse chops under cold running water and pat dry.

3. Heat oven to 350°F. Sprinkle chops with pepper; dredge in flour. Heat a 12-inch ovenproof skillet over high heat 2½ minutes, until very hot. Reduce heat to medium-high; add oil and chops. Cook chops 2 minutes per side, until browned. Arrange 1 lemon slice on center of each chop.

4. Mix together ketchup, water and brown sugar in a medium bowl. Pour over chops. Bake, uncovered, 25 minutes, until an instant-read meat thermometer inserted 1½ inches deep into side of each chop registers 155°F. (You may need to add a little water in the latter part of baking if sauce cooks down too much.) Makes 6 servings.

Per serving: 445 calories, 14.5 g total fat, 4.5 g saturated fat, 166 mg cholesterol, 1,273 mg sodium, 15 g carbohydrates, 59 g protein, 66 mg calcium, 1 g fiber

chicken pot pie

This delectable pot pie, with its flaky-rich crust and creamy filling, has been a family favorite for generations.

Prep time: 1 hour • Baking time: 30 minutes

10	cups water
1	whole chicken (about 3½ lbs.)
1	carrot, cut into thick slices
1	celery rib, cut into thick slices
1	medium onion, halved
½	bay leaf
¼	teaspoon freshly ground pepper
3	tablespoons butter or margarine, divided
½	pound white mushrooms, quartered
½	cup diced peeled carrot
½	cup diced celery
1	cup frozen pearl onions
1	red bell pepper, diced (¾ cup)
½	cup frozen peas
3	tablespoons flour
½	cup milk
1	teaspoon Worcestershire sauce
1	teaspoon salt
	Dash hot red pepper sauce
1	sheet from 1 package (17¼ oz.) frozen puff pastry, thawed according to package directions
1	large egg, lightly beaten

1. Combine water, chicken, sliced carrot, sliced celery, onion, bay leaf and ground pepper in a large saucepot. Bring to boil. Reduce heat to low and skim surface. Simmer, partially covered, 1 hour, turning chicken after 30 minutes. Remove chicken. Cool; strain broth and remove fat. Reserve 2 cups strained broth.

2. Heat 1 tablespoon of the butter in a large skillet. Add mushrooms and cook over medium-high heat 5 to 6 minutes, until golden; set aside.

3. Remove skin and bones from chicken; tear meat into large pieces. Transfer meat to a large bowl.

4. Bring reserved chicken broth to boil in a large saucepan. Add diced carrot and celery; reduce heat and simmer 5 minutes. Add pearl onions and bell pepper; simmer 2 minutes. With slotted spoon, add vegetables to chicken. Add mushrooms and peas to chicken. Reserve broth.

5. Melt remaining 2 tablespoons butter in a medium saucepan over medium-high heat. Add flour and cook, stirring and pressing flour paste, 1 minute. Remove from heat and gradually whisk in reserved chicken broth, the milk, Worcestershire sauce, salt and hot pepper sauce. Simmer 5 minutes, whisking occasionally. Add to chicken and vegetables and stir to combine.

6. Heat oven to 425°F. On a lightly floured surface, roll out puff pastry to an 11-inch square. Spoon chicken mixture into a 10-inch square (2½-quart) baking dish. Cover with pastry, pressing to sides of baking dish. Cut 3 or 4 small vents in top of pastry. Brush with egg and bake 30 minutes, until deep golden and bubbly. Makes 6 servings.

Per serving: 560 calories, 35 g total fat, 8.5 g saturated fat, 145 mg cholesterol, 754 mg sodium, 26 g carbohydrates, 35 g protein, 73 mg calcium, 2 g fiber

poached salmon with green sauce

Because meat was rationed in the U.S. during the first and second World Wars, recipes for fish were popular. After rationing ended, recipes for salmon still held their appeal. This one has passed the test of time. Pictured on page 8.

Prep time: 15 minutes • Cooking time: 6 to 8 minutes

    Water
1 **lemon, thinly sliced**
2 **teaspoons salt**
6 **salmon steaks (5 oz. each)**

GREEN SAUCE:
 ¾ **cup mayonnaise**
 ¼ **cup loosely packed fresh parsley leaves**
 3 **tablespoons chopped fresh chives**
 2 **tablespoons fresh lemon juice**
 ¼ **teaspoon salt**
 ¼ **teaspoon freshly ground pepper**
 1 **cucumber, peeled, seeded and diced**
   Fresh chives (optional)

1. Bring 1 inch water, lemon and 2 teaspoons salt to boil in a 12-inch skillet over high heat. Add salmon. Reduce heat to low; cover and simmer 6 to 8 minutes, until each salmon steak is opaque throughout.

2. *Make green sauce:* Meanwhile, combine mayonnaise, parsley, chives, lemon juice, salt and pepper in blender. Puree until smooth. Transfer to a bowl; stir in cucumber. Makes 1½ cups.

3. Drain salmon. Top each salmon steak with 2 tablespoons of the green sauce. Serve with additional sauce. Garnish with chives, if desired. Makes 6 servings.

Per serving with 2 tablespoons sauce: 380 calories, 28.5 g total fat, 4.5 g saturated fat, 79 mg cholesterol, 377 mg sodium, 2 g carbohydrates, 29 g protein, 68 mg calcium, 0 g fiber

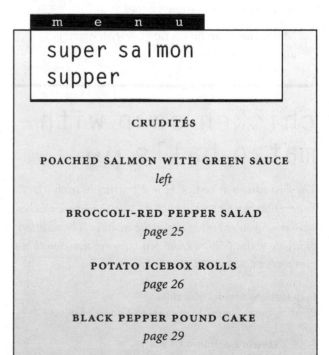

m e n u

super salmon supper

CRUDITÉS

POACHED SALMON WITH GREEN SAUCE
left

BROCCOLI-RED PEPPER SALAD
page 25

POTATO ICEBOX ROLLS
page 26

BLACK PEPPER POUND CAKE
page 29

much ado about matzo meal

If you're unfamiliar with matzo meal, you'll appreciate this brief rundown of what it is, what it's used for, and where it came from.

Matzo meal is ground matzo—a thin and brittle unleavened bread made with water and flour. The bread is consumed during the Jewish Passover holiday in accordance with the tradition that prohibits products containing yeast.

Bread is not the only food made with matzo meal. It's also used in pancakes, gefilte fish (a Jewish dish made with ground fish, matzo meal and seasonings) and matzo balls (see our delicious Chicken Soup with Matzo Balls recipe, below).

The tradition of prohibiting leavened products during the Jewish Passover goes back to the book of Exodus, when, according to the Bible, the Jews' speedy departure from Egypt left no time to prepare leavened bread.

Matzo meal can be found in Jewish markets and most supermarkets.

chicken soup with matzo balls

The food editors at Ladies' Home Journal *have always known that there's nothing better than homemade chicken soup when you're feeling under the weather. The addition of hearty matzo balls to broth is a Passover tradition that's also perfect for any cold, damp day.*

Prep time: 30 minutes plus chilling
Cooking time: 4 hours 10 minutes to 4 hours 15 minutes

- 1 **stewing chicken (4 lbs.)**
  Cold water
- 3 **carrots, cut into 1-inch pieces**
- 3 **celery ribs, cut into 1-inch pieces**
- 2 **medium onions, halved**
- 1 **parsnip, cut into 1-inch pieces**
- 3 **garlic cloves, peeled and halved**
- 10 **black peppercorns**
- 2 **fresh parsley sprigs**
- 4 **teaspoons salt**

MATZO BALLS:
- 4 **large eggs, lightly beaten**
- ½ **cup water**
- ⅓ **cup rendered chicken fat,* melted, or vegetable oil**
- 1 **cup matzo meal**
- 1 **teaspoon salt**
- ⅛ **teaspoon freshly ground pepper**
  Pinch nutmeg
  Water
  Fresh parsley sprigs, for garnish (optional)

1. Place chicken and 10 cups cold water in a large saucepot; bring to boil. Reduce heat; cover and simmer 30 minutes. Skim broth. Add vegetables, garlic, peppercorns, 2 parsley sprigs and salt; cover and simmer 2½ hours. Cool slightly and remove chicken meat. (Reserve meat for another use.)

2. Strain soup; reserve a few carrot pieces and cut into thin slices for garnish. Refrigerate overnight. Skim off fat using a slotted spoon. *(Can be made ahead. Cover and refrigerate up to 3 days.)*

3. *Prepare matzo balls:* Combine eggs, water and melted fat in a medium bowl. Stir in matzo meal, salt, pepper and nutmeg. Cover and refrigerate 1 hour.

4. Bring 6 quarts water to boil in a large saucepan. With wet palms, roll matzo mixture into 1-inch balls and drop into boiling water. Simmer, covered, 40 to 45 minutes. Meanwhile, reheat soup in large saucepot. Remove matzo balls with a slotted spoon and add to hot soup in serving bowls. If desired, garnish with parsley sprig and reserved carrot slices. Makes 10 cups soup and 22 matzo balls.

*To render chicken fat: Remove large pieces of fat from around cavity of raw chicken. Cut into small pieces and melt in a small saucepan over medium-low heat. Cool and use for matzo balls.

Per serving (1 cup soup and 2 matzo balls): 180 calories, 10 g total fat, 3 g saturated fat, 91 mg cholesterol, 1,035 mg sodium, 12 g carbohydrates, 9 g protein, 22 mg calcium, 0 g fiber

chicken and dumplings

It's the best chicken stew you'll ever taste, and it comes with a bonus—a batch of tender parsley dumplings on top.

Prep time: 30 minutes • Cooking time: 1 hour

- 1 3½-pound chicken, cut into 8 pieces and skin removed
- 1 teaspoon salt, divided
- ½ teaspoon freshly ground pepper, divided
- ½ cup all-purpose flour
- 1 teaspoon poultry seasoning, divided
- 2 tablespoons olive oil
- 2 large leeks, trimmed and sliced
- 1 small onion, chopped
- 1 can (14½ oz.) chicken broth
- 4 carrots, sliced
- 2 large celery ribs, diced
- 1 cup frozen green peas

DUMPLINGS:

- 1½ cups all-purpose flour
- 2 tablespoons chopped fresh parsley
- 2 teaspoons baking powder
- ½ teaspoon salt
- 1 cup half-and-half cream

1. Sprinkle chicken with ½ teaspoon of the salt and ¼ teaspoon of the pepper. Combine flour and ½ teaspoon of the poultry seasoning in a heavy-duty plastic bag. Add chicken and shake to coat.

2. Heat oil in a Dutch oven over medium-high heat. Add half of the chicken; reduce heat to medium and cook until well browned on each side. Transfer to a plate. Repeat with remaining chicken. Discard drippings from Dutch oven. Add leeks and onion to same Dutch oven and cook 5 minutes, until softened. Add enough water to chicken broth to equal 2½ cups and add to Dutch oven. Add chicken, carrots, celery, remaining ½ teaspoon each salt and poultry seasoning and ¼ teaspoon pepper; bring to boil. Reduce heat and simmer, covered, 30 minutes, until chicken is tender. Stir in peas.

3. *Make dumplings:* Combine flour, parsley, baking powder and salt in a medium bowl. Add cream; stir with a fork until dough is moistened. Drop dough

by heaping tablespoons into Dutch oven, making 8 dumplings. Cover and simmer 12 minutes, until a toothpick inserted in dumplings comes out clean. Makes 4 servings.

Per serving: 725 calories, 21.5 g total fat, 7 g saturated fat, 156 mg cholesterol, 1,830 mg sodium, 77 g carbohydrates, 54 g protein, 323 mg calcium, 7 g fiber

clam know-how

When buying live clams, look for moist shells without cracks and chips. Select clams that are tightly shut. If the shell is open slightly, tap it. If it doesn't close up, that means the clam is dead and must be thrown away. It's best to purchase clams the day of cooking.

linguine with white clam sauce *LOW FAT EASY*

Littleneck clams are the smallest, sweetest and most tender variety of hard-shell clams.

Prep time: 20 minutes • Cooking time: 18 minutes

1	bottle (8 oz.) clam juice
½	cup white wine
3	dozen littleneck clams, scrubbed
2	tablespoons extra-virgin olive oil
1	cup finely chopped onions
½	cup finely chopped carrot
½	cup finely chopped celery
2	teaspoons minced garlic
1	teaspoon finely chopped fresh thyme
⅛	teaspoon red pepper flakes
2	tablespoons chopped fresh parsley
1	pound linguine or spaghetti, cooked according to package directions
	Additional olive oil, for serving (optional)

1. Bring clam juice and wine to boil in a large Dutch oven. Add clams; cover and cook 5 to 8 minutes, until shells open. With a slotted spoon, transfer clams to a bowl; cool. (Discard any unopened clams.)

2. Remove clams from shells and coarsely chop. Pour clam juice-wine mixture through a sieve into a 2-cup measure. Rinse and dry Dutch oven. Heat oil in same Dutch oven over medium heat. Add onions, carrot and celery; cook 15 minutes, until tender. Add garlic and cook 1 minute. Add clam juice-wine mixture, thyme and red pepper flakes. Bring to boil; boil 2 minutes.

3. Stir in chopped clams and parsley. Toss sauce with hot pasta in a large serving bowl. Serve immediately with additional olive oil, if desired. Makes 6 servings.

Per serving without additional olive oil: 390 calories, 6 g total fat, 1 g saturated fat, 16 mg cholesterol, 135 mg sodium, 62 g carbohydrates, 16 g protein, 53 mg calcium, 3 g fiber

shrimp and sausage jambalaya *EASY*

French in origin, andouille sausage is a smoked sausage that is a staple in many Cajun dishes such as this jambalaya. Serve a bottle of hot sauce alongside for those who desire an added kick.

Prep time: 20 minutes • Cooking time: 45 to 50 minutes

1	pound andouille sausage, thinly sliced
1	cup chopped celery
¾	cup chopped fresh parsley
⅔	cup chopped green bell pepper
3	tablespoons olive oil
2	garlic cloves, minced
2	cans (16 oz. each) tomatoes
2	cups chicken broth
1	cup sliced green onions
1	tablespoon Creole seasoning*
1	teaspoon dried oregano
1	teaspoon dried thyme
1	bay leaf
⅛	teaspoon ground red pepper
⅛	teaspoon freshly ground black pepper
2	cups long-grain rice
3	pounds medium shrimp, peeled and deveined

1. Cook sausage in a heavy ovenproof 5-quart Dutch oven until meat is no longer pink. With a slotted spoon, transfer sausage to a bowl. Add celery, parsley, bell pepper, oil and garlic to sausage drippings in Dutch oven; cook 5 minutes.

2. Chop tomatoes, reserving liquid. Add tomatoes with reserved liquid, chicken broth and green onions to Dutch oven. Stir in Creole seasoning, oregano, thyme, bay leaf, ground red pepper and black pepper. Stir in uncooked rice and sausage and cook, covered, over low heat, 20 minutes, stirring occasionally to prevent rice from sticking. When most of the liquid has been absorbed, add shrimp.

3. Heat oven to 350°F. Bake 25 to 30 minutes, just until rice is tender. Remove bay leaf. Makes 8 to 10 servings.

To make Creole seasoning: Combine 1½ teaspoons salt, 1 teaspoon chili powder, ¼ teaspoon ground red pepper and ¼ teaspoon freshly ground black pepper.

Per serving: 550 calories, 23.5 g total fat, 7 g saturated fat, 207 mg cholesterol, 1,651 mg sodium, 42 g carbohydrates, 40 g protein, 145 mg calcium, 3 g fiber

classic bouillabaisse

Bouillabaisse means "fish soup" in French. This version boasts not only three different kinds of fish, but clams and shrimp too.

Prep time: 30 minutes • Cooking time: 50 minutes

- 3 tablespoons extra-virgin olive oil
- 1 fennel bulb, chopped
- 1 cup chopped onions
- ½ cup chopped leek
- 1 tablespoon minced garlic
- 1 3-inch strip orange peel
- 1 teaspoon finely chopped fresh thyme
  Pinch saffron threads
- 4 bottles (8 oz. each) clam juice
- 1 can (28 oz.) tomatoes, drained
- ½ cup white wine
- ½ teaspoon salt
- 1 dozen cherrystone or littleneck clams, scrubbed and rinsed
- ¾ pound skinless monkfish fillets, cubed
- ¾ pound red snapper fillets, cubed
- ¾ pound skinless cod fillets, cubed

- 1 dozen medium shrimp, peeled and deveined
- 1 tablespoon Pernod or ouzo liqueur
- ½ teaspoon freshly ground pepper
  Aïoli (recipe follows)

1. Heat oil in a large Dutch oven over medium heat. Stir in fennel, onions and leek; cook, stirring frequently, 10 minutes, until vegetables are tender. Stir in garlic, orange peel, thyme and saffron; cook 1 minute. Add clam juice, tomatoes, wine and salt; bring to boil. Reduce heat and simmer, uncovered, 30 minutes.

2. Increase heat to high and stir in clams. Cover and cook 5 minutes, just until clams open. Stir in fish, shrimp, Pernod and pepper. Cover and simmer 5 minutes more, just until fish is opaque. (Discard any unopened clams.) Ladle into large bowls and top each serving with a dollop of Aïoli. Makes 6 servings.

Per serving without Aïoli: 340 calories, 10 g total fat, 1.5 g saturated fat, 129 mg cholesterol, 922 mg sodium, 13 g carbohydrates, 45 g protein, 133 mg calcium, 6 g fiber

aïoli

The recipe for this garlic-flavored mayonnaise comes from the Provence region of France.

Total prep time: 10 minutes

- ⅓ cup mayonnaise
- 1 teaspoon extra-virgin olive oil
- 1 teaspoon fresh lemon juice
- ½ teaspoon minced garlic
- ⅛ teaspoon salt
- ⅛ teaspoon freshly ground pepper

Combine all ingredients in a small bowl, mixing with a fork until mixture is blended. Refrigerate until ready to serve. Makes ⅓ cup.

Per tablespoon: 95 calories, 10.5 g total fat, 1.5 g saturated fat, 4 mg cholesterol, 115 mg sodium, 0 g carbohydrates, 0 g protein, 1 mg calcium, 0 g fiber

all about the onion family

The immediate onion family includes green onions and "dry" onions (mature onions with a dry, paperlike skin). Relatives of the onion family include chives, leeks and shallots. Here are some tips on flavor and selection.

GREEN ONIONS (also known as scallions) have a white base and long green leaves. Select green onions that boast crisp, brightly colored green tops and a firm base. Both the white and green parts have a mild flavor.

DRY ONIONS offer an extensive range of flavor. Mild-flavored onions include the Bermuda onion (peak season March through June) and the Spanish onion (August to May). Both can be either yellow or white. Red onions (also known as Italian onions) have a stronger flavor and are available year-round. Vidalia, Walla Walla, Maui and other sweet onions (available spring and early summer) are known for their sweetness and juicy flesh. Choose onions that feel heavy for their size and have no soft spots or apparent moisture.

CHIVES are a long, green tubular herb that belongs to the onion family. They have a mild onion flavor and can be purchased fresh, frozen or freeze-dried. Use these forms interchangeably.

LEEKS, which look like oversized green onions, have a mild flavor that lends itself well to a variety of dishes. Purchase leeks that have wide, dark green leaves that appear crisp and colorful, and white portions without spots.

SHALLOTS, like onions, come with dry papery skins. They are similar to garlic in that each comes with a head of many cloves encased. The flesh ranges from pale brown to rose with slight tinges of green or purple. When selecting, check that shallots are firm.

quiche lorraine

Americans traveled more in the 1960s than ever before, and they brought home a taste for foods they discovered abroad, such as this savory pie. In the Lorraine region of France, quiche serves as a first course or appetizer. Our version makes a perfect entrée for a light luncheon.

Prep time: 40 minutes plus chilling
Baking time: 35 to 43 minutes

PASTRY:

- 1⅓ cups all-purpose flour
- ¼ teaspoon salt
- ½ cup butter or margarine, cut up
- 2 tablespoons vegetable shortening
- 2 to 3 tablespoons ice water

   •
- 6 slices bacon, cooked and crumbled
- 1 cup shredded Swiss cheese
- 2 cups milk
- 3 large eggs
- 1 tablespoon flour
- ½ teaspoon salt
- ⅛ teaspoon nutmeg
- 1 tablespoon butter or margarine

1. *Make pastry:* Combine flour and salt in a medium bowl. With pastry blender or 2 knives, cut in butter and shortening until mixture resembles fine crumbs. Sprinkle on water, tossing with fork until pastry holds together. Shape into ball; flatten into disk. Wrap well in plastic wrap; refrigerate 1 hour.

2. Heat oven to 425°F. On lightly floured surface, roll pastry into an 11-inch circle. Fit into a 9-inch pie plate; flute edge. Freeze 5 minutes. Line pastry with foil and fill with dried beans or pie weights. Bake 12 minutes. Remove foil and beans and bake pastry 5 minutes more. Cool.

3. Reduce oven temperature to 375°F. Sprinkle bacon and cheese evenly on bottom of pastry shell. Whisk together milk, eggs, flour, salt and nutmeg in a large bowl until combined; pour over cheese. Melt butter in saucepan until lightly browned but not burned; drizzle over top.

4. Bake 35 to 43 minutes, until center is puffed and a knife inserted near center of quiche comes out

clean. Cool on wire rack 15 minutes. Serve warm.
Makes 6 main dish or 12 appetizer servings.

Per main dish serving: 480 calories, 35 g total fat,
18.5 g saturated fat, 184 mg cholesterol, 698 mg sodium,
25 g carbohydrates, 16 g protein, 301 mg calcium, 1 g fiber

split pea soup with garlic croutons

*Here's a great soup to have stored in your freezer when a
dose of delicious warmth is needed. If you prefer, use
yellow split peas instead of green.*

Prep time: 30 minutes • Cooking time: 1 hour

- 1 tablespoon vegetable oil
- 2 cups peeled, chopped carrots
- 1 cup chopped onions
- 1 cup chopped celery
- ½ pound baked ham, diced
- 1 tablespoon minced garlic
- ¼ teaspoon cloves
- ¼ teaspoon ground red pepper
- 10 cups water
- 1 pound green split peas, rinsed and picked over
- 2 cans (14½ oz. each) chicken broth
- 1 bay leaf
- 1 teaspoon salt
- ½ teaspoon freshly ground black pepper

GARLIC CROUTONS:
- 3 tablespoons olive oil
- 1 teaspoon minced garlic
- ½ teaspoon salt
- ½ teaspoon freshly ground black pepper
- 4 cups bread cubes*

1. Heat oil in a Dutch oven over medium-high
heat. Add carrots, onions, celery and ham. Cook,
stirring, 10 minutes, until vegetables are softened.
Stir in garlic, cloves and red pepper; cook
30 seconds. Add water, split peas, broth, bay leaf,
salt and pepper; bring to boil. Reduce heat and
simmer, uncovered, 1 hour, until peas are tender,
stirring occasionally and skimming off foam with
a spoon.

2. *Make garlic croutons:* Meanwhile, heat oven to
425°F. Combine oil, garlic, salt and pepper in a
large bowl. Add bread and toss to coat. Spread on a
15½×10½-inch jelly-roll pan and bake 10 minutes,
until golden, stirring halfway through. Cool.

3. Remove bay leaf. Puree 6 cups of the soup in a
blender in 2 batches and return to Dutch oven.
Spoon soup into bowls and serve with garlic
croutons. Makes 8 servings.

*Note: Use French or Italian bread or 6 slices firm
white bread.

Per serving: 400 calories, 11.5 g total fat, 2.5 g saturated fat,
17 mg cholesterol, 1,340 mg sodium, 51 g carbohydrates,
25 g protein, 79 mg calcium, 17 g fiber

fettuccine alfredo

*Seek out the incomparable imported Parmigiano Reggiano
cheese when preparing this classic dish. Fresh fettuccine is
the authentic choice for the pasta, but this rich, creamy
sauce also partners well with ravioli or tortellini.*

Prep time: 5 minutes • Cooking time: 5 minutes

- ¼ cup butter (no substitutes)
- 2 cups heavy or whipping cream
- 1 teaspoon salt
- ½ teaspoon freshly ground pepper
  Pinch nutmeg
- 1 pound fettuccine, cooked according to
  package directions
- ¾ cup freshly grated Parmesan cheese

1. Combine butter, heavy cream, salt, pepper and
nutmeg in a medium skillet. Bring to boil over
medium-high heat. Reduce heat and simmer
4 minutes.

2. Toss sauce with hot pasta and Parmesan cheese
in a large serving bowl. Serve immediately. Makes
6 servings.

Per serving: 685 calories, 42.5 g total fat, 26 g saturated fat,
144 mg cholesterol, 653 mg sodium, 59 g carbohydrates,
16 g protein, 193 mg calcium, 2 g fiber

colcannon

Colcannon is a popular Irish dish of mashed potatoes, chopped onions and cabbage (see recipe, below). This highly regarded peasant dish traces back to the 19th century, when the potato had long since become an established staple in Ireland. The Spanish brought the potato to Europe in the late 1500s, introducing it to Ireland in the 1600s. In time the Irish deemed it an essential food source, since it was both inexpensive and plentiful. While colcannon, also known as "Irish potatoes," isn't as popular in the United States as corned beef and cabbage, it's most certainly a tried-and-true Gaelic favorite.

colcannon

For centuries, this traditional southern Irish potato dish has been much loved. So loved, in fact, poems and songs have been written in its honor. Studded with chopped green cabbage and onions, it's irresistible.

Prep time: 15 minutes • Cooking time: 25 minutes

1½	pounds all-purpose potatoes, peeled and cut into 2-inch chunks
	Cold water
1	teaspoon salt, divided
1½	cups chopped green cabbage or kale leaves
⅓	cup finely chopped green onions
2	cups boiling water
⅔	cup milk
2	tablespoons butter or margarine
⅛	teaspoon freshly ground pepper

1. Place potatoes and cold water to cover by 2 inches and ½ teaspoon of the salt in a large saucepan. Bring to boil; boil 5 minutes. Add cabbage and boil 10 minutes more, until potatoes are tender.

2. Meanwhile, place green onions in sieve; pour boiling water over them and drain. Add drained green onions to a medium saucepan with milk, butter, remaining ½ teaspoon salt and the pepper; bring to boil. Remove from heat.

3. Drain cooked potatoes and cabbage; return to large saucepan. Beat on low speed with hand-held mixer until coarsely mashed. Increase speed to high; gradually add milk and green onion mixture and continue to beat until potatoes are light and fluffy. Makes 4 cups.

Per cup: 220 calories, 7 g total fat, 4.5 g saturated fat, 19 mg cholesterol, 683 mg sodium, 35 g carbohydrates, 5 g protein, 84 mg calcium, 3 g fiber

scalloped leeks and potatoes

Our scalloped potatoes feature the mild, oniony flavor of leeks. The popularity of leeks in early 20th century recipes reflects the strong influence Britain had on American cooking.

Prep time: 50 minutes • Baking time: 70 to 80 minutes

6	tablespoons butter, divided (no substitutes)
3	pounds leeks, diced, white and pale green parts only (6 cups)
⅓	cup all-purpose flour
3¼	cups milk
1¾	teaspoons salt, divided
1	teaspoon paprika
¼	teaspoon freshly ground pepper
1	cup shredded sharp Cheddar cheese
4	pounds baking potatoes, peeled and very thinly sliced
¼	cup plain dry bread crumbs

1. Heat oven to 375°F. Butter a 13×9-inch baking dish. Melt 2 tablespoons of the butter in a large skillet over medium-high heat. Add leeks and cook 5 minutes, until softened.

2. Melt 3 tablespoons of the butter in a large saucepan over medium heat. Whisk in flour and cook

1 minute. Gradually whisk in milk, 1 teaspoon of the salt, the paprika and pepper. Bring to boil, whisking; boil 1 minute. Remove from heat and stir in cheese.

3. Spread one quarter of the potatoes in prepared baking dish and sprinkle with ¼ teaspoon of the salt. Top with one-third of the leeks, then one-third of the sauce. Repeat, layering 2 more times.

4. Bake, covered, 45 minutes. Melt remaining 1 tablespoon butter; toss with bread crumbs. Sprinkle over potatoes and bake, uncovered, 25 to 35 minutes, until golden and tender. Let stand 15 minutes before serving. Makes 12 servings.

Per serving: 290 calories, 11 g total fat, 6.5 g saturated fat, 31 mg cholesterol, 555 mg sodium, 41 g carbohydrates, 9 g protein, 192 mg calcium, 3 g fiber

broccoli-red pepper salad

Broccoli's popularity soared in the health-conscious 1980s, when it became known as a high-fiber, "anticancer" or cruciferous vegetable. And as red peppers became more available, salad fixings took a colorful turn.

Total prep time: 20 minutes

DRESSING:
- 3 tablespoons white wine vinegar
- 1 teaspoon Dijon mustard
- ¾ teaspoon salt
- ½ teaspoon minced garlic
- 6 tablespoons olive oil
- 1 tablespoon chopped fresh parsley

- 2 large bunches (2½ lbs.) broccoli
  Water
- 1 teaspoon salt
- 1 large head romaine lettuce (1¾ lbs.), leaves torn
- 1 head Boston lettuce (½ lb.), leaves torn
- 2 red bell peppers, cut into strips

1. *Make dressing:* Whisk together the vinegar, mustard, salt and garlic in a small bowl. Gradually whisk in oil. Stir in parsley. Makes ½ cup.

2. Cut broccoli into small florettes. (Reserve stalks for another use.) Bring 2 quarts water and salt to

boil in saucepot. Add broccoli and cook 30 seconds. Drain and rinse under cold water.

3. Combine torn lettuces, peppers and broccoli in a large salad bowl. *(Salad and dressing can be made ahead. Cover and refrigerate separately up to 4 hours.)* Add dressing; toss well. Makes 22 cups.

Per cup: 55 calories, 4 g total fat, 0.5 g saturated fat, 0 mg cholesterol, 125 mg sodium, 5 g carbohydrates, 2 g protein, 43 mg calcium, 2 g fiber

vegetable salad

This tried-and-true vegetable salad makes an ample—and colorful—side dish. Pictured on page 5.

Total prep and cooking time: 20 minutes

  Water
- 2 cups peeled and diced carrots
- 2 cups diced pickled beets
- 2 cups finely shredded romaine lettuce
- 2 cups finely shredded green cabbage
- 1 green bell pepper, finely chopped
- ¼ cup finely chopped fresh flat-leaf parsley
- 3 tablespoons olive oil
- 3 tablespoons vegetable oil
- 2 tablespoons red wine vinegar
- 1½ teaspoons salt
- ⅛ teaspoon freshly ground pepper
- ¼ cup minced onion
- ¼ cup mayonnaise
- 1 large egg, hard-cooked and grated
- ½ cup pimiento-stuffed olives, sliced (optional)

1. Bring 1½ quarts water to boil in a medium saucepan. Add carrots; cook 5 minutes. Drain in colander under cold running water until cool. Transfer to a large serving bowl. Stir in beets, lettuce, cabbage, bell pepper and parsley.

2. Whisk olive and vegetable oils, vinegar, salt and pepper together in a small bowl. Whisk in onion and mayonnaise to blend.

3. Toss vegetables with mayonnaise dressing to coat. Sprinkle top with grated egg and olives, if desired. Makes 8 servings.

Per serving: 190 calories, 16.5 g total fat, 2.5 g saturated fat, 29 mg cholesterol, 523 mg sodium, 9 g carbohydrates, 2 g protein, 35 mg calcium, 3 g fiber

potato icebox rolls

These golden, lighter-than-air rolls celebrate the world's best-known, most versatile vegetable. Pictured on page 5.

Prep time: 65 minutes plus rising
Baking time: 12 to 15 minutes per batch

- ¾ **pound baking potatoes, peeled and quartered**
  Water
- 1 **package active dry yeast**
- ½ **cup warm water (105°F. to 115°F.)**
- 1 **cup milk**
- ½ **cup vegetable shortening**
- 2 **large eggs**
- ⅓ **cup sugar**
- 1½ **teaspoons salt**
- 5½ **to 7 cups all-purpose flour, divided**

1. Place potatoes and enough water to cover in a saucepan. Bring to boil over high heat. Reduce heat to low; cover and simmer 15 to 20 minutes, until tender. Drain. Press potatoes through ricer, food mill or sieve.

2. Sprinkle yeast over warm water in a small bowl; let stand 5 minutes, until bubbly. Heat milk and vegetable shortening in a small saucepan over medium heat until bubbles form around edge of pan; remove from heat. Cool to lukewarm.

3. Beat eggs, sugar and salt together in a large mixer bowl on medium speed. Add yeast mixture, milk mixture and riced potatoes; beat until well blended. Gradually beat in 4 cups of the flour. Stir in 1½ cups more flour with a wooden spoon.

4. Grease a large bowl. On a lightly floured surface, knead dough 8 to 10 minutes, until smooth and elastic, adding enough of the remaining flour to prevent dough from sticking. Gather dough into a ball. Place in prepared bowl, turning to grease top. Cover with plastic wrap and weigh down with a heavy plate; refrigerate overnight or up to 48 hours.

5. About 2½ hours before baking time, punch down dough. Grease 32 (2½-inch) muffin-pan cups or 3 cookie sheets. Divide dough into 32 equal pieces; roll each piece into a ball and place each into a prepared muffin-pan cup or on cookie sheet.

Cover with clean kitchen towels; let rise in a warm, draft-free place until doubled in bulk, 2 to 2½ hours.

6. Heat oven to 425°F. Bake rolls 12 to 15 minutes, until golden brown. Makes 32 rolls.

Per roll: 125 calories, 4 g total fat, 1 g saturated fat, 14 mg cholesterol, 118 mg sodium, 19 g carbohydrates, 3 g protein, 15 mg calcium, 1 g fiber

banana-nut bread

Great banana-nut bread is moist and full of rich banana flavor but not gummy or overly sweet. Getting this perfect balance of taste and texture is surprisingly simple! The key is to start with fully ripe bananas. Pictured on page 6.

Prep time: 20 minutes
Baking time: 1 hour 10 minutes to 1 hour 12 minutes

- 1 **cup pecan halves**
- 2½ **cups all-purpose flour**
- 1¼ **teaspoons baking powder**
- ¾ **teaspoon baking soda**
- 1 **teaspoon cinnamon**
- ¾ **teaspoon salt**
- ⅛ **teaspoon nutmeg**
  Pinch cloves (optional)
- 1½ **cups (about 3 large) mashed very ripe bananas**
- ¼ **cup buttermilk (or ¼ cup milk plus 1 teaspoon vinegar or fresh lemon juice)**
- 1 **teaspoon vanilla extract**
- ½ **cup butter or margarine, softened**
- ¾ **cup firmly packed brown sugar**
- ½ **cup granulated sugar**
- 3 **large eggs, at room temperature**

1. Heat oven to 350°F. Grease and flour a 9×5-inch loaf pan. Pulse nuts in food processor until chopped. (Some will be finely chopped; some will be larger chopped pieces.) Set aside.

2. Whisk together flour, baking powder, baking soda, cinnamon, salt, nutmeg and cloves (if desired) in a medium bowl. Combine bananas, buttermilk and vanilla in another bowl.

3. Beat butter and sugars in a large mixer bowl on medium-high speed 5 minutes, until light and fluffy. Add eggs, one at a time, beating 30 seconds to 1 minute after each addition. Reduce speed to medium-low. Gradually beat in half of the flour mixture just until combined. Beat in half of the banana mixture just until combined. Repeat with remaining flour and banana mixtures. Fold in nuts.

4. Scrape batter evenly into the prepared pan. Bake 1 hour 10 minutes to 1 hour 12 minutes, until a toothpick inserted in center comes out almost clean (moist crumbs are fine). Cool in pan 5 minutes. Cut around sides of pan to loosen; unmold bread onto a wire rack. Turn top side up; cool completely. *(Can be made ahead. Wrap well in plastic wrap; store at room temperature up to 2 days.)* Makes 12 servings.

Per serving: 355 calories, 16.5 g total fat, 6 g saturated fat, 75 mg cholesterol, 376 mg sodium, 48 g carbohydrates, 5 g protein, 66 mg calcium, 2 g fiber

whole wheat bread

This hearty loaf became a home-baked favorite in the 1900s.

Prep time: 20 minutes plus rising
Baking time: 42 to 50 minutes

 1   cup milk
 ¼   cup sugar
 1½ teaspoons salt
 ½   cup warm water (105°F. to 115°F.)
 2   packages active dry yeast
 3½ to 4 cups whole wheat flour

1. Heat milk in a small saucepan over medium-high heat just to boil. Add sugar and salt; stir until dissolved. Cool to lukewarm. Combine water and yeast in a large bowl. Let stand 5 minutes, until bubbly. Add cooled milk mixture. Stir in flour, 1 cup at a time, until dough pulls away from sides of bowl. Grease a large bowl. On lightly floured surface, knead dough 8 to 10 minutes, until smooth and elastic, adding remaining flour as necessary. Place in prepared bowl, turning to grease top. Cover with plastic wrap and let rise in a warm, draft-free place until doubled in bulk, 30 minutes. Punch down dough; cover and let rise again until doubled in bulk, 30 minutes more.

2. Grease an 8½×4½-inch loaf pan. Punch down dough. Divide in half. Shape each half into a ball.

Place balls in prepared pan. Cover and let rise until doubled in bulk, about 25 minutes.

3. Meanwhile, heat oven to 400°F. Place pan in oven and reduce temperature to 375°F. Bake 42 to 50 minutes, until bread sounds hollow when tapped on bottom. Cool on a wire rack 5 minutes. Remove from pan and cool completely on wire rack. Cut into ½-inch slices. Makes 16 slices.

Per slice: 110 calories, 1 g total fat, 0.5 g saturated fat, 1 mg cholesterol, 228 mg sodium, 23 g carbohydrates, 4 g protein, 28 mg calcium, 3 g fiber

sally lunn

Who was Sally Lunn? No one knows for sure, but some say she sold this yeast-raised batter bread in her shop.

Prep time: 20 minutes plus rising
Baking time: 32 to 40 minutes

 1   package active dry yeast
 ¼   cup warm water (105°F. to 115°F.)
 ¾   cup milk, heated (105°F. to 115°F.)
 4   cups all-purpose flour
 1   teaspoon salt
 ½   cup butter or margarine, softened
 ⅓   cup sugar
 3   large eggs

1. Sprinkle yeast over warm water. Let stand 5 minutes, until bubbly. Stir in milk. Combine flour and salt in a medium bowl. Beat butter and sugar in a large mixer bowl until creamy. Beat in eggs, one at a time. Beat in flour mixture alternately with yeast mixture, beginning and ending with flour mixture, until well mixed. Cover completely with plastic wrap; let rise in a warm, draft-free place until doubled in bulk, 1 to 1½ hours. Stir well.

2. Grease a 10-inch tube pan or 12-cup Bundt pan. Spread dough in prepared pan. Cover with plastic wrap; let rise until doubled in bulk, 40 to 60 minutes.

3. Meanwhile, heat oven to 350°F. Bake 32 to 40 minutes, until bread is golden and sounds hollow when tapped on bottom. Unmold and cool on wire rack. Makes 20 slices.

Per slice: 155 calories, 6 g total fat, 3.5 g saturated fat, 46 mg cholesterol, 181 mg sodium, 21 g carbohydrates, 4 g protein, 20 mg calcium, 1 g fiber

éclairs

A dessert-lover's dream. Cream puff pastry, vanilla filling and chocolate glaze come together to create classic éclairs, the ultimate French pastry that is truly magnifique!

Prep time: 45 minutes plus standing and chilling
Baking time: 30 minutes

CREAM PUFF PASTRY:

- 1½ cups water
- 10 tablespoons butter or margarine, cut up
- 2 teaspoons sugar
- ½ teaspoon salt
- 1½ cups all-purpose flour
- 6 large eggs, at room temperature

VANILLA CREAM:

- 2¼ cups milk
- 6 egg yolks
- 1 cup sugar
- 3 tablespoons cornstarch
- 4½ teaspoons flour
- ¼ teaspoon salt
- 1½ teaspoons vanilla extract

CHOCOLATE GLAZE:

- 2 ounces unsweetened chocolate squares
- 1 teaspoon butter or margarine
- 1 cup confectioners' sugar
- 3 to 4 tablespoons hot water

1. Arrange oven racks to lower and upper thirds of oven. Heat oven to 400°F. Grease 2 large cookie sheets or line with parchment paper.

2. *Make cream puff pastry:* Combine water, butter, sugar and salt in a medium saucepan. Bring to boil over medium-high heat. Remove from heat and stir in flour all at once. Return to heat; cook, stirring constantly, until dough pulls away from sides of pan, 30 seconds. Remove from heat. Add eggs, one at a time, beating with a wooden spoon after each addition until smooth. Spoon into pastry bag fitted with a ⅝-inch plain tip. Holding bag at a 45° angle 1 inch above cookie sheet, pipe a 5×1-inch log,

twisting tip back as you finish to prevent a pointed end. Repeat, piping 23 more logs 2 inches apart. Bake 20 minutes; switch pans. Bake 10 minutes more, until golden. Turn off oven and let stand in oven 15 minutes. *(Do not open oven door.)* Transfer pastries to wire racks and cool completely. *(Can be made ahead. Freeze fully cooled pastries in heavy-duty plastic storage bags up to 1 month. Thaw on baking sheet in a single layer at room temperature 30 minutes; place in 350°F. oven for 8 minutes. Transfer to wire racks and cool completely.)*

3. *Make vanilla cream:* Rinse a large heavy-duty saucepan with cold water. Do not dry. Pour in milk and scald. Meanwhile, beat egg yolks and sugar in a small mixer bowl on medium speed until very light. Beat in cornstarch, flour and salt just until smooth. Reduce speed to low. Gradually beat in milk, scraping sides of bowl. Return mixture to saucepan. Cook over low heat, whisking constantly, until mixture comes to boil. (Don't worry if lumps form; the mixture will smooth out.) Cook and stir another 3 minutes. Remove from heat and stir in vanilla. Cover surface with plastic wrap and refrigerate 2 hours, until chilled. Makes 3 cups.

4. *To fill:* Make a small hole at each end of each éclair. Spoon filling into pastry bag fitted with a ¼-inch plain tip. Squeeze filling into hole in each end (or cut off tops of éclairs and fill each with 2 tablespoons of the vanilla cream).

5. *Make chocolate glaze:* Melt chocolate and butter in a small saucepan over very low heat. Remove from heat. Stir in confectioners' sugar and enough of the hot water for a smooth spreadable consistency. With a small spatula, spread over tops of éclairs. Refrigerate 15 minutes to set glaze. Makes 24 éclairs.

Per éclair: 185 calories, 10 g total fat, 5 g saturated fat, 122 mg cholesterol, 156 mg sodium, 21 g carbohydrates, 4 g protein, 45 mg calcium, 1 g fiber

MERINGUE:

3 large egg whites, at room temperature

¼ teaspoon cream of tartar

6 tablespoons sugar

•

1 9-inch purchased pie shell, baked

1. *Make filling:* Combine sugar, flour and salt in a medium saucepan. Add milk and stir with a whisk. Cook over medium heat, stirring constantly, until mixture begins to boil. Cook 1 minute more, stirring constantly. Remove from heat.

2. Beat ¼ cup of the hot milk mixture into egg yolks. Pour yolk mixture into saucepan, stirring quickly to prevent lumping. Return to low heat; cook 3 minutes more, stirring constantly *(do not boil)*. Remove from heat; stir in butter and vanilla until butter is melted. Fold in bananas.

3. Adjust oven rack to center position. Heat oven to 350°F.

4. *Make meringue:* Beat egg whites and cream of tartar in a small mixer bowl on high speed until foamy. Gradually beat in sugar, 1 tablespoon at a time, until sugar is completely dissolved and whites are stiff but not dry.

5. Pour filling into baked pie shell. Spread meringue over hot filling, sealing it well to crust (covering filling completely). Bake 15 minutes. Cool on wire rack; refrigerate until well chilled, at least 4 hours or overnight. Makes 8 servings.

Per serving: 400 calories, 19 g total fat, 10 g saturated fat, 117 mg cholesterol, 324 mg sodium, 51 g carbohydrates, 8 g protein, 93 mg calcium, 1 g fiber

classic tart cherry pie

Cherry hails as king of the fruit pies, especially when the filling features fabulous, fresh tart cherries! Tart cherries are available from late June through July.

Prep time: 25 minutes plus chilling and standing
Baking time: 75 to 80 minutes

Old-Fashioned Vinegar Pastry (see recipe, page 35)

1 cup plus 1 tablespoon sugar, divided

3 tablespoons cornstarch

⅛ teaspoon cinnamon

Pinch salt

5 cups fresh pitted sour (tart) cherries, 1½ pounds frozen sour (tart) cherries or 2 cans (16 oz. each) pitted sour (tart) cherries*

2 tablespoons fresh lemon juice

1 tablespoon butter or margarine, cut up

1. Make Old-Fashioned Vinegar Pastry as directed.

2. Adjust oven rack to lowest position. Place a cookie sheet on rack. Heat oven to 425°F. Roll the larger pastry disk into an 11-inch circle between 2 sheets of waxed paper and fit into a 9-inch pie plate, letting pastry overhang the edge.

3. Combine 1 cup of the sugar, cornstarch, cinnamon and salt in a large bowl. Add cherries and lemon juice; toss gently to combine. Spoon into pastry shell. Dot with butter. Trim pastry, leaving a 1-inch overhang.

4. Roll remaining pastry into a 9-inch circle between 2 sheets of waxed paper. Cut into ½-inch-wide strips and arrange in a lattice pattern on top of cherries. Trim the lattice ends. Fold overhanging pastry over lattice ends and flute. Sprinkle lattice with remaining 1 tablespoon sugar.

5. Place pie on cookie sheet and bake 20 minutes. Reduce oven temperature to 375°F. and bake 55 to 60 minutes more, until filling is bubbly in center. (Cover pie loosely with foil, if necessary, to prevent overbrowning.) Cool on a wire rack at least 1 hour before serving. Makes 8 servings.

*For canned cherries: Drain cherries, reserving ½ cup juice. In step 3: Combine 1 cup sugar, 3 tablespoons flour, ⅛ teaspoon cinnamon and a pinch of salt in a medium saucepan. Stir in reserved cherry juice and 2 tablespoons fresh lemon juice. Bring to boil over medium heat, stirring constantly; boil 1 minute. Remove from heat; stir in cherries. Cool completely. Proceed with recipe.

Per serving: 430 calories, 19 g total fat, 10 g saturated fat, 37 mg cholesterol, 306 mg sodium, 62 g carbohydrates, 4 g protein, 25 mg calcium, 2 g fiber

plum frangipane tart

Fresh plums star in this nutty tart that's fragrant with orange and a touch of cloves.

Prep time: 40 minutes plus chilling
Baking time: 45 to 55 minutes
Microwave used

PASTRY:

- 1¼ cups all-purpose flour
- ⅛ teaspoon salt
- ½ cup cold unsalted butter, cut up (no substitutes)
- 3 tablespoons ice water

FILLING:

- ¾ cup blanched almonds
- ⅓ cup confectioners' sugar
- 1 tablespoon all-purpose flour
  Pinch cloves
- 1 large egg
- 1 tablespoon butter, softened, cut up (no substitutes)
- ¼ teaspoon grated orange peel (optional)
- 1½ pounds small ripe plums, quartered (about 6)
- 2 tablespoons granulated sugar

- 2 tablespoons apricot or peach preserves
- 1 teaspoon water

1. *Make pastry:* Combine flour and salt in a medium bowl. Gradually add butter, tossing gently until all pieces are coated with flour. With a pastry blender or 2 knives, cut in butter until mixture resembles fine crumbs. Sprinkle with the ice water, 1 tablespoon at a time, tossing vigorously with a fork until pastry just begins to hold together.

2. On a smooth surface, shape pastry into a ball, kneading lightly if necessary. Flatten into a thick disk. Wrap tightly in plastic wrap and refrigerate 1 hour or overnight.

3. On a lightly floured surface with a floured rolling pin, roll the pastry into a 14-inch circle about ⅛ inch thick. Fold pastry in half. Carefully transfer pastry to a 10-inch tart pan with a removable bottom. Gently press pastry with fingertips along the bottom and up the side of the pan. With scissors, trim pastry to 1 inch above the edge of the pan. Fold overhanging pastry to the inside of crust and gently press edge up to extend ¼ inch above side of pan. Freeze pastry shell 20 minutes.

4. Adjust oven rack to lowest position. Place a cookie sheet on rack. Heat oven to 375°F.

5. *Make filling:* Meanwhile, combine the almonds, confectioners' sugar, flour and cloves in a food processor and process 2 minutes, until finely ground. Add egg, butter and orange peel (if using) and process until combined. Spoon and spread evenly into prepared pastry shell. Arrange plums on top and sprinkle with granulated sugar. Bake 45 to 55 minutes, until plums are tender and crust is golden brown.

6. Microwave preserves with water in a microwaveproof glass measure on High 30 seconds or until melted. Brush over warm tart. Remove side of pan and cool completely on a wire rack, about 2 hours. Makes 8 servings.

Per serving: 380 calories, 22.5 g total fat, 9.5 g saturated fat, 64 mg cholesterol, 64 mg sodium, 39 g carbohydrates, 7 g protein, 52 mg calcium, 4 g fiber

lickety-split apricot whip

This delightful recipe for apricot whip won't get in the way of your busy day. The original 1950s recipe required the toilsome task of pushing the apricots through a sieve to puree them. Thanks to the food processor, you can whip up this whip in a matter of minutes.

Prep time: 10 minutes plus freezing
Cooking time: 10 to 12 minutes

- 2 cans (17 oz. each) apricots in syrup
- ¼ cup sugar
- ⅛ teaspoon salt
- 1 cup heavy or whipping cream

APRICOT SAUCE:

- ½ cup sugar
- 2 tablespoons rum (optional)
- 1 teaspoon fresh lemon juice

1. Drain apricots, reserving syrup for sauce. Puree apricots in a food processor with sugar and salt. Whip cream in large mixer bowl on medium speed to stiff peaks; fold in apricot puree. Pour into a 9×9-inch metal pan and freeze at least 2 hours.

2. *Make apricot sauce:* Meanwhile, combine reserved syrup and sugar in a large saucepan. Bring to boil over medium-high heat; boil 10 to 12 minutes, until reduced to 1 cup. Remove from heat; stir in rum (if desired) and lemon juice. Cool to room temperature. Makes 1¼ cups.

3. *To serve:* Scoop frozen whip into 6 dessert bowls and top each with apricot sauce. Makes 6 servings.

Per serving: 365 calories, 15 g total fat, 9 g saturated fat, 55 mg cholesterol, 81 mg sodium, 60 g carbohydrates, 2 g protein, 41 mg calcium, 3 g fiber

crêpes suzette

Crêpes sound fancy but they're really just pancakes. Every country has a pancake, and in France, crêpes are often served for dessert. In the 1930s, Americans fell in love with crêpes suzette, which are filled with an orange-butter mixture and served with a brandy sauce for a dramatic dinner party finale.

Prep time: 1½ hours • Baking time: 6 minutes

CRÊPES:

- 3 large eggs
- 1½ teaspoons sugar
- ½ teaspoon salt
- 2 cups milk
- 1 cup all-purpose flour
- 6 tablespoons butter, melted (no substitutes)

FILLING:

- ¾ cup unsalted butter, divided (no substitutes)
- 1 cup confectioners' sugar
- 1 tablespoon orange-flavored liqueur
- 1 teaspoon grated orange peel
- ½ cup fresh orange juice
- ½ cup brandy or rum

1. *Make crêpes:* Whisk eggs, sugar and salt in a large bowl. Whisk in milk, flour and 3 tablespoons of the butter. Heat a 7- or 8-inch nonstick skillet over medium-high heat. Brush lightly with melted butter. Add just enough of the batter, about 3 tablespoons, to coat bottom of pan, swirling to cover evenly. Cook 30 to 60 seconds, until lightly browned. Turn crêpe and cook 30 to 60 seconds more, until golden. Transfer to waxed paper. Repeat with remaining batter, stacking cooked crêpes. *(Can be made ahead. Wrap and refrigerate up to 24 hours. Return to room temperature before filling.)*

2. *Make filling:* Beat ½ cup of the butter in a medium bowl until smooth. Beat in confectioners' sugar, orange liqueur and orange peel. Spread 1 teaspoon of the filling in center of each crêpe and fold into quarters. *(Can be made ahead. Cover and refrigerate up to 24 hours.)*

3. Heat oven to 325°F. Melt remaining filling with remaining ¼ cup butter, the orange juice and brandy in a large shallow roasting pan or bottom of a broiler pan; bring to boil. Remove from heat. Arrange crêpes, slightly overlapping, in 3 rows. Heat in oven 6 minutes, until hot. With a large spatula, transfer crêpes to a serving platter and pour sauce in pan over crêpes. Serve immediately. Makes about 2 dozen.

Per crêpe: 150 calories, 10 g total fat, 6 g saturated fat, 53 mg cholesterol, 99 mg sodium, 10 g carbohydrates, 2 g protein, 32 mg calcium, 0 g fiber

old-fashioned chocolate malt

Pour this soda-fountain favorite into pretty glasses and top with crispy chocolate wafers. If you're feeling particularly decadent, add whipped cream and, of course, a cherry.

Total prep time: 5 minutes

- 1½ cups premium vanilla ice cream
- 1 cup milk
- 5 tablespoons chocolate-flavored syrup
- ¼ cup plain instant malted milk

Combine all ingredients in a blender. Blend 30 seconds on high speed. Makes 3 cups.

Per cup: 405 calories, 16 g total fat, 9.5 g saturated fat, 57 mg cholesterol, 250 mg sodium, 60 g carbohydrates, 9 g protein, 273 mg calcium, 1 g fiber

old-fashioned rice pudding

A heavenly reminder of home, rice pudding has comforted the masses for the past century.

Prep time: 15 minutes plus chilling
Cooking time: 57 to 67 minutes

- 6 cups milk
- ¾ cup long-grain rice
- 1 cup heavy or whipping cream
- ¾ cup sugar
- 3 large egg yolks, beaten
- 2 teaspoons vanilla extract
- ¼ teaspoon salt
- About 1 teaspoon cinnamon

1. Rinse a medium saucepan with water (do not dry); pour in milk and bring to boil over medium heat. Stir in rice and return to boil. Reduce heat to medium-low. Bring to low boil; boil, uncovered, 55 minutes, until rice is tender and mixture is thick and the consistency of oatmeal, stirring occasionally. (If using converted rice, cook 65 minutes.)

2. Meanwhile, combine cream, sugar, egg yolks, vanilla and salt in a small bowl; set aside. When rice is tender and thickened, stir in cream mixture until completely combined. Return to boil; boil 2 minutes. Remove from heat and pour into a 2-quart serving dish. Sprinkle top generously with cinnamon. Cover with plastic wrap and refrigerate at least 4 hours or overnight. Makes 6 cups.

Per ½ cup: 235 calories, 11 g total fat, 6.5 g saturated fat, 90 mg cholesterol, 119 mg sodium, 28 g carbohydrates, 6 g protein, 173 mg calcium, 0 g fiber

baked indian pudding

This dish originated in New England. Serve it the traditional way, topped with whipped cream or vanilla ice cream and a sprinkle of cinnamon.

Prep time: 15 minutes
Baking time: 1 hour 15 minutes to 1 hour 25 minutes

- 2 cups milk
- 3 tablespoons yellow cornmeal
- ¼ cup molasses
- 1 tablespoon butter or margarine
- 2 large eggs, beaten
- ¼ cup sugar
- ½ teaspoon salt
- ½ teaspoon cinnamon
- ¼ teaspoon ginger

Heat oven to 300°F. Butter a 1-quart baking dish. Scald milk in a heavy saucepan. Gradually add cornmeal to milk and cook, stirring constantly, just until mixture comes to boil. Remove from heat. Add molasses and butter. Combine eggs, sugar, salt, cinnamon and ginger in a small bowl. Stir into milk mixture. Pour into prepared baking dish. Bake 1 hour 15 minutes to 1 hour 25 minutes, until center is puffed and top is a deep caramel color. Makes 6 to 8 servings.

Per serving: 145 calories, 4.5 g total fat, 2.5 g saturated fat, 71 mg cholesterol, 241 mg sodium, 21 g carbohydrates, 4 g protein, 118 mg calcium, 0 g fiber

WHITE AND
GREEN CHILI
PG. 53

daily dinner inspirations

ROASTED COD
WITH
PEPPERS AND
POTATOES
PG. 63

Whipping up a great-tasting meal needn't take more time or effort than it does to turn out ho-hum fare. If the question is what to make, you'll find answers here: inspired, satisfying recipes that are big on flavor, light on effort.

if it's true that **you**
are what you eat . . .

BRAISED BEEF
PG. 49

TANGY CHICKEN
PG. 61

...then be
something
to look
forward to!

GRILLED HAM
WITH FRUIT SALSA
PG. 55

how do you beat a
busy schedule?

CRAB CAKE
SANDWICHES
WITH CAPER
MAYONNAISE
PG. 67

CILANTRO
TURKEY
BURGERS
PG. 62

eat well—
it's the best antidote

SHRIMP GUMBO
PG. 66

set an extra place and **invite** someone to dinner

SALMON AND SOBA
NOODLES
PG. 65

good food makes

a *loving* world

have
breakfast
for dinner—
no pj's required!

HAM AND
CHEESE
OMELET
PG. 55

braised beef

Chuck is a flavorful and diverse cut of beef. When slowly braised with wine, herbs and vegetables as it is here, it becomes deliciously tender. During the last 10 minutes, stir Swiss chard into the stew for added color and taste. Pictured on page 42.

Prep time: 20 minutes
Roasting time: 1 hour 55 minutes to 2 hours 10 minutes

- **2 teaspoons salt**
- **1 teaspoon freshly ground pepper**
- **4 to 4½ pounds beef chuck shoulder steak, cut into 2-inch pieces**
- **1 tablespoon olive oil**
- **2 cups chopped onions**
- **3 parsnips, peeled and cut into 2-inch pieces**
- **1 cup coarsely chopped fennel**
- **4 garlic cloves**
- **1 large sprig fresh rosemary or 1 teaspoon dried rosemary**
- **2 tablespoons tomato paste**
- **1 4-inch strip orange peel**
- **2 cups red wine**
- **1½ cups chicken broth**
- **1 teaspoon sugar**
- **1 bunch Swiss chard, chopped**
- **Mashed potatoes (optional)**

1. Combine salt and pepper in a small cup. Sprinkle 2 teaspoons of the salt-and-pepper mixture over beef. Heat a large Dutch oven over medium-high heat. Add half of the beef and cook 3 to 5 minutes per side, until well browned. Transfer beef and juices to bowl. Repeat browning the remaining beef. Set beef aside.

2. Adjust an oven rack to lower third of oven. Heat oven to 350°F. Heat oil in same Dutch oven over medium heat. Add onions, parsnips, fennel, garlic, rosemary and remaining 1 teaspoon salt-and-pepper mixture. Cook 5 minutes, until vegetables soften. Return beef and any accumulated juices to Dutch oven; stir in tomato paste and orange peel; cook 1 minute. Add wine, broth and sugar; bring to boil. Remove from heat. Place a piece of parchment paper directly on top of beef mixture. (This will help reduce evaporation, keep corners of beef from drying out and give a deep and rich flavor.) Cover the Dutch oven with a tight-fitting lid. Bake 1 hour and 45 minutes to 2 hours, until beef is very tender.

3. When beef is tender, stir in Swiss chard. Cover and bake 10 minutes more. Skim any visible fat from the top. Serve with mashed potatoes, if desired. Makes 6 servings.

Per serving without mashed potatoes: 910 calories, 62 g total fat, 24.5 g saturated fat, 219 mg cholesterol, 1,406 mg sodium, 22 g carbohydrates, 63 g protein, 103 mg calcium, 5 g fiber

---

test kitchen tip

the skinny on swiss chard

Part of the beet family, Swiss chard features crisp green leaves and silvery celerylike stalks. The type with reddish stalks and dark green leaves, also known as "rhubarb chard," has a more intense flavor than the lighter variety. You may also see "ruby chard" with bright red stalks and a dark red leaf with green intertwined.

SELECTING AND STORING: Swiss chard can be found year-round, but its peak season is summertime. Choose chard that has crisp stalks and tender greens. Keep it refrigerated in a plastic storage bag for no more than 3 days.

PREPARING: Boil the stalks or roast them like asparagus; steam or boil the greens just as you would prepare fresh spinach.

HEALTH BONUS: Swiss chard contains iron as well as vitamins A and C.

meatloaf with roasted tomato sauce *EASY*

Canned tomatoes roasted with garlic, olive oil and red pepper flakes create a simple yet intensely flavorful sauce. Another great thing about this dish: There's no pot to fuss with; it's all done in the oven while the meatloaf bakes! Pictured on page 47.

Prep time: 15 minutes plus standing
Baking time: 70 to 75 minutes

MEATLOAF:
- 1 tablespoon olive oil
- 1 cup chopped onions
- ½ cup chopped celery
- 2 teaspoons chopped garlic
- 1 tablespoon chopped fresh flat-leaf parsley
- 1 teaspoon salt, divided
- 2¾ pounds unseasoned meatloaf mix or ground beef round
- ¾ cup fresh bread crumbs
- ⅓ cup ketchup
- 2 large eggs
- ¼ teaspoon nutmeg
- 4 slices bacon

ROASTED TOMATO SAUCE:
- 1 can (28 oz.) plum tomatoes in juice
- 1 tablespoon olive oil
- 1 large garlic clove, chopped
- ¼ teaspoon salt
- ¼ teaspoon red pepper flakes
- Cooked rice (optional)

1. Adjust oven racks to center and lower third of oven. Heat oven to 350°F. Heat oil in a large skillet over medium heat. Add onions, celery and garlic; cook 5 minutes, until vegetables soften. Stir in parsley and ½ teaspoon of the salt. Remove from heat; cool.

2. Combine ground meat, bread crumbs, ketchup, eggs, remaining ½ teaspoon salt, nutmeg and vegetables in large bowl until thoroughly blended.

3. Transfer meat mixture to a shallow roasting pan or the bottom half of a broiler pan; shape into a 9½×5-inch oval. Arrange bacon slices on top of meatloaf. Bake meatloaf on center rack 70 to 75 minutes, until an instant-read meat thermometer inserted in center of meatloaf registers 160°F.

4. *Make roasted tomato sauce:* Meanwhile, transfer tomatoes to a 9-inch square baking dish or large ovenproof skillet, breaking up tomatoes with back of spoon. Stir in oil, garlic, salt and red pepper flakes. Bake on lower rack with meatloaf 35 to 40 minutes, until sauce thickens. *(Can be made ahead. Cool sauce completely; cover and refrigerate up to 3 days. Reheat in microwave on High 3 to 5 minutes, until warm.)*

5. Let meatloaf stand 5 minutes before serving. Serve with roasted tomato sauce and rice, if desired. Makes 6 servings.

Per serving without cooked rice: 610 calories, 41.5 g total fat, 14.5 g saturated fat, 226 mg cholesterol, 1,124 mg sodium, 16 g carbohydrates, 42 g protein, 90 mg calcium, 2 g fiber

southwest bean stew *EASY*

Many chili seasoning kits found in the supermarket today go beyond flavoring ground beef with straight chili powder. The one we used contains several spice packs and masa, the corn flour so essential to achieving the proper taste and texture of Tex-Mex chili.

Prep time: 15 minutes • Cooking time: 25 minutes

- 1¼ pounds ground beef
- 1½ cups chopped onions, divided
- 1 can (14½ oz.) stewed tomatoes
- Water
- 1 package (3⅝ oz.) Wick Fowler's 2-Alarm Chili Kit or other chili seasoning kit
- 1 teaspoon salt
- ½ teaspoon ground red pepper (or more, if desired)
- 1 can (19 oz.) black beans, drained and rinsed
- 1 package (10 oz.) frozen corn, thawed
- 2 tablespoons chopped fresh cilantro
- Sour cream, for garnish (optional)

1. Heat a 12-inch nonstick skillet over medium-high heat; add beef and cook 4 to 5 minutes, until brown, breaking up with the back of a wooden spoon. Transfer beef with slotted spoon to a bowl; reserve 1 tablespoon drippings and discard remaining (if there are no drippings, add 1 tablespoon vegetable oil). Add 1 cup of the onions to skillet and cook 3 minutes, until beginning to brown. Return beef to skillet; stir in tomatoes, 2 cups water, 2-Alarm Chili Kit *except* the masa, the salt and red pepper. Bring mixture to boil; reduce heat and simmer 10 minutes.

2. Meanwhile, stir together masa and ¼ cup water. Place remaining ½ cup onion in a sieve and rinse under cold water; drain and pat dry. Stir beans, corn and masa mixture into skillet; cover and simmer 5 to 7 minutes more. Divide and spoon into 6 serving bowls. Top with reserved rinsed onion and sprinkle with cilantro. Garnish with sour cream, if desired. Makes 6 servings.

Per serving without sour cream: 385 calories, 14 g total fat, 4.5 g saturated fat, 59 mg cholesterol, 1,366 mg sodium, 40 g carbohydrates, 27 g protein, 116 mg calcium, 10 g fiber

braised short ribs

A generous serving of succulent beef short ribs, slow simmered in red wine until fork tender, may just be the ultimate comfort food experience. Select bone-in (versus boneless) ribs for maximum flavor.

Prep time: 30 minutes • Cooking time: 2 hours 25 minutes

- **3** **pounds bone-in beef short ribs, well trimmed of fat and cut into 3-inch lengths**
- **¾** **teaspoon salt, divided**
- **¼** **teaspoon freshly ground pepper**
- **1** **tablespoon olive oil**
- **2** **medium onions, halved and sliced**
- **2** **large carrots, diced**
- **1** **tablespoon minced garlic**
- **1** **can (14½ oz.) chicken broth**
- **½** **cup dried cherries**
- **½** **cup dry red wine**
- **½** **teaspoon dried thyme**
- **1** **bay leaf**
- **1** **tablespoon Dijon mustard**

- **1** **tablespoon prepared horseradish**
- **2** **tablespoons chopped fresh parsley, for garnish (optional)**
- **Mashed potatoes (optional)**

1. Heat oven to 350°F. Sprinkle the ribs with ½ teaspoon of the salt and the pepper. Heat oil in large Dutch oven over medium-high heat; brown ribs well on all sides, reducing heat if necessary. Discard drippings in Dutch oven. Reduce heat to medium-low. Add onions, carrots and garlic to same Dutch oven; cook 10 minutes, until softened.

2. Return ribs to Dutch oven. Add broth, cherries, wine, thyme, bay leaf and remaining ¼ teaspoon salt. Bring to boil and cover Dutch oven. Bake 2 hours, until meat is very tender and falls off the bones.

3. Remove ribs to a large, deep serving platter and cover to keep warm. With a spoon, skim all fat from Dutch oven; discard bay leaf and any bones that have fallen off ribs. If sauce is too thin, bring to boil and boil 5 minutes to reduce slightly (you should have about 2½ cups). Whisk in mustard and horseradish. Pour sauce over ribs. Sprinkle with parsley and serve with mashed potatoes, if desired. Makes 6 servings.

Per serving without parsley or mashed potatoes: 280 calories, 14 g total fat, 5 g saturated fat, 57 mg cholesterol, 696 mg sodium, 18 g carbohydrates, 21 g protein, 39 mg calcium, 2 g fiber

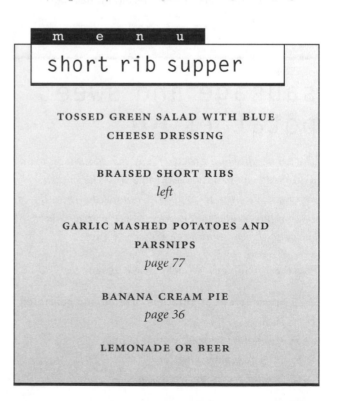

m e n u

short rib supper

TOSSED GREEN SALAD WITH BLUE CHEESE DRESSING

BRAISED SHORT RIBS
left

GARLIC MASHED POTATOES AND PARSNIPS
page 77

BANANA CREAM PIE
page 36

LEMONADE OR BEER

specialty sausages

ANDOUILLE: A peppery, smoked Cajun sausage made with pork and tripe, chitterlings, pepper and sometimes wine, onions and spices. Serve it grilled or in gumbos, stews or mixed with red beans.

BRATWURST: Smooth veal and pork sausage of German origin seasoned with an array of sweet and savory spices. Serve it hot with rice or vegetables, or make a hearty sandwich by topping it with sautéed onions.

CHORIZO: A Spanish (and Latin American) spicy hot pork sausage seasoned with ground red pepper, red bell pepper and sometimes garlic. Serve it with pasta; in casseroles, enchiladas, soups or stews; or on pizza.

KIELBASA: A smoked pork sausage, sometimes with beef added. Serve it with sauerkraut or add to potato casseroles.

ITALIAN: A spicy pork sausage flavored with garlic and fennel seed. Hot and sweet varieties are available. Serve it with pasta, in meatballs or on pizza.

sausage and sweet potatoes 🍽 EASY

The availability and variety of fully cooked sausages are a welcomed boon to busy weeknight cooks. The chicken sausage in this dish takes about 8 minutes to reheat. For a boost of flavor, the potatoes are drizzled with a reduced balsamic vinegar, a nice alternative to butter.

Prep time: 10 minutes • Cooking time: 20 minutes

- **2 pounds sweet potatoes, peeled and quartered**
  Salt
- **¼ teaspoon freshly ground pepper**
- **⅓ cup balsamic vinegar**
- **2 tablespoons brown sugar**

- **2 packages (13 oz. each) fully cooked chicken sausage (such as Chef Bruce Aidells or D'Artagnan)***
- **1 tablespoon extra-virgin olive oil**

1. Arrange a steamer basket in a saucepan. Add enough water to reach just below the steamer basket. Add sweet potatoes; cover pan and bring water to boil. Reduce heat and cook potatoes 15 to 20 minutes, until tender. Remove steamer basket from saucepan; discard water. Return potatoes and ½ teaspoon salt and the pepper to saucepan; mash with a potato masher. Set aside.

2. Meanwhile, bring vinegar, sugar and a pinch of salt to boil in small saucepan over medium heat. Cook 3 to 5 minutes, until mixture reduces to about 3 tablespoons. Set aside.

3. Arrange sausages in a single layer in a large nonstick skillet. Add oil and toss to coat well.

4. Cook the sausages over medium-high heat 8 minutes, until golden brown on both sides, turning sausages once. Transfer sweet potatoes to a large serving bowl; drizzle balsamic mixture over potatoes. Serve with the sausages. Makes 4 servings.

* Note: Available from Aidells Sausage Co. (877-243-3557) or D'Artagnan (800-327-8246).

Per serving: 620 calories, 32.5 g total fat, 10 g saturated fat, 164 mg cholesterol, 1,604 mg sodium, 49 g carbohydrates, 31 g protein, 83 mg calcium, 5 g fiber

spice-rubbed steak 🍽 EASY

Tasty do-ahead recipes such as this one satisfy the busiest of schedules. The flank steak is coated with a dry spice and herb mixture, then retreats to the refrigerator for 4 or more hours of chilling.

Prep time: 10 minutes plus chilling
Grilling time: 12 to 16 minutes

SPICE RUB:
- **3 tablespoons brown sugar**
- **1 tablespoon kosher salt**
- **2 teaspoons ground cumin**
- **2 teaspoons extra-virgin olive oil**
- **1 teaspoon coriander**

1 teaspoon chili powder
1 teaspoon dry mustard
1 teaspoon dried oregano
1 teaspoon dried thyme
½ teaspoon ground red pepper
■
2 flank steaks (1½ lbs. each)

1. ■ *Make spice rub:* Combine all ingredients in a small bowl. Rub spice mixture on both sides of each steak. Cover and refrigerate 4 hours or overnight.

2. ■ Remove steaks from refrigerator 30 minutes before grilling. Heat grill or grill pan. Oil grill or gill pan. Lightly rinse the steaks to remove excess rub, being careful not to wash away all of the seasoning. Pat dry with paper towels. Grill steaks over medium-high heat 6 to 8 minutes per side, until an instant-read meat thermometer inserted in the thickest portion of each steak registers 145°F. for medium rare. Let steaks stand 5 minutes. Slice steaks thinly across the grain. Makes 8 servings.

Per serving: 300 calories, 16.5 g total fat, 6.5 g saturated fat, 85 mg cholesterol, 470 mg sodium, 3 g carbohydrates, 33 g protein, 17 mg calcium, 0 g fiber

white and green chili ⓔⓐⓢⓨ

Whip up some serious chili without a lot of ingredients, thanks to convenient meatloaf mix and prepared green salsa. Pictured on page 41.

Total prep and cooking time: 30 minutes

1 pound unseasoned meatloaf mix or ground beef round or ⅓ pound each ground veal, pork and beef
1 small onion, chopped
2 cans (15 oz. each) Great Northern or white beans, drained and rinsed
1 jar (16 oz.) prepared green salsa
1 can (14½ oz.) chicken broth
1½ teaspoons ground cumin
4 tablespoons chopped fresh cilantro, divided
½ cup sour cream
Fresh cilantro sprigs, for garnish (optional)

1. ■ Heat a large Dutch oven over high heat. Add meat mixture and onion and cook 5 minutes, until brown, breaking up meat with spoon. Drain off any fat. Add beans, salsa, chicken broth and cumin. Bring to boil; reduce heat and simmer 15 minutes.

2. ■ Stir in 3 tablespoons of the chopped cilantro. Spoon into 4 serving bowls. Top with sour cream and remaining 1 tablespoon chopped cilantro. Garnish with cilantro sprigs, if desired. Makes 4 servings.

Per serving: 480 calories, 21 g total fat, 9 g saturated fat, 86 mg cholesterol, 1,536 mg sodium, 37 g carbohydrates, 32 g protein, 107 mg calcium, 9 g fiber

paprika and thyme rubbed pork tenderloin ⓔⓐⓢⓨ

A simple rub adds both color and flavor to pork tenderloin.

Prep time: 10 minutes plus standing
Baking time: 25 to 30 minutes

DRY RUB:
2 teaspoons minced fresh thyme or ½ teaspoon dried thyme
1 teaspoon paprika
1 teaspoon onion powder
1 teaspoon salt
¼ teaspoon freshly ground pepper
■
2 pork tenderloins (about 1 lb. each)
2 teaspoons olive oil

1. ■ Arrange rack in upper third of oven. Heat oven to 375°F.

2. ■ *Make dry rub:* Combine thyme, paprika, onion powder, salt and pepper in a cup.

3. ■ Arrange tenderloins on a broiler pan; brush with oil. Divide and sprinkle rub over all sides of each tenderloin. Roast on upper rack 25 to 30 minutes, until an instant-read meat thermometer inserted into center of each tenderloin registers 155°F. Let stand 5 minutes before slicing. Makes 6 servings.

Per serving: 220 calories, 9 g total fat, 3 g saturated fat, 99 mg cholesterol, 447 mg sodium, 1 g carbohydrates, 31 g protein, 11 mg calcium, 0 g fiber

southwest turkey fritters ⓔⓐⓢⓨ

Love those leftovers! Got 3 cups of cooked turkey? That's all you need to whip up this meal. Smoked chiles give these skillet patties a spicy kick. Serve them with cranberry relish to counter the heat.

Prep time: 30 minutes plus chilling
Cooking time: 6 minutes per batch

- ⅔ cup shredded Monterey Jack cheese
- ½ cup mayonnaise
- ½ teaspoon grated lime peel
- 2 tablespoons fresh lime juice
- 2 teaspoons minced chipotle chile in adobo sauce* (see tip, page 100)
- ¾ teaspoon salt
- 3 cups shredded cooked turkey
- 1 tablespoon plus 4 teaspoons olive oil, divided
- 1 cup minced red onions
- ¾ cup minced green bell pepper
- ½ cup minced celery
- 1¼ cups fresh bread crumbs

1. Combine cheese, mayonnaise, lime peel, lime juice, chipotle and salt in a bowl; stir in turkey.

2. Heat 1 tablespoon of the oil in a 12-inch nonstick skillet over medium-high heat. Add onions, bell pepper and celery. Cook 5 minutes. Stir onion mixture into turkey mixture.

3. Spread bread crumbs in a plate. Spoon ½ cup of the turkey mixture into crumbs, turning to coat. Pat into a 2½×1-inch fritter. Repeat with remaining turkey mixture. Refrigerate 1 hour.

4. Heat 2 teaspoons of the oil in same skillet over medium heat. Cook 4 fritters 3 minutes per side, until golden. Transfer to platter; cover and keep warm. Repeat with the remaining 2 teaspoons oil and fritters. Makes 8 fritters.

Note: Can be found in the ethnic sections of supermarkets or in Spanish or Latino specialty stores.

Per fritter: 295 calories, 20 g total fat, 4.5 g saturated fat, 53 mg cholesterol, 443 mg sodium, 7 g carbohydrates, 20 g protein, 98 mg calcium, 1 g fiber

capellini with sausage and spinach ⓔⓐⓢⓨ

Sausage and spinach lend their flavors to capellini in this one-pot dish that sauces itself as it cooks. Tip: The pasta is al dente when it is tender but still slightly firm when you bite into it.

Prep time: 15 minutes · Cooking time: 10 to 13 minutes

- 2 teaspoons olive oil
- 1 pound sweet Italian sausage, cut into ½-inch-thick slices
- 1 large onion, chopped
- 2 large garlic cloves, chopped
- 2 cans (14 oz. each) chicken broth
- ¼ cup water
- ½ pound capellini or vermicelli pasta, broken in half
- 2 bags (10 oz. each) or 1 bag (20 oz.) fresh spinach, coarsely chopped
- ¼ teaspoon freshly ground pepper
- ⅓ cup heavy or whipping cream

1. Heat oil in a Dutch oven or stockpot over medium-high heat; add the sausage and cook 3 to 4 minutes, turning as it browns. Add the onion and garlic and cook 2 to 3 minutes, until lightly browned.

2. Add broth and water to Dutch oven or pot; cover and bring to boil. Stir in pasta and cook 3 minutes, stirring frequently. Stir in spinach and pepper and cook 2 to 3 minutes more, until pasta is al dente and spinach is wilted. Stir in cream. Makes 4 to 6 servings.

Per serving: 615 calories, 38.5 g total fat, 14.5 g saturated fat, 91 mg cholesterol, 1,441 mg sodium, 44 g carbohydrates, 24 g protein, 159 mg calcium, 5 g fiber

ham and cheese omelet (EASY)

We call for Parmesan cheese for this breakfast, lunch or dinner omelet, but Swiss, Gruyère or Romano works deliciously as well. Pictured on page 48.

Prep time: 5 minutes
Cooking time: 1 minute 30 seconds to 2 minutes

PER OMELET:

- 2 **large eggs**
- 2 **tablespoons water**
- **Pinch salt**
- **Pinch freshly ground pepper**
- ¼ **cup ricotta, at room temperature**
- 2 **tablespoons coarsely shredded Parmesan cheese**
- ½ **tablespoon butter or margarine**
- 1 **large slice (1 oz.) rosemary ham or ham plus ⅛ teaspoon crushed dried rosemary**
- 1 **tablespoon chopped fresh chives**

1. Whisk together eggs, water, salt and pepper in a small bowl until blended. Combine ricotta and Parmesan in another small bowl.

2. Melt butter in a 10-inch nonstick skillet over medium heat, swirling to coat bottom and sides of skillet. Heat until bubbles begin to subside.

3. Pour in egg mixture. Swirl the skillet to evenly coat the bottom with egg. With skillet handle facing you, as eggs begin to set on bottom, gently push back cooked egg and tilt pan slightly to allow uncooked egg to flow onto exposed skillet. Return pan to heat and cook eggs a total of 1 minute, until the top is almost set (could be slightly wet).

4. With handle of skillet facing you, place ham on one side on top of omelet; dollop ricotta mixture down center. Sprinkle with some of the chives. Run a narrow spatula around edge of egg. (Don't worry if edge tears; when omelet is folded over you won't see it.) Roll one side of omelet over the ricotta into center, then over the opposite side. Slide onto plate,

flipping to encase the filling. Sprinkle with remaining chives. Makes 1 omelet. Repeat steps 1 through 4 for each additional omelet.

Per omelet: 415 calories, 30.5 g total fat, 15 g saturated fat, 498 mg cholesterol, 977 mg sodium, 5 g carbohydrates, 30 g protein, 353 mg calcium, 0 g fiber

grilled ham with fruit salsa (EASY)

The days of ham and pineapple are taking a well-deserved break. For a change of pace, rub the ham steak with cumin and pepper and replace the pineapple with a sumptuous mango-apple-cilantro salsa. Pictured on page 43.

Prep time: 10 minutes • Grilling time: 2 to 4 minutes

FRUIT SALSA:

- 1 **mango, peeled and diced**
- ½ **of a Granny Smith apple, cored and diced**
- 1 **tablespoon chopped fresh cilantro**
- 2 **teaspoons fresh lime juice**
- 1 **teaspoon sugar**
- **Pinch salt**

HAM:

- 1¾ **pounds bone-in, thick-cut ham steak**
- ½ **teaspoon ground cumin**
- ½ **teaspoon sugar**
- ½ **teaspoon olive oil**
- ¼ **teaspoon freshly ground pepper**

- **Cooked rice (optional)**

1. *Make the fruit salsa:* Combine all ingredients in bowl. *(Can be made ahead. Cover salsa and refrigerate overnight.)*

2. Heat grill or grill pan over medium-high heat.

3. Rinse ham steak and pat dry. Combine cumin, sugar, oil and pepper in a cup. Brush on both sides of steak. Grill ham over medium-high heat 1 to 2 minutes per side, until heated through and grill marks are dark.

4. Serve with fruit salsa and cooked rice, if desired. Makes 4 servings.

Per serving without cooked rice: 280 calories, 12 g total fat, 4 g saturated fat, 74 mg cholesterol, 1,909 mg sodium, 13 g carbohydrates, 29 g protein, 20 mg calcium, 1 g fiber

braciole basics

Braciole (also spelled "braciola") is the Italian word for roulade—a French term for thinly sliced meat that's rolled around a filling, such as sautéed vegetables with cheese. As directed in our "Pork Braciole with Polenta" (see recipe below), these rolled delights are normally held together with a toothpick or, in some recipes, string. Although we use thinly sliced boneless pork loin in our recipe, braciole is also often made with beef top round or top sirloin, flank steak or even thinly sliced veal. In fact, bracioles are sometimes described as Italian beef rolls. Regardless of the meat you use, just be sure to pound it to about ¼ inch thickness (or ask a butcher to do the honors).

pork braciole with polenta *EASY* *LOW FAT*

Most supermarket butchers will prepare braciole filets for you if they're not offered in the meat case. For this recipe, we suggest preparing them from boneless pork chops.

Prep time: 30 minutes • Cooking time: 45 minutes

BRACIOLE FILLING:
- 1 tablespoon olive oil
- ½ pound shiitake or white mushrooms, sliced
- ½ cup thinly sliced onion
- ¼ teaspoon salt
- ⅛ teaspoon freshly ground pepper
- ¼ cup freshly grated Parmesan cheese
- 2 tablespoons chopped fresh parsley
- ½ teaspoon chopped fresh rosemary or
    - ⅛ teaspoon dried rosemary

TOMATO SAUCE:
- 1 tablespoon olive oil
- 1 small onion, chopped
- 1 tablespoon chopped garlic
- ¼ cup white wine
- ⅓ cup water
- 1 can (28 oz.) crushed tomatoes in thick puree

- 2 cans (8 oz. each) tomato sauce
- 1 teaspoon salt
- ¼ teaspoon freshly ground pepper
- ⅛ teaspoon red pepper flakes
- ⅛ teaspoon crushed fennel seeds
    - ▪
- 8 very thin slices boneless pork loin (¾ lb.)

POLENTA:
- 2 cups water
- 1 can (14½ oz.) chicken broth
- 1½ cups instant polenta
- 2 tablespoons butter or margarine
    - ▪

    Freshly grated Romano or Parmesan cheese

1. *Make braciole filling:* Heat oil in a 4-quart saucepan. Add mushrooms and onion and cook over medium heat 10 minutes, until tender and lightly browned. Sprinkle with salt and pepper; transfer to a medium bowl and combine with cheese, parsley and rosemary.

2. *Make tomato sauce:* Heat oil in same pan. Add onion and garlic and cook 3 minutes, until tender. Add wine; bring to boil and boil 1 minute. Stir in remaining ingredients. Bring to boil; reduce heat, cover and simmer 15 minutes while finishing the braciole.

3. Meanwhile, arrange pork slices on a work surface. Divide braciole filling among slices, mounding in the center of each. Fold in two sides and roll up. Secure with toothpicks. Add pork rolls to sauce; cover and simmer 15 minutes. *(Can be made ahead. Cool and transfer to an airtight container. Refrigerate up to 4 days or freeze up to 2 weeks. If frozen, thaw overnight in refrigerator. Remove from refrigerator and let stand at room temperature 1 hour. Bring to simmer; cover and cook 30 minutes, until heated through.)*

4. *Make polenta:* Bring water and broth to boil in a deep, heavy-bottomed saucepot. Whisking constantly, slowly sprinkle polenta into liquid. Reduce heat to medium and cook 5 minutes, until thickened, stirring constantly with a wooden spoon. Stir in butter until melted. Immediately divide among 4 serving plates. Add 2 braciole to each plate and top with ½ cup of the tomato sauce; sprinkle each with 1 teaspoon of the grated cheese. Serve with remaining sauce and additional grated cheese, if desired. Makes 4 servings.

Per serving without additional sauce or grated cheese: 795 calories, 22 g total fat, 8 g saturated fat, 70 mg cholesterol, 2,301 mg sodium, 107 g carbohydrates, 38 g protein, 222 mg calcium, 16 g fiber

ham steak hash

Looking for a quick weeknight supper? Ham steak hash couldn't be easier. Our version comes together with leeks, onions, bell pepper, jalapeño, thyme and kale. Add a dash of red pepper sauce if you want to boost the heat.

Prep time: 15 minutes • Cooking time: 38 to 43 minutes

- 2 **tablespoons olive oil, divided**
- 1 **cup sliced leeks (white part only)**
- ½ **cup chopped onion**
- ½ **cup chopped yellow bell pepper**
- 2 **teaspoons chopped jalapeño chile (see tip, page 92)**
- 1 **teaspoon fresh thyme leaves or ½ teaspoon dried thyme**
- ¼ **teaspoon salt**
- ⅛ **teaspoon freshly ground pepper**
- 1 **pound russet potatoes, peeled and diced**
- 1 **can (14½ oz.) chicken broth, divided**
- 2 **cups chopped kale**
- 1 **pound boneless ham steak, diced**
  Hot red pepper sauce (optional)

1. Heat 1 tablespoon of the oil in a large nonstick skillet over medium heat. Add leeks, onion, bell pepper and jalapeño; cook 5 minutes, until vegetables soften. Stir in thyme, salt and pepper. Increase heat to medium-high. Add potatoes and cook 8 to 10 minutes, until potatoes begin to brown, stirring occasionally. Stir in 1½ cups of the broth. Cover skillet; reduce heat to medium-low and simmer 15 minutes, until potatoes are tender.

2. Uncover skillet; increase heat to medium-high. Add kale, ham and remaining broth. Cook until liquid evaporates, 10 minutes. Add remaining

1 tablespoon oil, stirring to keep potatoes from sticking. Cook hash 5 to 13 minutes, until potatoes are well browned. Serve with hot red pepper sauce, if desired. Makes 4 servings.

Per serving: 415 calories, 18 g total fat, 4.5 g saturated fat, 67 mg cholesterol, 2,200 mg sodium, 31 g carbohydrates, 32 g protein, 88 mg calcium, 4 g fiber

pasta with hot sausage, pepper and mushroom marinara

Here's a tomato sauce made with the works. It's chock full of spicy sausage and chunky veggies to satisfy hearty appetites.

Prep time: 5 minutes • Cooking time: 15 minutes

- ½ **pound hot Italian sausage, casings removed**
- 1 **green bell pepper, diced**
- ½ **pound mushrooms, sliced**
- 1 **jar (14 oz.) marinara sauce**
- 1 **pound rigatoni or ruote (wheels), cooked according to package directions**

1. Crumble sausage into a large nonstick skillet. Cook over medium-high heat 10 minutes, until browned.

2. Add bell pepper and mushrooms; cook 5 minutes more. Stir in marinara sauce; bring to boil.

3. Toss sauce with hot pasta in a large serving bowl. Serve immediately. Makes 6 servings.

Per serving: 455 calories, 14.5 g total fat, 4 g saturated fat, 30 mg cholesterol, 610 mg sodium, 65 g carbohydrates, 17 g protein, 39 mg calcium, 3 g fiber

friday night fried chicken dinner

SLICED CHEESE AND CRACKERS

CRISPY FRIED CHICKEN
below

PERFECT CORN BREAD
page 78

WARM RED POTATO AND CORN SALAD
page 115

WATERMELON SLICES

LEMONADE

crispy fried chicken

Marinating the chicken in buttermilk and red pepper sauce is the secret to this moist, tender picnic treat. Use a cast-iron skillet to cook the chicken—it maintains a constant, even heat for crisp results.

Prep time: 15 minutes plus chilling
Cooking time: 20 to 30 minutes

- 1 **teaspoon salt**
- 1 **whole chicken (3 to 3½ lbs.), cut into 8 pieces (see tip, page 19)**
- 2 **cups buttermilk**
- ½ **teaspoon hot red pepper sauce**
- 1½ **cups all-purpose flour**
- 2 **tablespoons Old Bay seasoning**
- ¾ **teaspoon freshly ground pepper**
- 2 **cups vegetable shortening**

1. Sprinkle salt on both sides of chicken. Combine buttermilk and red pepper sauce in a 1-gallon resealable plastic storage bag or a 13×9-inch glass baking dish; add chicken. Seal bag and turn chicken with buttermilk mixture to coat. If using a baking dish, cover with plastic wrap. Refrigerate 1 hour or overnight, turning once.

2. Arrange a large sheet of waxed paper on work surface. Arrange 2 wire racks on paper. Combine flour, Old Bay seasoning and pepper in pie plate or shallow dish. Working with several pieces of chicken at a time, remove chicken from buttermilk, shaking off excess; add to flour mixture, turning to coat evenly. Transfer pieces to wire rack. Repeat process with remaining chicken.

3. Meanwhile, heat oven to 250°F. Melt shortening in a 10-inch cast-iron skillet over medium heat until temperature reaches 360°F. on a deep-fat thermometer. Add several pieces of chicken, skin sides down, to hot shortening. Cover skillet and cook 5 minutes, until undersides are lightly golden. Turn pieces and cook, covered, until deep-golden and cooked through, turning every 4 to 5 minutes. Allow 7 to 10 minutes more for white meat and 12 to 15 minutes more for dark meat. For even cooking, keep heat adjusted to medium-low (medium for electric stovetop) to maintain a 275°F. to 300°F. temperature. Drain pieces on paper towels; transfer to baking sheet and keep warm in oven. Repeat process to cook remaining chicken. Makes 4 to 6 servings.

Per serving: 630 calories, 40 g total fat, 11 g saturated fat, 147 mg cholesterol, 1,483 mg sodium, 17 g carbohydrates, 49 g protein, 135 mg calcium, 0.5 g fiber

easy chicken cacciatore

This simple dish combines some of the most delicious and nutritious of foods. Red peppers and tomatoes provide vitamins A and C; tomatoes impart the anticancer phytochemical lycopene; and onions contribute their detoxifying effect with allicin. We used fire-roasted tomatoes, a new tomato product, for more robust flavor.

Prep time: 20 minutes • Cooking time: 20 to 25 minutes

- 1¼ **pounds boneless, skinless chicken thighs, cut into 1-inch chunks**
- 1 **teaspoon salt, divided**
- ⅛ **teaspoon plus ¼ teaspoon freshly ground pepper, divided**

1   tablespoon olive oil
2   medium red bell peppers, cut into
      1-inch cubes
1   pound small white onions, peeled and trimmed
1   tablespoon finely chopped garlic
⅓   cup white wine
2   cans (14½ oz. each) fire-roasted
      crushed tomatoes
1   box (13.2 oz.) 5-minute polenta
      Chopped fresh parsley, for garnish (optional)

1. Sprinkle chicken with ½ teaspoon of the salt and ⅛ teaspoon of the pepper.

2. Heat a 12-inch nonstick skillet over high heat. Add chicken and cook 3½ minutes, until browned, turning once. Transfer to a bowl.

3. Heat oil in same skillet. Add bell peppers and onions; reduce heat to medium-high and cook 4 minutes, until lightly browned. Add garlic and cook 30 seconds. Add wine and boil 1 minute. Add tomatoes, chicken with any accumulated juices, remaining ½ teaspoon salt and ¼ teaspoon pepper; bring to boil. Reduce heat to medium; cover and cook 10 minutes. Uncover and cook 10 to 15 minutes more, until sauce is slightly thickened and chicken is tender.

4. Meanwhile, cook polenta during last 5 minutes of the sauce's cooking time, following the package directions for soft polenta.

5. Divide polenta among 4 shallow serving bowls; top with chicken cacciatore. Sprinkle with parsley, if desired. Makes 4 servings.

Per serving: 625 calories, 9.5 g total fat, 2 g saturated fat, 118 mg cholesterol, 1,176 mg sodium, 89 g carbohydrates, 39 g protein, 97 mg calcium, 13 g fiber

chicken and red rice burritos EASY LOW FAT

We used easy-to-grab ingredients for these low-fat burritos. Since it's a quick recipe, feel free to make substitutions that suit your pantry or palate. For example, black beans for pink and flavored tortillas for a change of color.

Total prep and cooking time: 30 minutes

1   tablespoon vegetable oil
½   cup long-grain or medium-grain rice
1½   cups water
1½   cups prepared salsa, divided
1   cup canned pink beans, drained and rinsed
½   teaspoon salt
2   cups shredded cooked chicken
4   large lettuce leaves
4   burrito-size (10-inch) flour tortillas, softened
½   cup grated plain or pepper Monterey
       Jack cheese
       Additional salsa (optional)

1. Heat oil in large skillet over high heat. Add rice and cook 1 minute. Add water, 1 cup of the salsa, the beans and salt. Bring to boil. Cover and simmer 15 to 20 minutes, until rice is tender.

2. Toss chicken with remaining ½ cup salsa. Arrange a lettuce leaf on 1 tortilla. Spoon ¾ cup of the rice mixture down center of the lettuce leaf. Arrange ½ cup of the chicken mixture on top of rice; sprinkle with 2 tablespoons of the cheese. Roll up burrito and cut in half. Repeat with remaining tortillas, lettuce, rice, chicken and cheese. Serve with additional salsa, if desired. Makes 4 servings.

Per serving without additional salsa: 540 calories, 18 g total fat, 6 g saturated fat, 88 mg cholesterol, 832 mg sodium, 56 g carbohydrates, 37 g protein, 211 mg calcium, 4 g fiber

salts of the earth

Once upon a time, salt was rare and highly prized; in fact, Roman soldiers were paid, in part, with salt. Today it is inexpensive and plentiful, and perhaps the most often-used seasoning in the world. While most recipes call for table salt, there are other varieties. Here are some types commonly available, plus hints for storing salt:

TABLE SALT contains additives to help keep it from clumping and to give it its pure whiteness. Iodine, an essential dietary nutrient, is added to many table salts. Uniodized salt is also available.

KOSHER SALT has no additives and is more coarsely ground than table salt. Some of the recipes in this book call for kosher salt for its enhanced texture and less salty flavor.

SEA SALT is derived from the evaporation of seawater. This process is more costly than mining the mineral from salt mines; but some cooks prefer its flavor despite the added cost.

ROCK SALT, often called for in the freezing of homemade ice cream, is inedible. Because it is unrefined, it has a grayish hue.

CANNING AND PICKLING SALT is additive-free and does not cloud brines. It is more finely ground than regular table salt.

SEASONED SALTS are simply blends of salt and other seasonings.

STORING SALT: With the exception of seasoned salts, all salts can be stored indefinitely at room temperature. Store seasoned salts tightly capped at room temperature and use within 1 year.

fusilli with beans and chicken

A great source of calcium and iron, this fun and tasty pasta dish is an easy way to introduce beans to children. We used navy beans, which are small and creamy. Canned beans may be substituted for dried.

Prep time: 20 minutes plus standing · Cooking time: 1 hour

- 1 **cup dried navy beans, rinsed and picked over**
- 3 **teaspoons olive oil, divided**
- 1 **medium onion, chopped**
- 1 **tablespoon finely chopped garlic**
- 1 **can (14½ oz.) chicken broth**
- 1 **cup water**
- ¼ **teaspoon dried thyme**
- 1 **pound boneless, skinless chicken thighs, cut into ½-inch cubes**
- ½ **teaspoon salt**
- ¼ **teaspoon freshly ground pepper**
- ½ **cup white wine**
- 1 **can (14½ oz.) diced tomatoes**
- ¾ **pound fusilli, rotelle or cavatappi (corkscrew) pasta, cooked according to package directions**
- 1 **tablespoon chopped fresh flat-leaf parsley**

1. Cover dried beans with 2 inches of cold water. Refrigerate overnight. *(To quick soak:* Combine beans with water to cover by 2 inches in a 3-quart saucepan. Bring to boil; boil 2 minutes. Remove from heat. Cover and let stand 1 hour.) Drain beans in colander; set aside.

2. Heat 2 teaspoons of the oil in a 3-quart saucepan over medium heat. Add onion and cook 5 minutes, until softened; add garlic and cook 30 seconds, until fragrant. Add broth, water, beans and thyme. Cover and cook 45 minutes, until beans are almost tender.

3. Meanwhile, sprinkle chicken with salt and pepper. Heat the remaining 1 teaspoon oil in a large nonstick skillet over high heat. Add chicken and cook 3 to 4 minutes, turning as pieces brown. Add wine and boil 1 minute.

4. Stir chicken mixture and tomatoes into beans; bring to simmer. Simmer, uncovered, 10 to 12 minutes more.

5. Transfer hot pasta to a large serving bowl. Pour bean and chicken mixture over top and sprinkle with parsley. Makes 6 servings.

Per serving: 490 calories, 7 g total fat, 1.5 g saturated fat, 60 mg cholesterol, 585 mg sodium, 69 g carbohydrates, 32 g protein, 105 mg calcium, 10 g fiber

tangy chicken

This easy-on-the-cook dish comes together in 15 minutes and roasts unattended. Pictured on page 43.

Prep time: 15 minutes • Roasting time: 45 minutes

- 1 **teaspoon salt**
- ½ **teaspoon freshly ground pepper**
- 3 **pounds chicken thighs, excess fat discarded**
- 1 **teaspoon olive oil**
- 1 **large sweet onion (8 oz.), cut into ½-inch-thick slices**
- 1 **large red onion (8 oz.), cut into ½-inch-thick slices**
- 2 **shallots, quartered**
- ¼ **cup plus 1 tablespoon chopped fresh sage, divided**
- 4 **tablespoons sherry vinegar, divided**
  Fresh herb sprigs, for garnish (optional)
  Cooked polenta (optional)

1. Heat oven to 400°F. Combine salt and pepper in cup. Sprinkle 1 teaspoon of the salt-and-pepper mixture over both sides of chicken.

2. Brush oil on the bottom of a broiler pan or shallow roasting pan; add onions, shallots, ¼ cup of the sage and remaining ½ teaspoon salt-and-pepper mixture to prepared pan. Arrange chicken, skin sides up, on top of onions. Pour 3 tablespoons of the vinegar evenly over chicken. Sprinkle remaining 1 tablespoon sage over top.

3. Roast 45 minutes, until chicken is golden brown and cooked through. Pour remaining 1 tablespoon vinegar over chicken. Transfer chicken and onion

mixture to large serving plate. Garnish with fresh herb sprigs, if desired. Serve with polenta, if desired. Makes 4 to 6 servings.

Per serving without garnish or polenta: 575 calories, 39 g total fat, 11 g saturated fat, 208 mg cholesterol, 665 mg sodium, 10 g carbohydrates, 44 g protein, 62 mg calcium, 2 g fiber

test kitchen tip
fresh herb hints

REFRIGERATE most fresh herbs, whole leaves intact and dry, in a resealable plastic storage bag. (If the herbs come with stems or roots, store them with the roots immersed in water and the leaves loosely covered with a plastic bag.) Store basil as directed above, *except* do not refrigerate.

FOR MAXIMUM FLAVOR, chop herbs just before you're ready to use them. In no-cook sauces, herbs retain their delicate flavors and can be mixed in any time, but for cooked sauces, it's best to add herbs toward the end of the cooking time.

SUBSTITUTE dried herbs if need be, but use restraint when measuring the amount; their flavor is more potent. As a basic rule of thumb, substitute ¼ the amount of dried herb for the fresh plus 4 times that amount of chopped fresh flat-leaf parsley. For example: If the recipe calls for 1 teaspoon chopped fresh oregano, substitute ¼ teaspoon dried oregano and 1 teaspoon chopped fresh flat-leaf parsley.

CREATE an herb brush. Simply tie kitchen string around the stem ends of assorted fresh herbs (rosemary, thyme, sage, oregano or marjoram). Dip the sprigs in olive oil or vinaigrette dressing and brush over chicken, beef or vegetables while grilling.

cheers to cilantro

This zesty herb from the coriander plant has an earthy-lime flavor and is a staple in Asian cooking (it's also widely used in Caribbean and Latin American cooking). It comes in bunches (like parsley) and has a wonderfully pungent fragrance.

LOOK FOR bright, evenly colored cilantro leaves that are not wilted.

STORE CILANTRO in a plastic bag and keep in the refrigerator up to 1 week. (Another option is to place the stems in a container of water, cover the leaves with a plastic bag and place in the refrigerator; change the water every few days.)

USE fresh cilantro in all sorts of entrées (see recipe below); it particularly complements spicy foods. Wash the leaves with water and dry well with paper towels just before use.

cilantro turkey burgers

It's easy to jazz up your burgers tonight with the fresh, lively taste of cilantro. Just add the chopped herb to the burgers and zesty topping. Pictured on page 44.

Prep time: 20 minutes • Grilling time: 16 to 18 minutes

BURGERS:

- 1½ **pounds ground raw turkey (a blend of dark and white meat)**
- 1 **cup packed fresh cilantro leaves with stems or 1 cup packed fresh flat-leaf parsley leaves and 1 teaspoon dried cilantro, chopped**
- ¼ **cup finely chopped onion**
- 2 **teaspoons minced garlic**
- ¾ **teaspoon salt**
- ¼ **teaspoon freshly ground pepper**
-    ▪
- 1 **tablespoon olive oil**

MAYONNAISE:

- 1 **cup mayonnaise**
- 1 **cup packed fresh cilantro leaves with stems or 1 cup packed fresh flat-leaf parsley leaves and 1 teaspoon dried cilantro, chopped**
- ½ **teaspoon grated orange peel**
- 1 **teaspoon fresh orange juice**
-    ▪
- 4 **kaiser rolls, split**
   Lettuce
   Red onion, sliced, for garnish (optional)

1. ▪ *Make burgers:* Gently combine all ingredients in large bowl. Shape into four ¾-inch-thick patties. Brush tops of burgers with oil.

2. ▪ Oil large grill pan or cast-iron skillet; heat over medium-high heat. Grill burgers, oiled sides down, 8 minutes. Turn and grill 8 to 10 minutes more, until instant-read meat thermometer registers 165°F. when inserted 1 inch from edge of each burger. Transfer burgers to a plate. Grill rolls, cut sides down, 30 to 60 seconds, until lightly toasted.

3. ▪ *Make mayonnaise:* Meanwhile, combine all ingredients in a small bowl. *(Can be made ahead. Cover and refrigerate up to 3 days.)* Spread 1 tablespoon of the mayonnaise on cut sides of each roll. Top bottoms of rolls with lettuce, burgers, red onion (if desired) and tops of rolls. Makes 4 servings.

Per serving with 1 tablespoon mayonnaise: 570 calories, 31.5 g total fat, 6.5 g saturated fat, 92 mg cholesterol, 915 mg sodium, 32 g carbohydrates, 37 g protein, 103 mg calcium, 2 g fiber

tamale pie

Here's a turkey chili bake with a fluffy cornmeal topping the whole family will love. Substitute ground beef for the turkey, if desired.

Prep time: 25 minutes plus standing
Cooking time: 50 minutes

- 1 **pound ground raw turkey (a blend of dark and white meat)**
- 1 **large red bell pepper, coarsely chopped**
- 1 **medium red onion, chopped**
- 2 **tablespoons chili powder**

2 teaspoons minced garlic
1½ teaspoons ground cumin
½ teaspoon salt
¼ teaspoon freshly ground pepper
1 can (14½ oz.) diced tomatoes in juice
1 can (15 oz.) pink or black beans, drained and rinsed
1 tablespoon minced jarred pickled jalapeño chiles

TOPPING:

2½ cups milk
¾ cup cornmeal
1 cup frozen whole-kernel corn
½ teaspoon salt
1 large egg
1 cup shredded Cheddar cheese, divided
½ cup shredded jalapeño Jack cheese
   Shredded lettuce, sliced pimento-stuffed green olives, shredded cheese, diced tomato and sour cream, for garnish (optional)

1. Heat a 12-inch nonstick skillet over high heat. Add turkey, bell pepper and onion and cook 7 to 8 minutes, until turkey is brown and liquid evaporates, stirring frequently to break up turkey. Stir in chili powder, garlic, cumin, salt and pepper; cook 1 minute. Stir in tomatoes, beans and pickled jalapeño. Cover and simmer 10 minutes, stirring occasionally. Spread evenly into a shallow 3-quart baking dish; cover with foil and set aside.

2. *Make topping:* Heat oven to 375°F. Wipe out skillet; add milk and gradually whisk in cornmeal. Bring to boil, whisking until smooth. Cook 5 minutes, until thickened, stirring constantly. Stir in corn and salt. Remove skillet from heat. Beat egg with a fork in a small bowl. Add 1 cup of the cornmeal mixture and stir until blended. Return to skillet and stir until blended. Stir in ½ cup of the Cheddar cheese.

3. Uncover baking dish. Spoon cornmeal mixture by heaping tablespoonfuls on top of turkey mixture. Bake 15 minutes. Sprinkle topping with remaining ½ cup Cheddar cheese and the jalapeño cheese. Bake pie 15 minutes more, until bubbly at edges. Let stand 10 minutes before serving. Serve with garnishes, if desired. Makes 8 servings.

Per serving without garnishes: 350 calories, 15.5 g total fat, 7 g saturated fat, 101 mg cholesterol, 734 mg sodium, 30 g carbohydrates, 23 g protein, 297 mg calcium, 4 g fiber

roasted cod with peppers and potatoes EASY

If you like, garnish this fish lover's delight with fresh herb sprigs and edible flowers. Pictured on page 41.

Prep time: 10 minutes • Roasting time: 15 to 20 minutes

1 pound fingerling or small red potatoes, halved
1 yellow bell pepper, cut into 1-inch-wide strips
1 red bell pepper, cut into 1-inch-wide strips
4 garlic cloves, skins on
4 tablespoons olive oil, divided
1 teaspoon salt, divided
½ teaspoon freshly ground pepper, divided
1¾ pounds center-cut cod fillets, skin on, cut into 4 pieces (6 to 7 oz. each)
4 sprigs fresh rosemary
   Lemon wedges

1. Adjust oven rack to lower third of oven. Heat to 450°F.

2. Arrange potatoes, bell peppers and garlic on a jelly-roll pan. Toss with 2 tablespoons of the oil, ¼ teaspoon of the salt and ¼ teaspoon of the pepper. Roast 15 to 20 minutes, until potatoes are fork tender and bell peppers are golden. Transfer bell peppers and garlic to cutting board. Squeeze garlic out of skin; finely chop garlic and bell peppers. Toss the potatoes with 1 tablespoon of the oil. Cover with foil to keep warm.

3. Meanwhile, rinse cod fillets and pat dry with paper towels. Sprinkle remaining ¾ teaspoon salt and ¼ teaspoon pepper on both sides of each fillet. Heat remaining 1 tablespoon oil in a large ovenproof nonstick skillet over medium-high heat. Add cod, skin sides down; cook 2 to 3 minutes, until skin is crisp and golden brown. Arrange rosemary on top of fish. Transfer skillet to oven and cook 3 minutes. Turn fish; roast 3 minutes more, until fish is opaque and cooked through.

4. Spoon bell pepper mixture evenly on top of each fillet and serve with potatoes. Makes 4 servings.

Per serving: 375 calories, 15 g total fat, 2 g saturated fat, 78 mg cholesterol, 691 mg sodium, 24 g carbohydrates, 35 g protein, 42 mg calcium, 3 g fiber

mushroom matters

Here's a short list of some popular mushroom varieties and how to handle them with care:

PORTOBELLO: Rich in flavor with a dense, meaty texture. An extremely mature form of cremini mushrooms. Large, with an open flat cap with dark gills. Available whole or packaged sliced or caps only. Remove stems before cooking.

SHIITAKE: Meaty and slightly smoky in flavor with a large, dark brown cap. The stems are usually tough; discard them or use to flavor stocks or soups.

WHITE: Mild, earthy flavor, ranging in color from white to beige. ("Button" mushrooms are simply young white cultivated mushrooms.)

CLEANING AND STORING: Cool air is vital for keeping mushrooms fresh. Arrange them on a tray in a single layer, cover with a damp paper towel and store in the refrigerator no longer than 3 days. To clean, wipe with a damp paper towel (do not soak them in water because they will become soggy).

shiitake-coated salmon with green onion compote EASY

This dish may be prepared restaurant-style, but it is easy enough for the home cook. Before searing the salmon in a hot skillet, the fillets are coated with finely ground dried mushrooms.

Prep time: 25 minutes • Cooking time: 8 to 12 minutes

GREEN ONION COMPOTE:

- 1 tablespoon vegetable oil
- 1 pound shiitake mushrooms, sliced
- 1 tablespoon chopped garlic
- 2 teaspoons chopped fresh ginger
- ¼ cup sake or white wine
- 1 bunch green onions, sliced into ½-inch diagonal pieces
- 2 tablespoons soy sauce
- 1 tablespoon rice wine vinegar
  Pinch red pepper flakes

SALMON:

- 2 packages (0.5 oz. each) dried shiitake mushrooms
- ½ teaspoon salt
- ¼ teaspoon freshly ground pepper
- 6 salmon fillets (6 oz. each)
- 2 tablespoons vegetable oil, divided

1. *Make green onion compote:* Heat oil in a large skillet over medium-high heat 1 to 2 minutes, until very hot. Add mushrooms; cook, stirring often, 4 minutes, until tender and golden. Add garlic and ginger and cook 30 seconds to 1 minute, just until fragrant. Stir in sake and cook 3 to 4 minutes, until liquid evaporates and mixture is dry. Transfer to a large bowl. Stir in green onions, soy sauce, vinegar, and red pepper flakes. Cool to room temperature, 15 to 20 minutes.

2. *Make salmon:* Meanwhile, heat oven to 350°F. Process dried shiitakes in a spice grinder to a fine powder. Transfer to a pie plate. Combine salt and pepper in small cup and sprinkle on both sides of each salmon fillet. Generously coat both sides of each fillet with mushroom powder.

3. Heat 1 tablespoon of the oil in a large nonstick, ovenproof skillet over medium-high heat 1 to 2 minutes, until hot. Cook half of the fillets 2 to 3 minutes per side, until golden brown and crisp. Transfer to a large cookie sheet. Wipe out skillet with paper towels. Repeat with remaining 1 tablespoon oil and salmon. Place fillets in the oven on cookie sheet and bake 4 to 6 minutes, just until fish flakes easily with a fork in center of fillets. Serve with green onion compote. Makes 6 servings.

Per serving: 415 calories, 25.5 g total fat, 4.5 g saturated fat, 100 mg cholesterol, 641 mg sodium, 10 g carbohydrates, 37 g protein, 41 mg calcium, 2 g fiber

trout amandine

This buttery combination of trout and sliced almonds from Arnaud's in New Orleans has been a Big Easy favorite for generations. Tip: Bake the nuts in a toaster oven at 350°F. 8 to 10 minutes, until golden and fragrant. Pictured on page 47.

Prep time: 10 minutes
Cooking time: 4 to 6 minutes per batch

6	trout fillets with skin (4 to 6 oz. each)
1½	cups all-purpose flour
12	tablespoons butter, divided (no substitutes)
1	tablespoon fresh lemon juice
	Whole fresh green beans, cooked (optional)
1½	cups sliced almonds, toasted
6	lemon wedges

1. Heat oven to 250°F.

2. Dip each fillet in flour, shaking off excess. Melt 3 tablespoons of the butter in a 12-inch nonstick skillet over medium-high heat until bubbly. Add 3 fillets, skin sides down, and cook 2 to 3 minutes, until golden brown and skin is crisp. Turn and cook 2 to 3 minutes more, until golden brown. Transfer fillets to a platter; keep warm in oven.

3. Wipe out the skillet with paper towels. Melt 3 tablespoons of the butter in skillet and repeat cooking remaining fillets.

4. Meanwhile, melt remaining 6 tablespoons butter in small saucepan over medium heat. Stir in lemon juice. Serve trout over green beans, if desired. Spoon almonds, then butter sauce over each fillet. Serve with lemon wedges. Makes 6 servings.

Per serving without green beans: 600 calories, 41 g total fat, 14.5 g saturated fat, 134 mg cholesterol, 272 mg sodium, 22 g carbohydrates, 37 g protein, 141 mg calcium, 2 g fiber

salmon and soba noodles

Don't be put off by the number of fat grams in a serving of this Asian-inspired creation (most of it comes from the salmon, so it's predominately the healthy omega-3 fat). Plus, poaching salmon in an aromatic broth with ginger, soy sauce and red pepper flakes is a great way for calorie-conscious cooks to make it. Pictured on page 46.

Prep time: 20 minutes • Cooking time: 10 minutes

8	ounces soba noodles
2	bags (10 oz. each) fresh spinach, rinsed
2	teaspoons Asian sesame oil
	Pinch salt
1	teaspoon grated fresh ginger
1	teaspoon finely chopped garlic
4	skinless salmon fillets (4 oz. each)

BROTH:

1	can (14½ oz.) chicken broth
1	star anise
1	large garlic clove, sliced
2	quarter-size slices unpeeled fresh ginger
2	tablespoons sake
2	teaspoons soy sauce
¼	teaspoon red pepper flakes
⅓	cup sliced green onions

1. Cook noodles according to package directions. During last 2 minutes of cooking, add spinach to same pot; cover and cook just until wilted. Drain and toss in a bowl with the sesame oil and salt. Spoon noodles and spinach into 4 bowls; keep warm.

2. Rub ginger and garlic over salmon.

3. *Make broth:* Combine all ingredients in a deep 12-inch skillet. Add fish and bring to simmer. Cover and simmer 4 to 5 minutes; let stand 2 minutes. Transfer salmon to bowls. Remove star anise, garlic and ginger slices. Ladle hot broth into bowls. Sprinkle with green onions. Makes 4 servings.

Per serving: 535 calories, 19.5 g total fat, 4 g saturated fat, 84 mg cholesterol, 1,289 mg sodium, 51 g carbohydrates, 42 g protein, 190 mg calcium, 6 g fiber

mediterranean tuna

Tired of the same brown bag lunch? We combined canned tuna with fruity olive oil, fresh lemon juice and capers for a taste of the Mediterranean. To keep the bread from getting soggy, spread each slice with a bit of butter.

Total prep time: 15 minutes

- 1 can (6⅛ oz.) solid white tuna, packed in water, drained
- 2 tablespoons extra-virgin olive oil
- 1 teaspoon fresh lemon juice
- ½ teaspoon capers, drained
- Pinch freshly ground pepper
- 1 teaspoon butter or margarine
- 4 slices whole wheat bread
- Tomato slices
- Lettuce

Combine tuna, oil, lemon juice, capers and pepper in a small bowl. Spread butter evenly on one side of each slice of bread. Layer one bread slice with sliced tomato, lettuce and half of the tuna mixture. Arrange second slice of bread, buttered side down, on top of tuna. Repeat with remaining ingredients. Makes 2 sandwiches.

Per sandwich: 510 calories, 23 g total fat, 4.5 g saturated fat, 42 mg cholesterol, 690 mg sodium, 49 g carbohydrates, 29 g protein, 46 mg calcium, 6 g fiber

shrimp gumbo

Shrimp and spicy sausage join forces in this delectably, speedy Cajun-spiced rice bowl. Pictured on page 45.

Total prep and cooking time: 30 minutes

- ½ pound andouille or Cajun sausage, coarsely chopped
- 1 medium onion, chopped
- 1 green bell pepper, diced
- 1 can (14½ oz.) whole tomatoes in juice
- 1¼ cups water
- ½ cup long-grain rice
- 1½ teaspoons minced garlic
- 1 teaspoon Cajun or Creole seasoning
- 1 pound medium shelled and deveined shrimp

1. ■ Heat a large Dutch oven over high heat. Add sausage, onion and bell pepper and cook 5 minutes, until onion begins to brown. Add tomatoes and juice, water, rice, garlic and Cajun seasoning, stirring to break up tomatoes. Bring to boil; reduce heat and simmer, covered, 15 minutes, until rice is tender.

2. ■ Stir in shrimp; return to boil. Reduce heat and simmer, covered, 2 to 3 minutes more, until shrimp are cooked through, stirring occasionally. Makes 4 servings.

Per serving: 400 calories, 17.5 g total fat, 6 g saturated fat, 178 mg cholesterol, 1,178 mg sodium, 30 g carbohydrates, 29 g protein, 118 mg calcium, 2 g fiber

linguine with scallops and bacon

The smoky flavor of crispy bacon complements the sweetness of sea scallops in this speedy seafood-and-pasta combination.

Prep time: 5 minutes • Cooking time: 10 minutes

- 4 slices bacon, diced
- 1 pound sea scallops, if large cut in half
- 1 tablespoon minced shallots
- 1 bottle (8 oz.) clam juice
- ¼ teaspoon salt
- 1 pound linguine or tagliatelle, cooked according to package directions
- ¼ cup chopped fresh parsley
- 2 tablespoons olive oil

1. ■ Cook bacon in a large skillet over medium-high heat until crisp. Transfer to a large serving bowl. Discard all but 1 tablespoon of the drippings from skillet.

2. ■ Add scallops and shallots to skillet. Cook 4 minutes, until scallops are browned. Transfer scallops to bowl with bacon. Add clam juice and salt to skillet; bring to boil. Reduce heat and simmer for 2 minutes; add to scallops and bacon.

3. Add hot pasta, parsley and olive oil to scallop mixture in serving bowl; toss gently. Serve immediately. Makes 6 servings.

Per serving: 415 calories, 8.5 g total fat, 1.5 g saturated fat, 29 mg cholesterol, 383 mg sodium, 59 g carbohydrates, 24 g protein, 36 mg calcium, 2 g fiber

crab cake sandwiches with caper mayonnaise

Looking for an informal yet special summer dish? Crab cakes are the perfect indulgence. These cakes boast large pieces of crab that burst with flavor. Don't be afraid to use your hands to gently press the patties together while coating them; then cover and refrigerate them. Pictured on page 44.

Prep time: 20 minutes plus chilling
Cooking time: 16 to 17 minutes

CRAB CAKES:

- 2 slices firm white bread
- ⅓ cup mayonnaise
- ¼ cup finely chopped red bell pepper
- 2 tablespoons finely chopped green onions
- 1 tablespoon fresh lemon juice
- 1 large egg
- 1 tablespoon chopped fresh parsley
- 1 tablespoon grainy mustard
- ½ teaspoon salt
- ¼ teaspoon ground red pepper
- 1 pound cooked fresh lump or jumbo crabmeat or 1 can (16 oz.) refrigerated, pasteurized lump crabmeat, picked over

CAPER MAYONNAISE:

- ¼ cup mayonnaise
- 1 teaspoon grated lemon peel
- 1 teaspoon fresh lemon juice
- 1 teaspoon capers, chopped
- ⅛ teaspoon salt

- ½ cup plain dry bread crumbs
- 2 tablespoons olive oil, divided

- 6 soft rolls, split and lightly toasted
  Lettuce leaves (optional)
- 6 slices tomato
  Fresh herb sprigs, for garnish (optional)

1. *Make crab cakes:* Pulse bread in food processor to fine crumbs. Whisk all the remaining ingredients *except* the fresh bread crumbs and crab in a medium bowl. Gently fold in crab, then the crumbs. Cover and refrigerate 2 hours, until cold.

2. *Make caper mayonnaise:* Meanwhile, combine all ingredients in a small bowl. *(Can be made ahead. Cover and refrigerate up to 1 day.)*

3. Spread dry bread crumbs in 9-inch pie plate. Lightly pack a level ½ cup measure with crab mixture and drop onto bread crumbs; press lightly and gently turn to coat and shape into a 3×1-inch cake. Place on a cookie sheet. Repeat to form 5 more crab cakes.

4. Heat oven to 350° F. Heat 1 tablespoon of the oil in a large nonstick skillet over medium heat. Add 3 crab cakes and cook 2 minutes per side, until browned and crisp. Transfer to cookie sheet. Wipe out skillet. Repeat with remaining 1 tablespoon oil and crab cakes. *(Can be made ahead. Cover and refrigerate up to 6 hours.)* Bake crab cakes 8 to 9 minutes (12 to 14 minutes, if refrigerated), until heated through.

5. Spread cut sides of roll bottoms with some of the caper mayonnaise. Arrange lettuce (if using) and crab cakes on roll bottoms. Top with tomato, remaining caper mayonnaise, fresh herb sprigs (if desired) and roll tops. Makes 6 sandwiches.

Per sandwich without lettuce or garnish: 520 calories, 28.5 g total fat, 4.5 g saturated fat, 124 mg cholesterol, 1,108 mg sodium, 42 g carbohydrates, 23 g protein, 189 mg calcium, 2 g fiber

choice cheddar

Cheddar, a hard cow's-milk cheese, ranges in color from white to pale yellow to orange (if colored with the natural dye annatto). Good Cheddar is flavorful, but not bitter, with a creamy aftertaste. Basically, the longer a Cheddar cheese matures, the sharper its flavor becomes (9 to 24 months is the norm). Although it's a firm cheese, Cheddar should never be dry or cracked. Store Cheddar wrapped in plastic in the refrigerator. Like many cheeses, Cheddar's true flavor comes through when the cheese is allowed to stand for about an hour before serving. It's delicious served with crackers, crusty breads, apples or pears, toasted walnuts or olives, and is commonly used in casseroles, soups and sauces.

no-boil macaroni and cheese

This all-time comfort food is going through a slight change. We simplified the preparation without compromising the taste. By using oven-ready lasagne noodles, there's no pot of water to bring to a boil.

Prep time: 15 minutes • Baking time: 50 minutes

- 3 cups grated Cheddar cheese, divided
- ½ cup grated Parmesan cheese
- 1½ cups fresh bread crumbs, toasted
- 2 tablespoons chopped fresh flat-leaf parsley
- 4 cups milk, divided
- ⅓ cup all-purpose flour
- 2 tablespoons butter or margarine
- 1 teaspoon salt
- ½ teaspoon Worcestershire sauce
- ¼ teaspoon ground red pepper
- 1 box (9 oz.) oven-ready lasagne noodles

1. Heat oven to 350°F. Grease a 13×9-inch baking dish. Combine 1 cup of the Cheddar and the Parmesan cheese in a small bowl. Combine bread crumbs and parsley in another bowl. Set both aside.

2. Whisk together ½ cup of the milk and the flour in a medium saucepan until smooth. Stir in remaining 3½ cups milk, butter, salt, Worcestershire sauce and ground red pepper; bring to boil over medium heat. Stir in remaining 2 cups Cheddar cheese; remove from heat and stir until cheese is melted and sauce is smooth.

3. Spoon 1 cup of the cheese sauce on bottom of prepared dish. Arrange one third of the noodles in a single layer on top of sauce; sprinkle one third of the Cheddar-Parmesan mixture over noodles, then enough sauce to cover noodles. Repeat 2 more times with remaining noodles, cheese and sauce, ending with sauce. Cover pan with foil; bake 45 minutes, until noodles are tender when pierced with the tip of a sharp knife.

4. Remove foil and sprinkle top with bread crumb mixture. Bake 5 minutes more, until crumbs are golden brown. Makes 10 servings.

Per serving: 365 calories, 19 g total fat, 11.5 g saturated fat, 59 mg cholesterol, 626 mg sodium, 31 g carbohydrates, 18 g protein, 425 mg calcium, 1 g fiber

penne vodka

A classic from Rome, this dish rises to the occasion of spur-of-the-moment entertaining.

Prep time: 10 minutes • Cooking time: 8 minutes

- 2 tablespoons butter or margarine
- ⅓ cup vodka
- ½ teaspoon red pepper flakes
- 1 cup canned plum tomatoes
- ½ teaspoon salt
- ½ cup heavy or whipping cream
- ¼ cup freshly grated Parmesan cheese
- 1 pound penne, penne rigati or ziti, cooked according to package directions

1. Heat butter in a large skillet over medium-low heat. Stir in vodka and red pepper flakes; heat gently for 2 minutes, until vodka comes to simmer. Carefully add tomatoes and salt. Increase heat to high and cook 5 minutes more, until thickened, breaking up tomatoes with the back of a wooden spoon. Stir in heavy cream and Parmesan.

2. Toss sauce with hot pasta in a large serving bowl. Serve immediately. Makes 6 servings.

Per serving: 445 calories, 14 g total fat, 8 g saturated fat, 43 mg cholesterol, 355 mg sodium, 59 g carbohydrates, 12 g protein, 81 mg calcium, 2 g fiber

pasta primavera

This classic dish blossoming with fresh spring vegetables first appeared at the elegant New York City restaurant Le Cirque.

Prep time: 15 minutes • Cooking time: 8 minutes

 Water
½ pound asparagus, cut into 1½-inch pieces
4 ounces snow peas, trimmed
2 tablespoons olive oil
½ cup minced onion
1 yellow summer squash, thinly sliced
2 plum tomatoes, diced
1½ cups heavy or whipping cream
1 cup chicken broth
¾ teaspoon salt
½ teaspoon freshly ground pepper
¾ pound capellini (angel hair) or thin spaghetti, cooked according to package directions
½ cup freshly grated Parmesan cheese

1. Bring a large saucepan of water to boil. Add asparagus and cook 30 seconds. Add snow peas and cook 30 seconds more. With a slotted spoon, transfer asparagus and snow peas to a colander. Rinse under cold running water; drain.

2. Heat oil in a large skillet over medium-high heat. Add onion and summer squash and cook 2 minutes. Add asparagus, snow peas and tomatoes; cook 2 minutes. Stir in the heavy cream and chicken broth; bring to boil. Reduce heat to medium and cook at low boil 2 minutes more. Stir in salt and pepper.

3. Toss sauce with hot pasta and Parmesan cheese in a large serving bowl. Serve immediately. Makes 6 servings.

Per serving: 535 calories, 30.5 g total fat, 16.5 g saturated fat, 91 mg cholesterol, 554 mg sodium, 50 g carbohydrates, 14 g protein, 155 mg calcium, 3 g fiber

penne arrabiata

At Papa Razzi Restaurant in Westbury, New York, Chef Luigino Tripodi prepares this spicy dish. The handy tomato sauce with white wine, basil, garlic and red pepper flakes can be tossed with any medium-size pasta, such as ziti, shells or rigatoni.

Prep time: 15 minutes • Cooking time: 34 to 35 minutes

3 medium garlic cloves, divided
3 tablespoons extra-virgin olive oil, divided
2 tablespoons tomato paste
1 can (28 oz.) whole tomatoes in juice, chopped
1 bay leaf
1 tablespoon chopped fresh parsley
1 tablespoon chopped fresh basil
½ teaspoon red pepper flakes
¼ cup white wine
1 teaspoon salt
1 pound penne, cooked according to package directions
 Freshly grated Parmesan cheese (optional)
 Chopped fresh parsley and basil (optional)

1. Chop 1 of the garlic cloves. Heat 1 tablespoon of the oil in 3-quart saucepan over medium heat. Add chopped garlic and cook 30 seconds. Add tomato paste and cook, stirring, 2 minutes. Add tomatoes in juice; simmer 30 minutes.

2. Thinly slice remaining 2 cloves garlic. Heat 1 tablespoon of the oil in a 12-inch skillet over medium heat. Add thinly sliced garlic and cook 30 seconds, just until beginning to turn pale golden. Add 1 tablespoon parsley, 1 tablespoon basil and red pepper flakes; cook about 30 seconds. Add white wine and boil 30 seconds. Stir in tomato sauce and salt; simmer 4 to 5 minutes.

3. Toss sauce with hot pasta in a large serving bowl. Drizzle pasta with remaining 1 tablespoon oil. Serve with freshly grated Parmesan cheese and additional chopped fresh parsley and basil, if desired. Makes 4 servings.

Per serving without additional Parmesan, parsley or basil: 575 calories, 13 g total fat, 2 g saturated fat, 0 mg cholesterol, 980 mg sodium, 96 g carbohydrates, 17 g protein, 86 mg calcium, 5 g fiber

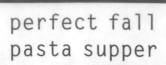

perfect fall pasta supper

BAKED ZITI WITH THREE CHEESES
below

GREEN SALAD WITH MANGO
page 117

FRENCH BREAD AND BUTTER

**CARROT CAKE WITH
CREAM CHEESE ICING**
page 32

baked ziti with three cheeses

Roasting the tomato and onions brings out their natural sweetness. Penne or any other tube shaped pasta can be substituted for the ziti.

Prep time: 45 minutes • Baking time: 35 to 40 minutes

- 2 tomatoes (8 oz. each), quartered
- 2 onions, quartered
- ¼ cup plus 1 tablespoon olive oil, divided
- ¾ pound ziti or penne
- 1 teaspoon salt, divided
- 2 tablespoons chopped garlic
- 3 tablespoons chopped shallots
- ½ cup white wine
- 2 cups heavy or whipping cream
- ¾ cup crumbled Gorgonzola cheese
- ½ cup grated fontina cheese
- 1 cup freshly grated Parmesan cheese
- ¼ teaspoon freshly grated pepper
  Chopped fresh flat-leaf parsley

1. Heat oven to 425°F. Combine tomatoes, onions and ¼ cup of the oil in a 13×9-inch glass baking dish. Roast 30 minutes, until tomatoes blister. Remove the tomatoes to a bowl. Continue roasting the onions in the oven 10 to 15 minutes more, until tender and golden. Transfer onions and

accumulated juices to bowl with tomatoes. Do not wash baking dish. Coarsely chop the vegetables. Set aside.

2. Meanwhile, cook pasta 2 minutes less than package directions. Drain and toss with chopped vegetables, accumulated juices and ¼ teaspoon of the salt. Spoon pasta and vegetables into baking dish.

3. Heat remaining 1 tablespoon oil in medium saucepan over medium-high heat. Add garlic and shallots; cook 30 seconds. Stir in the wine and cook 3 minutes, until liquid reduces by half. Add cream, stirring until the mixture thickens and coats the back of a spoon, 5 minutes. Remove from heat. Stir in cheeses until melted; stir in remaining ¾ teaspoon salt and the pepper. Transfer sauce to a large bowl; cool to room temperature, about 15 minutes.

4. Pour cream sauce over pasta, stirring to coat. Cover with foil and bake 35 to 40 minutes, until sauce is bubbly. Remove foil and stir until pasta is well coated with sauce. Sprinkle with chopped parsley. Makes 6 servings.

Per serving: 790 calories, 54 g total fat, 28 g saturated fat, 145 mg cholesterol, 1,007 mg sodium, 56 g carbohydrates, 23 g protein, 438 mg calcium, 3 g fiber

tuscan swiss chard with pasta and beans

Swiss chard, with its broad green leaves and hearty flavor and texture, is a favorite among Italian cooks. You can use fresh spinach as an alternative in this recipe, but then cut the cooking time by half.

Prep time: 10 minutes • Cooking time: 13 minutes

- 3 tablespoons olive oil
- 6 anchovy fillets, chopped
- 1 tablespoon minced garlic
- ½ teaspoon red pepper flakes
- 1 bunch (1 lb.) Swiss chard, finely chopped
- 1 cup chicken broth
- 1 teaspoon salt

1 can (19 oz.) cannellini beans, drained and
   rinsed
1 pound cavatelli or orecchiette, cooked
   according to package directions

1. Heat oil in a large skillet over high heat. Stir in anchovies, garlic and red pepper flakes; cook 30 seconds. Add Swiss chard, chicken broth and salt. Cover and cook on medium-low heat 10 minutes, until Swiss chard is tender, stirring occasionally. Stir in cannellini beans and cook 2 minutes, until heated through.

2. Toss sauce with hot pasta in a serving bowl. Serve immediately. Makes 6 servings.

Per serving: 425 calories, 9 g total fat, 1.5 g saturated fat, 3 mg cholesterol, 957 mg sodium, 72 g carbohydrates, 18 g protein, 86 mg calcium, 7 g fiber

orecchiette with broccoli rabe EASY LOW FAT

Broccoli rabe, an assertive leafy green with a somewhat sharp flavor, pairs well with orecchiette, a short pasta that originates from southern Italy. You'll need to peel off any of the rabe's large, coarse stems.

Prep time: 5 minutes • Cooking time: 8 to 10 minutes

   Water
1 tablespoon plus 1 teaspoon salt, divided
1 bunch (1 lb.) broccoli rabe, trimmed (see
   tip, right)
¼ cup olive oil
1 tablespoon minced garlic
½ teaspoon red pepper flakes
1 pound orecchiette or cavatelli, cooked
   according to package directions

1. Bring a large pot of water and 1 tablespoon of the salt to boil. Add broccoli rabe and cook 3 minutes, until barely tender. Drain in a colander; cool slightly and coarsely chop.

2. Heat oil in a large skillet over medium-high heat. Add garlic, remaining 1 teaspoon salt and the red pepper flakes and cook 30 seconds. Add broccoli rabe and cook, stirring, 3 minutes more.

3. Toss broccoli rabe mixture with hot pasta in a large serving bowl. Serve immediately. Makes 6 servings.

Per serving: 385 calories, 10.5 g total fat, 1.5 g saturated fat, 0 mg cholesterol, 798 mg sodium, 61 g carbohydrates, 12 g protein, 53 mg calcium, 4 g fiber

---

test kitchen tip

broccoli rabe primer

WHAT IT IS...A relative of the cabbage and turnip family, broccoli "rabe" or broccoli "raab" is known for its tender young leaves and stems that form clusters of very small buds similar to regular broccoli. Unlike regular broccoli, the flavor of broccoli rabe is pungent and slightly bitter.

HOW TO USE... Prepare it as you would regular broccoli. Or, take a lesson from Italian cooks who love to fry, steam and even braise broccoli rabe. It's also good in salads, soups and stews and with pasta, such as orecchiette (see recipe, left).

WHEN IN SEASON... Available in many supermarkets that have large produce sections and specialty goods, the season for broccoli rabe begins in the fall and continues through spring. Refrigerate in plastic storage bags for up to 5 days.

creamy three-cheese and walnut pasta *EASY*

The heat from the hot pasta melts the Gorgonzola, ricotta and Parmesan cheeses in this truly luxurious sauce.

Prep time: 5 minutes • Cooking time: 8 to 10 minutes

- ¾ **cup crumbled Gorgonzola cheese, at room temperature**
- ⅔ **cup ricotta cheese, at room temperature**
- ¼ **cup freshly grated Parmesan cheese**
- 2 **tablespoons butter or margarine, softened**
- ¾ **cup frozen peas, thawed**
- ¾ **cup walnuts, toasted and chopped**
- ½ **teaspoon salt**
- ½ **teaspoon freshly ground pepper**
- 1 **pound farfalle (bow ties) or penne rigati, cooked according to package directions, reserving ¼ cup hot cooking liquid**

Combine the Gorgonzola, ricotta, Parmesan and butter in a large serving bowl. Stir in peas, walnuts, salt and pepper. Stir in reserved cooking liquid from pasta. Toss sauce with hot pasta. Serve immediately. Makes 6 servings.

Per serving: 535 calories, 22.5 g total fat, 8.5 g saturated fat, 34 mg cholesterol, 538 mg sodium, 63 g carbohydrates, 21 g protein, 227 mg calcium, 4 g fiber

lentil-vegetable soup *EASY* *LOW FAT*

Chock full of veggie goodness—mushrooms, onion, carrots, celery and fresh spinach, to name a few—this hearty, meatless meal more than satisfies.

Prep time: 25 minutes • Cooking time: 55 to 60 minutes

- 3 **tablespoons olive oil**
- ½ **cup chopped onion**
- 1 **tablespoon chopped garlic**
- 1 **cup diced carrots**
- 1 **cup diced celery**
- ½ **pound mushrooms, chopped**
- 1 **teaspoon chopped jalapeño chile (see tip, page 92)**
- 1 **teaspoon fresh thyme leaves or ½ teaspoon dried thyme**
- ½ **teaspoon salt**
- ½ **teaspoon freshly ground pepper**
- 1 **bag (16 oz.) lentils, rinsed and picked over**
- 2 **tablespoons ground cumin**
- ¼ **teaspoon celery seed**
- ¼ **teaspoon turmeric**
- 4 **cans (14½ oz. each) chicken broth**
- 3 **cups water**
- 1 **pound fresh spinach, chopped**
- 2 **tablespoons balsamic vinegar**
  Cooked rice (optional)
  Chopped fresh cilantro, for garnish (optional)

Heat oil in medium Dutch oven over medium heat. Add onion and garlic and cook 2 minutes, until garlic is fragrant. Add carrots and celery; cook 2 minutes, until softened. Add mushrooms, jalapeño, thyme, salt and pepper; cook 4 minutes, until vegetables soften. Stir in lentils, cumin, celery seed and turmeric; cook 2 to 3 minutes, until vegetables and spices are well combined. Add broth and water. Bring to boil; reduce heat and simmer 40 to 45 minutes, until lentils are tender. Add spinach and vinegar; cook 15 minutes more, until soup thickens. Serve with rice and sprinkle with cilantro, if desired. Makes 6 servings.

Per serving without rice or garnish: 400 calories, 10.5 g total fat, 1.5 g saturated fat, 0 mg cholesterol, 1,458 mg sodium, 54 g carbohydrates, 27 g protein, 156 mg calcium, 12 g fiber

golden onion soup EASY

Meet a lighter version of the typical French onion soup. The sweetness of the apple complements the savory notes of the onion.

Prep time: 15 minutes • Cooking time: 20 to 23 minutes

- 1 cup diced sourdough bread
- 1½ tablespoons butter or margarine
- 1 medium (¾ lb.) Spanish onion, thinly sliced
- 1 Granny Smith apple, peeled, cored and thinly sliced
- 1 teaspoon salt
- ⅛ teaspoon freshly ground pepper
- 2 cans (14½ oz. each) chicken broth
- ½ cup coarsely shredded Gruyère or Swiss cheese
- ¼ cup half-and-half cream
- 2 tablespoons apple-flavored brandy

1. Heat oven to 375°F. Line a cookie sheet with foil. Spread bread in single layer on prepared sheet. Bake 8 to 10 minutes, until toasted. Cool on cookie sheet. Leave oven on.

2. Meanwhile, heat butter in a 4-quart saucepot over medium-high heat. Add onion and apple; cover and cook 10 to 12 minutes, until mixture is tender and just starting to brown, stirring occasionally. Uncover; sprinkle with salt and pepper and cook 3 to 4 minutes more, until lightly caramelized. Add broth. Bring to boil; reduce heat to medium and simmer 5 minutes.

3. Meanwhile, arrange bread cubes in a single layer with sides touching; sprinkle cheese evenly over top. Bake 5 minutes, until cheese is melted.

4. Stir cream and apple-flavored brandy into soup; heat through. Ladle soup into 4 serving bowls. Divide and top each serving with cheese croutons. Makes 4 servings.

Per serving: 220 calories, 12 g total fat, 7 g saturated fat, 30 mg cholesterol, 1,456 mg sodium, 15 g carbohydrates, 9 g protein, 142 mg calcium, 2 g fiber

---

test kitchen tip

in an emergency

Don't get caught without something to prepare for fast weeknight meals. If you keep a variety of ingredients on hand, you'll be able to fix something for dinner in short order.

in the cabinet...

GRAINS AND GRAIN PRODUCTS: various pastas, rices, couscous and quick-cooking barley and polenta.

CANNED AND JARRED FOODS: sun-dried tomatoes, beans; tomato products; roasted red peppers; chicken, beef and vegetable broths; tuna; salmon; anchovies and clams.

FRESH FOODS: onions, potatoes and garlic.

SAUCES AND SEASONINGS: vinegars, oil (olive and vegetable), soy sauce, teriyaki sauce, marinara sauce, salsa, salad dressings, chutney, dry mustard, herbs and spices.

BAKING SUPPLIES: flour, sugars, cornmeal, cornstarch, baking powder and baking soda.

in the fridge...

DAIRY PRODUCTS: milk, butter or margarine, cheeses, yogurt and sour cream.

OTHER ITEMS: eggs, bacon, olives, mayonnaise, parsley, mustard, hot pepper sauce, salad greens and other fresh vegetables and fruits, such as lemons, green onions, carrots, apples and oranges.

in the freezer...

MISCELLANEOUS: frozen vegetables, nuts, ice cream and sorbet.

winter minestrone

Want to make a big batch of soup? Eight kinds of veggies (plus beans) mingle in this soothing concoction. It's so thick and hearty you'll consider it a meal. Simmer the mix with a piece of Parmesan rind for extra flavor.

Prep time: 45 minutes plus standing · Cooking time: 1 hour

BEANS:

- 1 cup dried Great Northern beans, picked over and rinsed
  Water
- 1 teaspoon minced garlic
- ½ teaspoon dried thyme
- ½ teaspoon dried rosemary
- ½ teaspoon salt
- 1 bay leaf

- 3 tablespoons olive oil, divided
- 1 large onion, chopped
- 2 large carrots, chopped
- 1 large celery rib, diced
- 2 teaspoons minced garlic
- 1½ teaspoons salt, divided
- ½ teaspoon freshly ground pepper
- 1 pound butternut squash, peeled, seeded and cut into ¾-inch chunks
- ½ pound green beans, trimmed, cut into ¾-inch pieces
- 4 cups thinly sliced savoy or green cabbage
- 3 cans (14½ oz. each) chicken broth
- 1 quart water
- 1 piece (3×4-inch) Parmesan cheese rind (optional)
- 2 medium zucchini, quartered lengthwise and sliced
- ½ of a small head cauliflower, cut into tiny florettes
- 1 can (14½ oz.) whole tomatoes in juice, drained and chopped
- 4 slices sourdough bread
- ½ cup freshly grated Parmesan cheese

1. *Make beans:* Bring the beans and enough cold water to cover by 1 inch to boil in a large Dutch oven. Remove from heat, cover and let stand 1 hour. Drain the beans; return to Dutch oven and cover with 2 inches cold water. Add remaining ingredients. Bring to boil; reduce heat and simmer, covered, 30 minutes, until beans are tender. Drain beans; discard bay leaf. Set aside.

2. Heat 2 tablespoons of the oil in same Dutch oven over medium heat. Add onion, carrots, celery, garlic, ½ teaspoon of the salt and the pepper and cook 8 minutes, until garlic is golden. Add drained beans, squash, green beans, cabbage, chicken broth, water, Parmesan rind (if desired) and remaining 1 teaspoon salt. Bring to boil; reduce heat and simmer, partially covered, 30 minutes.

3. Stir in zucchini and cauliflower. Return to boil; reduce heat and simmer, partially covered, 20 minutes more, until beans and vegetables are very tender. Add tomatoes and cook 10 minutes. Remove and discard Parmesan rind. Transfer 2 cups of the soup, 1 cup at a time, to a blender and puree; return to Dutch oven. *(Can be made ahead. Cool. Cover and refrigerate up to 24 hours.)*

4. Heat oven to 375°F. Brush bread with remaining 1 tablespoon oil; arrange on a cookie sheet. Sprinkle with grated Parmesan. Bake 15 to 18 minutes, until golden brown and toasted. Cut each piece in half and serve with soup. Makes 8 servings.

Per serving: 285 calories, 9 g total fat, 2.5 g saturated fat, 5 mg cholesterol, 1,546 mg sodium, 41 g carbohydrates, 13 g protein, 222 mg calcium, 13 g fiber

butternut soup with cilantro (EASY)

For a velvety texture, puree the soup in 2 batches. Start on the blender's lowest speed and increase to the highest. Stop to scrape and redistribute the squash as necessary.

Prep time: 20 minutes • Cooking time: 30 to 35 minutes

- 1 medium (2 lbs.) butternut squash, peeled and cut into 2-inch chunks
- 3 teaspoons olive oil, divided
- 1 tablespoon butter or margarine
- ½ cup finely chopped onion
- 3 tablespoons finely chopped shallot
- 1 tablespoon finely chopped jalapeño chile with seeds (see tip, page 92)
- 2 teaspoons grated fresh ginger
- 2 cans (14½ oz. each) chicken broth
- ½ cup chopped fresh cilantro
- ⅔ cup unsweetened coconut milk

1. Heat oven to 400°F. Toss the squash with 2 teaspoons of the oil on a large jelly-roll pan. Roast 30 to 35 minutes, until tender when pierced with a knife.

2. Meanwhile, melt butter in a 3-quart saucepan over medium-high heat. Add onion and shallot; cook 2 to 3 minutes, until starting to brown. Add jalapeño and ginger; cook 1 minute more. Pour in the broth.

3. Remove 3 tablespoons of the broth mixture from saucepan to a blender. Add cilantro and remaining 1 teaspoon oil to blender and puree, scraping mixture with a spatula, until smooth. Transfer cilantro puree to a cup and set aside. Wash blender.

4. Add roasted squash to remaining broth mixture in saucepan and bring to boil. Cook 5 minutes, then remove from heat and cool 5 minutes. Puree squash mixture in blender, in 2 batches, until very smooth. Return puree to saucepan; stir in coconut milk and heat through. Ladle soup into serving bowls. Drop about 1 teaspoon of the cilantro puree into center of each and swirl with the tip of a knife. Makes 10 servings.

Per serving: 105 calories, 6 g total fat, 4 g saturated fat, 3 mg cholesterol, 284 mg sodium, 10 g carbohydrates, 4 g protein, 37 mg calcium, 2 g fiber

spinach salad with pear-thyme vinaigrette (EASY)

Take advantage of conveniently bagged baby spinach. Just give it a wash and a quick spin in the salad spinner. Any extra vinaigrette can be stored in the refrigerator up to 2 days.

Prep time: 10 minutes • Cooking time: 4 to 5 minutes

VINAIGRETTE:
- 1 Bartlett pear, peeled, cored and quartered
- ¼ cup white wine
- ¼ cup rice wine vinegar
- 1 shallot, minced
- 2 teaspoons chopped garlic
- 2 teaspoons Dijon mustard
- ¼ teaspoon salt
- ⅛ teaspoon freshly ground pepper
- ¾ cup extra-virgin olive oil
- 2 teaspoons chopped fresh thyme leaves

- 2 bags (10 oz. each) baby spinach
- 1 small head radicchio, chopped
- ½ pound white mushrooms, sliced
- 2 Bartlett pears, cored and sliced

1. *Make vinaigrette:* Cook the pear and wine in a small skillet over medium-high heat 4 to 5 minutes, until the pear is tender, stirring often. Transfer the pear to a blender or food processor. Add the vinegar, shallot, garlic, mustard, salt and pepper and puree until smooth. With the machine running, slowly add the oil, then add the thyme. Transfer vinaigrette to an airtight container. Refrigerate up to 2 days.

2. Toss the spinach, radicchio and mushrooms in a large bowl. Divide among 6 salad plates; arrange pear slices on top and drizzle each salad with 1 tablespoon of the vinaigrette. Serve immediately. Makes 6 servings.

Per serving: 360 calories, 28.5 g total fat, 4 g saturated fat, 0 mg cholesterol, 320 mg sodium, 27 g carbohydrates, 4 g protein, 86 mg calcium, 8 g fiber

sautéed cabbage

Here's a quick side dish that livens up any grilled chicken or steak dinner.

Prep time: 15 minutes • Cooking time: 12 minutes

- 1 tablespoon butter or margarine
- ½ cup chopped onion
- 1 bag (16 oz.) coleslaw mix
- ⅓ cup chicken broth
  Generous pinch crushed cumin seed
- 1½ teaspoons cider vinegar
- ½ teaspoon salt
- ⅛ teaspoon freshly ground pepper

Melt butter in a 12-inch skillet over medium-high heat. Add onion and cook 3 minutes, until browned. Add coleslaw mix, chicken broth and cumin seed. Cover and cook 7 minutes, until slaw is just tender. Stir in cider vinegar, salt and pepper. Cook 3 minutes more, until tender and excess moisture has evaporated, stirring occasionally. Makes 4 servings.

Per serving: 65 calories, 3.5 g total fat, 2 g saturated fat, 8 mg cholesterol, 407 mg sodium, 8 g carbohydrates, 2 g protein, 60 mg calcium, 3 g fiber

polenta with parmesan cheese

Excessive time and effort are not required ingredients for fabulous polenta. Need proof? Check out this recipe.

Prep time: 5 minutes • Microwave time: 7 minutes
Microwave used

- ½ cup yellow cornmeal
- 1 can (14½ oz.) low-sodium chicken broth plus enough water to equal 2 cups
- ⅛ teaspoon freshly ground pepper
- 2 tablespoons grated Parmesan cheese

Whisk cornmeal, broth mixture and pepper in a 2-quart microwaveproof bowl. Microwave on High 4 minutes; whisk vigorously. Microwave 3 minutes

more, until smooth and thickened; whisk in cheese. Serve immediately. Makes 2 servings.

Per serving: 165 calories, 2.5 g total fat, 1 g saturated fat, 4 mg cholesterol, 420 mg sodium, 28 g carbohydrates, 7 g protein, 84 mg calcium, 3 g fiber

roasted shoestring potatoes with lemon

Here's a great new take on French fries! To cut paper-thin strips of potato and lemon, use an inexpensive hand-held plastic slicer. Roast the potatoes with just a touch of olive oil until golden and crisp.

Prep time: 15 minutes • Roasting time: 40 minutes

- 4 tablespoons olive oil, divided
- ½ teaspoon salt
- ¼ teaspoon freshly ground pepper
- 1 small lemon, scrubbed
- 2 pounds baking potatoes, scrubbed

1. Arrange oven racks on middle and lower third of oven. Heat oven to 400°F. Brush 1 tablespoon of the oil on each of 2 large cookie sheets.

2. Combine remaining 2 tablespoons oil, salt and pepper in a bowl. Using slicing blade on a hand-held slicer, slice lemon ⅛ inch thick. Discard seeds and toss with oil mixture.

3. Insert ⅛-inch-wide matchstick blade into slicer and cut potatoes. Pat potatoes dry on paper towels; toss with lemon-oil mixture. Divide and spread evenly on prepared cookie sheets; roast 20 minutes.

4. Turn potatoes with metal spatula. Switch pans on racks and roast 20 minutes more, until golden and crisp. Makes 4 servings.

Per serving: 290 calories, 14 g total fat, 2 g saturated fat, 0 mg cholesterol, 298 mg sodium, 38 g carbohydrates, 6 g protein, 38 mg calcium, 5 g fiber

garlic mashed potatoes and parsnips

Everyone loves our mashed potatoes. The secret? We added parsnips and a hint of garlic. For the fluffiest texture, use a food mill or ricer for mashing.

Prep time: 20 minutes • Cooking time: 16 minutes

- **2 pounds all-purpose potatoes, peeled and cut into 2-inch pieces**
- **1 pound parsnips, peeled and chopped**
- **1 teaspoon salt, divided**
- **1 cup milk**
- **3 medium garlic cloves, thinly sliced**
- **2 tablespoons butter or margarine, cut up**
- **⅛ teaspoon white pepper**

1. Combine potatoes, parsnips, ½ teaspoon of the salt and cold water to cover by 1 inch in a large Dutch oven. Bring to boil; reduce heat and simmer 15 minutes, until vegetables are tender.

2. Meanwhile, combine milk, remaining ½ teaspoon salt and garlic in saucepan. Bring to boil. Remove from heat; cover and let stand 15 minutes.

3. Drain potatoes and parsnips. Return to Dutch oven and cook 1 minute to dry. Spoon vegetables into a food mill or ricer and press into bowl. Strain milk mixture into potatoes. Stir in butter and pepper until smooth. Makes 6 servings.

Per serving: 230 calories, 5.5 g total fat, 3 g saturated fat, 14 mg cholesterol, 461 mg sodium, 41 g carbohydrates, 6 g protein, 95 mg calcium, 6 g fiber

perfect
corn bread

If you want to try your hand at baking bread, corn bread couldn't be easier to master. Just mix the dry ingredients in one bowl and the wet in another, and with a few strokes of a spoon the batter is ready. We discovered that baking corn bread in a heated cast-iron skillet (versus a baking pan) produces the crispest crust while retaining a moist, tender interior. Cornmeal is available in a variety of textures from fine to coarse (sometimes labeled "stone ground") with each producing a bread of slightly different texture. Corn bread is best eaten fresh from the oven, so it's a great last-minute addition to any meal, but it also can be frozen up to 1 month and reheated.

Prep time: 5 minutes • Baking time: 20 to 22 minutes

 1   **cup yellow cornmeal**
 1   **cup all-purpose flour**
 2   **tablespoons sugar**

 1   **tablespoon baking powder**
 ½   **teaspoon salt**
 ⅛   **teaspoon ground red pepper**
 1   **cup buttermilk or dry buttermilk blend***
 ¼   **teaspoon baking soda**
 2   **large eggs**
 5   **tablespoons melted butter or margarine**
 1   **tablespoon vegetable shortening**

1. Heat oven to 400°F. Heat a 10-inch cast-iron skillet in oven 10 minutes.

2. Whisk together the cornmeal, flour, sugar, baking powder, salt and ground red pepper in a large bowl. Combine buttermilk and soda in a 2-cup glass measuring cup. Beat eggs and butter in small bowl until blended. Add wet ingredients to cornmeal mixture, gently stirring with a rubber spatula just until combined.

3. Add shortening to the hot skillet; return skillet to oven 1 minute, until shortening is melted. Pour batter into hot skillet. Bake 20 to 22 minutes, until toothpick inserted in center comes out clean. Cool on wire rack 5 minutes. Serve hot, warm or at room temperature. Cut into 8 wedges. Makes 8 servings.

*Note: Prepare recipe as directed *except* mix dry buttermilk blend with other dry ingredients and substitute 1 cup water for liquid buttermilk.

Per serving: 240 calories, 10.5 g total fat, 3.5 g saturated fat, 74 mg cholesterol, 488 mg sodium, 31 g carbohydrates, 6 g protein, 148 mg calcium, 1.5 g fiber

For corn sticks: Prepare corn bread as directed *except* heat 12 corn-stick molds 10 minutes in oven. Brush molds with 1 tablespoon shortening. Return molds to oven and heat 1 minute. Divide batter among molds, spreading batter with back of small spoon to fill each. Bake 13 to 15 minutes, until tops are golden and toothpick inserted in center of corn sticks comes out clean. Cool corn sticks in pan on a wire rack 5 minutes, then unmold onto rack. Makes 12 corn sticks.

chocolate praline bread pudding with cinnamon cream

Charlie Trotter is author of Charlie Trotter Cooks at Home *(Ten Speed Press) and is chef of Charlie Trotter in Chicago, Illinois. "When my family comes together for a celebration, it is a house full of chocolate lovers. Thanksgiving is no exception. This dessert offers a hefty dose of hot chocolate topped with cinnamon and crunchy nuts. This is perfect for a dinner party. Make the praline ahead, combine all of the ingredients for the pudding and cover with plastic wrap. Just before sitting down, put the pudding in the oven and serve it piping hot as dinner is finished."*

Prep time: 30 minutes • Baking time: 45 minutes

PRALINE:

- ¾ cup granulated sugar
- ¼ cup water
- ¾ cup pecan halves, toasted

BREAD PUDDING:

- 8 ounces crustless day-old bread, cut into 1-inch cubes
- 3 cups heavy or whipping cream
- 3 large eggs
- 3 large egg yolks
- ½ cup granulated sugar
- 9 ounces bittersweet chocolate, chopped, divided
- ⅛ teaspoon salt

CINNAMON CREAM:

- ½ cup heavy or whipping cream
- ½ teaspoon cinnamon
- 2 tablespoons confectioners' sugar

1. *Make praline:* Grease a cookie sheet; set aside. Combine sugar and water in a heavy medium skillet and cook over medium heat 10 minutes, until golden brown (do not stir). Stir in pecans. Immediately pour praline onto prepared cookie sheet. Cool completely, about 45 minutes. Chop into small pieces. *(Can be made ahead. Store in an airtight container at room temperature up to 1 week.)*

2. *Make pudding:* Heat oven to 350°F. Butter a 9-inch square baking dish. Place cubed bread in a large bowl. Set both aside.

3. Bring the cream to boil in a medium saucepan over medium heat. Meanwhile, whisk together the eggs, egg yolks and sugar in a medium bowl. Slowly whisk 1 cup of the hot cream into egg mixture. Then whisk cream-egg mixture back into saucepan with remaining cream; cook 1 to 2 minutes, until sugar dissolves. Add 3 ounces of the chocolate, stirring until chocolate is completely melted. Pour mixture over bread; let stand 10 minutes, until the bread absorbs all the liquid, stirring occasionally. Stir in remaining 6 ounces chocolate, salt and 1 cup of the praline.

4. Spoon mixture into prepared baking dish. Place in a large roasting pan. *(Make sure there is at least 1 inch of space between edges of baking dish and roasting pan.)* Carefully pour enough hot water into roasting pan to reach halfway up sides of baking dish. Bake 45 minutes, until a knife inserted in center comes out clean. Remove pudding from water bath; cool on wire rack 10 to 20 minutes. *(Can be made ahead. Cool completely. Cover with plastic wrap and refrigerate overnight. Remove from refrigerator 30 minutes before serving. Microwave on High 2 to 3 minutes, until center is warm.)*

5. *Make cinnamon cream:* Meanwhile, beat cream and cinnamon in a medium mixer bowl on medium-high speed until soft peaks form. Beat in confectioners' sugar just until combined. *(Can be made ahead. Cover and refrigerate up to 3 hours.)*

6. *To serve:* Cut pudding into 3-inch squares. Spoon 1 tablespoon of the cinnamon cream over each serving of pudding and sprinkle each with 1 tablespoon of the remaining praline. Makes 9 servings.

Per serving: 745 calories, 55 g total fat, 29 g saturated fat, 270 mg cholesterol, 247 mg sodium, 61 g carbohydrates, 10 g protein, 114 mg calcium, 4 g fiber

almond granola

This flavorful granola, from the Marriott Hotel in Albuquerque, New Mexico, makes a hearty meal served with milk, a nutty topping for ice cream or yogurt and a great snack by the handful.

Prep time: 10 minutes • Baking time: 20 to 25 minutes

- 2 **cups firmly packed brown sugar**
- ⅔ **cup butter or margarine**
- ½ **cup honey**
- 4 **cups uncooked oats**
- 2 **cups crisp rice cereal**
- 2 **cups sliced blanched almonds**
- 2 **tablespoons cinnamon**
- 2 **cups raisins**
- 1 **cup dried apples, diced**
  Milk, vanilla soy milk or frozen yogurt (optional)

1. Arrange oven racks in center and upper third of oven. Heat oven to 350°F. Line 2 large jelly-roll pans with foil.

2. Heat sugar, butter and honey in a medium saucepan over medium-high heat 5 minutes, until butter is melted and sugar is dissolved, stirring occasionally.

3. Meanwhile, combine oats, crisp rice cereal, almonds and cinnamon in a large bowl.

4. Pour melted butter mixture over oat mixture and toss to coat. Divide and spread oat mixture between prepared pans. Bake 20 to 25 minutes, until granola is well toasted, stirring every 10 minutes and rotating sheets between racks.

5. Cool granola on pans 5 minutes, then transfer to a large bowl. Stir in raisins and apples and cool completely. *(Can be made ahead. Store in resealable plastic storage bags up to 2 weeks.)* Serve with milk, vanilla soy milk or frozen yogurt, if desired. Makes 14 cups.

Per 1-cup serving without milk or frozen yogurt: 500 calories, 18.5 g total fat, 6.5 g saturated fat, 24 mg cholesterol, 149 mg sodium, 83 g carbohydrates, 8 g protein, 102 mg calcium, 5 g fiber

---

test kitchen tip
easy as 1-2-3 b-fast for dinner

Try these fun ideas for a fresh take on dinner, lunch or for your morning repast. (They make great snacks, too!)

USE UP ripe fruit by whirling it in the blender with some yogurt and milk or orange juice for a deliciously nutritious smoothie.

SWIRL applesauce and a little brown sugar into a bowl of hot oatmeal.

INDULGE by making a chocolate croissant: Slice 1 croissant in half horizontally. Sprinkle the bottom half with 1 tablespoon chocolate chips. Replace the top half, and microwave on High about 30 seconds.

SLICE a bagel in half and spread peanut butter on each; sprinkle with raisins.

TOP French toast or pancakes with jam or jelly instead of syrup.

PREPARE healthy parfaits: Spoon alternating layers of fruit and vanilla yogurt and top with broken graham cracker pieces or crunchy cereal for a fantastic finish.

DRESS UP scrambled eggs by adding your favorite sautéed veggies (such as mushrooms, onions and bell peppers) and wrapping them in a warmed flour tortilla. When you want to really indulge, include bacon or sausage pieces.

ADD chocolate chips and/or peanut butter chips to pancake batter.

MAKE a Southwest scramble: Split a kaiser roll, sprinkle some Cheddar cheese on top and toast in a toaster oven. Meanwhile, scramble an egg, spoon the egg over the toasted roll and top with a little salsa!

BARLEY
WALDORF SALAD
PG. 120

market fresh and fabulous

Simply put, fresh market ingredients are the best, whether they're from the garden or the sea ... fresh tastes better, feels better, looks better! What's more, the fresh stuff is so full of flavor, it needs little effort to become a sensational dish. So go ahead, get fresh with these ideas.

WHITE PIZZA
WITH BROCCOLI
PG. 106

take your **taste**
buds for a spin...

WARM RED
POTATO AND
CORN SALAD
PG. 115

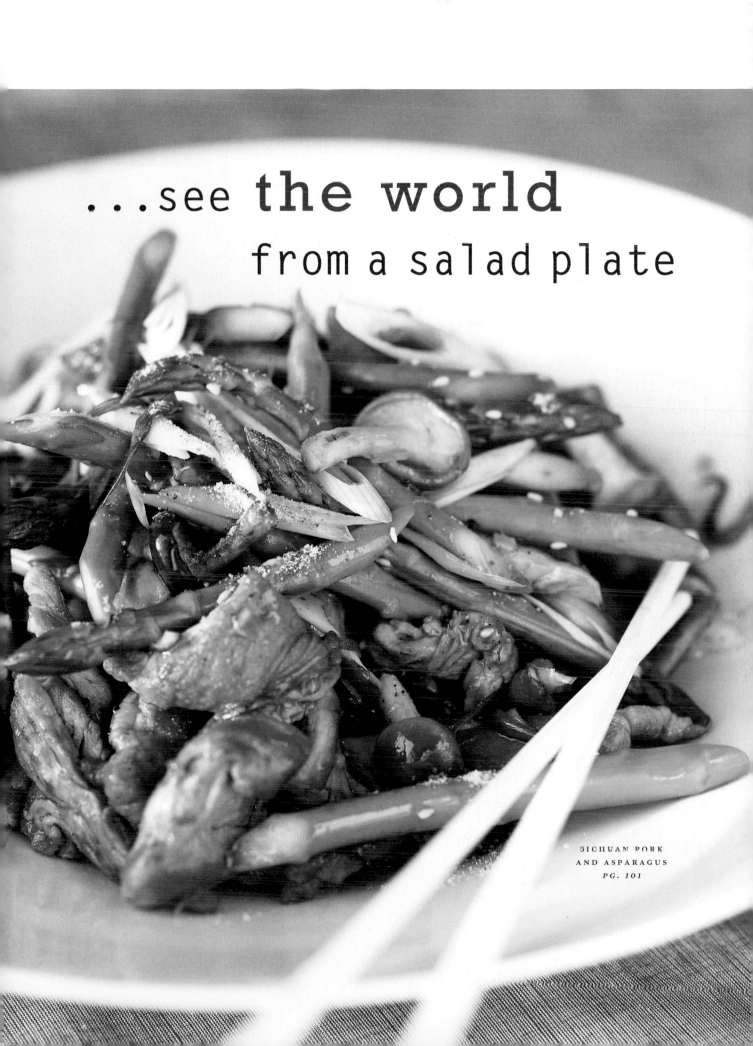

...see **the world**
from a salad plate

SICHUAN PORK
AND ASPARAGUS
PG. 101

what's the secret
to eating good stuff?

SPRING LASAGNE
PG. 104

SHRIMP WITH
ASPARAGUS
AND BARLEY
PG. 102

SALMON AND
BABY BROCCOLI WITH
MISO DRESSING
PG. 102

shopping for the good stuff!

eat your **veggies!**

and fall in love...

SOYFUL
SCALLOPED
POTATOES
PG. 116

CHICKEN
FIESTA SALAD
PG. 96

with **flavor,** oh yes

CREAMY
COLESLAW
PG. 114

cradled by earth,
raised by **sun...**
fresh tastes best

ROASTED
VEGETABLE
FRITTATA
PG. 108

VEGETABLE-BEAN
QUESADILLAS
PG. 107

tropical sunrise smoothie LOW FAT EASY

Look for guava nectar in the juice aisle of your neighborhood supermarket.

Total prep time: 10 minutes

- **1 cup cold guava nectar**
- **2 cups peeled and cubed cold cantaloupe**
- **½ cup cold plain or vanilla low-fat yogurt**

Blend all ingredients in a blender on high speed until smooth. Makes 2 servings.

Per serving: 110 calories, 1 g total fat, 0.5 g saturated fat, 2 mg cholesterol, 38 mg sodium, 24 g carbohydrates, 3 g protein, 86 mg calcium, 1 g fiber

creamy cantaloupe crush LOW FAT EASY

If getting your 5-a-day fruits and veggies seems daunting, you'll be happy to know you can check off three servings in a single shake. Precut cantaloupe from the produce aisle makes this a speedy treat.

Total prep time: 10 minutes

- **3 cups peeled and cubed cold cantaloupe**
- **1 cup cold orange-peach-mango 100% juice**
- **2 tablespoons cold plain or vanilla low-fat yogurt**
- **½ cup ice**

Blend cantaloupe, juice and yogurt in a blender on high speed until smooth. With motor running, add ice, one cube at a time, through feed tube, blending until smooth. Makes 2 servings.

Per serving: 155 calories, 1 g total fat, 0.5 g saturated fat, 1 mg cholesterol, 58 mg sodium, 36 g carbohydrates, 3 g protein, 65 mg calcium, 2 g fiber

test kitchen tip
power foods: melon

Full of good-for-you nutrients with few calories, melons are a refreshing treat that beats the heat of summer. And with high levels of potassium, melon is a smart food choice to help lower high blood pressure. Cantaloupe leads with the highest amount of potassium at 495 mg per serving, honeydew has 460 mg and watermelon 185 mg. Cantaloupe also contains beta-carotene, a powerful antioxidant that fights against blood and circulatory diseases and certain cancers. This antioxidant also can be found in other orange melons, such as Crenshaws. With only 50 calories, one serving of cantaloupe (about one-fourth of a medium melon) gives you 100% of your daily needs for vitamin A and 80% for vitamin C, which is good for enhancing immunity. Honeydew (50 calories in one-tenth of a melon) provides you with half your daily value of vitamin C, and watermelon (80 calories in 1 cup cubed) gives you one-fourth of your daily C needs.

Different varieties of melons are available sporadically all year. When selecting melons, choose those that feel heavy for their size and yield to slight pressure at the blossom end (except for watermelons). They should be evenly ripe, with no soft, water-soaked areas or mold. Look for cantaloupe with a slightly golden undercolor and a netting pattern that stands out prominently and covers the melon. Also check for a distinctive, sweet aroma.

People allergic to ragweed or grass pollen may develop an itchy throat or mouth after eating cantaloupe. Those allergic to tomatoes may have a similar reaction to honeydew or watermelon.

Melons are often sold underripe and need to be ripened at room temperature to develop maximum flavor. If your melon is slightly soft, it's ready to eat. Once ripe, whole melons keep for 2 to 3 days in the refrigerator. Once cut, wrap in plastic wrap and refrigerate up to 5 days.

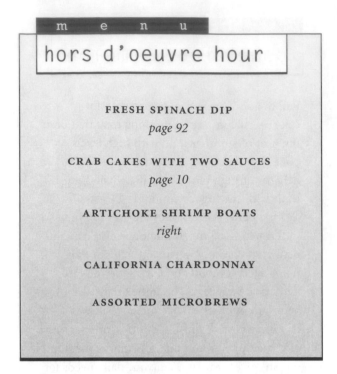

m e n u

hors d'oeuvre hour

FRESH SPINACH DIP
page 92

CRAB CAKES WITH TWO SAUCES
page 10

ARTICHOKE SHRIMP BOATS
right

CALIFORNIA CHARDONNAY

ASSORTED MICROBREWS

asparagus with tarragon dipping sauce EASY

All the joys (and flavors) of spring are found in this dip. We used slender asparagus stalks no more than ½ inch in diameter. If your stalks are larger, adjust the cooking time.

Prep time: 10 minutes • Cooking time: 2 minutes

> **Water**
> 1 **tablespoon salt**
> 3 **pounds thin asparagus, trimmed to 5-inch spears**

TARRAGON SAUCE:
> ½ **cup mayonnaise**
> ¼ **cup sour cream**
> 2 **tablespoons minced shallots**
> 2 **tablespoons chopped fresh tarragon**
> 1 **teaspoon fresh lemon juice**
> ¼ **teaspoon salt**
> ¼ **teaspoon freshly ground black pepper**
> **Pinch ground red pepper**

1. Bring water and salt to boil in a large pot over medium-high heat. Add asparagus and return to boil; cook 2 minutes, just until tender. Transfer asparagus to a colander; rinse and drain under cold

running water. Pat asparagus dry with paper towels. *(Can be made ahead. Wrap; refrigerate up to 24 hours.)*

2. *Make tarragon sauce:* Combine all ingredients in a small bowl. Stir together until well mixed. *(Can be made ahead. Cover and refrigerate up to 24 hours.)*

3. Arrange asparagus on a serving platter and serve with tarragon sauce. Makes 20 servings.

Per serving with 1 teaspoon sauce: 60 calories, 5 g total fat, 1 g saturated fat, 3 mg cholesterol, 120 mg sodium, 3 g carbohydrates, 1 g protein, 14 mg calcium, 1 g fiber

artichoke shrimp boats LOW FAT EASY

These festive artichoke "boats" are filled with a delicious and elegant shrimp stuffing.

Prep time: 45 minutes • Baking time: 20 minutes

> 4½ **quarts water**
> 2 **tablespoons olive oil**
> 2 **garlic cloves, thinly sliced**
> 1 **teaspoon salt**
> 1 **teaspoon sugar**
> 6 **medium artichokes**

STUFFING:
> 2 **tablespoons olive oil**
> ½ **teaspoon minced garlic**
> 1 **pound medium shrimp, peeled, deveined and chopped**
> ¼ **cup chopped green onions**
> ½ **teaspoon salt**
> ½ **teaspoon freshly ground pepper**
> 1 **cup fresh bread crumbs (2 slices firm white sandwich bread)**
> ¼ **cup chopped fresh flat-leaf parsley**
> 2 **teaspoons fresh lemon juice**

1. Bring water, oil, garlic, salt and sugar to boil in a Dutch oven. Cut tops and stems off artichokes. With scissors, snip off tips of leaves. Add artichokes to Dutch oven; return water to boil. Reduce heat and simmer, covered, 25 minutes, until a leaf near center pulls out easily. Drain and cool.

2. Heat oven to 325°F. Remove center leaves of artichokes; scrape out fuzzy centers (chokes) using a tablespoon and discard.

3. *Make stuffing:* Heat oil in a large skillet. Add garlic; cook 1 minute. Add shrimp, green onions, salt and pepper; cook, stirring, 3 to 4 minutes, until shrimp turn pink and are opaque. Remove from heat; stir in bread crumbs, parsley and lemon juice.

4. Grease a 13×9-inch baking dish. Spoon about ⅓ cup stuffing into each artichoke. Arrange in prepared dish; cover with foil. Bake 20 minutes. Makes 6 servings.

Per serving: 185 calories, 6 g total fat, 1 g saturated fat, 86 mg cholesterol, 434 mg sodium, 19 g carbohydrates, 17 g protein, 101 mg calcium, 7 g fiber

braised artichokes with mint

EASY

Serve this perfectly seasoned dish at room temperature as an irresistible, slightly exotic appetizer.

Prep time: 20 minutes • Cooking time: 25 to 30 minutes

4	artichokes (2 lbs. total), quartered
½	lemon
½	cup water
3	tablespoons olive oil
2	tablespoons chopped fresh flat-leaf parsley
1	teaspoon minced garlic
½	teaspoon salt
¼	teaspoon dried mint
¼	cup chopped fresh mint
1	teaspoon minced lemon peel

1. Remove outer leaves of the artichokes and trim stems to 1 inch, then peel stems with a small, sharp knife. Slice off top half of artichokes; discard top half. Carefully scrape out fuzzy centers (chokes) using a tablespoon and discard. Rub all sides of artichoke quarters with cut side of lemon.

2. Arrange artichokes in a single layer in a medium skillet. Drizzle with the water and oil. Combine parsley, garlic, salt and dried mint in a cup and sprinkle evenly over artichokes; bring to boil over medium-high heat. Reduce heat to medium-low and simmer, covered, 20 minutes, until tender. Uncover and continue to cook until all but 2 tablespoons of the liquid has evaporated, if necessary.

3. Transfer artichokes and liquid to a serving dish. Combine fresh mint and lemon peel in a cup and sprinkle on top. Makes 4 servings.

Per serving: 155 calories, 10.5 g total fat, 1.5 g saturated fat, 0 mg cholesterol, 407 mg sodium, 15 g carbohydrates, 4 g protein, 68 mg calcium, 7 g fiber

test kitchen tip

artichokes

Unfamiliar with the almighty artichoke? You've come to the right place.

how to prepare

• First, cut off the artichoke's stem, then discard the small bottom leaves. Next, cut off the top quarter of the artichoke. Trim the tips of the leaves with scissors, and rub the exposed cut leaves and stem with lemon.

• To cook whole artichokes, place them in a deep saucepan or pot with 3 inches boiling water. Cover and boil gently 25 to 40 minutes (depending on size), until a leaf near the center pulls out easily.

how to eat a whole artichoke

• Starting from the base of the cooked artichoke, pull off one leaf.

• Put the base of the leaf in your mouth and pull it through your teeth to remove the soft, pulpy portion at the base of the petal. Discard the petal, and continue eating the remaining leaves.

• With a spoon, carefully scrape out and discard the fuzzy center (choke). Cut the bottom (heart) of the artichoke into small pieces and eat (it's especially delicious dipped in melted butter).

chile peppers

Chile peppers add extra spark to many dishes, but they require extra precautions.

HANDLING: Because chile peppers, such as jalapeños, contain volatile oils that can burn your skin and eyes, avoid direct contact with them as much as possible. When working with chile peppers, wear plastic or rubber gloves. If your bare hands touch the chile peppers, wash your hands well with soap and water.

COOKING: As they cook, chile peppers release fumes that can irritate breathing passages and cause coughing. Avoid breathing these fumes.

1. Peel husks of corn down to the bottom of each ear without detaching, and remove silk. Replace husks and secure with twine. Soak corn in a large bowl of cold water 30 minutes before grilling.

2. Heat grill. Drain corn. Grill corn and chiles over high heat 12 to 15 minutes, until tender and evenly charred, turning every 5 minutes. Remove from grill; cover and let stand 10 minutes.

3. When cool enough to handle, peel the skin from the chiles, then discard membranes and seeds; finely dice. Remove husks from corn and discard. Carefully cut kernels from each cob, then transfer the corn to a medium bowl. Stir in diced chiles, zucchini, tomato, green onions, oregano, lime juice, oil, garlic and salt. Makes 5 cups.

Per ½ cup: 40 calories, 1.5 g total fat, 0 g saturated fat, 0 mg cholesterol, 62 mg sodium, 7 g carbohydrates, 1 g protein, 11 mg calcium, 1 g fiber

grilled corn and chile salsa

Charring the poblano chiles—large, medium-hot chile peppers—on the grill adds a rich, smoky flavor to this summer-harvest salsa. The corn and zucchini cool things off. Serve the salsa with tortilla chips, crackers or a platter of cut-up vegetables.

Prep time: 35 minutes plus soaking
Grilling time: 12 to 15 minutes

- **3** ears corn
- **2** poblano chiles (see tip, above)
- **1** cup diced zucchini
- **1** plum tomato, seeded and finely diced (½ cup)
- **¼** cup thinly sliced green onions
- **1** tablespoon chopped fresh oregano or
  ½ teaspoon dried oregano
- **1** tablespoon fresh lime juice
- **1** tablespoon olive oil
- **½** teaspoon minced garlic
- **¼** teaspoon salt

fresh spinach dip

We've lightened this popular dip by using reduced-fat sour cream. Serve with crackers, or for a beta-carotene bonanza, serve with carrot sticks and broccoli florettes.

Total prep time: 10 minutes plus chilling

- **2** cups packed fresh spinach leaves
- **½** cup reduced-fat sour cream
- **½** teaspoon salt
  Pinch ground red pepper
- **¼** cup finely chopped green onions

Combine spinach, sour cream, salt and red pepper in a food processor; process until smooth. Transfer to a serving bowl and stir in green onions. Cover and refrigerate for at least 3 hours, until thickened. *(Can be made ahead. Cover and refrigerate overnight.)* Makes 1 cup.

Per tablespoon: 10 calories, 0.5 g total fat, 0.5 g saturated fat, 3 mg cholesterol, 83 mg sodium, 1 g carbohydrates, 1 g protein, 19 mg calcium, 0.5 g fiber

zucchini fritters with coriander chutney EASY

Spice up these fritters with a delectable partner. Our Indian-style chutney is a tangy puree of cilantro (another name for coriander), fresh lime and poblano chile.

Prep time: 35 minutes
Cooking time: 2 to 3 minutes per batch

CHUTNEY:

- 1 poblano chile (see tip, opposite page)
- 1 cup packed fresh cilantro leaves
- ½ cup packed fresh parsley leaves
- 2 tablespoons olive oil
- 1 tablespoon fresh lime juice
- ½ teaspoon salt

FRITTERS:

- 2 medium zucchini (½ lb.)
- 1 large egg, separated, at room temperature
- 6 tablespoons milk
- ¼ cup shredded pepper Jack cheese
- 1 green onion, sliced
- ¾ cup all-purpose flour
- ½ teaspoon baking powder
- ½ teaspoon ground cumin
- ½ teaspoon salt
  •
- 3 tablespoons olive oil, divided, for frying

1. *Make chutney:* Roast the chile directly on a gas or electric burner over medium-high heat until evenly charred. Place in a brown paper bag; fold over opening and cool 10 to 15 minutes.

2. When chile is cool enough to handle, peel and remove stem and seeds. Place chile and remaining chutney ingredients in a blender. Blend until smooth; set aside.

3. Heat oven to 200°F. Line a cookie sheet with paper towels.

4. *Make fritters:* Coarsely shred 2 cups zucchini onto several layers of paper towels. Whisk together egg yolk, milk, cheese and green onion in a medium bowl. Pat zucchini dry and add to egg yolk mixture. Beat egg white to stiff peaks in a small mixer bowl on high speed.

5. Combine flour, baking powder, cumin and salt in a small bowl. Stir into zucchini mixture, then gently fold in beaten egg white with a rubber spatula just until mixed.

6. Heat 1 tablespoon of the oil in a 12-inch nonstick skillet. Carefully drop batter by slightly rounded tablespoonfuls, 10 at a time, into skillet. Cook 2 to 3 minutes, until golden, turning once halfway through cooking. Transfer fritters to prepared cookie sheet and keep warm in oven. Repeat twice. Serve hot with chutney. Makes about 2½ dozen fritters.

Per fritter: 45 calories, 3 g total fat, 0.5 g saturated fat, 8 mg cholesterol, 97 mg sodium, 3 g carbohydrates, 1 g protein, 22 mg calcium, 0 g fiber

---

test kitchen tip

shake the salt

High-salt diets are associated with calcium loss and, for those who are salt sensitive, high blood pressure. The American Heart Association and other health organizations recommend no more than 2,400 milligrams of sodium (that's the offending compound in salt) each day. Surprisingly, processed and prepared foods, rather than the table shaker, are the greatest source of salt and sodium in our diets. And often these foods don't even taste salty. For example, there is more sodium in a McDonald's milk shake than in a serving of its fries! If you eat a lot of prepared foods, get in the habit of reading nutrition labels and limit very high-sodium choices. If you eat canned vegetables, simply rinse them to wash away most of the sodium. Another tip: Always taste before reaching for the shaker.

a fresh start

To ensure your diet is the best it can possibly be, keep this trio of tips in mind.

GO VEGETARIAN SOMETIMES One of the reasons Asian women don't have problems with osteoporosis to the extent American women do may be their vegetable-based diets. Replacing a meat-based meal two or three times a week with one built on vegetables is not only economical but also healthy. Be sure to include some nonmeat protein such as eggs, beans or some form of soybeans in these meals.

DRINK WATER Humans are 55 to 75 percent water—that's 10 to 12 gallons. (How much water your body contains depends on your age, gender and how much fat you have.) Studies show that when humans think they're hungry, often they're actually thirsty. Dehydration is a major cause of fatigue. So if you find yourself reaching for a "little pick-me-up," drink a glass of water first. This is especially important in air-conditioned and heated buildings where moisture is removed from the air—and thus your body. The average adult loses about 2½ quarts of water a day. So drink up.

SHRINK SERVING SIZES By now we all know that it's not just what you eat but how much, that's important. But it's getting more difficult to know how much is too much. Americans are eating out and ordering take-out more often, and restaurant portion sizes are HUGE! For example, burgers average 8 ounces (4 ounces is recommended by nutritionists); meat, poultry and fish are sold in 8- to 12-ounce portions (versus the recommended 4); bakery muffins are 5½ ounces instead of the recommended 1½ ounces. Put meals back into proper perspective: One serving of protein (lean meat, poultry, eggs or fish) is 3 to 4 ounces, starch ½ to 1 cup, and fruits and vegetables ½ cup. When eating out, kid size it—don't super size.

white bean sandwich spread

Canned white beans work beautifully in spread and dip recipes. To keep prep quick and simple, mash the beans with a potato masher.

Total prep time: 10 minutes

- **1 cup canned white beans, drained and rinsed**
- **2 tablespoons extra-virgin olive oil**
- **¼ cup thinly sliced fresh basil leaves**
- **½ teaspoon fresh lemon juice**
- **¼ teaspoon salt**
- **Pinch freshly ground pepper**

Coarsely mash beans with a potato masher or 2 forks. Stir in remaining ingredients. Use 2 tablespoons per sandwich. Cover and refrigerate up to 3 days. Makes ¾ cup.

Per 2 tablespoons: 70 calories, 5 g total fat, 0.5 g saturated fat, 0 mg cholesterol, 182 mg sodium, 5 g carbohydrates, 2 g protein, 16 mg calcium, 2 g fiber

chipotle mayonnaise

Chipotles are smoked jalapeño chiles and are available chopped or whole in adobo sauce. We used the canned variety. Use them sparingly; a small amount provides a healthy zap of heat.

Total prep time: 5 minutes

- **½ cup mayonnaise**
- **1 tablespoon chopped chipotle chile**
- **1 tablespoon minced onion**
- **½ teaspoon grated orange peel**

Combine all ingredients in a small bowl. Cover and refrigerate up to 3 days. Use 1 tablespoon per sandwich. Makes ½ cup.

Per 1 tablespoon: 100 calories, 11 g total fat, 1.5 g saturated fat, 8 mg cholesterol, 94 mg sodium, 1 g carbohydrates, 0 g protein, 4 mg calcium, 0 g fiber

peanut hummus

This hummus uses peanuts rather than the classic chickpeas.

Total prep time: 5 minutes

- ½ cup unsalted peanuts
- ¼ cup tahini (sesame seed paste)
- 1 garlic clove, crushed
- 3 tablespoons fresh lemon juice
- 3 tablespoons water
- 1 tablespoon lite soy sauce
- Pinch salt
- 1 tablespoon chopped fresh cilantro
- Pita bread wedges or crackers (optional)

Puree all ingredients *except* cilantro in blender until smooth. Stir in cilantro. Use 2 tablespoons per sandwich, or, if desired, serve with pita bread wedges or crackers. Cover and refrigerate up to 3 days. Makes ¾ cup.

Per 2 tablespoons: 135 calories, 11.5 g total fat, 1.5 g saturated fat, 0 mg cholesterol, 136 mg sodium, 6 g carbohydrates, 5 g protein, 51 mg calcium, 2 g fiber

raspberry whirl

As an alternative, try this recipe with cranberry-cherry juice and frozen, dark sweet cherries.

Total prep time: 10 minutes plus freezing

- ¾ cup fresh raspberries
- 1¼ cups cranberry-raspberry juice
- 1 large banana
- ½ cup ice

1. Freeze raspberries in a single layer on a cookie sheet 2 hours or overnight.

2. Blend juice, raspberries and banana in a blender on high speed until smooth. With motor running, add ice, one cube at a time, through feed tube, blending 1 minute, until smooth and color lightens. Makes 2 servings.

Per serving: 180 calories, 0.5 g total fat, 0 g saturated fat, 0 mg cholesterol, 23 mg sodium, 45 g carbohydrates, 1 g protein, 15 mg calcium, 5 g fiber

zucchini fettuccine with chicken

It's the perfect entrée for a hot summer evening. The "fettuccine" is made from thin strips of zucchini, then tossed with chicken (cook your own, or pick up a rotisserie chicken at the supermarket).

Total prep and cooking time: 30 minutes

- 5 tablespoons rice vinegar, divided
- Salt
- ½ teaspoon freshly ground pepper
- ¼ teaspoon sugar
- ¼ cup finely chopped onion
- 1 pound zucchini, trimmed
- 3 tablespoons mayonnaise
- 1 tablespoon chopped fresh flat-leaf parsley
- 1 pound cooked boneless smoked chicken breast, skin removed and coarsely chopped
- 1 medium tomato, coarsely chopped

1. Whisk together 3 tablespoons of the vinegar, ½ teaspoon salt, the pepper and sugar in a large bowl. Stir in onion.

2. Using a wide-blade vegetable peeler, cut zucchini lengthwise into wide, flat slices. Dice the first slice and middle portion. Add both sliced and diced zucchini to bowl with vinegar mixture and gently toss to coat. Let stand 15 minutes.

3. Combine mayonnaise, remaining 2 tablespoons vinegar, parsley and a pinch of salt in a medium bowl. Add chicken, tossing to coat.

4. *To serve:* Arrange zucchini slices with vinegar mixture on 4 serving plates. Spoon chicken, then tomato on top. Makes 4 servings.

Per serving: 230 calories, 12.5 g total fat, 3 g saturated fat, 51 mg cholesterol, 1,401 mg sodium, 7 g carbohydrates, 24 g protein, 31 mg calcium, 1 g fiber

fajita fiesta

Fajitas make the perfect party food because you can prepare all the ingredients ahead of time. When you're ready to eat, set everything out in individual bowls and let your guests assemble their own fajita dinners.

GRILLED CORN AND CHILE SALSA
page 92

GUACAMOLE
page 98

OVEN-BAKED TORTILLA CHIPS
page 131

CHICKEN FIESTA SALAD *below* **OR**
GRILLED CHICKEN FAJITAS
page 98

FROZEN MARGARITAS
ASSORTED MEXICAN BEERS

NORTHWEST BERRY SHORTCAKE
page 174

chicken fiesta salad

A specialty of Ruby Tuesday in Pueblo, Colorado, this hearty salad showcases flour tortillas baked until crisp in special molds. The shells are filled with a combo of Cajun-spiced chicken, lettuce, shredded cheese and tomato. To top it off, it's all drizzled with creamy ranch dressing. Pictured on page 87.

Prep time: 30 minutes • Cooking time: 24 to 26 minutes

- **4** **burrito-size (12-inch) tortillas**
- **4** **boneless, skinless chicken breast halves (5 to 6 oz. each)**
- **4** **teaspoons Cajun seasoning**
- **1** **tablespoon vegetable oil**

- **1** **pound iceberg lettuce, cut into 1-inch slices (8 packed cups)**
- **6** **ounces romaine lettuce, cut into 1-inch slices (4 packed cups)**
- **1** **cup coarsely shredded carrots**
- **¼** **cup sliced red cabbage**
- **½** **cup coarsely shredded Monterey Jack cheese**
- **½** **cup coarsely shredded Cheddar cheese**
- **½** **cup prepared ranch salad dressing**
- **2** **cups diced tomatoes**

1. Heat oven to 375°F. Lightly coat 2 tortilla/taco shell molds* or medium ovenproof bowls with vegetable cooking spray. Carefully press tortilla into each mold, making sure the tortilla follows the shape of the mold. Bake 10 to 12 minutes, until golden. Let cool in molds 5 minutes. Carefully remove tortilla shells and cool on wire rack. Repeat with remaining 2 tortillas.

2. Meanwhile, sprinkle both sides of chicken with Cajun seasoning. Heat oil in a large skillet over medium-high heat. Add chicken and cook 7 minutes per side, until cooked through.

3. Toss the lettuces, carrots and cabbage in a large bowl. Toss cheeses together in another bowl. Fill each tortilla shell with 3 cups of the packed lettuce mixture; top with 2 tablespoons of the dressing, ¼ cup of the cheese mixture, ½ cup of the tomatoes and 1 of the chicken breasts, sliced. Pass remaining dressing. Makes 4 servings.

*Note: Look for these molds at kitchenware shops or Spanish or Latino specialty stores.

Per serving: 800 calories, 38.5 g total fat, 10 g saturated fat, 128 mg cholesterol, 1,829 mg sodium, 60 g carbohydrates, 54 g protein, 434 mg calcium, 6 g fiber

grilled chicken salad with summer fruit EASY

A warm-weather delight! Toss smoky, grilled chicken and fresh fruits together in a ginger-lime dressing for an intriguing contrast of flavors and textures.

Prep time: 15 minutes plus marinating
Grilling time: 8 minutes

MARINADE:

- ½ teaspoon fennel seeds
- 1 tablespoon vegetable oil
- 1 tablespoon fresh lime juice
- ½ teaspoon salt
- ¼ teaspoon freshly ground pepper
- 4 chicken cutlets (6 to 8 oz. each), ¼ inch thick

LIME DRESSING:

- 3 tablespoons vegetable oil
- ⅛ teaspoon grated lime peel
- 1 tablespoon fresh lime juice
- ½ teaspoon salt
- ⅛ teaspoon red pepper flakes

- 2 nectarines, very thinly sliced
- 2 plums, very thinly sliced
- 2 green onions, minced
- 2 tablespoons fresh lime juice
- 2 teaspoons grated fresh ginger

- 3 cups tightly packed fresh spinach leaves
- 2 cups tightly packed watercress, trimmed
  Lime peel, cut into thin strips, for garnish (optional)

1. *Make marinade:* Heat a large skillet over medium-high heat. Add fennel seeds and toast, shaking skillet, 2 minutes, until fragrant. Transfer seeds to a cutting board and crush with the back of a knife.

2. Combine oil, lime juice, salt, pepper and fennel seeds in a shallow bowl. Add chicken and turn to coat. Cover and marinate in the refrigerator 15 to 30 minutes.

3. *Make lime dressing:* Meanwhile, whisk together all ingredients in a bowl.

4. Toss together sliced nectarines, plums, green onions, the 2 tablespoons lime juice and ginger in another bowl.

5. Heat grill for direct heat, or heat broiler. Grill chicken over medium heat, or broil chicken 4 inches from heat source, 4 minutes per side. Slice chicken into ½-inch-thick strips. Toss greens with the lime dressing and arrange on a serving platter. Top with chicken and spoon on fruit. Garnish with lime peel strips, if desired. Makes 4 servings.

Per serving: 395 calories, 17.5 g total fat, 3 g saturated fat, 99 mg cholesterol, 734 mg sodium, 19 g carbohydrates, 42 g protein, 76 mg calcium, 5 g fiber

---

test kitchen tip

nectarine know-how

Similar in flavor and texture to peaches (but without the fuzz), nectarines are one of the special treats of summer. They usually peak between June and September. Here's how to enjoy them at their best:

CHOOSE nectarines that have a healthy golden yellow skin with no tinges of green. The skin's pretty blush color has to do with the variety of nectarine, not ripeness. Nectarines should be firm and unblemished in the store. Complete ripening them at home in a loosely closed paper bag for several days at room temperature.

USE the ripened fruit as soon as possible. Refrigerate ripe nectarines for up to 5 days.

SERVE nectarines at room temperature for best flavor. As with peaches, whether or not you peel them is a personal choice.

ahhh, avocado

Avocados, contrary to popular belief, are a fruit and not a vegetable. Native to the tropics and now grown abundantly in California, the avocado is known for its rich, buttery texture and mildly nutty flavor. There are several different types of avocado available today on the market. The black Hass and the green Fuerte are perhaps the most widely distributed in the United States.

When selecting avocados, look for blemish-free fruit that feels heavy for its size. Ripe avocados yield to gentle pressure, but the ones typically found in stores are unripe. To ripen quickly, place avocados in a paper bag, close the bag and store at room temperature for 2 to 4 days.

Discoloring occurs extremely quickly when an avocado's flesh is exposed to air. When used in a dish that calls for mashed avocado, such as guacamole (see recipe, right), a touch of lemon or lime juice helps stop discoloration. If using pieces of avocado, add them just prior to serving.

grilled chicken fajitas EASY

Salsa cruda and guacamole garnish this grilled fajita dish. For maximum flavor, let the chicken marinate at least an hour in the refrigerator.

Prep time: 30 minutes plus marinating
Grilling time: 10 to 12 minutes

- ½ **cup fresh lime juice**
- 2 **teaspoons minced garlic**
- 1 **teaspoon red pepper flakes**
- 2 **pounds boneless, skinless chicken breasts**

SALSA CRUDA:

- 6 **plum tomatoes, diced (3 cups)**
- ½ **cup minced red onion**
- ¼ **cup chopped fresh cilantro**
- 2 **medium jalapeño chiles, minced (4 teaspoons) (see tip, page 92)**
- 1 **teaspoon salt**

GUACAMOLE:

- 2 **ripe avocados, peeled and pitted**
- ¼ **cup minced red onion**
- 2 **tablespoons fresh lime juice**
- ½ **teaspoon salt**
- ¼ **teaspoon red pepper sauce**
- •
- ¾ **teaspoon salt**
- 12 **(6- to 8-inch) flour tortillas, warmed**

1. Combine lime juice, garlic and red pepper flakes in a glass bowl. Add the chicken; cover and marinate in the refrigerator 1 hour, turning occasionally.

2. *Make salsa cruda:* Combine all ingredients in a serving bowl. Makes 3 cups.

3. *Make guacamole:* Mash all ingredients together with a potato masher or a large fork in a bowl. Makes 1¾ cups.

4. Heat grill. Remove chicken from marinade and sprinkle with the ¾ teaspoon salt.

5. Grill over medium heat 5 to 6 minutes per side, until cooked through. Slice and serve with warm tortillas, salsa cruda and guacamole. Makes 6 servings.

Per serving with 1 tablespoon salsa cruda and 1 tablespoon guacamole: 485 calories, 17 g total fat, 3 g saturated fat, 88 mg cholesterol, 1,214 mg sodium, 43 g carbohydrates, 42 g protein, 104 mg calcium, 5 g fiber

warm chicken and pesto vegetable sandwich EASY

You'll love this crunchy sweet pepper, radish and carrot slaw on top of warm chicken cutlets.

Prep time: 20 minutes • Cooking time: 4 to 6 minutes

- 1 **green onion, finely chopped (2 tablespoons)**
- ¼ **cup sour cream**

2 tablespoons pesto (recipe, below)
1 teaspoon fresh lemon juice
¼ teaspoon salt
½ red bell pepper, thinly sliced
½ yellow bell pepper, thinly sliced
¼ cup julienned radish
¼ cup shredded carrot
1 green onion, thinly sliced on the diagonal
1 tablespoon olive oil
4 boneless, skinless chicken cutlets (¾ lb.), ½ inch thick
8 slices pumpernickel bread, toasted

1. Combine chopped green onion, sour cream, pesto, lemon juice and salt in a medium bowl. Add bell peppers, radish, carrot and thinly sliced green onion and stir until well combined.

2. Heat oil in a large skillet over medium-high heat. Add chicken and sauté 4 to 6 minutes, until cooked through, turning once.

3. Place each cutlet on a slice of bread. Spoon vegetable mixture over cutlets and top with remaining bread. Makes 4 servings.

Per serving: 360 calories, 12.5 g total fat, 3 g saturated fat, 55 mg cholesterol, 661 mg sodium, 35 g carbohydrates, 27 g protein, 92 mg calcium, 5 g fiber

pesto

Here's a homemade pesto that's not only easy to make, it's a nice alternative to the usual tomato sauce. Toss with cooked chicken or pasta for a fresh summertime dish. Tip: A little pesto goes a long way. For 1 serving (4 oz. uncooked) pasta, toss 2 tablespoons pesto and 1 teaspoon pasta water with cooked, drained pasta. Drizzle with 1 teaspoon olive oil, if desired.

Total prep time: 15 minutes

2 cups fresh basil leaves, rinsed and patted dry
⅓ cup walnuts, toasted and cooled
¼ cup freshly grated Parmesan cheese
1 garlic clove, sliced
¼ teaspoon salt
¼ teaspoon freshly ground pepper
⅓ cup olive oil

Combine basil, walnuts, Parmesan, garlic, salt and pepper in a food processor. Process 30 seconds. With machine running, pour oil through feed tube and process 15 seconds, until smooth. Transfer to bowl; cover and refrigerate until ready to use. *(Can be made ahead. Cover and refrigerate up to 4 days or place in an airtight container and freeze up to 1 month.)* Makes 1 cup.

Per tablespoon: 65 calories, 6.5 g total fat, 1 g saturated fat, 2 mg cholesterol, 55 mg sodium, 1 g carbohydrates, 1 g protein, 27 mg calcium, 0 g fiber

test kitchen tip

carbs are ok

Pasta lovers needn't despair. Despite the emphasis on high-protein, low-carbohydrate diets, there are plenty of good reasons to enjoy a plate of penne. Carbohydrates, in pastas as well as other foods, are a great source of energy. For an added benefit, buy whole wheat pastas which deliver fiber too. But pasta in itself is not a complete meal. Just as you wouldn't eat 3 or 4 slices of bread and call it dinner, you need to add other foods to the pasta on your plate to balance the nutrients. Add a source of protein such as tuna, ground meat, beans or tofu. Serving size counts too: A 16-ounce package of pasta serves 6 to 8 people, not 4.

chipotle chiles

You've seen the name "chipotle" on restaurant menus, in recipes and at your local market. Here's the dish.

WHAT ARE THEY? Chipotles are dried, smoked jalapeño chiles (also known as chile ahumado or chile meco). Their flavor is smoky, yet sweet. Heat level: relatively mild.

WHAT FOODS ARE CHIPOTLES BEST FOR? Soups, salsas and stews.

WHAT FORMS ARE AVAILABLE? Chipotles are available whole, in packages or canned in adobo sauce.

tacos with grilled green onions *EASY*

These spicy tacos get their delicious smoky-savory flavor from charred green onions. For a lighter version of this dish, substitute ground raw turkey or chicken for the ground beef. Serve with Mexican beer and cold margaritas for a real fiesta.

Total prep and cooking time: 1 hour 15 minutes

- 2 bunches (8 oz. total) green onions
- 3 tablespoons vegetable oil, divided
  Salt
- 1 tablespoon chopped garlic
- 1 pound ground beef
- 1 jar (16 oz.) mild salsa, divided
- 2 teaspoons minced chipotle in adobo sauce, divided, plus 1 teaspoon adobo sauce*
- ¼ teaspoon cumin seed, crushed
- 1 cup canned black beans, drained and rinsed
- 1 package (8 oz.) corn tortillas

GARNISHES:
- 2 cups shredded iceberg lettuce
- 1½ cups quartered cherry tomatoes
- 1 avocado (12 oz.) pitted, peeled and diced
  Sour cream
  Lime wedges

1. Heat oven to 200°F. Oil a grill pan or cast-iron skillet; heat over medium-high heat.

2. Toss green onions with 1 teaspoon of the oil and a generous pinch of salt. Grill onions in prepared pan 3 minutes, turning as they char. Transfer to a cutting board and chop.

3. Heat 1 teaspoon of the oil in a large nonstick skillet over medium-high heat. Add garlic and cook 20 seconds, until fragrant. Add beef and cook 3 to 4 minutes, until no longer pink, breaking up with the side of a wooden spoon. Transfer beef to a bowl. Wipe out skillet. Add 2 teaspoons of the oil to skillet and heat over high heat just until starting to smoke. Carefully pour in ¾ cup of the salsa, 1 teaspoon of the minced chipotle, the adobo sauce, ½ teaspoon salt and cumin seed (mixture should sizzle); boil 40 seconds. Add beans and return beef to skillet; heat through. Combine salsa and remaining 1 teaspoon minced chipotle in a bowl; set aside.

4. Brush both sides of tortillas with remaining 2 teaspoons plus 1 tablespoon oil. Grill, one or two at a time, in grill pan just until lightly browned and softened. Holding tortilla in a paper-towel-lined hand, fill center of each tortilla with ⅓ cup of the beef mixture; add ½ teaspoon of the green onions and fold over. Transfer folded tortilla to ovenproof platter or jelly-roll pan and place in oven until all tortillas are filled.

5. Serve tortillas with bowls filled with each garnish. Serve with reserved salsa mixture. Makes about 12 tacos.

*Note: Can be found in ethnic sections of supermarkets or in Spanish or Latino specialty stores.

Per taco: 195 calories, 11 g total fat, 3 g saturated fat, 24 mg cholesterol, 346 mg sodium, 15 g carbohydrates, 11 g protein, 53 mg calcium, 3 g fiber

sichuan pork and asparagus

Roasting Sichuan peppercorns, a mildly hot spice from China, with salt brings out their flavor. Pictured on page 83.

Prep time: 15 minutes • Cooking time: 15 minutes

PEPPER-SALT:
- ¼   cup kosher salt
- 2   tablespoons Sichuan peppercorns

SAUCE:
- ½   cup chicken broth
- 4   teaspoons soy sauce
- 1   tablespoon cream sherry
- 1½   teaspoons sugar
- 1½   teaspoons rice wine vinegar
- ¼   teaspoon salt
- 1   teaspoon cornstarch

   •

- 2   tablespoons peanut or vegetable oil, divided
- 1   bunch (1 to 1¼ lbs.) asparagus, trimmed and cut diagonally into 1½-inch pieces
- 1   tablespoon sesame seeds
- 1   pound pork tenderloin or firm tofu,* cut into 1½×¼-inch strips
- 2   teaspoons minced fresh ginger
- ½   pound shiitake mushrooms, stems discarded and caps sliced
- 1   tablespoon chicken broth
- ¼   cup sliced green onions

1. *Make pepper-salt:* Toast kosher salt and Sichuan peppercorns in a large, dry skillet over medium heat 4 to 5 minutes, until fragrant and slightly darkened. Transfer to a mini food processor or electric spice or coffee grinder; process until fine. Makes ¼ cup.

2. *Make sauce:* Combine all ingredients *except* cornstarch in a 1-cup measure; with a fork, whisk in cornstarch.

3. Heat 1½ teaspoons of the oil in a 12-inch nonstick skillet over high heat. Add asparagus and sesame seeds and stir-fry 3 to 4 minutes, just until tender. Transfer to a bowl. Set aside.

4. Heat 1½ teaspoons of the oil in same skillet. Add half of the pork, 1 teaspoon of the ginger and ¼ teaspoon of the pepper-salt; stir-fry 2 minutes.

Transfer to another bowl. Repeat with 1½ teaspoons of the oil, remaining pork, ginger and ¼ teaspoon of the pepper-salt.

5. Heat remaining 1½ teaspoons oil in skillet. Add mushrooms and broth; stir-fry 2 minutes, until mushrooms are tender. Whisk sauce again until well combined and pour into skillet; bring to boil. Boil 30 seconds; stir in pork and heat 10 to 20 seconds more (no longer, pork will overcook). Transfer pork mixture to a large platter; top with asparagus and sprinkle with green onions and ½ teaspoon of the pepper-salt (reserve remaining pepper-salt for another use). Makes 4 servings.

To use tofu: Prepare recipe as directed *except* stir-fry ginger with asparagus and sesame seeds. Add the sauce and ½ teaspoon of the pepper-salt to the mushrooms, then add the tofu and stir-fry 1 to 2 minutes, until heated through.

Per serving with pork: 285 calories, 14.5 g total fat, 3.5 g saturated fat, 75 mg cholesterol, 1,017 mg sodium, 11 g carbohydrates, 29 g protein, 58 mg calcium, 2 g fiber
Per serving with tofu: 295 calories, 18 g total fat, 3 g saturated fat, 0 mg cholesterol, 1,161 mg sodium, 16 g carbohydrates, 23 g protein, 287 mg calcium, 2 g fiber

---

test kitchen tip

positively pork

Whether you sauté, braise, grill, broil or roast your pork, here are a few tips to get the ultimate result on your dinner plate.

STORE IT SAFE AND SOUND: Before cooking, store pork, in the package in which it was purchased, in the refrigerator for up to 5 days (ground pork up to 2 days). Pork chops can be frozen up to 6 months, ground pork up to 4 months and roasts up to 12 months.

COOK IT RIGHT: Fresh pork is now leaner than ever. That's why it's important to resist the tendency to overcook pork loin and tenderloin. Cook the cuts to an internal temperature of 155°F. (Upon standing, the temperature of the meat will increase to 160°F.) The juices should run clear when the meat is pierced with a fork.

eat more fish

Fish is the best source of omega-3 fatty acids, heart-healthy fats in short supply in the American diet. Due to breeding practices, our meats, poultry and eggs no longer contain these fats. The best dietary source today is fish, though flaxseeds and canola oil also contain some omega-3s. Without them, risk of heart disease creeps up; so do mood disorders, decreased immune response, weight gain and risk of diabetes. The American Heart Association's dietary guidelines recommend eating fish twice a week.

salmon and baby broccoli with miso dressing

Three of the reasons to make this recipe are a one-step blender dressing, a foolproof cooking method for salmon and a pretty presentation. Great flavor and great for you, fish contains the good fat—omega-3 fatty acids— which helps reduce the incidence of strokes and heart disease. Pictured on page 85.

Prep time: 15 minutes • Cooking time: 19 minutes

- **1 teaspoon olive oil**
- **4 (4 to 5 oz. each) center-cut salmon fillets**
- **½ teaspoon salt**
- **¼ teaspoon freshly ground pepper**
- **⅓ cup sliced almonds**

DRESSING:
- **¼ cup chicken broth**
- **3 tablespoons miso***
- **1 tablespoon sugar**
- **1 tablespoon sake or vermouth**
- **2 teaspoons mayonnaise**
- **¼ teaspoon grated fresh ginger**
  - •
- **1½ pounds baby broccoli or broccoli, trimmed and cut into 3-inch spears**
- **½ pound mesclun salad greens**

1. Heat oven to 300°F. Lightly brush a jelly-roll pan with oil. Sprinkle both sides of salmon with salt and pepper; arrange, skin side up, on one half of prepared pan. Bake 5 minutes. Spread the almonds on the other half of the pan and bake 14 minutes more, until fish flakes with a fork but is still slightly rosy toward center.

2. *Make dressing:* Meanwhile, puree all ingredients in blender until smooth. Makes ½ cup.

3. Place a large steamer basket in a large saucepan or stockpot. Arrange baby broccoli in basket. Add enough water to reach just under the basket. Cover and bring to boil; steam 5 minutes, just until stems are tender.

4. Toss mesclun in a large bowl with 3 tablespoons of the dressing. Evenly arrange mesclun, baby broccoli and salmon on 4 serving plates and sprinkle with almonds. Pass remaining dressing. Makes 4 servings.

*Note: Can be found in the ethnic sections of supermarkets or in Asian specialty stores.

Per serving: 395 calories, 22.5 g total fat, 3.5 g saturated fat, 68 mg cholesterol, 949 mg sodium, 19 g carbohydrates, 31 g protein, 160 mg calcium, 6 g fiber

shrimp with asparagus and barley

Pearl barley, a great source of soluble and insoluble fiber, helps lower the absorption of cholesterol and fat into the body. Pictured on page 84.

Prep time: 15 minutes • Cooking time: 30 to 35 minutes

- **2 tablespoons vegetable oil, divided**
- **½ cup sliced shallots**
- **3 coin-size slices fresh ginger**
- **1 tablespoon chopped garlic**
- **1 cup pearl barley**
- **3 cups water**
- **¾ teaspoon salt, divided**
- **1 pound asparagus, ends trimmed and cut into 1½-inch pieces**
- **½ teaspoon curry powder**
- **¼ teaspoon freshly ground pepper**

1 pound large shrimp, shelled and deveined
½ cup cooked, shelled edamame beans (fresh
   soy beans, from about 8 oz. pods)
½ teaspoon grated lime peel

1. Heat 1 tablespoon of the oil in a large skillet over medium heat. Add shallots, ginger and garlic and cook 3 to 5 minutes, until vegetables soften. Stir in barley, tossing to coat grains. Add water and ½ teaspoon of the salt; bring to boil. Cover and simmer 30 to 35 minutes, until barley is tender. Remove from heat and let stand, covered, 5 minutes.

2. Meanwhile, heat oven to 425°F. Arrange asparagus on cookie sheet and toss with 2 teaspoons of the oil. Roast asparagus 10 to 11 minutes, until tender and lightly golden. Set aside.

3. Heat a 12-inch nonstick skillet over high heat 2 minutes. Combine curry, remaining ¼ teaspoon salt and pepper in a cup. Toss shrimp with remaining 1 teaspoon oil and curry mixture. Add shrimp to hot skillet and cook 1 minute per side, until golden brown.

4. Remove ginger from barley. Transfer barley to large serving bowl and stir in asparagus, shrimp, edamame and lime peel. Makes 4 servings.

Per serving: 405 calories, 10.5 g total fat, 1.5 g saturated fat, 140 mg cholesterol, 585 mg sodium, 50 g carbohydrates, 30 g protein, 129 mg calcium, 10 g fiber

shrimp couscous salad with carrot-ginger vinaigrette

This unusual seafood salad, prepared with fresh carrot juice, is the "something different" you've been looking for.

Prep time: 20 minutes plus cooling
Cooking time: 10 minutes

COUSCOUS:
2¼ cups fresh carrot juice
½ stick cinnamon
½ teaspoon salt
1 box (10 oz.) couscous (1⅓ cups)
½ cup frozen peas, thawed
½ cup finely diced jicama
3 green onions, thinly sliced

CARROT-GINGER VINAIGRETTE:
½ cup fresh carrot juice
3 tablespoons olive oil
1 teaspoon grated fresh ginger
½ teaspoon salt
⅛ teaspoon freshly ground pepper
   •
8 cups assorted baby lettuces
1 pound shrimp, cooked, peeled and deveined
   Lemon wedges

1. *Make couscous:* Bring carrot juice, cinnamon stick and salt to boil in a medium saucepan. Stir in couscous. Remove from heat; cover and let stand 5 minutes. Fluff couscous with a fork. Transfer to a large bowl and cool to room temperature. Stir in peas, jicama and green onions.

2. *Make carrot-ginger vinaigrette:* Bring carrot juice to boil in a small saucepan and boil until reduced to ¼ cup, about 2 minutes. Transfer juice to a medium bowl and cool to room temperature. Whisk in oil, ginger, salt and pepper.

3. Toss lettuces with 2 tablespoons of the vinaigrette in a large bowl. Arrange lettuce mixture on a large serving platter or 6 dinner plates. Toss shrimp in a small bowl with another 2 tablespoons of the vinaigrette. Add remaining vinaigrette to couscous and toss with a fork to combine.

4. Spoon couscous over greens and top with shrimp. Serve with lemon wedges. Makes 6 servings.

Per serving: 370 calories, 8.5 g total fat, 1 g saturated fat, 86 mg cholesterol, 528 mg sodium, 53 g carbohydrates, 20 g protein, 91 mg calcium, 5 g fiber

seafood and potato salad with watercress dressing

With lobster, shrimp, artichoke hearts and red potatoes, this is not your ordinary potato salad.

Prep time: 20 minutes • Cooking time: 27 to 30 minutes

- 2¼ **pounds small red potatoes, scrubbed**
- 2 **lemons, halved, divided**
- 4 **large artichokes**

WATERCRESS DRESSING:

- 1 **large bunch (6 oz.) watercress, trimmed**
- 6 **tablespoons extra-virgin olive oil**
- 5 **tablespoons fresh lemon juice**
- 2 **tablespoons chopped fresh mint**
- ¾ **teaspoon salt**
- ¼ **teaspoon coarsely ground pepper**
- 1 **teaspoon finely chopped garlic**
  - •
- 1 **pound cooked lobster meat**
- ½ **pound large shelled and deveined cooked shrimp**
- 1 **cup radishes (8 oz.), cut into thin strips**

1. Bring potatoes and enough water to cover to boil in a large saucepan. Boil 14 to 16 minutes, just until tender (skins should stay intact). Drain; cool and cut into ¼-inch slices. Cover and set aside.

2. Fill medium saucepan two thirds with cold water; squeeze juice from 2 of the lemon halves into saucepan. Trim artichoke stems to 1 inch and peel. Bend back tough outer petals of artichoke until they snap off near the base and a layer of tender yellow petals is exposed. Discard outer petals. Cut off top quarter of each artichoke and discard. With small, sharp knife, peel outer dark green layer from base. Halve artichokes. Scrape out fuzzy centers (chokes) using a tablespoon and discard. Rub all sides of artichoke halves with remaining 2 lemon halves. Drop artichokes into saucepan with lemon-water. Bring water to boil; boil artichokes 13 to 14 minutes, until knife pierces each base easily. Drain; cool and slice.

3. *Make watercress dressing:* Chop enough of the watercress to equal ½ cup; set remaining aside. Combine chopped watercress and remaining ingredients *except* garlic in blender; puree until smooth. Stir in garlic. Makes ¾ cup.

4. Arrange remaining watercress on 6 serving plates; top with overlapping potatoes. Arrange lobster, shrimp and artichoke hearts on opposite sides of plates. Drizzle each serving with 1 tablespoon of the dressing. Sprinkle radishes in centers. Pass remaining dressing. Makes 6 servings.

Per serving with 1 tablespoon dressing: 430 calories, 15.5 g total fat, 2 g saturated fat, 154 mg cholesterol, 712 mg sodium, 40 g carbohydrates, 34 g protein, 164 mg calcium, 9 g fiber

spring lasagne

This version of lasagne uses a combination of vegetables and oven-ready lasagne noodles. For quick assembly, the vegetables can be prepared a day ahead. Pictured on page 84.

Prep time: 30 minutes • Baking time: 50 minutes

- **Olive oil**
- 1 **bunch (8 oz.) escarole, chopped**
- 1 **tablespoon chopped garlic**
- 1 **container (15 oz.) part-skim ricotta**
- 2 **small yellow summer squash, halved crosswise and sliced lengthwise, ¼ inch thick**
- 1 **bunch (1½ lbs.) Swiss chard, trimmed and chopped**
- 2 **cups chopped onions**
- ¼ **teaspoon salt**
- ¼ **teaspoon fennel seeds**
- 2 **cups prepared marinara sauce**
- ½ **cup sliced fresh basil leaves**
- 12 **oven-ready lasagne noodles**
- 1 **cup shredded Fontina cheese**

1. Heat 1 teaspoon oil in large nonstick skillet over medium-high heat. Add escarole and cook 5 minutes, until tender. Add garlic and cook 1 minute more. Drain off liquid. Cool escarole. Transfer to medium bowl; stir in ricotta. Set aside.

2. Heat same skillet over medium heat. Toss squash slices with 1 teaspoon oil. Cook squash 1½ to 2 minutes per side, just until tender and light golden. Transfer to large plate.

3. Heat 1 teaspoon oil in skillet over medium-high heat. Add Swiss chard and cook 3 to 5 minutes, until wilted. Stir in onions and salt; cook 5 minutes, until onions soften. Transfer vegetables to a large plate and cool. *(Can be made ahead. Cover the ricotta mixture, squash and chard with plastic wrap and refrigerate overnight. To use, bring vegetables and ricotta to room temperature.)*

4. Heat 1 teaspoon oil in small saucepan over medium heat; add fennel seeds and cook 1 minute. Stir in marinara sauce and basil and cook 5 minutes, until heated through.

5. Meanwhile, heat oven to 375°F. Spoon half of the marinara sauce mixture on bottom of a 13×9-inch baking dish. Arrange 3 of the noodles on top of sauce. Spread one-third of the ricotta mixture over noodles, then layer with all of the squash. Layer 3 more of the noodles over squash, then another one-third of the ricotta mixture. Sprinkle half of the Swiss chard mixture over ricotta and top with 3 more of the lasagne noodles. Spread remaining ricotta, then remaining Swiss chard mixture over noodles. Arrange remaining 3 lasagne noodles over chard. Spoon remaining marinara sauce mixture over noodles. Sprinkle Fontina cheese over sauce. Cover dish loosely with foil. Bake 50 minutes, until sauce is bubbly and noodles are tender. Let stand 15 minutes before cutting and serving. Makes 8 servings.

Per serving: 330 calories, 13.5 g total fat, 6 g saturated fat, 33 mg cholesterol, 748 mg sodium, 39 g carbohydrates, 17 g protein, 314 mg calcium, 5 g fiber

eggplant and mushroom sloppy joes EASY

A new take on a beefy sandwich, this vegetarian Sloppy Joe is best eaten with a knife and fork.

Prep time: 20 minutes • Baking time: 18 to 22 minutes

- 3 **tablespoons olive oil, divided**
- 1 **tablespoon chopped garlic**
- 1 **large (1½ lbs.) eggplant, peeled and diced**
- 3 **tablespoons water**
- 1 **teaspoon salt, divided**
- 1 **cup prepared marinara sauce**
- 4 **medium (4 to 5 oz. each) portobello mushroom caps**
- 2 **5-inch squares plain or herbed focaccia, split**
- ½ **cup 4-cheese blend shredded cheese**
- 4 **very thin slices onion**

1. Arrange oven rack in top third of oven. Heat oven to 450°F.

2. Heat 2 tablespoons of the oil in a 12-inch nonstick skillet over medium heat. Add garlic and cook 30 to 40 seconds, just until it begins to color. Add the eggplant and water; sprinkle with ½ teaspoon of the salt. Cover and cook 7 minutes, until eggplant softens. Stir in marinara sauce and cook 7 minutes more, until eggplant is very tender.

3. Meanwhile, brush mushroom tops with remaining 1 tablespoon oil; sprinkle with remaining ½ teaspoon salt. Arrange mushrooms on the bottom of a broiler pan without the rack; roast on top rack of oven 15 to 18 minutes, until tender. Remove from oven.

4. Reduce oven temperature to 350°F. Arrange focaccia, cut sides up, on cookie sheet; bake on top rack 3 to 4 minutes, until toasted. Arrange 1 piece on each of 4 serving plates; top each with a mushroom.

5. Divide and spoon eggplant mixture over the mushrooms. Top each evenly with the cheese, then with the onion. Makes 4 servings.

Per serving: 425 calories, 20.5 g total fat, 5 g saturated fat, 19 mg cholesterol, 1,227 mg sodium, 51 g carbohydrates, 16 g protein, 236 mg calcium, 6 g fiber

white pizza with broccoli

Talk about pizza deluxe! With nonfat dry milk in the pizza crust and a cheesy topping, each serving of this pizza has about as much calcium as a 6-ounce glass of nonfat milk! This recipe makes enough dough for two pies, so freeze half for another meal. Pictured on page 81.

Prep time: 40 minutes plus standing
Baking time: 15 minutes

DOUGH:

- 1 package active dry yeast
- ¼ cup warm water (105°F. to 115°F.)
- ¾ cup water
- 2 tablespoons olive oil
- 2 tablespoons honey
- 3 cups all-purpose flour
- ⅓ cup nonfat dry milk
- 1 teaspoon salt

TOPPING:

- 1 tablespoon olive oil
- 1 large bunch (1 lb.) broccoli, trimmed and cut into 1-inch florettes
- ½ cup chicken broth
- 1 tablespoon chopped garlic
- 1 tablespoon cornmeal
- ½ cup part-skim ricotta cheese
- 2 tablespoons nonfat dry milk
- 1 cup shredded low-fat yogurt cheese or part-skim mozzarella cheese
- 2 tablespoons chopped sun-dried tomatoes in oil, patted dry

1. *Make dough:* Sprinkle yeast over warm water in a cup; let stand 5 minutes, until yeast is bubbly. Add the ¾ cup water, oil and honey.

2. Meanwhile, pulse together flour, dry milk and salt in food processor. With motor running, pour yeast mixture through feed tube; process until mixture forms a ball. Pulse dough 1 minute (or on a lightly floured surface, knead dough until smooth and elastic, 5 minutes). Place dough in a greased bowl, turning to grease top. Cover and let rise in a warm, draft-free place until doubled in bulk, about 1 hour.

3. Punch down dough and divide in half. *(Wrap one piece of dough in plastic wrap. Refrigerate overnight or freeze up to 1 month for another pizza.)*

4. Arrange oven rack on bottom shelf. Heat oven to 450°F.

5. *Make topping:* Heat oil in a large skillet over medium heat. Add broccoli; cook, stirring, 2 minutes. Stir in broth and garlic. Cover skillet; reduce heat to medium-low and cook 5 minutes, until broccoli is tender. Uncover and cool.

6. Sprinkle large cookie sheet with cornmeal. On a lightly floured surface, roll dough into a 12-inch circle. Transfer to prepared sheet. Combine ricotta, and dry milk in a small bowl. Spread ricotta mixture evenly on top of dough, then sprinkle evenly with cheese. Arrange broccoli mixture and sun-dried tomatoes on top. Bake pizza 15 minutes, until crust is golden brown. Makes 8 servings.

Per serving: 340 calories, 8.5 g total fat, 1.5 g saturated fat, 7 mg cholesterol, 432 mg sodium, 52 g carbohydrates, 13 g protein, 187 mg calcium, 3 g fiber

linguine with mint pesto and peas

Fresh mint and pistachios replace basil and pine nuts for a new twist on pesto.

Prep time: 10 minutes • Cooking time: 9 to 11 minutes

MINT PESTO:

- ¼ cup extra-virgin olive oil
- ¼ cup water
- 2 bunches (4 oz. total) fresh mint, trimmed (2 cups leaves)
- ½ cup freshly grated Parmesan cheese
- 3 tablespoons chopped pistachio nuts
- 1 teaspoon salt
- ¼ teaspoon freshly ground pepper
- •
- 1 pound linguine, cooked according to package directions, reserving ¼ cup pasta water
- 1 package (10 oz.) frozen peas, thawed

1. *Make mint pesto:* Puree all ingredients in blender until smooth.

2. Toss mint pesto, hot pasta, reserved hot pasta water and peas in a large serving bowl. Makes 6 servings.

Per serving: 465 calories, 15 g total fat, 3.5 g saturated fat, 6 mg cholesterol, 604 mg sodium, 66 g carbohydrates, 17 mg protein, 180 mg calcium, 4 g fiber

vegetable-bean quesadillas LOW FAT EASY

Shiitake mushrooms, beans and cheese grilled together in flour tortillas make up these vegetarian Southwest treats. Pictured on page 88.

Prep time: 20 minutes plus standing
Cooking time: 54 to 56 minutes

    1 cup dried cannellini, Great Northern or anasazi
       beans, or 2 cans (15 to 16 oz. each)
       cannellini beans, drained and rinsed
       Water

CORN SALSA:

    1 teaspoon olive oil
    1 cup fresh or frozen whole-kernel corn
    1 can (10 oz.) diced tomatoes and green chiles
    ¼ cup chopped fresh cilantro
    2 tablespoons orange juice
       •
    1 teaspoon olive oil
    ½ pound shiitake mushrooms, stems discarded
       and caps sliced
    ¼ teaspoon ground cumin
    ½ cup chopped onion
    ½ teaspoon salt
    ½ cup shredded Monterey Jack cheese
    8 (6- to 7-inch) flavored flour tortillas (such as
       spinach, whole wheat or red chile)

1. Cover dried beans with 2 inches of cold water. Refrigerate overnight. (*To quick soak:* Combine beans with water to cover by 2 inches in a 3-quart saucepan. Bring to boil; boil 2 minutes. Remove from heat. Cover and let stand 1 hour.) Drain beans in colander. Return beans to saucepan and add cold water to cover by 2 inches; bring to boil. Reduce heat and simmer 50 minutes, until beans are tender.

2. *Make corn salsa:* Meanwhile, heat a large nonstick skillet over high heat 2 minutes. Add oil and corn. Cook 3 minutes, until edges of corn brown. Stir in tomatoes and green chiles; cook 5 minutes, until mixture thickens slightly. Transfer to a bowl; stir in cilantro and orange juice. Set aside.

3. Wipe out skillet with paper towel. Heat skillet over high heat 1 minute; add 1 teaspoon oil, mushrooms and cumin. Cook 2 to 4 minutes, until mushrooms soften. Add onion and salt and cook 5 minutes more, until onion is softened.

4. Add soaked beans and ⅓ cup water (or add canned beans and ¼ cup water) to skillet.

5. For each quesadilla, sprinkle 1 tablespoon of the cheese on a tortilla; spoon ¾ cup of the bean mixture over top. Sprinkle beans with another 1 tablespoon of the cheese; top with another tortilla.

6. Oil a large grill pan or cast-iron skillet; heat over medium heat 2 to 3 minutes. Grill quesadillas, in batches, 2 to 3 minutes per side, until dark grill marks are formed and cheese has melted. Serve with corn salsa. Makes 4 servings.

Per serving: 455 calories, 12.5 g total fat, 4.5 g saturated fat, 15 mg cholesterol, 1,016 mg sodium, 67 g carbohydrates, 21 g protein, 208 mg calcium, 24 g fiber

test kitchen tip

softening tortillas

To make a roll, simple foldover, enchilada or burrito, start with a warm tortilla that's soft and pliable. There are three options for softening:

IN THE OVEN: Heat to 350°F. Stack 4 to 6 tortillas; wrap in foil. Bake 8 to 10 minutes.

IN THE MICROWAVE: Stack 4 tortillas between 2 damp paper towels on a microwaveproof plate. Microwave on High for 45 seconds to 1 minute.

IN THE SKILLET: Heat a skillet over medium heat. Add a tortilla and heat 30 to 45 seconds, turning frequently.

roasted vegetable frittata 🅴🅰🆂🆈

An assortment of vegetables fits into this skillet-baked version of "scrambled eggs." Roasting the bell peppers, onion and zucchini intensifies their flavor and can be done a day ahead. Pictured on page 88.

Prep time: 35 minutes • Baking time: 50 minutes

- 1 **tablespoon plus 1½ teaspoons olive oil, divided**
- 2 **red bell peppers, cored and cut into quarters**
- 2 **yellow bell peppers, cored and cut into quarters**
- 4 **garlic cloves, unpeeled**
- 2 **zucchini (1 lb. total), cut into 3×½-inch slices**
- 1 **medium onion, cut into ½-inch-thick slices**
- ¼ **cup chopped fresh flat-leaf parsley**
- 1 **teaspoon salt, divided**
- 8 **large eggs**
- ¼ **teaspoon ground red pepper**
- ⅓ **cup freshly grated Parmesan cheese**

1. Arrange oven racks in lower and center third of oven. Heat oven to 425°F. Line the bottoms of a broiler pan and a jelly-roll pan with foil. Brush the foil in each pan with ½ teaspoon of the oil.

2. Arrange bell peppers and garlic on one prepared pan and zucchini and onion on the other. Brush vegetables with 1 tablespoon of the oil. Roast zucchini and onion on lower rack and bell peppers and garlic on center rack 15 minutes. Remove zucchini and onion. Transfer bell peppers to lower rack; roast 10 minutes more, until lightly charred. Let vegetables cool 5 minutes. Remove garlic from skins. Coarsely chop garlic and vegetables. Transfer to medium bowl. Stir in parsley and ½ teaspoon of the salt. Reduce oven temperature to 350°F.

3. Brush a 9-inch nonstick round cake pan with remaining ½ teaspoon oil. Whisk together eggs, remaining ½ teaspoon salt and ground red pepper in a large bowl. Stir in roasted vegetables and Parmesan cheese. Pour mixture into prepared cake pan.

4. Bake 50 minutes, until center is set and top is light golden. Cool in pan on wire rack 5 minutes. Invert frittata onto a large plate, then invert again, right side up, onto a large serving plate. Makes 6 servings.

Per serving: 230 calories, 16.5 g total fat, 4 g saturated fat, 288 mg cholesterol, 480 mg sodium, 10 g carbohydrates, 12 g protein, 135 mg calcium, 2 g fiber

ratatouille omelet 🅴🅰🆂🆈

A savory omelet like this one can be enjoyed any time of day—as part of a hearty breakfast, lunch or light supper. Make the filling ahead of time and refrigerate up to 3 days or freeze up to 1 month. When you're ready to cook, measure the amount of filling you need and whip up as many omelets as you please.

Prep time: 20 minutes • Cooking time: 55 minutes

RATATOUILLE FILLING:

- 1 **unpeeled eggplant (about 1 lb.), finely diced**
- 2½ **teaspoons salt, divided**
- 1 **tablespoon olive oil**
- 3 **cups finely diced onions**
- 4 **cups finely diced zucchini**
- 1 **can (14½ or 16 oz.) whole tomatoes in puree**
- 1 **cup finely diced red bell pepper**
- ¾ **cup diced green bell pepper**
- 4 **garlic cloves, minced**
- 2 **sprigs fresh thyme**
- ½ **teaspoon freshly ground pepper**
- ½ **cup chopped fresh basil**

OMELET:

- 2 **large eggs**
- ⅛ **teaspoon salt**
- 1½ **teaspoons butter or margarine**
- 2 **tablespoons shredded Gruyère cheese**

1. *Make ratatouille filling:* Place a large colander over a medium bowl. Combine eggplant and 2 teaspoons of the salt in a colander. Drain 20 minutes; pat dry with paper towels.

2. ∎ Heat oil in a Dutch oven over medium-high heat. Add onions and cook 5 minutes, until tender. Stir in eggplant, remaining ½ teaspoon salt, zucchini, tomatoes, bell peppers, garlic, thyme and freshly ground pepper. Reduce heat to medium-low and simmer, uncovered, 35 minutes, until vegetables are tender, breaking up tomatoes with the back of a spoon. Remove thyme sprigs and discard. Stir in basil. *(Can be made ahead. Cover and refrigerate up to 3 days or divide into serving portions, place in airtight containers and freeze up to 1 month.)* Makes 6 cups.

3. ∎ *Make omelet:* Whisk together eggs and salt in a medium bowl until frothy. Melt butter in a 10-inch nonstick skillet over medium-low heat, swirling to coat bottom and sides of skillet. Heat until bubbles begin to subside. Pour in egg mixture. Swirl the skillet to evenly coat the bottom with eggs. When eggs begin to set, about 2 minutes, sprinkle with cheese and spoon ½ cup of the ratatouille filling down the center of omelet. Continue to cook 2 minutes more, until the bottom begins to brown and eggs are almost set. Gently fold the omelet in half and slide onto a serving plate. Makes 1 serving.

4. ∎ *For each additional omelet:* Wipe skillet clean with paper towels and repeat process with another recipe of egg mixture, an additional 2 tablespoons cheese and another ½ cup of the ratatouille filling.

Per serving: 315 calories, 22 g total fat, 10 g saturated fat, 457 mg cholesterol, 871 mg sodium, 12 g carbohydrates, 19 g protein, 227 mg calcium, 3 g fiber

whole wheat linguine with spring vegetables

This veggie-packed dish is jammed with nutrition, but all your taste buds will notice are the refreshing flavors.

Prep time: 20 minutes • Cooking time: 8 to 10 minutes

- **1** tablespoon extra-virgin olive oil
- **2** large shallots, thinly sliced
- **1** teaspoon minced garlic
- **1** jalapeño chile, seeded and minced (see tip, page 92)
- **¾** cup thinly sliced celery
- **¾** cup thinly sliced carrot
- **1** cup small broccoli florettes
- **½** pound asparagus, thinly sliced on the diagonal
- **1** small zucchini, thinly sliced on the diagonal
- **2** cups sliced fresh shiitake mushrooms (stems removed and discarded) or white mushrooms (¼ lb.)
- **¼** pound snow peas, trimmed and halved diagonally
- **¾** cup chicken or vegetable broth
- **8** ounces whole wheat linguine, cooked according to package directions
- **½** teaspoon salt
- **¼** teaspoon freshly ground pepper
- **2** tablespoons chopped chives
  Additional extra-virgin olive oil (optional)

1. ∎ Heat 1 tablespoon oil in a large skillet over high heat. Add shallots, garlic and jalapeño and cook 1 minute, until softened. Add celery and carrot; cook 1 minute. Stir in broccoli, asparagus, zucchini, mushrooms, snow peas and chicken broth. Cover and cook 3 minutes more.

2. ∎ Add hot linguine, salt and pepper to skillet, tossing gently to combine with vegetables. Transfer to a large serving bowl and sprinkle with chives. Drizzle with additional oil, if desired. Serve immediately. Makes 4 servings.

Per serving without additional oil: 330 calories, 5 g total fat, 1 g saturated fat, 0 mg cholesterol, 477 mg sodium, 63 g carbohydrates, 14 g protein, 83 mg calcium, 10 g fiber

greek-style greens pie *EASY*

Here's a wonderful meatless entrée that's perfect for lunch or as a light supper.

Prep time: 50 minutes • Baking time: 50 to 60 minutes

GREENS FILLING:
- ½ cup water
- 1 pound fresh spinach, stems removed, coarsely chopped
- ½ pound escarole, coarsely chopped
- ½ pound chicory, coarsely chopped
- 2 tablespoons butter or margarine
- 1 cup chopped onions
- ¼ cup chopped fresh flat-leaf parsley
- 3 tablespoons chopped fresh dill
- ½ teaspoon freshly ground pepper
- ¼ teaspoon salt
- Pinch nutmeg
- 4 ounces goat cheese, crumbled

- 4 ounces feta cheese, crumbled
- 1 large egg, lightly beaten

- ⅓ cup butter or margarine, melted
- 16 sheets (about ½ lb.) phyllo dough

1. Make greens filling: Bring water to boil in a large Dutch oven. Add the spinach, escarole and chicory. Cover and cook, stirring occasionally, 5 minutes, until greens are wilted. Drain greens in a colander, pressing out excess liquid.

2. Melt butter in a large skillet over medium-high heat. Add onions and cook 3 minutes, until tender. Add cooked greens, parsley, dill, pepper, salt and nutmeg; cook 2 minutes more. Cool greens mixture, then add goat cheese, feta and egg; mix well.

3. Arrange oven rack in lower third of oven. Place a cookie sheet on rack. Heat oven to 425°F. Brush a 9-inch metal or glass pie plate with melted butter. Place 1 phyllo sheet in the pie plate, letting sides overhang. Brush lightly with butter to 1 inch beyond edge of plate. Layer and butter 7 more sheets of phyllo. Spoon in greens filling. Layer and butter remaining 8 phyllo sheets on top, then trim edges of phyllo with scissors to form a 1-inch overhang. Tuck overhang under and flute edge. Bake 25 to 30 minutes. Cover edges of pie with foil. Reduce oven temperature to 375°F. and bake 25 to 30 minutes more, until pie is golden and center is puffed. Makes 8 servings.

Per serving: 320 calories, 20.5 g total fat, 12 g saturated fat, 75 mg cholesterol, 657 mg sodium, 25 g carbohydrates, 11 g protein, 184 mg calcium, 7 g fiber

penne with pomodoro crudo *LOW FAT* *EASY*

You won't believe the flavors that come out when hot pasta is tossed with this simple blend of ripe tomatoes, olive oil and fresh herbs. It's a summer favorite in Italy, but you can enjoy it all year by using canned plum tomatoes.

Prep time: 20 minutes plus standing
Cooking time: 8 to 10 minutes

- 2 pounds fresh plum tomatoes, diced into ¼-inch pieces, or 2 cans (28 oz. each) whole plum tomatoes, drained and chopped

¼ cup extra-virgin olive oil
¼ cup thinly sliced fresh basil
¼ cup sliced green onions
¾ teaspoon salt
½ teaspoon freshly ground pepper
1 pound penne or ziti, cooked according to package directions
Freshly grated Parmesan cheese

1. Combine tomatoes, oil, basil, onions, salt and pepper in a serving bowl. Let stand 30 minutes.

2. Toss tomato mixture with hot pasta. Serve immediately with Parmesan. Makes 6 servings.

Per serving: 415 calories, 12 g total fat, 2.5 g saturated fat, 4 mg cholesterol, 401 mg sodium, 64 g carbohydrates, 13 g protein, 96 mg calcium, 4 g fiber

triple potato chowder LOW FAT EASY

This soup can be made with just one type of potato, but we used three—red, purple and yellow—to entice the eye as well as the palate.

Prep time: 35 minutes • Cooking time: 25 to 30 minutes

1 tablespoon butter or margarine
1½ cups diced leeks
1 cup diced celery
1 cup diced carrots
1 teaspoon minced garlic
1½ cups diced, unpeeled red potatoes (½ lb.)
1½ cups diced, unpeeled purple potatoes (½ lb.)
1½ cups diced, unpeeled yellow potatoes (½ lb.)
2 cans (14½ oz. each) fat-free chicken broth plus enough water to equal 5 cups
¼ teaspoon chopped fresh thyme or dash dried thyme
½ bay leaf
¼ teaspoon freshly ground pepper
1 tablespoon chopped fresh flat-leaf parsley

1. Melt butter in a large saucepan over medium heat. Add leeks, celery, carrots and garlic. Cook 5 minutes, until vegetables have softened. Add potatoes, chicken broth-water mixture, thyme, bay leaf and pepper.

2. Bring chowder to boil over medium-high heat. Reduce heat to medium-low and simmer, partially covered, 20 to 25 minutes, until potatoes are tender. Remove bay leaf. Puree 1 cup of the chowder in blender until almost smooth. Return to saucepan and stir in parsley. Makes about 6 cups.

Per cup: 140 calories, 2.5 g total fat, 1.5 g saturated fat, 5 mg cholesterol, 323 mg sodium, 24 g carbohydrates, 5 g protein, 39 mg calcium, 3 g fiber

test kitchen tip

you say potato. I say: which one?

Now when you say potato, you're not just talking the reliable russet anymore. Check out these tasty varieties in the market.

- **RUSSETS** are the popular standby. Brown skin, dry and fluffy flesh. Best for baking.

- **RED POTATOES** have a white, moist flesh. Great for boiling and roasting. (The same type also comes with white, freckled skin.)

- **BLUE POTATOES** sport blue flesh to match their skin, which can range from blue-purple to purple-black. Good for boiling.

- **YUKON GOLDS** boast a firm, golden or yellow flesh. Their moist texture makes them perfect for mashed potatoes.

- **FINGERLING** varieties, named for their shape and size, include Australian Crescents (light yellow inside with a light brown skin), Ruby Crescents (tawny skin, yellow flesh) and Rosevales (red and yellow flesh). Fingerlings are terrific roasted. Or try them thinly sliced and sautéed or boiled in salads.

winter vegetable stew

While this veggie-rich stew is terrific the day you make it, the flavors blend and come together so well over time that if you can resist, we suggest you let it sit overnight.

Prep time: 35 minutes • Cooking time: 50 to 55 minutes

3	tablespoons olive oil
1½	tablespoons curry powder
4	medium celery ribs, cut diagonally into 1-inch pieces (2½ cups)
6	medium carrots, peeled and cut into 1-inch pieces (2 cups)
2	cups chopped leeks (white part only)
4	all-purpose potatoes (1¼ lbs.), peeled and cut into 1-inch pieces
3	medium white turnips (10 oz.), peeled and cut into 1-inch pieces
1	medium butternut squash (1½ lbs.), peeled and cut into 1-inch pieces
1	teaspoon salt
½	teaspoon dried thyme
1	bay leaf
2	cans (14½ oz. each) fat-free chicken or vegetable broth
1	cup water
3	cups small cauliflower florettes
1½	cups frozen peas

1. Heat oil in a large Dutch oven over medium-high heat. Add curry powder and cook, stirring, 1 minute. Add celery, carrots and leeks. Cook, stirring frequently, 10 minutes, until vegetables begin to brown. Add potatoes and turnips; cook, stirring occasionally, 5 minutes. Add squash, salt, thyme and bay leaf and cook 5 minutes more.

2. Stir chicken broth and the water into vegetable mixture. Bring to boil. Reduce heat and simmer, uncovered, 10 minutes. Remove bay leaf. Add cauliflower and peas and simmer 15 to 20 minutes, until all the vegetables are tender. *(Can be made ahead. Cover and refrigerate up to 2 days or store in airtight containers and freeze up to 1 month.)* Makes 14 cups.

Per cup: 120 calories, 3.5 g total fat, 0.5 g saturated fat, 0 mg cholesterol, 241 mg sodium, 21 g carbohydrates, 4 g protein, 56 mg calcium, 4 g fiber

fresh corn, zucchini and tomato chowder

When autumn nights turn chilly, what could be more warming than this harvest vegetable soup?

Prep time: 15 minutes • Cooking time: 20 minutes

1	tablespoon butter or margarine
1	cup chopped onions
1	teaspoon minced garlic
3	cups fresh corn kernels, divided (4 to 6 ears)
1	can (14½ oz.) chicken broth
1	tomato, seeded and diced (1 cup)
1	cup diced zucchini
¼	cup heavy or whipping cream
2	tablespoons thinly sliced fresh basil
2	tablespoons minced fresh chives
½	teaspoon salt
¼	teaspoon freshly ground pepper

1. Melt butter in a large saucepan over medium heat. Add onions and garlic; cover and cook 3 minutes, until onions are softened. Stir in 2 cups of the corn and the chicken broth; bring to boil over medium-high heat. Reduce heat to medium-low and simmer, covered, 5 minutes.

2. Puree soup in a blender in small batches, returning each batch to saucepan. Add remaining 1 cup corn, tomato and zucchini. Cover and simmer 5 minutes. Remove from heat and stir in cream, basil and chives. Stir in salt and pepper. Spoon soup into warm bowls. Makes 4 servings.

Per serving: 240 calories, 11 g total fat, 6 g saturated fat, 29 mg cholesterol, 680 mg sodium, 33 g carbohydrates, 8 g protein, 38 mg calcium, 5 g fiber

spinach salad with apples and pecans *EASY*

In this special salad from Spago in Chicago, Illinois, tender baby spinach, endive, apples and toasted nuts are tossed with creamy blue cheese and a light vinaigrette dressing—a perfect dish to serve with roast chicken or a grilled tenderloin or rib-eye steak.

Total prep time: 20 minutes

DRESSING:

- 1 small shallot, minced
- 2 tablespoons sherry vinegar
- 1 tablespoon red wine vinegar
- 2 teaspoons Dijon mustard
- ⅓ cup olive oil
- ¼ teaspoon salt
  Pinch freshly ground pepper

- 1 pound fresh baby spinach, stems removed, or 2 bags (8 oz. each) fresh spinach
- 1 large (5 oz.) Belgian endive, cut into thin strips
- 1 large apple or pear, cored, quartered and sliced
- ½ cup (2 oz.) crumbled Stilton or blue cheese
- ½ cup toasted pecan halves

1. *Make dressing:* Whisk together shallot, vinegars and mustard in a small bowl. Gradually whisk in oil, salt and pepper until blended. Makes about ⅔ cup.

2. Toss spinach, endive and apple with dressing in a large bowl. Divide mixture among 6 salad plates. Sprinkle with cheese and pecans. Makes 6 servings.

Per serving: 255 calories, 21 g total fat, 4 g saturated fat, 7 mg cholesterol, 397 mg sodium, 16 g carbohydrates, 5 g protein, 104 mg calcium, 6 g fiber

---

test kitchen tip
blue cheese basics

Not sure what's what when it comes to the blues? Blue cheese is treated with molds that make blue or green veins throughout the cheese and give it its tangy flavor. The various cheeses' rich flavors range in intensity and their textures vary from creamy to crumbly. Here's how they differ:

MAYTAG BLUE: From Iowa. Made from cow's milk. Has a peppery taste and creamy texture. Flavor gets more piquant with age.

GORGONZOLA DOLCE: Italian. Made from cow's milk. Creamy, moderately mild and slightly sweet; aged only 3 months.

STILTON: English. Made from cow's milk. Has a mellow flavor similar to cheddar accented with blue-cheese pungency. Rich and creamy texture, yet slightly crumbly.

ROQUEFORT: French. Made from sheep's milk. Texture is moist and creamy-rich. Flavor is quite strong with spicy and salty nuances.

CABRALES: Spanish. Made from goat's, cow's or sheep's milk. Crumbly interior with intense purple veining; rich, strong flavor.

calories versus fat

Research from the University of Vermont (published in 1998) illustrates how concentrating on the fat in food, in lieu of counting its calories, won't help control weight. A group of dieters was told to restrict fat dramatically, but no limits were put on how many calories they could eat. Another group restricted calories but was not told to count fat grams. After 6 months, the calorie counters lost more than twice as much weight as the fat restricters! One reason: Many low-fat and nonfat foods have exactly the same number of calories as the regular ones. The fat counters were eating too many calories, even though they were eating hardly any fat.

asian coleslaw with basil

Some describe the taste of basil as a cross between licorice and cloves. Tossed with cabbage, carrots and grated ginger, it adds a sweet touch to this refreshingly different salad. A sprinkling of toasted almonds provides a lively crunch.

Total prep time: 30 minutes
Microwave used

- ½ cup thinly sliced shallots
- 4 teaspoons safflower or vegetable oil, divided
- ¼ cup fresh lime juice
- 2 tablespoons rice wine vinegar
- 1½ teaspoons brown sugar
- 1 teaspoon soy sauce
- 1 teaspoon finely chopped fresh ginger
- ¾ teaspoon salt
- ⅛ teaspoon freshly ground pepper
- 1 small head (1½ lbs.) Napa or green cabbage, thinly sliced
- 1 cup coarsely shredded carrots
- 1 cup fresh basil leaves, thinly sliced, or 1 cup fresh parsley leaves and 1 tablespoon dried basil, chopped
- ⅓ cup whole blanched almonds, toasted and coarsely chopped

1. Toss shallots with 1 teaspoon of the oil in a 9-inch glass pie plate. Microwave on High 3 minutes, until tender-crisp.

2. Combine remaining 3 teaspoons oil, lime juice, vinegar, sugar, soy sauce, ginger, salt and pepper in a large bowl. Add the cabbage, carrots, basil and shallots and toss well. Sprinkle with almonds. Makes 7 cups.

Per ½-cup serving: 50 calories, 3 g total fat, 0 g saturated fat, 0 mg cholesterol, 158 mg sodium, 5 g carbohydrates, 2 g protein, 61 mg calcium, 1 g fiber

creamy coleslaw

We used more red cabbage than typical coleslaw salads do, making this salad as pretty as it is flavorful. Slice the cabbage thinly for a delicate texture. Pictured on page 87.

Total prep time: 25 minutes plus chilling

- ½ cup sour cream
- ½ cup mayonnaise
- ½ cup finely chopped sweet onion (such as Vidalia)
- ½ cup finely chopped celery
- ⅓ cup distilled white vinegar
- 2 tablespoons sugar
- 1¼ teaspoons salt
- ¾ teaspoon caraway seed, crushed
- ¼ teaspoon freshly ground pepper
- 1 medium head green cabbage, thinly sliced (8 cups)
- 1 small head red cabbage, thinly sliced (6 cups)
- 1 cup coarsely shredded carrots

Whisk together sour cream, mayonnaise, onion, celery, vinegar, sugar, salt, caraway seed and pepper in a large bowl. Fold in cabbages and carrots until well coated. Cover and refrigerate at least 1 hour or overnight. Makes 12 cups.

Per 1-cup serving: 125 calories, 9.5 g total fat, 2.5 g saturated fat, 10 mg cholesterol, 320 mg sodium, 10 g carbohydrates, 2 g protein, 60 mg calcium, 2 g fiber

warm red potato and corn salad

No summer gathering is complete without the addition of potato salad. The potatoes are tossed with corn for crunch and cooked bacon for a light, smoky flavor. The crushed red pepper just needs seconds in the vinaigrette to release its heat. Tip: Toss the still-warm potatoes with the heated dressing to help them absorb the flavor. Pictured on page 82.

Prep time: 20 minutes · Cooking time: 20 minutes

- 3 **pounds small red potatoes**
  Water
  Salt
- 3 **large ears corn, kernels removed (2¼ cups)**
- 5 **slices wood-smoked or thick-slice bacon, diced (about ⅔ cup)**
- 1 **medium red onion, cut into ½-inch dice**
- ¼ **teaspoon red pepper flakes**
- ⅓ **cup apple cider vinegar**
- ⅓ **cup chicken broth**
- ½ **cup fresh parsley leaves, coarsely chopped**

1. Bring the potatoes, enough water to cover by 2 inches, and 2 tablespoons salt to boil in a large stockpot. Cook 9 minutes. Add corn kernels and cook 1 to 2 minutes more, until the tip of a sharp knife can pierce the potatoes easily, but skins remain intact. Drain vegetables in colander; rinse just 30 seconds with cool water to stop cooking. Cut potatoes in half; place in a large serving bowl.

2. Meanwhile, cook bacon in large nonstick skillet over medium-high heat until crisp. Transfer with a slotted spoon to a double layer of paper towels and drain. Add onion to drippings in skillet and cook 5 minutes, until tender. Add red pepper and cook 10 seconds, just until slightly darkened. Pour in cider vinegar; let bubble, then add broth and bring to boil. Cool 5 minutes. Stir in 1¼ teaspoons salt and the parsley, and pour over potatoes; toss to combine. Makes 10 cups.

Per 1-cup serving: 255 calories, 11.5 g total fat, 4 g saturated fat, 13 mg cholesterol, 706 mg sodium, 33 g carbohydrates, 6 g protein, 12 mg calcium, 4 g fiber

---

test kitchen tip

keeping nutrients in fresh vegetables

Vegetables are loaded with vitamins, minerals and fiber; however, the process of preparing and cooking them breaks down these nutrients. Fortunately, there are some steps you can take to get the most from the garden's bounty.

SELECT THE BEST: Purchase vegetables with a bright, healthy-looking appearance. Avoid veggies with insect or other damage.

AVOID EXPOSURE: Elements such as heat, air, light and water hasten the loss of nutrients. When possible, keep fresh vegetables whole until the time you use them in a recipe.

MINIMIZE CHOPPING: The more surface area exposed, the more nutrients likely to be lost. Use larger pieces when possible.

COOK IT RIGHT: Cooking vegetables actually helps release minerals and phytochemicals, making these easier for your body to absorb. However, when vegetables are overcooked, these nutrients are lost. To strike the right balance, cook fresh or frozen vegetables in a small amount of water just until tender-crisp. Exceptions to this rule are potatoes and other root vegetables that are cooked until they become tender.

soy sensational

Soy foods have a low carbohydrate count and provide a fine source of protein, calcium, iron, fiber and B-vitamins. Many experts contend that soy is beneficial for pre- and post menopausal women, and that soybean isoflavones (natural compounds) also help prevent breast cancer and other estrogen-related cancers, as well as osteoporosis.

One way to further your quest for a well-rounded diet is to take advantage of the wide variety of soy foods in the marketplace today. Here are just a few:

SOY MILK: Higher in protein than cow's milk and cholesterol-free. Available in containers and in powder form (to be mixed with water at home).

SOY YOGURT: Made from soy milk. Comes in a variety of flavors.

WHOLE SOYBEANS: Yellowish or black in color. The dried ones need to be soaked before cooking (as most beans do). Their texture is slightly crunchier than regular beans.

MEAT ALTERNATIVES: Available frozen, canned or dried; consist of tofu or soy protein and other ingredients.

SOY NUTS: Whole soybeans, which have been soaked in water then roasted; similar to peanuts in taste and texture.

TOFU: Also known as soybean curd, made from soy milk. Comes in firm, soft and silken varieties.

soyful scalloped potatoes *EASY*

Use tofu and golden potatoes for this innovative dish that's as tasty as the traditional version. Pictured on page 86.

Prep time: 30 minutes plus standing
Baking time: 55 to 60 minutes

- 1 **package (19 oz.) firm tofu**
- 4 **teaspoons butter, divided**
- 1 **medium (12 oz.) sweet onion, cut into very thin wedges**
- ½ **teaspoon dried thyme**
- 2 **pounds Yukon Gold potatoes, peeled and cut into ¼-inch slices**
- ½ **teaspoon salt**
- ¼ **teaspoon freshly ground pepper**
- ¼ **cup freshly grated Parmesan cheese, divided**
- 1⅓ **cups chicken broth**

1. Line a large cookie sheet with 4 layers of paper towels. Arrange tofu on top in a single layer; top with a single layer of paper towels, another large cookie sheet and 2 large cans. Let stand 20 minutes.

2. Meanwhile, heat oven to 400°F. Heat 3 teaspoons of the butter in a 12-inch nonstick skillet over medium heat. Add the onion and cook 12 minutes, stirring occasionally. Sprinkle with the thyme; increase heat to medium-high and cook 3 to 4 minutes, until golden in spots and tender.

3. Toss potatoes, salt and pepper in a large bowl. Arrange half of the potatoes in the bottom of a shallow 2-quart baking dish, overlapping slightly. Crumble half of the tofu over the potatoes, then half of the onion and half of the cheese. Repeat. Pour in the broth and dot with the remaining 1 teaspoon butter. Cover dish with foil; bake 40 minutes. Uncover and bake 15 to 20 minutes more, until potatoes are tender when pierced with a knife. Let stand 10 minutes. Makes 6 servings.

Per serving: 280 calories, 10.5 g total fat, 3.5 g saturated fat, 10 mg cholesterol, 546 mg sodium, 33 g carbohydrates, 17 g protein, 231 mg calcium, 3 g fiber

grilled summer squash

There's nothing like fresh summer vegetables on the grill, and tender summer squash is no exception. It's a great side dish with any barbecued meat or fish.

Prep time: 25 minutes plus standing
Cooking time: 6 to 8 minutes

2½ pounds summer squash
1 large plum tomato, diced
⅓ cup diced red onion
1 jalapeño chile, seeded and minced (see tip, page 92)
4 tablespoons extra-virgin olive oil, divided
½ teaspoon grated lemon peel
1 tablespoon fresh lemon juice
½ teaspoon salt, divided
½ teaspoon freshly ground pepper, divided
1 garlic clove, crushed through a press

1. Finely dice enough of the squash to equal 1 cup. Combine diced squash, tomato, red onion, jalapeño, 2 tablespoons of the oil, the lemon peel, lemon juice, ¼ teaspoon of the salt and ¼ teaspoon of the pepper in a small bowl. Stir and let stand 1 hour, stirring occasionally.

2. Heat grill. Cut remaining squash lengthwise into ½-inch-thick slices. Stir together remaining 2 tablespoons oil, ¼ teaspoon salt, ¼ teaspoon pepper and the garlic in a small cup until blended. Brush mixture on one side of squash slices. Grill over medium heat 3 or 4 minutes per side, until tender, turning once. Arrange squash slices on a serving platter and top with tomato mixture. Makes 6 servings.

Per serving: 125 calories, 9.5 g total fat, 1.5 g saturated fat, 0 mg cholesterol, 200 mg sodium, 10 g carbohydrates, 3 g protein, 43 mg calcium, 4 g fiber

green salad with mango

This sweet, unique 5-ingredient dressing is simple to prepare and the perfect partner for baby greens.

Prep time: 5 minutes • Cooking time: 10 to 12 minutes

1 cup tamarind nectar*
1 tablespoon rice wine vinegar
½ teaspoon minced shallot
½ teaspoon salt
2 tablespoons safflower or vegetable oil
¾ pound mesclun greens
1 large ripe mango, peeled and diced

1. Bring nectar to boil in a small saucepan; boil until reduced to ¼ cup, 10 to 12 minutes.

2. Transfer nectar to a blender; add vinegar, shallot and salt. With machine running, gradually add oil through feed tube until dressing is blended and smooth. (Can be made ahead. Transfer to an airtight container and refrigerate overnight.) Toss dressing with greens and mango. Makes 8 servings.

*Note: Goya and Jumex make tamarind nectar. It can be found in the ethnic section of supermarkets or in Spanish or Latin specialty stores.

Per serving: 80 calories, 3.5 g total fat, 0.5 g saturated fat, 0 mg cholesterol, 151 mg sodium, 12 g carbohydrates, 1 g protein, 37 mg calcium, 1 g fiber

test kitchen tip
cutting up a mango

Love mangos but aren't sure how to go about cutting one? Getting around the elongated clingstone is a snap with this trick. Hold the mango on a cutting board with the stem end facing away from you and slice off the outer third of the fruit lengthwise, getting as close to the pit as you can. With the tip of a knife, score the flesh of the cut section in a crisscross pattern without cutting through the skin. Turn the mango inside out, and cut off cubes. Repeat the same procedure on the other side.

get your 5-a-day

The facts are loud and clear. Fruits and vegetables are nutritional gold mines. Yet on average, only one quarter of Americans eat the 5 servings of produce they need each day. And half of us eat no fruits at all on some days. Supplements can't replace the vitamins, minerals, fiber and other nutrients in fruits and vegetables. Plus, there are confirmed health benefits beyond the known nutritional components. Phytochemicals and other beneficial plant compounds have the antioxidant ability to help maintain health, improve immunity and reduce the effects of aging. Relax, a serving is only about half a cup. Fresh, frozen or canned, try to sneak in a serving whenever you have something to eat.

fruit and avocado salad with coriander dressing

You will hardly miss summer fruit with this healthful salad of winter citrus and avocado.

Total prep and cooking time: 30 minutes

DRESSING:

- ¼ **cup water**
- ¼ **cup sugar**
- 1 **teaspoon coriander seeds**
- 1 **1-inch strip lime peel**
- 4 **teaspoons fresh lime juice**
- 2 **teaspoons red wine vinegar**
- 1 **tablespoon olive oil**
- ¼ **teaspoon salt**

  •

- ¼ **pound mesclun greens**
- 3 **ruby grapefruit, sectioned**
- 2 **large oranges, sectioned**
- 3 **kiwi, peeled and sliced**

- 1 **avocado, halved, pitted, peeled and cut into wedges**
- 12 **strawberries**

1. *Make dressing:* Bring water, sugar, coriander and lime peel to boil, stirring to dissolve the sugar; boil 1 minute. Remove from heat and cool. Strain mixture through a sieve into a bowl; discard seeds and peel. Whisk in remaining ingredients. Makes 6 tablespoons.

2. Toss greens in a large bowl with 2 tablespoons of the dressing.

3. Divide greens among 6 serving plates. Arrange the assorted fruit evenly on greens. Divide and drizzle remaining dressing over each serving. Makes 6 servings.

Per serving: 170 calories, 7.5 g total fat, 1 g saturated fat, 0 mg cholesterol, 104 mg sodium, 26 g carbohydrates, 2 g protein, 44 mg calcium, 5 g fiber

fennel mashed potatoes LOW FAT EASY

The anise flavor of the fennel mellows as it cooks and brings out the best in this favorite side dish. When choosing fennel, choose clean, crisp bulbs with no signs of browning. To store, tightly wrap in a plastic bag and place in the vegetable crisper of your refrigerator for up to 5 days.

Prep time: 15 minutes • Cooking time: 35 to 37 minutes

- 2 **tablespoons butter or margarine, divided**
- 1 **large fennel bulb (1½ lbs.), stems and fronds removed and cut into ½-inch pieces**
- ¼ **cup chopped onion**
- 1½ **teaspoons salt, divided**
- ¼ **teaspoon freshly ground pepper**
  Water
- 2 **pounds all-purpose large potatoes, peeled and quartered**
- ⅔ **cup warm milk**
- 2 **tablespoons chopped fresh flat-leaf parsley**

1. Heat 1 tablespoon of the butter in a large skillet over medium-high heat. Add the fennel, onion, ½ teaspoon of the salt and the pepper. Cook, stirring occasionally, 10 minutes, until fennel is golden. Stir in 2 tablespoons water. Reduce heat to low; cover and simmer 10 minutes more, until the fennel is very tender.

2. Meanwhile, bring potatoes, ½ teaspoon of the salt and enough water to cover to boil in a large saucepan over medium-high heat. Cover and cook 15 to 17 minutes, until tender. Drain potatoes in a large colander; return to the saucepan.

3. With a potato masher, mash potatoes with remaining 1 tablespoon butter, ½ teaspoon salt, the milk and parsley. Mash the potatoes until smooth. Stir in fennel mixture. Makes 3½ cups.

Per ½-cup serving: 160 calories, 4 g total fat, 2.5 g saturated fat, 11 mg cholesterol, 571 mg sodium, 27 g carbohydrates, 4 g protein, 58 mg calcium, 3 g fiber

dutch lettuce

Total prep time: 20 minutes

- 1 head (1¼ lbs.) green-leaf lettuce, washed and drained
- ¼ pound sliced bacon, cut into squares
- 3 tablespoons cider vinegar
- 1 tablespoon water
- ½ teaspoon sugar
- ⅛ teaspoon salt
  Pinch freshly ground pepper
- 2 hard-cooked eggs, chopped

1. Tear lettuce into bite-size pieces. Place in a large salad bowl.

2. Cook bacon in a medium skillet until crisp, reserving bacon drippings (about 2½ tablespoons). Add vinegar, water, sugar, salt and pepper to skillet and immediately pour bacon mixture over lettuce. *(Be sure bacon fat is hot so vinegar bubbles immediately.)* Toss well to combine. Top with the eggs. Makes 8 servings.

Per serving: 50 calories, 3 g total fat, 1 g saturated fat, 56 mg cholesterol, 107 mg sodium, 3 g carbohydrates, 3 g protein, 46 mg calcium, 1 g fiber

gobble grains

People who eat lots of fiber generally weigh less than those who don't. So, if you want to weigh less, eat at least 6 servings of high-fiber foods every day. If you make half of those foods made with whole grains, such as whole wheat, oats, barley and brown rice, you'll get a healthy dose of fiber. Fiber is crucial for digestive health, and it may help you feel satisfied with eating less fat! We need to eat 25 to 35 grams of fiber each day, and most Americans eat a mere 11 grams. Children need more fiber, too. For them, the recommendation is 5 grams plus 1 gram for each year. Therefore, an eight-year-old would need 13 grams of fiber daily. Other bonuses you get when you eat whole grains: Vitamin E, B6, magnesium, zinc, copper, manganese and potassium—all vital nutrients that are often in short supply.

barley waldorf salad LOW FAT EASY

A serving of this snappy salad provides a quarter of your daily fiber needs. The trick to using barley is toasting the grains in a skillet to bring out the nutty flavor. Then, just like the classic Waldorf salad, the grains are tossed with crunchy apples, celery and grapes. Pictured on page 81.

Prep time: 25 minutes plus cooling
Cooking time: 27 to 35 minutes

- ¾ cup barley
- 3¾ cups water
- 1¼ teaspoons salt, divided
- 2 tablespoons light mayonnaise dressing
- 3 tablespoons plain low-fat yogurt
- ¼ teaspoon grated lemon peel
- 1 tablespoon fresh lemon juice
- ¼ teaspoon sugar
- 1½ cups green and red seedless grapes, cut in half
- 1 Gala or Fuji apple, cored and diced
- ½ cup finely chopped celery
- ¼ cup walnuts pieces, lightly toasted
  Grapes, for garnish (optional)
  Lemon peel strips, for garnish (optional)

1. Heat large skillet over medium heat 2 minutes. Add barley and toast 4 to 5 minutes, until barley is golden brown, stirring or shaking pan occasionally. Combine barley, water and ½ teaspoon of the salt in a 3-quart saucepan; bring to boil. Reduce heat to medium-low, cover and simmer 27 to 35 minutes, until tender; drain. Let cool 30 minutes.

2. Whisk together the mayonnaise, yogurt, grated lemon peel, juice, remaining ¾ teaspoon salt and the sugar in a large bowl. Stir in the barley, 1½ cups grapes, apple and celery.

3. Sprinkle salad with walnuts. Garnish with additional grapes and lemon peel strips, if desired. Makes 6 servings.

Per serving: 210 calories, 6 g total fat, 1 g saturated fat, 2 mg cholesterol, 257 mg sodium, 35 g carbohydrates, 6 g protein, 50 mg calcium, 7 g fiber

---

m e n u

eat your veggies

EGGPLANT AND MUSHROOM SLOPPY JOES
page 105

BARLEY WALDORF SALAD
left

ICED TEA OR LEMONADE

CUCUMBER RELISH
PG. 157
WATERMELON
AND RADISH RELISH
PG. 158
MOROCCAN-
FLAVORED CARROTS
PG. 156

gathering for good times

BEST BURGERS
PG. 140

The air buzzes with excitement ... there's a party on the horizon! Casual get-together or formal event, good food is always at the center of a memorable gathering. Read on to discover drinks and dishes that will add life to the party. They're fun to make, too!

raise the bar
make a toast,

SPICY
SHRIMP FRITTERS
PG. 136
JAMAICAN PATTIES
PG. 134
CARIBBEAN CHICKEN
AND BEEF SKEWERS
PG. 146

WILD SALMON
FILLETS
PG. 152

GRILLED HERB
CHICKEN
PG. 146

dance the **salsa**, bake some homemade chips

when **company's**
coming your way,

VEGETABLE
CURRY
PG. 155

turn up the
flavor to full blast

JERK PORK
PG. 144

Gathering for Good Times **125**

warm the soul,
make memories,

SHRIMP SALSA
VERDE
PG. 154

GRILLED PIZZA
PG. 150

round up great
people and good food

GRILLED PORK
CHOPS
PG. 142

second helpings inspire a **standing ovation,** so be ready

PINK BEANS
AND RICE
PG. 155

the soprano (campartini)

This new drink gets its unique flavor from the popular Italian liqueur called Campari, a bittersweet, citrus-herb infused apéritif. We combined it with vodka and came up with a refreshing, fruity martini. Salúte!

Total prep time: 5 minutes plus standing and freezing

- ⅓   cup water
- ⅓   cup sugar
- 2   strips (2×½-inch) fresh orange peel
- 4   dime-size pieces fresh lime peel
- ¾   cup vodka
- 2   tablespoons Campari liqueur
- 6   ice cubes
- 4   thin strips fresh lime peel, for garnish (optional)

1. Combine the water, sugar, orange peel and dime-size pieces lime peel in a small saucepan. Bring to boil; boil and stir 2 to 3 minutes, until the sugar dissolves. Remove from heat; cool completely. Remove peels.

2. Chill 4 martini glasses in the freezer 5 minutes. Meanwhile, combine the vodka, Campari and cooled sugar mixture in a cocktail shaker or jar. Add ice cubes and shake vigorously. Immediately pour into chilled glasses. Give each thin strip of lime peel a twist and add one to each glass as a garnish, if desired. Makes 4 servings.

Per serving: 180 calories, 0 g total fat, 0 g saturated fat, 0 mg cholesterol, 1 mg sodium, 18 g carbohydrates, 0 g protein, 1 mg calcium, 0 g fiber

mojito

Our version of this classic has a twist—peach liqueur.

Total prep time: 10 minutes plus standing and chilling

- ¼   cup water
- ¼   cup sugar
- 12   fresh mint leaves
- ¾   cup white rum
- ¼   cup Pecher Mignon or any peach-flavored liqueur
- ¼   cup fresh lime juice
- 16   ice cubes, finely crushed
- 4   fresh mint sprigs
- 2   cups cold sparkling water or seltzer

1. Combine ¼ cup water, sugar and mint leaves in a small saucepan; bring to boil, stirring until sugar is dissolved. Let stand until cooled.

2. Strain syrup into an airtight plastic container; stir in rum, peach liqueur and lime juice. Freeze 30 minutes, until very cold. Meanwhile, refrigerate 4 tall, narrow glasses.

3. *To serve:* Fill the prepared glasses halfway with the crushed ice; add a mint sprig. Pour ½ cup of the sparkling water into each glass and divide the rum mixture among them. Makes 4 servings.

Per serving: 195 calories, 0 g total fat, 0 g saturated fat, 0 mg cholesterol, 28 mg sodium, 18 g carbohydrates, 0 g protein, 9 mg calcium, 0 g fiber

strawberry daiquiri

If you like your drinks extra chilly, use the berries directly from the freezer.

Total prep time: 20 minutes plus standing

- 2   bags (12 oz. each) frozen whole strawberries
- 1   cup white rum or tropical fruit-blend drink
- 4   tablespoons superfine sugar or 5 tablespoons granulated sugar
- 2   teaspoons fresh lemon juice
- 2   tablespoons framboise (raspberry-flavored liqueur) or grenadine syrup

Combine all ingredients in a large bowl; let stand 30 minutes at room temperature. Transfer half of the mixture to a blender; puree until smooth. Pour into serving glasses. Repeat with remaining mixture. Makes 6 servings.

Per serving: 180 calories, 0 g total fat, 0 g saturated fat, 0 mg cholesterol, 9 mg sodium, 47 g carbohydrates, 1 g protein, 38 mg calcium, 0 g fiber

rosemary-spiced walnuts and almonds

These sweet and savory nuts, totally addictive on their own, have an added kick of heat that makes them even more so. Served with cocktails or as a snack, they'll disappear in no time.

Prep time: 5 minutes plus standing • Baking time: 10 minutes

- ½ **pound whole unsalted walnuts**
- ½ **pound whole blanched almonds**
- 4 **teaspoons butter, melted (no substitutes)**
- 2 **tablespoons finely chopped fresh rosemary, divided**
- 2 **teaspoons firmly packed brown sugar**
- 2 **teaspoons kosher salt**
- ½ **teaspoon ground red pepper**
- 1½ **teaspoons granulated sugar**

1. Heat oven to 350°F. Toss nuts with butter in a large bowl. Combine 1 tablespoon of the rosemary, the brown sugar, salt and ground red pepper in a cup. Sprinkle over nuts and toss to coat. Spread in a single layer on a large baking pan. Bake 10 minutes.

2. Remove nuts from the oven; sprinkle with remaining 1 tablespoon rosemary and the granulated sugar. Cool completely. Store in an airtight container at room temperature for up to 1 month. Makes 3 cups.

Per ¼-cup serving: 250 calories, 23 g total fat, 2.5 g saturated fat, 4 mg cholesterol, 341 mg sodium, 8 g carbohydrates, 7 g protein, 63 mg calcium, 3 g fiber

fruit salsa

The papaya supplies a surprise dash of sweet-tart flavor. It's great served with Caribbean Chicken and Beef Skewers (see recipe, page 146) or Jamaican Patties (see recipe, page 134).

Total prep time: 15 minutes

- 1 **navel orange**
- 1 **ripe avocado, peeled and diced**
- ¼ **cup finely chopped onion, rinsed under cold water**
- 1 **papaya, peeled, seeded and diced**
- ½ **of a banana, diced**
- 1 **tablespoon chopped fresh cilantro**
- 1 **tablespoon fresh lime juice**
- ⅛ **teaspoon salt**

Peel and section orange over a large bowl. Squeeze juice from orange membranes into bowl. Gently stir in orange sections and remaining ingredients. *(Can be made ahead. Cover and refrigerate up to 3 hours. Let stand at room temperature 30 minutes before serving.)* Makes 3½ cups.

Per ¼-cup serving: 40 calories, 2 g total fat, 0.5 g saturated fat, 0 mg cholesterol, 23 mg sodium, 6 g carbohydrates, 0.5 g protein, 12 mg calcium, 1 g fiber

the perfect guacamole

Few foods compare when it comes to the creaminess of a ripe avocado. Coarsely mashed with a few select ingredients, this simple fruit transforms into an all-time-favorite guacamole.

Total prep time: 10 minutes

- 1 **medium tomato, diced**
- ¼ **cup finely chopped white onion, rinsed under cold water**
- 2 **tablespoons chopped fresh cilantro**
- 2 **teaspoons finely chopped jalapeño chile with seeds (see tip, page 92)**
- ½ **teaspoon salt**
- 2 **ripe Hass avocados, pitted and peeled**
- 1 **tablespoon fresh lime juice**
  Chopped white onion, for garnish (optional)
  Tortilla chips (optional)

Combine tomato, ¼ cup onion, cilantro, jalapeño and salt in a small bowl. Coarsely mash the avocado with a fork or potato masher in a large bowl. Add the onion mixture and lime juice and stir until well mixed. Garnish with additional chopped onion and serve with tortilla chips, if desired. *(Can be made ahead. Cover and refrigerate up to 4 hours.)* Makes 2 cups.

Per 1-tablespoon serving: 20 calories, 2 g total fat, 0.5 g saturated fat, 0 mg cholesterol, 38 mg sodium, 1 g carbohydrates, 0 g protein, 2 mg calcium, 0 g fiber

crunchy jicama salsa

For maximum crunch, dice each ingredient into very small pieces and be sure to have plenty of tortilla chips for dipping. To use as a topping for chicken or fish, add 1 cup diced honeydew melon.

Total prep time: 30 minutes

- **2 cups finely diced jicama**
- **1 large yellow or red tomato, seeded and finely diced**
- **½ cup finely diced yellow bell pepper**
- **½ cup peeled, seeded and finely diced cucumber**
- **½ cup finely diced red onion**
- **¼ cup fresh lime juice**
- **2 tablespoons chopped fresh cilantro**
- **2 teaspoons minced jalapeño or serrano chile with seeds (see tip, page 92)**
- **¾ teaspoon salt**
- **½ teaspoon sugar**
   Oven-Baked Tortilla Chips (recipe follows)

Combine all ingredients *except* tortilla chips in a large serving bowl. Serve with Oven-Baked Tortilla Chips. Makes 4 cups.

Per 2-tablespoon serving: 10 calories, 0 g total fat, 0 g saturated fat, 0 mg cholesterol, 56 mg sodium, 2 g carbohydrates, 0 g protein, 2 mg calcium, 0 g fiber

oven-baked tortilla chips

Prep time: 5 minutes • Baking time: 5 to 7 minutes

- **8 corn tortillas**

Heat oven to 450°F. Cut each tortilla into 8 wedges and spread in a single layer on 2 cookie sheets. Bake 5 to 7 minutes, until crisp. Makes 4 servings.

Per serving: 115 calories, 1.5 g total fat, 0 g saturated fat, 0 mg cholesterol, 84 mg sodium, 24 g carbohydrates, 3 g protein, 91 mg calcium, 3 g fiber

garden salsa

Serve this salsa with Grilled Tex-Mex Chicken and Beef Kabobs (see recipe, page 147) or with tortilla chips.

Total prep time: 20 minutes

- **8 large plum tomatoes (1¼ lbs.), finely diced**
- **1 large cucumber, peeled, seeded and diced**
- **¾ cup chopped green onions**
- **¼ cup chopped fresh cilantro**
- **1 tablespoon minced jalapeño chile (see tip, page 92)**
- **1 tablespoon fresh lime juice**
- **1½ teaspoons minced garlic**
- **¾ teaspoon salt**
   Tortilla chips (optional)

Combine all ingredients *except* tortilla chips in a bowl. *(Can be made ahead. Cover and refrigerate up to 24 hours.)* Serve with tortilla chips, if desired. Makes about 5 cups.

Per 2-tablespoon serving: 5 calories, 0 g total fat, 0 g saturated fat, 0 mg cholesterol, 46 mg sodium, 1 g carbohydrates, 0 g protein, 4 mg calcium, 0 g fiber

double tomato jam

Two kinds of tomatoes—fresh and dried—come together in this colorful spread. It's perfect served as an appetizer with our homemade Garlic Toasts (right) or as an accompaniment to grilled chicken or beef.

Prep time: 20 minutes plus cooling
Cooking time: 25 to 30 minutes

- **14 plum tomatoes (about 2 lbs.)**
- **¼ cup sun-dried tomatoes packed in oil, well drained**
- **2 tablespoons extra-virgin olive oil**
- **1 cup thinly sliced shallots**
- **2 teaspoons minced garlic**
- **2 teaspoons grated fresh ginger**
- **2 tablespoons balsamic vinegar**
- **1 tablespoon firmly packed brown sugar**
- **½ teaspoon salt**
- **¼ teaspoon freshly ground pepper**
- **Garlic Toasts (recipe, right) or assorted crackers**

1. Heat grill or broiler. Grill plum tomatoes over medium-high heat or broil 3 inches from heat source for 2 to 5 minutes per side, until skin is blackened, turning occasionally. Cool slightly and chop coarsely; reserve liquid. Chop sun-dried tomatoes.

2. Heat oil in a large skillet over medium-high heat. Add shallots and cook 2 to 3 minutes, until golden. Stir in the garlic and ginger and cook 30 seconds. Reduce heat to medium. Carefully add plum and sun-dried tomatoes with their liquid; cook, stirring occasionally, 18 to 20 minutes, until mixture is thickened and most of the liquid is evaporated. Add vinegar, sugar, salt and pepper and cook 1 minute more. Transfer to a medium bowl and cool. *(Can be made ahead. Cover and refrigerate up to 3 days.)* Serve with Garlic Toasts or crackers. Makes 3 cups.

Per 1-tablespoon serving: 15 calories, 0.5 g total fat, 0 g saturated fat, 0 mg cholesterol, 28 mg sodium, 2 g carbohydrates, 0 g protein, 3 mg calcium, 0 g fiber

garlic toasts

These savory toasted rounds provide a crispy base for just about any topping. We suggest our Double Tomato Jam (left) or Tuscan Beans (below).

Prep time: 15 minutes • Cooking time: 1 to 2 minutes

- **1 loaf (1 lb.) French or Italian bread, split lengthwise**
- **1 garlic clove, peeled and halved**

Heat grill or broiler. Grill or broil bread 1 to 2 minutes, until deep golden. Rub garlic clove over cut sides of bread. Cut into ½-inch-thick slices. Makes 8 servings.

Per serving: 155 calories, 1.5 g total fat, 0.5 g saturated fat, 0 mg cholesterol, 345 mg sodium, 29 g carbohydrates, 5 g protein, 43 mg calcium, 2 g fiber

tuscan beans

This rustic dish is made with cannellini beans (white kidney beans), the most popular in Italian cooking. It makes a great topping for Garlic Toasts (above) or crackers.

Prep time: 5 minutes plus standing
Cooking time: 55 to 60 minutes

- **1½ cups dried cannellini or Great Northern beans, rinsed**
- **1 can (14½ oz.) chicken broth**
- **1½ cups water**
- **½ cup fresh sage leaves, thinly sliced, or 1 tablespoon dried sage plus 2 tablespoons chopped fresh parsley**
- **¼ teaspoon freshly ground pepper**
- **2 tablespoons olive oil**
- **1½ teaspoons minced garlic**
- **¾ teaspoon salt**
- **Garlic Toasts (recipe above) or assorted crackers**

1. Soak beans in water to cover by 2 inches in a large saucepan overnight. (*To quick-soak:* Combine beans with water to cover by 2 inches in a large saucepan. Bring to boil; boil 2 minutes. Cover and let stand 1 hour.) Drain beans in colander.

2. Combine drained beans, broth, 1½ cups water, sage and pepper in the saucepan; bring to boil. Reduce heat and simmer, covered, 40 minutes, until almost tender. Add oil, garlic and salt and simmer, uncovered, 12 to 15 minutes more, until beans are tender but not mushy. Serve warm or at room temperature. Makes 4½ cups.

Per ½-cup serving: 140 calories, 4 g total fat, 0.5 g saturated fat, 0 mg cholesterol, 389 mg sodium, 20 g carbohydrates, 7 g protein, 62 mg calcium, 6 g fiber

roasted red pepper baguette EASY

This tangy hors d'oeuvre, made with goat cheese, balsamic vinegar and roasted red peppers, is guaranteed to please at any party or gathering. For last-minute entertaining, substitute 2 jars (7 ounces each) roasted red peppers, drained and sliced, for the red bell peppers.

Prep time: 10 minutes plus standing
Broiling time: 23 to 27 minutes

- **4** red bell peppers
- **1** loaf (1 lb.) French bread (24-inch-long baguette)
- **⅓** cup pitted kalamata olives, quartered lengthwise
- **¼** cup extra-virgin olive oil
- **¼** cup minced shallots
- **2** tablespoons balsamic vinegar
- **1** tablespoon chopped fresh flat-leaf parsley
- **2** teaspoons chopped fresh rosemary or ½ teaspoon dried rosemary
- **½** teaspoon salt
- **½** teaspoon freshly ground pepper
- **4** ounces goat cheese, crumbled

1. Heat broiler. Rinse bell peppers; drain well on paper towels. Place on a foil-lined cookie sheet and broil 6 inches from heat 18 to 22 minutes, until skins are bubbly and evenly charred, turning occasionally. Immediately wrap foil around peppers. Let stand 20 to 30 minutes, until peppers are cool enough to handle. Cut peppers lengthwise

in half. Cut out stems, seeds and membranes and discard them. Remove blistered skin from peppers, using a sharp knife to gently pull it off in strips; discard skin. Cut peppers into ¼-inch-thick slices.

2. Slice bread in half lengthwise and place, cut sides up, on a broiler pan.

3. Combine bell peppers, olives, oil, shallots, vinegar, parsley, rosemary, salt and pepper in a medium bowl, stirring to mix well. Spoon evenly over cut sides of bread halves, then top with goat cheese. Broil 3 inches from heat source 5 minutes, until cheese begins to soften and edges of bread are lightly browned. Cut crosswise into 1-inch-thick slices and serve. Makes 48 appetizers.

Per appetizer: 50 calories, 2.5 g total fat, 0.5 g saturated fat, 2 mg cholesterol, 105 mg sodium, 6 g carbohydrates, 1 g protein, 16 mg calcium, 1 g fiber

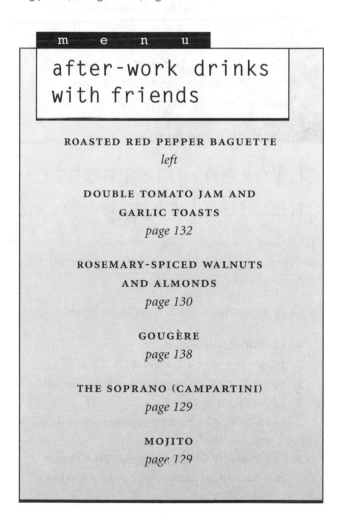

menu

after-work drinks with friends

ROASTED RED PEPPER BAGUETTE
left

DOUBLE TOMATO JAM AND GARLIC TOASTS
page 132

ROSEMARY-SPICED WALNUTS AND ALMONDS
page 130

GOUGÈRE
page 138

THE SOPRANO (CAMPARTINI)
page 129

MOJITO
page 129

test kitchen tip

nuts for pistachios

The pale green pistachio nut is a beloved favorite to eat out of hand and a great ingredient in all sorts of sweet and savory recipes.

In its natural form, the pistachio shell is tan, though some have been dyed red, and others blanched until they turn white. According to The California Pistachio Commission, pistachios are dyed to make them easier to find in a mixed-nuts bowl and also because consumers associate red shells with pistachios. The color of the shell doesn't affect the nut's flavor.

Pistachios come both unshelled and shelled, raw or roasted and salted and unsalted. If you are buying them unshelled, be sure the shells are partially opened. Nuts with closed shells are typically immature and should be discarded. Pistachios are available year-round.

2. Meanwhile, lightly brush 4 of the tortillas on one side with 1½ teaspoons of the oil. Place tortillas, oiled sides down, on a large cookie sheet.

3. Combine salsa and mayonnaise in a medium bowl. Add chicken and toss to coat.

4. Spread a generous ½ cup of the chicken mixture over the entire surface of each of the prepared tortillas on the cookie sheet. Top evenly with cheese, then sprinkle with nuts. Cover with remaining 4 tortillas and brush tops lightly with remaining 1½ teaspoons oil. Bake 11 to 12 minutes, until tortillas are crisp and golden. Cut each quesadilla into eighths. Makes 32 wedges.

Per wedge: 85 calories, 4.5 g total fat, 1.5 g saturated fat, 12 mg cholesterol, 161 mg sodium, 6 g carbohydrates, 5 g protein, 44 mg calcium, 0 g fiber

chicken-pistachio quesadilla

Make it easy on yourself: Use a deli rotisserie chicken, or roast your own the day before. Prepared green pepper salsa adds moisture and flavor in one step.

Prep time: 10 minutes • Baking time: 11 to 12 minutes

> 8 (7-inch) flour tortillas
> 3 teaspoons olive oil, divided
> 1 cup prepared green pepper or tomatillo salsa
> 2 tablespoons mayonnaise
> 2 cups coarsely shredded rotisserie or cooked chicken
> 1 cup coarsely shredded pepper Jack cheese
> ½ cup shelled pistachio nuts, lightly toasted and finely chopped

1. Adjust oven rack to lowest position. Heat oven to 425°F.

jamaican patties

These hearty meat turnovers can be served as appetizers or entrées. Filled with ground beef and spiced with traditional seasonings—allspice for sweetness and Scotch bonnet for heat—they impart a casual island feeling. Pictured on page 122.

Prep time: 30 minutes • Baking time: 20 to 25 minutes

FILLING:

> 1 pound lean ground beef
> ⅔ cup chopped green onions
> ½ cup chopped red bell pepper
> 1 tablespoon chopped garlic
> 1 tablespoon grated fresh ginger
> 1 teaspoon allspice
> 1 teaspoon salt
> ¼ to ½ teaspoon finely chopped Scotch bonnet chile (see tip, page 92) (optional)
>
> 1 recipe Roti dough (see recipe, page 159) or 2 packages (1 lb. 3 oz. each) large refrigerated biscuits
>   Whole fresh chiles, for garnish (optional)
>   Fruit Salsa (see recipe, page 130) (optional)

1. Heat oven to 375°F.

2. *Make filling:* Heat a large nonstick skillet over medium heat. Cook beef 5 to 8 minutes, until brown, breaking up into small pieces with back of spoon. Add remaining ingredients and cook 5 minutes, until vegetables soften. Cool.

3. Prepare Roti dough as directed *except* divide dough into 16 pieces. Working with one piece of dough at a time, roll on a lightly floured surface into a 6-inch circle. Spoon 3 tablespoons of the beef mixture in center of circle; brush edge with water. Fold circle in half, seal edges with fingertips, then trim with fluted pastry wheel. Transfer patties to an ungreased cookie sheet and refrigerate. Repeat with the remaining dough and filling.

4. Brush tops of patties with water. Bake 20 to 25 minutes, until golden brown (12 to 15 minutes for biscuit dough). Garnish with fresh chiles, if desired. Serve warm with fruit salsa, if desired. *(Can be made ahead. Cool and transfer to an airtight container and freeze up to 1 week. To reheat: Bake in a 350°F. oven 15 minutes.)* Makes 16 patties.

Per patty: 195 calories, 8.5 g total fat, 2.5 g saturated fat, 21 mg cholesterol, 277 mg sodium, 21 g carbohydrates, 8 g protein, 33 mg calcium, 1 g fiber

salmon and wasabi-caviar spirals

Use high-quality smoked salmon for this appetizer. The caviar can be a less expensive variety. The one we used was a notch above the most inexpensive kind found on the shelves in supermarkets. Fresh refrigerated caviar is available in fish stores or in the fish department of your local supermarket.

Total prep time: 20 minutes plus chilling

WASABI CREAM:

- 1 package (3 oz.) cream cheese, softened
- 1 teaspoon prepared wasabi paste

- 6 large slices (6 oz. total) smoked salmon (not lox)
- 1 jar (1 oz.) flying fish, American sturgeon or salmon roe
- 1 English (seedless) cucumber (about 13 inches long), peeled and cut into ⅜-inch-thick rounds

1. *Make wasabi cream:* Stir wasabi into the cream cheese in a small bowl until smooth.

2. On a large piece of waxed paper, arrange salmon slices separate and flat. With a small spatula or fingertips, spread about 2 teaspoons of the wasabi cream on the entire surface of 1 salmon slice. Lightly spread 1 teaspoon of the roe over the wasabi cream. Repeat with remaining salmon, wasabi cream and roe. From short end, roll up each salmon slice; wrap each roll in plastic wrap and refrigerate 2 hours.

3. Lightly pat cucumber rounds with paper towels. Arrange cucumber slices on a large serving platter. Unwrap salmon rolls. With a sharp knife, cut a ⅜-inch-thick round from one of the rolls and place, cut side up, on top of a cucumber slice. Repeat, topping all cucumber slices. Serve immediately or cover with plastic wrap and refrigerate up to 1 hour before serving. Makes 26 to 30 spirals.

Per spiral: 20 calories, 1.5 g total fat, 1 g saturated fat, 9 mg cholesterol, 62 mg sodium, 0 g carbohydrates, 2 g protein, 6 mg calcium, 0 g fiber

---

test kitchen tip

caviar

WHAT IS CAVIAR? Caviar is the roe (eggs) of fish. Sturgeon roe is considered premium caviar. Types of sturgeon roe include beluga, osetra and sevruga.

WHEN ONLY THE BEST WILL DO... Beluga, found in the Caspian Sea, is well known and appreciated for its large, soft eggs and is the most expensive caviar; its color ranges from pale silver to black.

NEXT IN LINE... Osetra is gray to brownish gray, with medium-size eggs, while sevruga has smaller grayish eggs. The less pricey varieties of caviar include lumpfish, whitefish and salmon or red caviar.

cape sante scallops EASY

Serve these plump, sweet scallops—lightly coated with bread crumbs, then cooked with a fragrant garlic butter until crisp and golden—as an appetizer or main dish.

Prep time: 10 minutes • Cooking time: 5 to 6 minutes

- ½ cup plain dry bread crumbs
- ¼ teaspoon salt
- 1 pound medium sea scallops
- 2 tablespoons olive oil
- 2 tablespoons butter or margarine
- 1 teaspoon chopped fresh flat-leaf parsley
- ½ teaspoon minced garlic
- ¼ cup white wine
- 2 tablespoons fresh lemon juice

1. Combine bread crumbs and salt in a medium bowl; add scallops and toss to coat.

2. Heat oil and butter in a large skillet over high heat. Add parsley and garlic; cook 20 seconds. Add scallops and cook 4 to 5 minutes, until browned, turning once. Add wine and lemon juice; cook 1 minute more. For appetizers, transfer to heated scallop shells, if desired. Makes 6 appetizer or 4 main-dish servings.

Per appetizer serving: 175 calories, 9.5 g total fat, 3.5 g saturated fat, 36 mg cholesterol, 438 mg sodium, 7 g carbohydrates, 14 g protein, 37 mg calcium, 0 g fiber
Per main-dish serving: 265 calories, 14.5 g total fat, 5 g saturated fat, 54 mg cholesterol, 657 mg sodium, 11 g carbohydrates, 20 g protein, 56 mg calcium, 0 g fiber

spicy shrimp fritters

Cooking the shrimp with jalapeño and garlic first gives the fritters a great flavor throughout. Pictured on page 122.

Prep time: 30 minutes
Cooking time: 2 to 3 minutes per batch
Microwave used

- 5 teaspoons olive oil, divided
- 1 pound medium shelled and deveined shrimp
- 2 teaspoons minced garlic
- ½ of a jalapeño chile with seeds, finely chopped (see tip, page 92)
- ¾ teaspoon salt, divided
- 2 large eggs, lightly beaten with 2 tablespoons water
- ¼ cup all-purpose flour
- ¼ teaspoon baking powder
- ⅛ teaspoon freshly ground pepper
- Assorted Sauces (such as Earth & Vine Provisions Red Bell Pepper and Ancho Chili Jam) (see Sauce Source tip, page 146)

1. Heat 1 teaspoon of the oil in a 12-inch nonstick skillet over high heat 2 minutes. Combine shrimp with garlic, jalapeño and ½ teaspoon of the salt on waxed paper, tossing to coat. Add shrimp to skillet and cook, stirring, 1 to 2 minutes, until partially cooked. Cool and chop.

2. Meanwhile, whisk eggs with water in medium bowl 10 seconds, until very frothy; stir in shrimp and any juices from skillet.

3. Combine flour, baking powder, remaining ¼ teaspoon salt and the pepper in a small bowl. Sift half of the flour mixture over the shrimp, then gently fold in with a rubber spatula. Repeat with remaining flour mixture.

4. Wipe skillet with paper towel. Add 1 teaspoon of the oil and heat over medium-high heat. Drop 12 level tablespoons of the shrimp mixture into skillet, spacing evenly. Cook 1 to 1½ minutes, until golden; turn fritters. Drizzle another 1 teaspoon of the oil into skillet and cook 1 to 1½ minutes more, until golden. Transfer to a serving platter. Repeat with remaining batter and 2 teaspoons oil. *(Can be made ahead. Transfer fritters to a cookie sheet and cool. Cover and refrigerate overnight. To reheat, bake in a 350°F. oven 10 minutes.)*

5. Microwave Red Bell Pepper and Ancho Chili Jam in a microwaveproof bowl on High 30 to 60 seconds to loosen. Serve immediately with fritters. Makes about 24 fritters.

Per fritter: 40 calories, 1.5 g total fat, 0.5 g saturated fat, 46 mg cholesterol, 111 mg sodium, 1 g carbohydrates, 5 g protein, 15 mg calcium, 0 g fiber

fried calamari with roasted tomato sauce

Here's the super-crispy calamari we all love, with a new dipping sauce. For those who like it hot, increase the heat by adding more chipotle chile.

Prep time: 20 minutes plus chilling
Cooking time: 1 minute per batch

ROASTED TOMATO SAUCE:

- 1 tablespoon olive oil
- 2 tablespoons sesame seeds
- 1 tablespoon finely chopped garlic
- 1 teaspoon chili powder
- 1 can (14½ oz.) fire-roasted diced tomatoes
- 1 teaspoon minced chipotle in adobo sauce
- 1 tablespoon grated unsweetened chocolate

CALAMARI:

- 1 pound cleaned squid
- ½ cup all-purpose flour
- ¼ cup cornstarch
- 1 teaspoon salt
- ¼ teaspoon freshly ground pepper
- Vegetable oil

1. *Make roasted tomato sauce:* Heat oil in a small saucepan over medium heat. Add sesame seeds and garlic; cook 1 to 1½ minutes, until golden. Add chili powder; cook 20 to 30 seconds. Stir in tomatoes and chipotle and bring to boil. Reduce heat slightly, keeping at a low boil, and cook 5 minutes more. Remove from heat and stir in chocolate; cover and set aside. Reheat before serving.

2. *Make calamari:* Cut squid bodies into ½-inch-thick rings, keeping tentacles intact. Whisk together flour, cornstarch, salt and pepper in a large bowl. Add half of the squid and toss to coat, shaking off excess flour mixture. Transfer to a cookie sheet. Repeat with remaining squid.

3. Heat 1½ inches oil to 375°F. on a deep-fry thermometer in a heavy, large pot or deep fryer. Add squid to pot, with a slotted spoon, a few pieces at a time. Cook squid about 1 minute, until deep golden. Transfer with slotted spoon to paper towels to drain. Repeat with remaining flour-coated squid. Transfer to a serving platter and serve immediately with roasted tomato sauce. Makes 6 servings.

Per serving: 305 calories, 18 g total fat, 3 g saturated fat, 176 mg cholesterol, 550 mg sodium, 21 g carbohydrates, 14 g protein, 82 mg calcium, 1 g fiber

shrimp canapés

These shrimp finger sandwiches are ideal as a part of an afternoon tea or as an accompaniment to your favorite soup for a satisfying lunch.

Prep time: 30 minutes plus chilling
Cooking time: 2 minutes

- ½ pound peeled medium shrimp
- ¼ cup mayonnaise or salad dressing
- ¼ teaspoon grated lemon peel
- 1 tablespoon fresh lemon juice
- 1 tablespoon dry sherry
- ⅛ teaspoon salt
- ¼ teaspoon freshly ground black pepper
- Pinch ground red pepper
- ⅓ cup chopped fresh parsley
- 14 slices firm white bread
- 2 tablespoons butter, softened (no substitutes)

1. Cook shrimp in boiling water 2 minutes, until shrimp turn pink and are opaque.

2. Place shrimp in food processor with mayonnaise, lemon peel, lemon juice, sherry, salt, black pepper and ground red pepper; process until smooth.

3. Place parsley on a plate. Spread 2 slightly rounded tablespoons of the shrimp mixture evenly onto 1 slice of bread. Cover with another bread slice. Lightly spread bread with butter and press into parsley, tapping off excess. Repeat, making 6 more sandwiches. Wrap in plastic wrap and chill at least 1 hour or up to 4 hours. Cut each into 4 triangles. Makes 28 canapés.

Per canapé: 65 calories, 3.5 g total fat, 1 g saturated fat, 15 mg cholesterol, 110 mg sodium, 7 g carbohydrates, 3 g protein, 16 mg calcium, 0 g fiber

swedish meatballs

One of the great classics in the world of hors d'oeuvres, these saucy meatballs will disappear in no time.

Prep time: 20 minutes • Cooking time: 33 to 35 minutes

- **4 tablespoons butter or margarine, divided**
- **1 cup finely chopped onions**
- **2 cups cubed fresh bread (4 slices)**
- **½ cup milk**
- **1½ pounds lean ground beef**
- **2 large eggs**
- **1 teaspoon salt**
- **1 teaspoon fines herbes**
- **1 teaspoon paprika**
- **1 teaspoon dry mustard**
- **¼ teaspoon nutmeg**
- **¼ teaspoon freshly ground pepper**
- **½ cup water, divided**
- **½ teaspoon minced garlic**
- **2 tablespoons flour**
- **1 teaspoon tomato paste**
- **1 cup beef broth**
- **½ cup sour cream**
- **2 tablespoons chopped fresh dill, divided**

1. Heat oven to 400°F. Lightly grease 2 jelly-roll pans.

2. Melt 2 tablespoons of the butter in a large skillet over medium heat. Add the onions and cook 8 minutes, until tender. Transfer to a large bowl and cool.

3. Soak bread cubes in milk in a small bowl 1 minute, then squeeze very dry; discard milk. Add bread to onions with beef, eggs, salt, fines herbes, paprika, mustard, nutmeg and pepper; mix well. Shape into forty 1½-inch balls. Arrange on prepared jelly-roll pans. Bake 18 to 20 minutes, until cooked through, turning meatballs once and rotating pans halfway through. Remove the meatballs from pans and set aside.

4. Pour 2 tablespoons of the water into each jelly-roll pan, scraping up browned bits from bottom. Heat remaining 2 tablespoons butter in a large skillet over medium heat. Add garlic and cook

30 seconds. Stir in flour and tomato paste; cook 1 minute. Whisk in beef broth and the remaining ¼ cup water. Strain drippings from jelly-roll pans into beef broth mixture. Bring to boil. Add meatballs to skillet. *(Can be made ahead. Cover and refrigerate up to 24 hours. Reheat in skillet with ¼ cup more water 20 minutes, until hot.)* Reduce heat to low and stir in sour cream and 1 tablespoon of the dill *(do not boil)*. Transfer to a serving bowl. Sprinkle with remaining 1 tablespoon dill. Makes 40 meatballs.

Per meatball: 65 calories, 4.5 g total fat, 2 g saturated fat, 24 mg cholesterol, 121 mg sodium, 2 g carbohydrates, 4 g protein, 12 mg calcium, 0 g fiber

gougère

These easy-to-bake classic French cheese puffs make a festive pull-apart appetizer.

Prep time: 20 minutes plus standing
Baking time: 30 minutes

- **1 cup all-purpose flour**
- **½ teaspoon salt**
- **½ teaspoon sugar**
- **⅛ teaspoon ground red pepper**
  Pinch nutmeg
- **1 cup water**
- **6 tablespoons butter or margarine**
- **4 large eggs**
- **1 cup (4 oz.) shredded Swiss or Jarlsberg cheese**
- **1 large egg, lightly beaten, for glaze**

1. Heat oven to 400°F. Grease and flour a large cookie sheet. Using a 9-inch round cake pan, trace a 9-inch circle on prepared sheet. Remove cake pan. Set aside.

2. Combine 1 cup flour, salt, sugar, red pepper and nutmeg in a small bowl.

3. Bring water and butter to boil in a medium saucepan over high heat; boil until butter has melted. Reduce heat to low; add flour mixture all at once. Stir vigorously with a wooden spoon until mixture leaves sides of pan and forms a ball; stir 1 minute to dry the mixture. Remove from heat. Beat in 4 eggs, one at a time, beating well after each addition, until completely smooth. Fold in cheese.

4. Drop dough by ¼ cupfuls inside marked ring on cookie sheet; brush tops with beaten egg. Bake 30 minutes, until puffed and golden. Turn off oven; leave in oven 30 minutes *(do not open oven)*. Transfer to wire rack. Serve warm or at room temperature. *(Can be made ahead. Cool. Wrap well and freeze up to 1 month. Unwrap and thaw at room temperature about 1 hour. Bake in heated 350°F. oven 8 to 10 minutes to crisp.)* Makes 12 appetizer servings.

Per serving: 160 calories, 11 g total fat, 6 g saturated fat, 115 mg cholesterol, 199 mg sodium, 8 g carbohydrates, 6 g protein, 97 mg calcium, 0 g fiber

smoked-salmon ribbon sandwiches

These pretty-as-a-picture salmon hors d'oeuvres brighten up a cocktail party.

Total prep time: 1 hour plus chilling

SMOKED-SALMON FILLING:
- 4 ounces cream cheese, softened
- 3 ounces smoked salmon, chopped
- 1 tablespoon heavy or whipping cream
- 2 teaspoons fresh lemon juice
- ⅛ teaspoon freshly ground pepper

WATERCRESS FILLING:
- 1 cup firmly packed watercress leaves
- ⅓ cup mayonnaise
- 1 ounce cream cheese, softened

- 15 very thin slices whole wheat bread
- 10 very thin slices white bread
- ¼ cup butter, softened (no substitutes)

1. *Make smoked-salmon filling:* Puree all ingredients in food processor until smooth. Spoon into small bowl and set side.

2. *Make watercress filling:* Process all ingredients in food processor until watercress is just finely chopped in a smooth cream filling.

3. Lightly spread 1 side of each bread slice with butter. Spread 1 generous tablespoon of the salmon filling on each of 10 slices whole wheat bread. Spread 1 tablespoon of the watercress filling on each of 10 slices white bread.

4. *Make sandwich stacks:* Arrange 1 salmon slice, spread side up, on a flat surface and cover with 1 watercress slice, spread side up; repeat with another salmon, then watercress slice and top with 1 whole wheat slice, buttered side down. Repeat, making 4 more sandwich stacks.

5. Wrap sandwich stacks well in waxed paper, covering all sides; arrange on a cookie sheet. Place another cookie sheet on top and weight lightly with two 1-pound cans. Refrigerate at least 1 hour or up to 24 hours. To serve, unwrap sandwiches, trim crusts and slice into ½-inch-wide strips. Arrange on trays. Makes 30 strips.

Per sandwich strip: 100 calories, 6 g total fat, 2.5 g saturated fat, 12 mg cholesterol, 162 mg sodium, 9 g carbohydrates, 3 g protein, 26 mg calcium, 1 g fiber

---

test kitchen tip
smoked salmon savvy

NOVA OR NOVA SCOTIA salmon is a term used in the United States to refer to cold-smoked salmon. (Fresh salmon is cold-smoked at a temperature of 70°F. to 90°F. in a smokehouse for at least 1 day or up to 3 weeks.)

LOX, a brine-cured cold-smoked salmon slightly saltier than other kinds, is one of the most popular kinds of smoked salmon. It's often served with bagels and cream cheese.

KIPPERED salmon is a steak or fillet that has been soaked in a mild brine and hot-smoked (the salmon is smoked at temperatures between 120°F. and 180°F. for a time range of 6 to 12 hours).

INDIAN-CURE salmon is a salmon jerky of sorts. It has been cold-smoked for up to 2 weeks.

DANISH-SMOKED, IRISH-SMOKED AND SCOTCH-SMOKED salmon are simply types of cold-smoked Atlantic salmon that are pinpointed geographically. The coho and chinook, two Pacific species, are usually just labeled generically as smoked salmon.

great grilling

TO ENSURE THOROUGH, EVEN COOKING, make sure coals are hot enough before placing food on the grill. Allow 25 to 30 minutes for the coals to burn evenly and develop a coating of gray ash. Preheat gas grills for 10 to 15 minutes.

DO NOT CROWD THE GRILL. Grilled foods need ample airflow to cook quickly and evenly. Leave at least a half inch between foods.

DO NOT ENCOURAGE FLARE-UPS or cook food over a flame. Doing so burns food and makes it taste bitter. Covering the grill helps tame the flame. If you don't have a cover, move the food to another part of the grill.

USE AN INSTANT-READ MEAT THERMOMETER to determine when meat, poultry and fish are properly cooked.

best burgers

Nothing says summer quite like a grilled burger. Flipping burgers frequently during cooking results in moist, char-free patties. For safe grilling, always use an instant-read meat thermometer to test each burger's doneness. Looks can be deceiving! Pictured on page 121.

Prep time: 10 minutes • Grilling time: 15 minutes

1½	pounds 80% lean ground beef
1	teaspoon kosher salt
½	teaspoon freshly ground pepper
4	super-size English muffins, split
1	garlic clove, halved
1	tablespoon extra-virgin olive oil
8	fresh basil leaves
4	tomato slices

1. Divide beef into quarters. Gently shape each piece into a ¾-inch-thick patty.

2. Heat grill. Combine salt and pepper in cup; sprinkle over both sides of patties. Grill patties over medium heat 15 minutes, until an instant-read meat thermometer inserted in the side of each burger registers 160°F., turning every 4 minutes.

3. While burgers are cooking, grill muffins, cut sides down, 1½ to 2 minutes, until toasted. Rub garlic on toasted sides, then brush each half with oil.

4. Place basil leaves on bottom halves of muffins. Top with burgers, tomato slices and top halves of muffins. Makes 4 servings.

Per serving: 610 calories, 35 g total fat, 11 g saturated fat, 123 mg cholesterol, 759 mg sodium, 39 g carbohydrates, 35 g protein, 123 mg calcium, 2 g fiber

peppercorn filets

For this company-special dish, from Ken Stewart's Grille in Akron, Ohio, cook beef tenderloin filets the easy way— in a skillet. The scrumptious sauce that goes with the filets has a touch of honey and brandy and is ready in less than 10 minutes.

Total prep and cooking time: 25 minutes

2	tablespoons olive oil
4	center-cut beef tenderloin filets (8 oz. each) about 1¼ inch thick
¾	teaspoon salt
2	teaspoons cracked black peppercorns
½	cup brandy or red wine
1	cup water
¼	cup prepared demiglace
1	tablespoon honey
2	tablespoons cold butter, cut up (no substitutes)

1. Heat oven to 450°F.

2. Heat oil in a large ovenproof skillet over medium-high heat just until starting to smoke, 3 to 4 minutes. Meanwhile, sprinkle both sides of filets with salt and one side with pepper. Place filets, peppered sides down, in skillet and cook 3 minutes until browned. Turn filets; transfer to oven and bake 7 to 9 minutes, until an instant-read meat thermometer inserted in center of each filet registers 140°F. for medium-rare.

3. Transfer filets to 4 serving plates; cover and keep warm. Add brandy to skillet and cook over high heat until reduced to 2 tablespoons, about 2 minutes. Add the water, demiglace and honey; bring to boil, stirring, and boil until reduced by half (to about ¾ cup), about 5 minutes. Remove skillet from heat and whisk in butter until blended. Pour sauce around filets. Makes 4 servings.

Note: Demiglace is available from More Than Gourmet (800-860-9385).

Per serving: 800 calories, 65 g total fat, 25.5 g saturated fat, 177 mg cholesterol, 667 mg sodium, 6 g carbohydrates, 41 g protein, 23 mg calcium, 0 g fiber

spiced leg of lamb

Leg of lamb—a rare indulgence for most—is a delicious way to impress your guests. Boneless leg of lamb is available in many markets, or ask the butcher to bone and tie the meat. Two rubs are combined to flavor the lamb: a seasoned garlic paste and a fragrant mixture of freshly ground peppercorns, mustard seeds and coriander seeds. Serve the roast with our rich port pan gravy.

Prep time: 10 minutes plus marinating
Roasting time: 1½ to 1¾ hours

- **1 tablespoon mustard seeds**
- **1 tablespoon coriander seeds**
- **1 tablespoon whole black peppercorns**
- **½ teaspoon dried thyme**
- **1½ teaspoons salt**
- **1 tablespoon chopped garlic**
- **¼ cup finely chopped fresh flat-leaf parsley**
- **1 lamb leg roast (5 to 6 lbs.), boneless, tied**
- **1 tablespoon olive oil**

PORT GRAVY:
- **¾ cup water**
- **3 tablespoons port**
- **1 tablespoon flour**

1. Combine mustard, coriander, peppercorns and thyme in food processor or blender; process 1 minute, until seeds are coarsely crushed. Set aside.

2. Sprinkle salt over chopped garlic and press with side of knife against cutting board to form a paste. Add parsley and mix until combined.

3. Rub lamb with oil, then spread with garlic-parsley paste. Press spice mixture onto meat. Place in a shallow dish covered with plastic wrap or in a 2-gallon resealable plastic storage bag. Seal and marinate in the refrigerator 4 hours or overnight.

4. Heat oven to 450°F. Place lamb in a 17×11-inch roasting pan. Roast lamb 15 minutes. Reduce heat to 350°F. Roast 1¼ to 1½ hours more, until instant-read meat thermometer inserted in center of roast registers 140°F. for medium-rare. Transfer to cutting board; cover loosely with foil. Let stand 15 to 20 minutes before slicing. Serve with port gravy. Makes 8 servings.

5. *Make port gravy:* Spoon fat from roasting pan; pour water into pan and bring to simmer, scraping up browned bits. Pour into small saucepan; keep warm. Stir port and flour together in a cup until smooth. Whisk into saucepan. Cook 1 minute, until gravy thickens. Makes about 1 cup.

Per serving: 575 calories, 33.5 g total fat, 13.5 g saturated fat, 204 mg cholesterol, 574 mg sodium, 3 g carbohydrates, 60 g protein, 43 mg calcium, 1 g fiber

---

test kitchen tip

on the lamb

Hailed for its tender meat, lamb is a sheep younger than 1 year of age. A baby lamb is usually between 6 and 8 weeks old; a spring lamb, from 3 to 5 months old; and a standard lamb, just under a year old. Between 1 year and 2 years, a lamb is referred to as a "yearling," and if over 2 years of age, it's called a mutton (and isn't as tender).

test kitchen tip

making the cut

Like beef, lamb is available ground as well as cut into steaks. You can also purchase chops and roasts. Wrap ground lamb and small cuts of lamb loosely and keep in the refrigerator up to 3 days. Ground lamb may be frozen up to 3 months; regular cuts, for up to 6 months. Store roasts in the refrigerator up to 5 days.

rack of lamb

Simple and elegant! The perfect example of a hassle-free, although admittedly extravagant, entrée for guests.

Prep time: 20 minutes plus standing
Roasting time: 30 minutes

- **2 trimmed racks of lamb, 8 ribs each (about 1½ lbs. total)**
- **1 tablespoon olive oil**
- **2 tablespoons Dijon mustard**
- **2 tablespoons white wine**
- **½ teaspoon salt**
- **¼ teaspoon freshly ground pepper**
- **1 cup fresh bread crumbs (2 slices firm white sandwich bread)**
- **½ cup chopped fresh flat-leaf parsley**

1. ■ Let lamb stand at room temperature 1 hour.

2. ■ Adjust oven rack in upper third of oven. Heat oven to 450°F. Rub lamb with oil and stand racks opposite each other in a shallow roasting pan, meaty portions out, bone tips up and interlaced. Roast 15 minutes.

3. ■ Meanwhile, combine mustard, wine, salt and pepper in a small bowl. Toss bread crumbs and parsley in another bowl to combine.

4. ■ Remove roasting pan from oven. Reduce temperature to 400°F. Brush each rack with mustard mixture. Pat bread crumbs over the meaty side of each rack. Return to oven and roast 15 minutes more, until an instant-read meat thermometer inserted into center of lamb but not

touching bone registers 140°F. for medium-rare. Remove from oven and let stand 5 minutes before carving. Makes 8 servings.

Per serving: 160 calories, 8.5 g total fat, 2.5 g saturated fat, 48 mg cholesterol, 239 mg sodium, 4 g carbohydrates, 15 g protein, 26 mg calcium, 0 g fiber

grilled pork chops

Marinating the pork chops in a brine—a mixture of salt, sugar, seasonings and water—for 24 hours yields incredibly moist, juicy results. Pictured on page 127.

Prep time: 5 minutes plus brining
Grilling time: 15 to 20 minutes

BRINE:

- **2 cups hot water**
- **¼ cup kosher salt**
- **¼ cup sugar**
- **6 quarter-size slices fresh ginger**
- **4 garlic cloves, crushed**
- **1 teaspoon fennel seeds**
- **1 small jalapeño chile, quartered (see tip, page 92)**
- **2 cups cold water**

■

- **4 center or rib cut pork chops, 1 inch thick**
- **2 teaspoons extra-virgin olive oil**
    Watermelon and Radish Relish (see recipe, page 158) (optional)

1. ■ *Make brine:* Stir together all ingredients *except* cold water in large bowl until salt and sugar dissolve. Add cold water. Let brine stand until room temperature. Pour brine into a large, heavy-duty resealable plastic freezer bag. Add pork chops. Seal bag, carefully pressing out air. Lay bag flat on tray or large plate and refrigerate 24 hours, turning bag several times. *(Can be frozen up to 1 month. Thaw in refrigerator 24 hours.)*

2. ■ Heat grill. Drain pork chops in colander. Discard brine and rinse pork under cold running water. Pat chops dry and brush both sides of each chop with oil.

3. Grill the chops over medium-high heat 15 to 20 minutes, until an instant-read meat thermometer inserted lengthwise in thickest portion of each chop registers 155°F., turning chops every 5 minutes. Transfer to serving plate; let stand 5 minutes before serving. Serve with Watermelon and Radish Relish, if desired. Makes 4 servings.

Per serving: 320 calories, 18.5 g total fat, 6 g saturated fat, 101 mg cholesterol, 440 mg sodium, 1 g carbohydrates, 35 g protein, 46 mg calcium, 0 g fiber

barbecue baby back ribs

These ribs are seasoned with a dry rub and allowed to marinate overnight. Then they're slowly cooked in the oven before they are slapped on the grill just before serving for that smoky flavor. We used the favorite cut of rib aficionados, pork back ribs, because they are meaty and easy to handle. Plan on 1 pound per person for great finger-lickin' eating.

Prep time: 10 minutes plus marinating
Baking time: 1 hour • Grilling time: 10 minutes

SPICE RUB:
- 2 tablespoons paprika
- 2 tablespoons firmly packed brown sugar
- 1 tablespoon salt
- 1 tablespoon ground cumin
- 1 tablespoon smoked jalapeño flakes* or
    - 1 canned chipotle chile in adobo sauce and
    - 1 tablespoon adobo sauce
- 2 teaspoons ground red pepper
- ½ teaspoon garlic powder

- 5 pounds pork back ribs (baby back ribs)

SAUCE:
- 2 tablespoons vegetable oil
- 1 jar (12 oz.) prepared barbecue sauce
- 3 sprigs fresh thyme

1. *Make spice rub:* Combine all ingredients in a small bowl. Rub spices on both sides of ribs. (If using chipotle chile in adobo sauce, finely chop with sauce. Combine with spices and rub onto ribs.) Transfer ribs to a jelly-roll pan and cover with plastic wrap. Marinate in the refrigerator 2 hours or overnight.

2. Heat oven to 300°F. Wrap ribs tightly in foil.

3. Return to clean jelly-roll pan. Bake 1 hour. Transfer drippings to a bowl. Skim off fat from drippings.

4. Heat grill. Oil grill. Remove ribs from foil. Grill over medium-high heat 10 minutes, turning ribs every 2 to 3 minutes and brushing each side with some of the reserved drippings. Serve immediately with warm sauce. Makes 4 to 6 servings.

5. *Make sauce:* Heat oil in small saucepan over medium heat 1 minute. Add barbecue sauce and thyme sprigs; cook 2 to 3 minutes. Remove thyme. Makes 1 cup.

*Note: Jalapeno flakes are available through Chile Today, Hot Tamale (800-468-7377).

Per serving: 960 calories, 73 g total fat, 25.5 g saturated fat, 261 mg cholesterol, 2,179 mg sodium, 17 g carbohydrates, 56 g protein, 139 mg calcium, 1 g fiber

m e n u

celebrate summer backyard barbecue

FRESH SPINACH DIP
page 92

BARBECUE BABY BACK RIBS
left

CREAMY COLESLAW
page 114

DELI BAKED BEANS
RASPBERRY-APRICOT TARTS
page 160

PALE ALE AND ICED TEA

jerk pork

Jerk is a seasoning used throughout the Caribbean islands for meat, poultry and fish. This pork is a "double" jerk, first seasoned with an American-influenced dry rub, then brushed with a prepared barbecue sauce after the meat is grilled. Look for fruit-based barbecue sauces, widely available in supermarkets and specialty stores. We used two of our favorites; both lend a moderate amount of heat. Pictured on page 125.

Prep time: 10 minutes • Grilling time: 20 to 30 minutes
Microwave used

DRY RUB:

- **1 tablespoon allspice**
- **2 teaspoons nutmeg**
- **2 teaspoons cinnamon**
- **2 teaspoons sugar**
- **1½ teaspoons salt**
- **½ teaspoon habañero chile powder* or ground red pepper**

- **2 packages (2 lbs. each) pork tenderloins (4 tenderloins)**
- **1 tablespoon olive oil**
  Assorted sauces (such as American Spoon Foods' Pumpkin Chipotle Roasting Sauce or Porcupine Island Company's Cranberry Honey BBQ Sauce) (see Sauce Source tip, page 146)
  Fresh rosemary sprigs and lime wedges, for garnish (optional)

1. Heat grill.

2. *Make dry rub:* Combine allspice, nutmeg, cinnamon, sugar, salt and habañero powder in a cup. Brush tenderloins with oil; sprinkle evenly with dry rub. *(Can be made ahead. Cover and refrigerate overnight.)*

3. Oil grill; add tenderloins and grill over medium heat 15 to 20 minutes, turning once. Brush each tenderloin with ¾ cup of the desired sauce and grill 5 to 10 minutes more, until an instant-read meat thermometer inserted into thickest section of each tenderloin registers 155°F. Let stand 5 minutes before serving.

4. Meanwhile, transfer ½ cup of each sauce to a microwaveproof cup; microwave on High 1 minute, just until warm. Transfer tenderloins to cutting board; slice and arrange on a serving platter with the same sauce you basted them with. Garnish with the rosemary sprigs and lime wedges, if desired. Makes 8 servings.

*Note: Habañero chile powder may be purchased from Chile Today, Hot Tamale (800-468-7377).

Per serving: 330 calories, 14.5 g total fat, 5 g saturated fat, 143 mg cholesterol, 536 mg sodium, 2 g carbohydrates, 46 g protein, 21 mg calcium, 0 g fiber

chipotle-cascabel roasted pork with sweet potatoes

The Chipotle-Cascabel Cooking Salsa from Frontera Foods (see note for source) gives the meat a smoky-sweet chile flavor without too much heat. A portion of the salsa is spooned onto the pork tenderloin during roasting; then more salsa is combined with fresh orange juice and spooned over the tenderloin for a fabulous finish.

Prep time: 15 minutes • Baking time: 24 to 30 minutes
Microwave used

- **2 pounds sweet potatoes, peeled**
- **1 tablespoon olive oil**
- **½ teaspoon salt, divided**
- **1 pork tenderloin (1 lb.)**
- **¼ teaspoon freshly ground pepper**
- **6 tablespoons Frontera Chipotle-Cascabel Cooking Salsa,* divided**
- **1 tablespoon butter or margarine, cut up**
- **¼ teaspoon grated orange peel**
- **3 tablespoons fresh orange juice**
  Finely chopped fresh parsley, for garnish (optional)

1. Adjust rack to upper third of oven. Heat oven to 475°F.

2. Cut potatoes in half lengthwise, then in half crosswise. Cut each piece into 3 spears. Toss with oil and ¼ teaspoon of the salt on a jelly-roll pan.

3. Sprinkle pork with remaining ¼ teaspoon salt and the pepper. Place on pan with potatoes, spreading potatoes around pork. Roast pork and potatoes 12 minutes.

4. Spoon 3 tablespoons of the cooking salsa on top of pork; return to oven and roast 10 to 15 minutes more, until an instant-read meat thermometer inserted 1½ inches into center of pork registers 155°F. Wrap pork in a sheet of foil and set aside.

5. Toss potatoes with butter and orange peel and bake 2 to 3 minutes more, until heated through.

6. Meanwhile, microwave remaining 3 tablespoons cooking salsa and orange juice in a microwaveproof cup on High 2 minutes.

7. Slice pork and arrange on serving platter with potatoes. Spoon warmed cooking salsa over pork; sprinkle with parsley, if desired. Makes 4 servings.

Note: Available in most supermarkets or from Frontera (800-509-4441).

Per serving: 445 calories, 9.5 g total fat, 3.5 g saturated fat, 75 mg cholesterol, 323 mg sodium, 58 g carbohydrates, 31 g protein, 59 mg calcium, 7 g fiber

country captain

No wonder this is a favorite for entertaining. It's loaded with everybody's favorites, like tender chicken, peppers, tomatoes and raisins. This recipe can be doubled for a larger crowd. Serve the saucy chicken with rice to soak up the delicious juices.

Prep time: 50 minutes • Baking time: 1 hour

CURRY MIX:

- 1 tablespoon curry powder
- ½ tablespoon ground cumin
- 1 teaspoon salt
- ½ teaspoon coriander
- ½ teaspoon cinnamon
- ½ teaspoon dried thyme
- ¼ teaspoon turmeric
- ¼ teaspoon ground red pepper
- ¼ teaspoon freshly ground black pepper

- ½ cup all-purpose flour
- 1½ teaspoons salt
- ¼ teaspoon freshly ground pepper
- 6 chicken thighs

- 3 whole chicken breasts, split
- 3 teaspoons olive oil, divided
- 2 cups chopped onions
- 1 large red bell pepper, chopped
- 1 large green bell pepper, chopped
- 1 tablespoon minced garlic
- 2 cans (16 oz. each) diced tomatoes
- 1 can (14½ oz.) chicken broth
- ½ cup raisins or currants
- ½ cup slivered almonds, toasted
  Cooked rice (optional)

1. *Make curry mix:* Combine all ingredients in a small bowl; set aside.

2. Heat oven to 375°F. Combine flour, salt and pepper in a large bowl. Coat chicken pieces in flour mixture, shaking off excess. Heat 1½ teaspoons of the oil in a 12-inch nonstick skillet over medium-high heat. Add chicken thighs, skin sides down, and cook 5 minutes per side, until browned. Transfer to an 8-quart Dutch oven. Repeat with the remaining 1½ teaspoons oil and chicken breasts. Drain off all but 3 tablespoons drippings from the skillet. Transfer 1 tablespoon drippings to a cup.

3. Add onions and bell peppers to skillet; cook 6 to 8 minutes, until softened. Add garlic, curry mix and reserved 1 tablespoon drippings; cook 1 minute. Transfer to Dutch oven. Stir in tomatoes, broth and raisins. Bring to boil. Cover and bake 1 hour, stirring once halfway through. Using a slotted spoon, transfer chicken to a large bowl. When cool enough to handle, remove meat from bones and tear into large pieces. Return chicken to Dutch oven and heat through. *(Can be made ahead. Cool. Transfer to airtight containers and freeze up to 2 weeks. Thaw overnight in refrigerator. Remove any fat from surface. Transfer to Dutch oven and let stand at room temperature 1 hour. Heat over medium-high heat, stirring frequently, 20 to 30 minutes, until heated through and bubbly.)* Sprinkle with almonds. Serve with rice, if desired. Makes 6 servings.

Per serving: 685 calories, 35.5 g total fat, 8.5 g saturated fat, 171 mg cholesterol, 1,630 mg sodium, 37 g carbohydrates, 53 g protein, 152 mg calcium, 5 g fiber

caribbean chicken and beef skewers

Chicken and beef skewers never fail to please a crowd. For fun, we used edible sugar cane sticks for skewers. If you like spicy foods, double the green pepper sauce in the rub. If you choose to do both chicken and beef, double the rub. We tried several of the interesting sauces available nationwide. Check the box above for mail-order sources. Pictured on page 122.

Prep time: 30 minutes • Grilling time: 8 to 10 minutes

2	packages (4 oz. each) sugar cane sticks* or 20 (6-inch) wooden or metal skewers
1½	pounds boneless, skinless chicken breasts or 2 pounds boneless beef sirloin
1	tablespoon safflower or vegetable oil
1½	teaspoons green pepper sauce
1	teaspoon minced garlic
¾	teaspoon dried thyme
½	teaspoon salt
½	teaspoon cinnamon
	Whole fresh chiles, for garnish (optional)

Assorted sauces (such as Bobby Flay's Smoked Yellow Pepper Sauce, Earth & Vine Provisions Red Bell Pepper and Ancho Chili Jam or Sweet Sides Blueberry BBQ Sauce) (see tip, left)

1. Cut each sugar cane stick in half crosswise with sharp heavy-duty scissors or knife. Then cut one end of each to form a point (or soak wooden skewers in enough water to cover in shallow pan 30 minutes).

2. Cut the chicken into 1¼-inch chunks (about 40 pieces), or cut beef into ¼-inch-thick slices (about 40 slices).

3. Toss chicken (or beef) with oil, pepper sauce, garlic, thyme, salt and cinnamon. *(Can be made ahead. Cover and refrigerate overnight.)*

4. Heat grill or grill pan.

5. Thread 1 piece of chicken or beef on each sugar cane stick or 2 pieces onto each skewer. Grill chicken over medium-high heat 8 to 10 minutes, until cooked through, turning as they brown (for beef, grill 3 minutes per side, until browned). Garnish with fresh chiles, if desired. Serve with assorted sauces. Makes 20 servings.

*Note: Can be purchased through Frieda's Finest (800-421-9477).

Per serving (chicken): 45 calories, 1 g total fat, 0 g saturated fat, 20 mg cholesterol, 85 mg sodium, 0 g carbohydrates, 8 g protein, 6 mg calcium, 0 g fiber
Per serving (beef): 65 calories, 4 g total fat, 1.5 g saturated fat, 21 mg cholesterol, 78 mg sodium, 0 g carbohydrates, 6 g protein, 5 mg calcium, 0 g fiber

grilled herb chicken

To reduce grilling time, the chicken is butterflied and flattened by removing the backbone. Pictured on page 123.

Prep time: 15 minutes • Grilling time: 30 minutes

1	tablespoon chopped fresh rosemary
1	tablespoon chopped fresh thyme leaves
1	tablespoon chopped fresh sage
2	tablespoons plus 1 teaspoon extra-virgin olive oil, divided

1 tablespoon chopped garlic

1 teaspoon grated lemon peel

1 teaspoon salt, divided

½ teaspoon freshly ground pepper

1 whole chicken (3¼ to 3½ lbs.) rinsed and
   patted dry

1. Combine herbs, 2 tablespoons of the oil, garlic, lemon peel and ½ teaspoon of the salt in a bowl. Combine remaining ½ teaspoon salt and the pepper in cup. Set both aside.

2. Using poultry shears or a large knife, cut chicken along both sides of backbone; discard backbone. Turn chicken breast side up, and push down the breastbone to flatten slightly. Gently lift skin from chicken. Spread herb mixture evenly under skin.

3. Heat grill. Brush chicken, skin side up, with remaining 1 teaspoon oil. Sprinkle both sides of chicken with salt and pepper mixture. Arrange chicken, skin side down, on grill. Close lid and grill over medium heat 10 minutes. Turn chicken and grill 20 minutes more, until an instant-read meat thermometer inserted in thigh registers 180°F., turning every 10 minutes.

4. Transfer chicken to a cutting board. Let stand 5 minutes before cutting. Makes 4 servings.

Per serving: 280 calories, 13.5 g total fat, 3 g saturated fat, 113 mg cholesterol, 399 mg sodium, 1 g carbohydrates, 37 g protein, 25 mg calcium, 0 g fiber

grilled tex-mex chicken and beef kabobs EASY

Prep time: 40 minutes plus marinating
Grilling time: 40 to 50 minutes

MARINADE:

⅔ cup olive oil

½ cup fresh lime juice

2 tablespoons minced garlic

4 teaspoons ground cumin

4 teaspoons coriander

1 teaspoon salt

1 teaspoon freshly ground pepper

½ teaspoon allspice

■

4 whole boneless, skinless chicken breasts
   (about 2 lbs.), split and cut into 2-inch
   pieces

12 boneless, skinless chicken thighs (about
   2½ lbs.), halved

1 large flank steak (2½ to 3 lbs.), cut crosswise
   into ½-inch-thick strips

44 12-inch wooden skewers

6 large bell peppers (2 each yellow, red and
   green), stemmed, seeded and cut into
   8 wedges each

4 medium onions, cut into 8 wedges each

24 (7-inch) flour tortillas

½ of a head romaine lettuce, shredded
   Garden Salsa (see recipe, page 131)

1. *Make marinade:* Whisk together all ingredients in a bowl.

2. Combine chicken breasts and thighs in a shallow glass dish. Add ⅔ cup of the marinade, tossing to coat. Coat steak with remaining marinade in another shallow dish. Cover and marinate 1 hour at room temperature. *(Can be made ahead. Cover and refrigerate up to 24 hours. Remove from refrigerator 1 hour before grilling.)* Soak skewers in water 30 minutes before using.

3. Heat grill. Loosely thread chicken pieces on double skewers. Loosely thread beef on single skewers. Thread bell peppers and onions separately on single skewers. Place skewers on grill rack, leaving 1 inch between skewers. Grill vegetables over medium heat 20 to 25 minutes, until evenly browned and tender, turning every 5 minutes. Transfer to a serving platter and cover with foil while grilling remaining kabobs. Grill chicken 15 to 20 minutes, until cooked through at center, turning every 5 minutes. Grill steak 7 to 10 minutes for medium-rare, turning halfway through. Heat tortillas on grill 1 to 2 minutes, until warm.

4. Just before serving kabobs, grill tortillas until toasted. Serve kabobs with grilled tortillas, romaine lettuce and Garden Salsa. Makes 16 servings.

Per serving: 525 calories, 21 g total fat, 5 g saturated fat, 120 mg cholesterol, 495 mg sodium, 34 g carbohydrates, 48 g protein, 105 mg calcium, 4 g fiber

near east chicken with cucumber relish ⊘ EASY

Best known for its use as a baking spice, warm, spicy-sweet cardamom is also common in Indian dishes such as this simple marinated chicken with yogurt and garlic. Cardamom is available either in pods or ground. The pods offer the most flavor, as the seeds begin to lose their essential oils as soon as they're ground.

Prep time: 10 minutes plus marinating
Grilling time: 20 minutes

- 1 tablespoon green cardamom pods (about 20) or 1 tablespoon ground cardamom
- ½ teaspoon salt
- ¼ teaspoon freshly ground pepper
- 2½ pounds skinless chicken thighs
- 1 container (8 oz.) plain yogurt
- 6 quarter-size slices fresh ginger
- 4 garlic cloves, crushed
- 1 tablespoon sliced jalapeño chile (see tip, page 92)
- ½ teaspoon paprika

CUCUMBER RELISH:

- ½ of an English (seedless) cucumber, peeled and sliced (about 1 cup)
- 1 cup thinly sliced fennel
- ½ cup thinly sliced onion, rinsed under cold water
- 1 tablespoon cider vinegar
- 2 teaspoons olive oil
- ½ teaspoon salt
- ½ teaspoon sugar
- Pinch cumin seed

1. Toast cardamom pods in small skillet, shaking pan occasionally, over low heat 2 to 3 minutes, until fragrant. (For ground cardamom, toast 1 minute.) Transfer to plate and cool. Pinch pods with fingers to open slightly.

2. Sprinkle salt and pepper over chicken. Combine yogurt, ginger, garlic, jalapeño, paprika and cardamom in a large bowl. Add chicken, turning chicken pieces several times until well coated. Cover bowl with plastic wrap and marinate chicken in the refrigerator overnight.

3. Remove chicken from refrigerator 30 minutes before grilling. Drain chicken, discarding marinade.

4. *Make cucumber relish:* Combine all ingredients in medium bowl.

5. Heat covered grill. Oil grill. Arrange chicken on cooking grate. Cover grill and grill chicken over medium heat 20 minutes, until chicken is lightly charred and an instant-read meat thermometer registers 180°F. when inserted in thickest part of chicken, turning chicken every 5 minutes. Serve with cucumber relish. Makes 4 servings.

Per serving: 335 calories, 12.5 g total fat, 3.5 g saturated fat, 180 mg cholesterol, 797 mg sodium, 10 g carbohydrates, 44 g protein, 118 mg calcium, 2 g fiber

relleno-stuffed chicken with black beans ⊘ EASY

Serving chicken for company is a safe choice, since almost everyone likes it. We removed the bone from this stuffed chicken breast and left the skin on for extra juiciness and flavor.

Prep time: 30 minutes • Baking time: 25 to 30 minutes

- 1½ cups shredded Monterey Jack cheese
- 3 tablespoons minced green onions
- 4 teaspoons chopped fresh cilantro
- 1 teaspoon minced garlic
- ¾ teaspoon ground cumin
- 8 boneless chicken breast halves with skin (about 3½ lbs.)
- 4 teaspoons olive oil
- ½ teaspoon salt
- ½ teaspoon freshly ground pepper

BLACK BEAN SALAD:

- 3 cans (15 oz. each) black beans, drained and rinsed
- 4 plum tomatoes, seeded and chopped (2 cups)
- 2 avocados, peeled, pitted and diced
- ½ cup sliced green onions
- 2 tablespoons fresh lime juice
- 1 tablespoon vegetable oil

½ teaspoon ground cumin

½ teaspoon salt

¼ teaspoon freshly ground pepper

CREAMY CILANTRO DRESSING:

2 cups lightly packed fresh cilantro leaves or
2 cups fresh parsley plus 2 tablespoons
dried cilantro

1 cup sour cream

½ cup mayonnaise

2 tablespoons fresh lime juice

¼ teaspoon minced garlic

¼ teaspoon grated lime peel

Salt

Freshly ground pepper

■

Small romaine lettuce leaves

1. Heat oven to 425°F. Combine cheese, minced
green onions, cilantro, garlic and cumin in a medium
bowl. Loosen skin from 1 chicken breast half and
spoon 2 tablespoons of the cheese filling under skin.
Repeat with remaining chicken breasts and filling.
Arrange stuffed breasts, skin sides up, in a single layer
in a broiler pan or shallow roasting pan.

2. Drizzle chicken with oil and sprinkle with salt
and pepper. Bake 25 to 30 minutes, until skin is
golden and juices run clear when chicken is pierced
with a fork. Let stand 5 minutes before slicing.

3. *Make black bean salad:* Combine black beans,
tomatoes, avocados, green onions, lime juice,
vegetable oil, cumin, salt and pepper in a medium
bowl. Toss to coat well. Makes 8 cups.

4. *Make creamy cilantro dressing:* Combine cilantro,
sour cream, mayonnaise, lime juice and garlic in a
blender; blend until smooth. Stir in lime peel. Salt
and pepper to taste. Cover and refrigerate until
ready to use. Makes 1½ cups.

5. *To serve:* Cut each chicken breast into ½-inch-
thick slices. Arrange some romaine lettuce on each
of 8 dinner plates, then top with 1 cup of the black
bean salad, 1 sliced chicken breast half and
3 tablespoons of the creamy cilantro dressing.
Makes 8 servings.

Per serving: 740 calories, 46.5 g total fat, 15 g saturated fat,
167 mg cholesterol, 1,062 mg sodium, 27 g carbohydrates,
60 g protein, 323 mg calcium, 10 g fiber

chicken
san remese

*This skillet dinner, from That's Amore in Rockville,
Maryland, is perfect for a dinner party. Bottled marinara
sauce, frozen artichoke hearts, bagged fresh spinach and
cheese tortellini cut down on prep time.*

Prep time: 15 minutes • Cooking time: 23 minutes

4 boneless, skinless chicken breast halves
(4 oz. each)

½ teaspoon salt

¼ teaspoon freshly ground pepper

2 tablespoons flour

1 tablespoon butter or margarine

½ cup (2 oz.) diced pancetta or thick-sliced
bacon

½ cup diced onion

1 bag (10 oz.) fresh spinach

½ pound sliced white mushrooms

3 tablespoons Marsala wine

1 cup heavy or whipping cream

3 tablespoons prepared marinara sauce

1 package (9 oz.) frozen artichoke hearts,
thawed

1/2 pound prepared cheese tortellini, cooked
according to package directions

1. Sprinkle chicken with salt and pepper; lightly
coat with flour. Melt butter in a 12-inch nonstick
skillet over medium-high heat. Add chicken and
cook 4 minutes per side, until golden; transfer to
a plate.

2. Add pancetta and onion to same skillet; cook,
stirring frequently, 3 minutes, until onion is golden
and pancetta is crisp. Add spinach and mushrooms;
cook 3 minutes, until spinach is wilted. Add
Marsala and bring to boil. Stir in cream and
marinara sauce; stir in artichokes. Reduce heat
slightly and simmer 7 minutes.

3. Return chicken to skillet; spoon sauce and
vegetables over chicken and cook 2 minutes more,
until heated through. Stir in hot tortellini. Divide
chicken, sauce and pasta among 4 dinner plates.
Makes 4 servings.

Per serving: 710 calories, 39.5 g total fat, 20.5 g saturated fat,
188 mg cholesterol, 869 mg sodium, 46 g carbohydrates,
42 g protein, 213 mg calcium, 8 g fiber

marinated turkey breast with prosciutto

Here's a lovely (and delicious) addition to your buffet table. Tip: Ask the butcher at your local meat market or supermarket to bone the turkey for you.

Prep time: 35 minutes plus marinating and standing
Cooking time: 1 hour 27 minutes
Microwave used

- ½ of a boneless, skinless turkey breast (3 to 3½ lbs.)

MARINADE:
- ⅓ cup olive oil
- ¼ cup fresh lemon juice
- ¼ cup chopped fresh basil leaves
- 1 tablespoon chopped fresh oregano
- 2 teaspoons minced garlic
- ½ teaspoon salt
- ¼ teaspoon freshly ground pepper

  •

- 4 ounces thinly sliced prosciutto
- 1 cup loosely packed basil leaves
- ¼ cup olive oil

SAUCE:
- 1 can (14½ oz.) chicken broth
- ¼ cup (0.3 oz.) dried porcini mushrooms, rinsed well

  ▪

  Fresh oregano sprigs, for garnish (optional)

1. Butterfly and pound turkey breast ¾ inch thick between 2 sheets of plastic wrap.

2. *Make marinade:* Whisk together oil, lemon juice, basil, oregano, garlic, salt and pepper in a bowl. Pour one-third of marinade into a 13×9-inch glass baking dish; add turkey and pour remaining marinade over turkey, spreading to coat. Cover and refrigerate 2 to 4 hours, turning once.

3. Place turkey, skin side down, on work surface. Arrange prosciutto down center of turkey and top with basil. Starting from one long side, roll up turkey jelly-roll style. Secure ends with toothpicks and tie roll with string at ½-inch intervals. Return to marinade in dish; cover and refrigerate overnight.

4. Heat oven to 350°F. Dip an 18×8-inch double thickness of cheesecloth in the ¼ cup olive oil and drape over turkey to cover. Bake the turkey 1 hour 15 minutes, until an instant-read meat thermometer inserted in the center registers 160°F., basting every 15 minutes. Let turkey stand at least 10 minutes.

5. *Make sauce:* Meanwhile, combine chicken broth, porcini mushrooms and any defatted turkey drippings in a saucepan. Bring mixture to boil; reduce heat and simmer 10 minutes. Remove mushrooms with a slotted spoon; finely chop and set aside. Strain sauce through a strainer lined with a double thickness of cheesecloth into a 2-cup glass measure or a small microwaveproof bowl. Add mushrooms and microwave sauce on High 1 to 2 minutes, until hot.

6. Discard toothpicks and string from turkey and cut into ¼-inch-thick slices. Arrange slices on a serving platter and garnish with oregano sprigs, if desired. Serve warm with mushroom sauce. Makes 8 servings.

Per serving: 340 calories, 15.5 g total fat, 2.5 g saturated fat, 115 mg cholesterol, 756 mg sodium, 2 g carbohydrates, 47 g protein, 37 mg calcium, 0 g fiber

grilled pizza

Yes, you can grill dough on the barbecue, and no, it will not fall through the grate! Tip: The dough cooks quickly, so have all the topping ingredients ready before you start the grill. Pictured on page 127.

Prep time: 30 minutes plus rising
Grilling time: 12 to 14 minutes

DOUGH:
- 1 package active dry yeast (do not use rapid rise yeast)
  Sugar
- 1 cup warm water (105°F. to 110°F.)
- 2 tablespoons extra-virgin olive oil
- 3 cups all-purpose flour
- 1 teaspoon salt
- ½ teaspoon freshly ground pepper

  ▪

  Cornmeal
- 2 tablespoons extra-virgin olive oil

MARGHERITA TOPPINGS:

- **4** ounces fresh mozzarella cheese, thinly sliced
- **1** medium tomato, sliced and blotted dry
- **⅓** cup thinly sliced fresh basil leaves

HAM AND CHEESE TOPPINGS:

- **2** ounces Camembert or Brie cheese, cut into ½-inch pieces
- **1** ounce thinly sliced prosciutto or smoked ham
- **1** tablespoon coarsely chopped fresh sage

PROVENÇAL TOPPINGS:

- **2** ounces goat cheese, crumbled (about ½ cup loosely filled)
- **⅓** cup pitted oil-cured olives, coarsely chopped
- **½** of a small yellow bell pepper, thinly sliced (¼ cup)
- **½** cup chopped tomatoes

MESCLUN TOPPINGS:

- **1** teaspoon chopped fresh rosemary
- **½** cup freshly grated Parmesan cheese
- **¼** cup mesclun salad greens
- **1** teaspoon extra-virgin olive oil

1. *Make dough:* Sprinkle yeast and a pinch of sugar over water in small bowl. Let stand 5 minutes, until yeast is bubbly. Stir in oil.

2. Pulse together flour, 1 teaspoon sugar, the salt and pepper in a food processor. With motor running, pour yeast mixture through feed tube; process 1 minute. Place dough in a greased bowl, turning to grease top. Cover and let rise in a warm draft-free place until doubled in bulk, 1 hour. *(Can be made ahead. Cover and let rise overnight in refrigerator.)*

3. Punch down dough. Divide dough into 4 equal pieces. Cover and let rest 15 minutes.

4. Heat grill for indirect grilling. On a lightly floured surface, roll each piece of dough into an 8-inch circle. Stack dough between sheets of waxed paper that have been lightly dusted with cornmeal. Brush tops of dough with oil. Grill dough, oiled sides down, over medium-high heat 6 minutes, until browned and firm. Transfer dough to clean surface and arrange desired toppings on grilled side of dough.

5. Arrange your choice of toppings on each individual pizza as follows:

- *Margherita:* mozzarella cheese, sliced tomatoes and basil
- *Ham and Cheese:* Camembert, prosciutto and sage
- *Provençal:* goat cheese, olives, bell peppers and chopped tomatoes
- *Mesclun:* rosemary and Parmesan cheese. Toss mesclun greens with oil in a small bowl. After pizza is grilled, arrange salad on top.

6. Return pizza to grill and grill 6 to 8 minutes, until underside is browned and cheese is melted. Makes 4 servings.

Per serving Margherita: 580 calories, 22 g total fat, 6.5 g saturated fat, 25 mg cholesterol, 704 mg sodium, 77 g carbohydrates, 17 g protein, 180 mg calcium, 4 g fiber
Per serving Ham and Cheese: 540 calories, 19.5 g total fat, 4.5 g saturated fat, 16 mg cholesterol, 836 mg sodium, 76 g carbohydrates, 16 g protein, 74 mg calcium, 3 g fiber
Per serving Provençal: 580 calories, 23.5 g total fat, 5.5 g saturated fat, 11 mg cholesterol, 1,051 mg sodium, 78 g carbohydrates, 14 g protein, 66 mg calcium, 4 g fiber
Per serving Mesclun: 550 calories, 20 g total fat, 4.5 g saturated fat, 10 mg cholesterol, 813 mg sodium, 76 g carbohydrates, 16 g protein, 186 mg calcium, 3 g fiber

---

test kitchen tip

pizza pizazz

Here are some more pizza toppings to try:

BBQ CHICKEN: Spread your favorite bottled barbecue sauce on the grilled side of dough. Top with deli-roasted chicken, red onion and shredded provolone.

HAWAIIAN: Lightly top the crust with tomato-based pizza sauce. Then add drained pineapple cubes, slices of Canadian bacon and shredded mozzarella and, if desired, Parmesan.

VEGGIE: Sauté your favorite vegetables (mushrooms, zucchini and eggplant make good choices) in olive oil, salt and pepper. Brush the crust with additional olive oil, top with the veggies and finish with a sprinkling of freshly grated Parmesan.

caribbean snapper LOW FAT

Spicy and sweet play off each other in island cooking. The sweet potatoes and snapper balance the heat of the two kinds of peppers. All are wrapped together in foil or parchment for a great steamed dish.

Prep time: 25 minutes • Baking time: 17 to 18 minutes
Microwave used

- **1 pound sweet potatoes, peeled and cut into ½-inch-thick slices**
- **1 tablespoon water**
- **8 tablespoons fresh lime juice, divided**
- **½ teaspoon salt, divided**
- **Olive oil**
- **½ cup finely chopped onion**
- **¼ teaspoon freshly ground black pepper**
- **⅛ teaspoon ground red pepper**
- **4 snapper fillets (8 oz. each), each cut in half crosswise**

GREEN SAUCE:
- **2 tablespoons olive oil**
- **1 cup fresh cilantro leaves with stems**
- **1 teaspoon grated fresh ginger**
- **¼ teaspoon salt**

1. Arrange oven racks in upper and lower thirds of oven. Heat oven to 400°F.

2. Spread potatoes in a 9-inch glass pie plate; add water. Cover with plastic wrap, turning back 1 section to vent. Microwave the potatoes on High 2 minutes. Let stand until cool enough to handle. *(Can be made ahead. Cover and refrigerate overnight.)* Cut potatoes into ½-inch dice, then toss with 1 tablespoon of the lime juice and ¼ teaspoon of the salt in pie plate.

3. Heat 1 teaspoon oil in a large nonstick skillet over high heat. Add onion and cook 2 minutes, until lightly charred at edges. Combine remaining ¼ teaspoon salt and peppers in a cup.

4. Tear off eight 12-inch sheets of parchment paper or heavy-duty foil. Lightly brush center (6-inch square) of each sheet with oil. Divide potatoes among centers of prepared sheets; top each with a piece of fish. Divide onion over fish, then sprinkle with the salt-and-pepper mixture. Divide and drizzle remaining 7 tablespoons lime juice over each. Fold up each sheet to make a package, leaving an air pocket over fish. Arrange packages on two large cookie sheets and bake 17 to 18 minutes, just until fish flakes with a fork in center of fillets and potatoes are tender.

5. *Make green sauce:* Meanwhile, puree all ingredients in a blender or mini food processor. Carefully open packages and serve with green sauce. Makes 8 servings.

Per serving: 200 calories, 5.5 g total fat, 1 g saturated fat, 42 mg cholesterol, 295 mg sodium, 12 g carbohydrates, 24 g protein, 51 mg calcium, 1 g fiber

wild salmon fillets EASY

Alaskan salmon, caught in the wild, is not as fatty as farm-raised salmon and, therefore, cooks a bit faster. To guarantee perfect results, we recommend using a timer. Pictured on page 122.

Prep time: 15 minutes plus marinating
Grilling time: 8 to 10 minutes

MARINADE:
- **½ cup sake**
- **2 tablespoons rice wine vinegar**
- **2 tablespoons lite soy sauce**
- **1 tablespoon vegetable oil**
- **1 tablespoon miso paste**
- **1 teaspoon whole black peppercorns, crushed**

- **6 Alaskan salmon fillets with skin (5 to 6 oz. each)**
- **1 tablespoon vegetable oil**
- **12 sprigs fresh tarragon**

DRESSING:
- **2 tablespoons rice wine vinegar**
- **4 teaspoons lite soy sauce**
- **1 tablespoon sugar**
- **½ teaspoon miso paste**
- **1 tablespoon vegetable oil**

- **Fresh herb sprigs, for garnish (optional)**

1. *Make marinade:* Combine all ingredients in a small bowl.

2. Arrange salmon fillets in a single layer in baking dish. Pour marinade over salmon and cover dish with plastic wrap. Marinate in the refrigerator 2 hours or overnight, turning fillets once.

3. Heat grill. Oil grill. Remove fillets from marinade, reserving marinade. Brush skin side of each fillet with oil. Arrange fillets, skin sides down, on grill; top each fillet with 2 sprigs of tarragon. Brush salmon with reserved marinade. Close lid and grill fillets over medium heat 8 to 10 minutes, just until fish flakes with a fork in center of fillets.

4. *Make dressing:* Meanwhile, whisk together all ingredients in small bowl.

5. Transfer salmon to large serving plate. Drizzle dressing evenly over the fish and garnish with fresh herb sprigs, if desired. Makes 6 servings.

Per serving: 340 calories, 22 g total fat, 4.5 g saturated fat, 94 mg cholesterol, 524 mg sodium, 5 g carbohydrates, 30 g protein, 47 mg calcium, 0 g fiber

spiced grilled trout (EASY)

Trout is often sold cleaned and whole, but most stores and fish departments in supermarkets will save you the extra step by filleting it at no charge. To ensure freshness, look for bright eyes and shiny skin.

Prep time: 15 minutes • Grilling time: 4 to 5 minutes

- **3 tablespoons coriander seeds**
- **1 tablespoon fennel seeds**
- **1 tablespoon cumin seeds**
- **1 teaspoon olive oil**
- **6 trout fillets (4 to 5 oz. each)**
- **Salt**
- **6 teaspoons butter or margarine**

1. Toast coriander, fennel and cumin in a medium skillet over medium-high heat until fragrant and slightly darkened, 1 to 2 minutes. Transfer to a mortar and pestle or electric spice grinder. Process until ground.

2. Heat grill. Oil grill.

3. Meanwhile, rub the 1 teaspoon oil over skin sides of fillets; sprinkle each with 1 teaspoon of the ground spices and ⅛ teaspoon salt. Arrange fillets on grill, skin sides down. Sprinkle top of each fillet with ½ teaspoon of the ground spices and a pinch of salt. Cover and grill over medium-high heat 4 to 5 minutes, just until fish flakes with a fork in center of fillets. Dot 1 teaspoon of the butter onto each fillet. With a large spatula, transfer fillets to a serving platter. Makes 6 servings.

Per serving: 225 calories, 13 g total fat, 4 g saturated fat, 76 mg cholesterol, 540 mg sodium, 2 g carbohydrates, 24 g protein, 91 mg calcium, 2 g fiber

---

test kitchen tip

fish tips

Fresh fish makes a healthy and satisfying meal. To best store and thaw it, follow these guidelines:

KEEPING FISH FRESH: To store fresh fish steaks and fillets, wrap each piece tightly in plastic wrap or in a sealed plastic storage bag. Place the wrapped fish in a colander set in a shallow dish. Fill the dish around the colander with ice. Place in the refrigerator and refrigerate (between 32°F. and 38°F.) up to 2 days, adding more ice as it melts. Never allow the fish to have direct contact with the ice or water, as this can affect flavor and texture.

THE DEEP FREEZE: If your fish is frozen, thaw it in the refrigerator, not at room temperature. (The same holds true for meat and poultry.)

shrimp salsa verde *EASY*

To keep shrimp from spinning when flipping on the grill, thread them on two skewers per serving. Tip: Soak the wooden skewers in water 30 minutes before cooking so they don't burn. Pictured on page 126.

Prep time: 20 minutes plus soaking
Grilling time: 4 to 8 minutes

- 20 **wooden skewers**

SALSA VERDE:

- 2 **cups fresh mint leaves**
- 1 **cup fresh flat-leaf parsley leaves**
- 3 **anchovy fillets, drained**
- 2 **shallots, peeled and quartered**
- ⅓ **cup olive oil**
- 2 **tablespoons water**
- ¼ **teaspoon freshly ground pepper**
  Pinch salt

- 1 **pound large shrimp, peeled and deveined, with tails intact**
  Cucumber Relish (see recipe, page 157) (optional)

1. Soak 20 wooden skewers in enough water to cover for 30 minutes.

2. *Make salsa verde:* Puree all ingredients in blender or food processor until smooth. Set aside. *(Can be made ahead. Cover and refrigerate overnight. Remove from refrigerator 30 minutes before grilling.)*

3. Thread 3 shrimp on 1 skewer; thread another skewer through shrimp in the opposite direction. Repeat with remaining shrimp and skewers. Brush both sides of shrimp with salsa verde. *(Can be assembled ahead. Cover and refrigerate up to 4 hours.)*

4. Heat grill. Grill shrimp over medium-high heat 2 to 4 minutes, until shrimp turn pink and are lightly charred. Turn skewers and grill 2 to 4 minutes more. Serve with Cucumber Relish, if desired. Makes 4 servings.

Per serving without cucumber relish: 245 calories, 15.5 g total fat, 2 g saturated fat, 141 mg cholesterol, 255 mg sodium, 5 g carbohydrates, 21 g protein, 137 mg calcium, 3 g fiber

basil shrimp and noodles *EASY* *LOW FAT*

In this scrumptious Asian curry, we toss pungent basil-chili paste with quick-cooking angel hair pasta, creamy coconut milk and seared shrimp.

Prep time: 15 minutes · Cooking time: 10 to 15 minutes

CHILI PASTE:

- 2 **cups packed fresh basil leaves (3 oz.) or 2 cups packed fresh parsley leaves and 1 tablespoon dried basil**
- 2 **tablespoons water**
- 1 **tablespoon fresh lime juice**
- 1 **tablespoon Asian chile paste**
- 1 **garlic clove, crushed**
- 1 **teaspoon grated fresh ginger**

- 3 **teaspoons olive oil, divided**
- 1 **pound large shrimp, peeled and deveined**
- ½ **cup coconut milk**
- ½ **cup chicken broth**
- 1 **teaspoon grated lime peel**
- ½ **teaspoon salt**
- 8 **ounces angel hair pasta, cooked according to package directions**

1. *Make chili paste:* Puree all ingredients in blender; transfer to small bowl. Remove ¼ cup of the paste and rub on shrimp; place in another bowl. Set both aside.

2. Heat 1½ teaspoons of the oil in large nonstick skillet over medium-high heat. Add half of the shrimp and cook 1 to 2 minutes per side, until golden brown. Transfer shrimp to a large plate. Wipe out skillet with paper towel; repeat with remaining 1½ teaspoons oil and shrimp.

3. Combine coconut milk, broth, lime peel, salt and remaining chili paste in same skillet; bring to boil over medium heat. Cook 2 to 3 minutes, until sauce thickens slightly. Remove skillet from heat; add hot pasta, tossing to coat.

4. Divide pasta among 4 shallow bowls; top each with shrimp. Serve immediately. Makes 4 servings.

Per serving: 420 calories, 13 g total fat, 6.5 g saturated fat, 140 mg cholesterol, 582 mg sodium, 47 g carbohydrates, 28 g protein, 98 mg calcium, 2 g fiber

vegetable curry

Serve this delicious curry with Roti (see recipe, page 159). Pictured on page 124.

Prep time: 20 minutes • Cooking time: 30 minutes

- 2 tablespoons vegetable oil
- 1½ cups chopped onions
- 1 tablespoon thinly sliced fresh ginger
- 1 tablespoon curry powder
- ½ teaspoon salt
- 1 pound plum tomatoes, coarsely chopped
- ¾ cup chicken broth
- ¾ pound green beans or 1 pound okra, trimmed and cut into 1-inch pieces
- 1 pound zucchini or yellow summer squash, cut into ¾-inch-thick pieces

1. Heat oil in a large, deep skillet over medium heat. Add onions and ginger and cook 5 minutes, until softened. Stir in curry and salt; cook 2 minutes. Add tomatoes; stir until they are coated with spices. Add broth; bring mixture to boil. Reduce heat to medium-low; stir in green beans and cook 10 minutes, until green beans are just tender. (If using okra, cook 15 minutes.)

2. Add zucchini. Cover skillet and simmer 8 to 10 minutes more, until squash is tender but still retains its shape. *(Can be made ahead. Transfer to a microwaveproof bowl and cool completely. Cover and refrigerate overnight. To reheat, microwave on High 5 to 6 minutes, stirring once halfway through.)* Makes 6 cups.

Per 1-cup serving: 50 calories, 2.5 g total fat, 0.5 g saturated fat, 0 mg cholesterol, 168 mg sodium, 7 g carbohydrates, 2 g protein, 23 mg calcium, 2 g fiber

pink beans and rice

Pictured on page 128.

Prep time: 20 minutes • Cooking time: 15 minutes

- 4 quarts water (16 cups)
- 1½ teaspoons salt, divided
- 1 cup long-grain rice
- 1 tablespoon vegetable oil
- 1 cup chopped onions
- 2 tablespoons chopped garlic
- ¼ teaspoon coriander
- ½ of a bay leaf
- 1 can (15 oz.) pink beans, drained and rinsed
- ½ cup chicken broth
  Sliced lime, for garnish (optional)

1. Bring water and 1 teaspoon of the salt to boil in a large Dutch oven. Add the rice; reduce heat to medium and gently boil 12 to 15 minutes, until tender but not soft. Drain. Transfer rice to a large cookie sheet and spread in a single layer. Cool.

2. Meanwhile, heat oil in a large skillet over medium-high heat. Add onions, garlic, coriander and bay leaf; cook 8 minutes, until onions are almost golden. Stir in beans, broth and remaining ½ teaspoon salt. Simmer 10 to 15 minutes, until beans are heated through and well seasoned.

3. Transfer rice to a large serving bowl. Stir in bean mixture. *(Can be made ahead. Cover and refrigerate overnight. Let the rice stand at room temperature 1 hour before serving.)* Garnish top with lime, if desired. Makes about 5 cups.

Per ½-cup serving: 120 calories, 2 g total fat, 0 g saturated fat, 0 mg cholesterol, 455 mg sodium, 22 g carbohydrates, 4 g protein, 22 mg calcium, 2 g fiber

---

test kitchen tip

fresh ginger

There are two types of fresh ginger: young and mature. Mature ginger is widely available in supermarkets. It has a tough skin, which is peeled to reveal the tender flesh. When selecting, be sure the skin is smooth. Young ginger, also known as spring ginger, for the most part can only be found in Asian markets during the spring. It has a paler, thinner skin and milder flavor than mature ginger and does not need to be peeled. Store fresh ginger well wrapped in the refrigerator with its skin on for up to 3 weeks, or freeze it for up to 6 months.

polenta gratin

This layered casserole combines polenta with vegetables and cheese and partners well with grilled meat.

Prep time: 50 minutes plus standing
Baking time: 35 minutes

- **4 cups milk**
- **1 cup yellow cornmeal**
- **⅔ cup freshly grated Parmesan cheese**
- **¼ cup chopped green onions**
- **2 tablespoons butter or margarine**
- **1 teaspoon salt, divided**
- **½ teaspoon freshly ground pepper, divided**
- **1 tablespoon olive oil**
- **3 carrots, halved, cut lengthwise into ¼-inch-thick slices**
- **1 garlic clove, finely chopped**
- **Water**
- **2 medium zucchini (¾ lb.), halved and cut lengthwise into ¼-inch-thick slices**
- **2 red bell peppers, cut into ¼-inch-thick strips**
- **2 teaspoons chopped fresh thyme**
- **1¼ cups shredded Gruyère cheese, divided**

1. Bring milk to boil in a heavy saucepan over medium-high heat. Reduce heat to very low and gradually whisk cornmeal into milk until smooth. Cook, stirring occasionally, 15 minutes. Stir in the Parmesan, onions, butter, ¾ teaspoon of the salt and ¼ teaspoon of the pepper. Spread in an 11×7-inch buttered baking dish.

2. Heat oil in a large skillet over medium-high heat. Add carrots, garlic and ⅓ cup water. Cover and cook 5 minutes. Add zucchini and bell peppers; cover and cook 5 minutes, until tender. Cook, uncovered, just until liquid evaporates, 1 to 2 minutes more, if needed. Add thyme and remaining ¼ teaspoon salt and pepper. Remove from heat. Sprinkle ¾ cup of the Gruyère cheese evenly over polenta. Arrange vegetables in an even layer over cheese. Top with remaining ½ cup Gruyère. *(Can be made ahead. Cover and refrigerate overnight.)*

3. Heat oven to 375°F. Bake 35 minutes, until heated through. Let stand 15 minutes before serving. Makes 10 servings.

Per serving: 240 calories, 12.5 g total fat, 7 g saturated fat, 34 mg cholesterol, 485 mg sodium, 21 g carbohydrates, 12 g protein, 369 mg calcium, 3 g fiber

moroccan-flavored carrots

It's the cumin that reveals this relish recipe's place of origin. The carrots are microwaved to soften slightly, then plunged into a bowl of ice water to prevent further cooking. Pictured on page 121.

Total prep time: 15 minutes plus standing
Microwave used

- **1 pound carrots, peeled and cut into ½-inch diagonal pieces**
- **2 tablespoons water**
- **2 tablespoons plus 2 teaspoons cider vinegar, divided**
- **¾ pound sweet onions, sliced**
- **1 tablespoon extra-virgin olive oil**
- **2 teaspoons ground cumin**
- **¾ teaspoon kosher salt**
- **½ teaspoon coriander**
- **Pinch ground red pepper**
- **½ cup fresh cilantro leaves, coarsely chopped**

1. Microwave carrots, water and 2 tablespoons of the vinegar in microwaveproof bowl on High 2 minutes. Transfer carrots and liquid to a bowl filled with ice water. Let stand 5 minutes. Drain and pat carrots dry.

2. Rinse onions under hot water 1 minute. Drain and pat dry.

3. Combine carrots, onions and remaining ingredients in a medium bowl. Let stand at room temperature 1 hour, stirring twice. *(Can be made ahead. Cover and refrigerate for up to 2 days.)* Makes 3 cups.

Per ½-cup serving: 75 calories, 2.5 g total fat, 0.5 g saturated fat, 0 mg cholesterol, 215 mg sodium, 13 g carbohydrates, 2 g protein, 44 mg calcium, 3 g fiber

steamed artichokes with herb mayonnaise EASY

Serve these artichokes at room temperature or chilled. Lime juice and cilantro make the perfect pair in our herb mayonnaise, but you can substitute lemon juice for the lime and basil for the cilantro for a nice variation.

Prep time: 10 minutes plus standing and chilling
Microwave time: 15 to 17 minutes
Microwave used

- 1 lemon, halved crosswise
- 4 large artichokes (½ lb. each), stems removed and leaf tips trimmed
- ¼ cup chicken broth
- 1 tablespoon thinly sliced garlic

HERB MAYONNAISE:

- ½ cup mayonnaise
- ½ cup chopped fresh cilantro
- 2 teaspoons fresh lime juice

1. Cut 1 lemon half into quarters; reserve other lemon half. Rub each artichoke with cut side of lemon quarter. Place in an 8-inch square microwaveproof dish, stem sides up. Add broth and garlic. Cover with the plastic wrap, turning back 1 corner to vent. Microwave on High 15 to 17 minutes, until tender when pierced with a fork, rotating dish once. Let stand, covered, for 3 minutes. Chill artichokes, if desired.

2. *Make herb mayonnaise:* Combine all ingredients in a bowl; chill until ready to serve. Makes ⅔ cup.

3. *To serve:* Cut reserved lemon half into 4 slices or wedges. Place each artichoke on a serving plate. Serve with lemon slices and herb mayonnaise. Makes 4 servings.

Per serving: 255 calories, 22.5 g total fat, 3.5 g saturated fat, 16 mg cholesterol, 307 mg sodium, 14 g carbohydrates, 4 g protein, 61 mg calcium, 6 g fiber

minted fruit EASY LOW FAT

A simple syrup infused with mint adds flavor to fruit salad.

Total prep time: 15 minutes

- ½ cup sugar
- ½ cup water
- ⅓ cup firmly packed mint leaves
- 1 small ripe pineapple (2¾ lbs.), cubed
- 1 pint strawberries, halved
- ½ of a honeydew melon (2¼ lbs.), cubed
- 3 tablespoons fresh lemon juice
- 2 tablespoons bourbon or rum
- 2 tablespoons chopped fresh mint

Combine sugar, water and ⅓ cup mint leaves in saucepan. Boil and stir 1 minute, until sugar dissolves; strain into a bowl. Add remaining ingredients; toss to combine. Makes 8 servings.

Per serving: 120 calories, 0.5 g total fat, 0 g saturated fat, 0 mg cholesterol, 8 mg sodium, 28 g carbohydrates, 1 g protein, 15 mg calcium, 2 g fiber

cucumber relish

Pictured on page 121.

Total prep time: 10 minutes plus standing

- 2 medium cucumbers, peeled, seeded and cut in half lengthwise, then cut into ¼-inch-thick crosswise slices
- ¼ cup rice wine vinegar
- 2 tablespoons thinly sliced fresh basil
- 2 teaspoons sugar
- 1 teaspoon kosher salt
- 1 teaspoon grated lime peel
- 1 teaspoon grated fresh ginger
- ¼ to ½ teaspoon red pepper flakes

Stir together all ingredients in a medium bowl. Let stand 15 minutes. Makes 2½ cups.

Per ½-cup serving: 20 calories, 0 g total fat, 0 g saturated fat, 0 mg cholesterol, 300 mg sodium, 5 g carbohydrates, 1 g protein, 21 mg calcium, 1 g fiber

watermelon and radish relish

The sweet watermelon and peppery radish make an unusual yet perfect match. For a colorful contrast, use yellow tomatoes instead of red. Pictured on page 121.

Total prep time: 10 minutes

- **3   cups cubed seedless watermelon**
- **1   cup halved red or yellow cherry tomatoes**
- **½   cup radishes, thinly sliced**
- **1   tablespoon fresh tarragon leaves**
- **2   teaspoons balsamic vinegar**
- **1   teaspoon extra-virgin olive oil**
  Pinch salt

Combine all ingredients in a large bowl. Let stand 15 minutes. Makes 4 cups.

Per ½-cup serving: 30 calories, 1 g total fat, 0 g saturated fat, 0 mg cholesterol, 22 mg sodium, 5 g carbohydrates, 1 g protein, 9 mg calcium, 1 g fiber

mango and apple chutney

This unforgettable chutney, served with roast pork, once held a place on the menu of New York City's Tavern on the Green. It displays a wonderful contrast of spices and fresh and dried fruits. Double the recipe so you can stock up!

Prep time: 20 minutes • Cooking time: 35 minutes

- **¾   cup diced onion**
- **¾   cup sugar**
- **¾   cup red wine vinegar**
- **½   of a lemon, seeded and thinly sliced**
- **¼   cup golden raisins**
- **1   garlic clove, minced**
- **¾   teaspoon cinnamon**
- **½   teaspoon salt**
- **¼   teaspoon cloves**
- **¼   teaspoon allspice**
- **¼   teaspoon ground red pepper**
- **2   ripe mangoes, peeled and diced**
- **2   tart green apples, peeled, cored and diced**

1. Combine onion, sugar, vinegar, lemon, raisins, garlic, cinnamon, salt, cloves, allspice and ground red pepper in a large saucepan. Bring to boil; reduce heat to medium. Cook, stirring occasionally, 20 minutes.

2. Stir in mangoes and apples. Increase heat and cook 15 minutes, until fruit is tender and chutney is thickened, stirring frequently. Spoon into 3 clean 8-ounce jars; cover and refrigerate. Makes 2¾ cups.

Per ¼-cup serving: 105 calories, 0 g total fat, 0 g saturated fat, 0 mg cholesterol, 108 mg sodium, 28 g carbohydrates, 1 g protein, 15 mg calcium, 2 g fiber

focaccia

The fresh rosemary makes this yeast bread, served at the Camberley Brown Hotel in Louisville, Kentucky, delectable.

Prep time: 25 minutes plus rising
Baking time: 30 to 40 minutes

- **2   packages active dry yeast**
- **1⅓ cups lukewarm water (105°F. to 115°F.)**
- **4   to 5 cups bread or all-purpose flour**
- **1   tablespoon chopped fresh rosemary**
- **1   teaspoon salt**
- **½   cup lukewarm milk (105°F. to 115°F.)**
- **¼   cup plus 1 tablespoon olive oil, divided**
- **2   teaspoons kosher salt**
- **1   tablespoon fresh rosemary leaves (optional)**

1. Sprinkle yeast over lukewarm water in a large bowl. Stir briefly, then let stand 5 minutes to dissolve. Attach a paddle to a large, heavy-duty mixer. At low speed, stir in 2 cups of the flour, chopped rosemary and salt; beat 1 minute, until smooth. (Or combine ingredients in a large bowl and beat vigorously with a wooden spoon 2 minutes, until smooth.) Add milk and ¼ cup olive oil. Stir in enough of the remaining flour, ½ cup at a time, to make a soft dough that begins to pull away from the side of the bowl.

2. On a lightly floured surface, knead dough 8 to 10 minutes, until smooth and elastic. Place dough in a large, lightly oiled bowl, turning to oil top. Cover bowl with plastic wrap; let rise in a warm, draft-free place, until doubled in bulk, 1 hour.

3. Heat oven to 375°F. Lightly oil a 15½×10½-inch jelly-roll pan. With a lightly floured rolling pin, shape dough into 12×4-inch rectangle. Carefully transfer to prepared pan. Cover and let stand 5 minutes.

4. Gently stretch and press dough to edges of pan with fingers (if dough resists stretching, let stand 5 minutes). Press top of dough with fingertips, leaving ½-inch indentations. Brush dough with 1 tablespoon olive oil and sprinkle with kosher salt and rosemary leaves, if desired. Bake 30 to 40 minutes, until top is golden and bottom sounds hollow when removed from pan and tapped on bottom. Cool slightly. Cut into 3¾×2½-inch pieces. Makes 12 servings.

Per serving: 255 calories, 7.5 g total fat, 1 g saturated fat, 1 mg cholesterol, 447 mg sodium, 39 g carbohydrates, 7 g protein, 23 mg calcium, 2 g fiber

roti ❤ LOW FAT

Roti is an unleavened bread brought to the Caribbean islands by East Indian laborers. It's wonderful wrapped around grilled meat skewers, or use the dough for Jamaican Patties (see recipe, page 134). Good news—this bread can be baked up to 2 hours ahead.

Prep time: 30 minutes plus standing
Cooking time: 20 minutes total

　　All-purpose flour
1¼　**teaspoons baking powder**
½　**teaspoon salt**
1¼　**cups lukewarm water (84° F.)**
　　Vegetable oil

1. Whisk together 3 cups flour, baking powder and salt in large bowl. Stir in lukewarm water with a spoon (dough will be sticky). Transfer dough to a floured surface and knead gently 5 minutes, adding more flour as needed to keep dough from sticking to hands. Transfer dough to a large plate. Cover with a clean kitchen towel and let stand 15 minutes.

2. Divide dough in half. On a floured surface, roll each piece into a 14×12-inch rectangle, about ⅛ inch thick. Brush each rectangle with

1 tablespoon oil and sprinkle with 1 teaspoon flour. Lightly flour a large cookie sheet. Roll each rectangle from one short end jelly-roll style. Place rolls, seam sides down, on a cutting board. Cut each into 1¼-inch-thick slices. Transfer slices, cut sides down, to prepared sheet and sprinkle lightly with 2 teaspoons flour. Let stand 10 minutes.

3. Roll each slice into an 8-inch circle. Heat a large nonstick skillet over medium heat 2 minutes. Add 1 circle of dough; cook 20 to 30 seconds, turn, brush lightly with oil and cook 30 to 45 seconds more, until lightly golden and roti is still pliable and soft. Turn circle again and brush lightly with oil; cook 45 seconds more, until lightly browned. Wrap in foil to keep warm. Repeat. *(Can be made ahead. Store at room temperature up to 2 hours. To reheat, bake in 350°F. oven 5 minutes.)* Makes 12 roti.

Per roti: 110 calories, 1 g total fat, 0 g saturated fat, 0 mg cholesterol, 140 mg sodium, 22 g carbohydrates, 3 g protein, 30 mg calcium, 1 g fiber

m　e　n　u

come to the caribbean

SPICY SHRIMP FRITTERS
page 136

JAMAICAN PATTIES
page 134

CARIBBEAN CHICKEN AND BEEF SKEWERS
page 146

GREEN SALAD WITH MANGO
page 117

STRAWBERRY DAIQUIRI
page 129

raspberry-apricot tarts

These fruit-filled tarts are a refreshing end to any summer celebration.

Prep time: 40 minutes plus chilling
Baking time: 27 to 30 minutes
Microwave used

PASTRY:

- 1 cup unsalted butter, softened and cut up (no substitutes)
- ⅔ cup sugar
- 2 large eggs
- 2 teaspoons vanilla extract
- 3 cups all-purpose flour
- 1 teaspoon salt
- 3 ounces semisweet chocolate squares, chopped

FILLING:

- 1 cup heavy or whipping cream
- 2 tablespoons sugar
- 2 tablespoons framboise (raspberry-flavored liqueur)
- 2 pints raspberries
- 8 fresh apricots, sliced

1. *Make pastry:* Beat butter in a large bowl until light and fluffy. Add sugar and beat until combined. Add eggs, one at a time, beating well after each addition. Add vanilla and beat until combined. With mixer at low speed, blend in flour and salt. Divide pastry in half. Shape each half into a ball and flatten into a ½-inch-thick disk. Wrap well in plastic wrap and refrigerate 1 hour or overnight.

2. Roll 1 pastry disk between 2 sheets of waxed paper to an 11-inch circle. Peel off top sheet of waxed paper, invert pastry and center over a 10-inch tart pan. Remove second piece of waxed paper. Gently press pastry into tart pan and to top edge of pan, if necessary. Repeat with remaining pastry for second tart. Refrigerate 30 minutes.

3. Heat oven to 375°F. Prick bottom of each pastry with a fork several times. Line each pan with foil; fill with dried beans or pie weights. Bake

15 minutes. Remove the foil and beans; bake 12 to 15 minutes more, until deep golden.

4. Meanwhile, microwave chocolate in a microwaveproof bowl on High 1 to 1½ minutes, until melted. Stir until smooth. While shells are still hot, brush inside bottom and sides with chocolate. Cool completely on wire rack. Remove tart shells from pans. *(Can be made ahead. Wrap well in plastic wrap and freeze up to 1 week. Thaw unwrapped at room temperature.)*

5. *Make filling:* Meanwhile, beat cream in a large bowl on medium-high speed 2 to 3 minutes, until thickened. Add sugar and framboise; beat to stiff peaks. Cover and refrigerate. Arrange raspberries and apricot slices in shells. Serve with flavored whipped cream. *(Tarts and cream can both be made ahead. Cover and refrigerate up to 2 hours.)* Makes 2 tarts (16 servings).

Per serving: 350 calories, 20.5 g total fat, 12 g saturated fat, 80 mg cholesterol, 161 mg sodium, 37 g carbohydrates, 5 g protein, 29 mg calcium, 4 g fiber

test kitchen tip

just desserts

For a casual or impromptu get-together, whip up one of these delicious quick desserts.

- Top premium coffee ice cream with Heath bar candy pieces and crème de cacao.

- Pour crème de menthe over lemon sorbet.

- Dip strawberries in sour cream and then in brown sugar (of course, melted chocolate is always a tasty treat, too).

- Add fresh fruit (such as ripe mango) to a vanilla shake and pour into large snifters or wine glasses for a sophisticated presentation.

- Dip bananas into melted chocolate, roll in chopped peanuts or granola, then freeze on a stick (fun for kids to make—and eat!).

- Grate 1 ounce semisweet chocolate as a topping for rice pudding.

THE PERFECT
OATMEAL COOKIE
PG. 182

sweets
for all
seasons

TAPIOCA
PUDDING WITH
CARAMELIZED
PEARS
PG. 193

Treats based on fruit, nuts and flavors of the season are some of the best and most beloved—not to mention a luscious reminder to enjoy the day at hand. Jewels of the orchard, gems of the vine—put them together with our recipes . . . aaahh, simply divine.

...summer sun,
autumn breeze

VANILLA-APPLE
BREAD PUDDING
PG. 180

162 *Recipes 2001*

...taste the **season**
from your fork

FRESH GINGER CAKE
WITH SAUTÉED APPLES
PG. 174

We're **fools** for love,

RHUBARB
FOOL
PG. 179

BAKED
RICOTTA
PG. 200

and berries...

PAVLOVA
PG. 181

Take a **break . . .**

FIG AND PEAR
TART
PG. 185

THE PERFECT
BISCOTTI
PG. 180

...with a crunchy
cookie, a creamy cake

NEW ORLEANS
CHEESECAKE
PG. 170

Rise to
the occasion,
my sweet

TIRAMISU
PG. 171

TROPICAL
TULIPES
PG. 199

guava
cheesecake

Dazzle guests with this tropical delight, perfect for summertime entertaining.

Prep time: 20 minutes plus standing and chilling
Baking time: 1 hour 30 minutes
Microwave used

CRUST:

1⅓	cups graham-cracker crumbs
⅓	cup melted butter or margarine
1	large egg white, lightly beaten

4	packages (8 oz. each) cream cheese, at room temperature
1¼	cups sugar
4	large eggs, at room temperature
1	teaspoon vanilla extract
⅓	cup sour cream
1	can (21 oz.) guava paste,* divided
¼	cup all-purpose flour

1. Heat oven to 350°F.

2. *Make crust:* Combine crumbs and butter in a small bowl. Press crumbs into bottom of a 9-inch springform pan. Brush bottom with egg white. Bake 8 to 10 minutes, until crust is golden brown. Cool on a wire rack. Wrap pan in heavy-duty foil. Set aside. Reduce oven temperature to 325°F.

3. Beat cream cheese and sugar in a large mixer bowl on medium-high speed 5 minutes, until creamy. Scrape side of bowl with rubber spatula. Add eggs, one at a time, beating just until blended and mixture is smooth. At low speed, beat in vanilla and sour cream.

4. Place 1 cup of the guava paste in a microwaveproof bowl; microwave on High 1 minute. Whisk until smooth. Transfer 3 cups of the filling to a large bowl. Whisk in warmed guava paste and flour until smooth. Pour guava filling into prepared pan. Pour remaining filling over guava layer. Place springform pan in a large baking pan. (Make sure there is at least 1 inch between springform and edges of baking pan.) Place baking pan on oven rack. Carefully pour enough very hot tap water into baking pan to come 1 inch up side of springform pan.

5. Bake 1 hour 30 minutes. Turn oven off. Let cheesecake stand in oven 1 hour. (Do not open door.) Remove from water bath and discard foil. Cool completely on wire rack. Cover cheesecake with plastic wrap and refrigerate overnight.

6. Run a knife around inside edge of springform pan to loosen. Remove ring from pan. Transfer cake to a flat serving plate. Place remaining 1 cup guava paste in a small microwaveproof bowl; microwave on High 1 minute. Whisk until smooth. Transfer guava paste to a small plastic storage bag. Snip a small hole in one corner of bag. Drizzle guava paste on top of cheesecake. Makes 12 servings.

Note: Guava paste is available in the ethnic sections of supermarkets or in Latin specialty stores.

Per serving: 630 calories, 35.5 g total fat, 21.5 g saturated fat, 171 mg cholesterol, 358 mg sodium, 69 g carbohydrates, 9 g protein, 82 mg calcium, 3 g fiber

---

test kitchen tip

go for guava

GROWN in its place of origin, South America, as well as in Hawaii, California and Florida, guava is an oval-shape tropical fruit appreciated for its sweetness and fragrance. Its skin color ranges from yellow or red to dark purple; its flesh ranges from light yellow to red.

LOOK for ripe guavas (ripe fruit yields slightly when pressed gently) that do not have any spots. If not ripe when purchased, ripen at room temperature.

STORE guavas in the refrigerator up to 4 days.

USE for sauces or in jams and preserves. If you cannot find fresh guavas, look for canned whole guavas at your supermarket.

new orleans cheesecake *EASY*

Pictured on page 167.

Prep time: 30 minutes plus chilling
Baking time: 1 hour 30 minutes to 1 hour 40 minutes

CRUST:
- 2 **cups pecans, finely chopped**
- ¼ **cup butter or margarine, melted**
- 2 **tablespoons firmly packed brown sugar**

FILLING:
- 4 **packages (8 oz. each) cream cheese, softened**
- 2 **cups firmly packed brown sugar**
- ½ **cup cornstarch**
- ½ **cup bourbon**
- 1 **teaspoon vanilla extract**
- 4 **large eggs, at room temperature**

GANACHE:
- 8 **ounces semisweet chocolate squares, cut up**
- ½ **cup half-and-half cream**

1. *Make crust:* Heat oven to 350°F. Combine all ingredients in a bowl until evenly moistened. Press mixture into bottom of a 9-inch springform pan. Wrap bottom and side of pan with heavy-duty foil.

2. *Make filling:* Beat cream cheese in a large mixer bowl on high speed until smooth. Scrape side of bowl with a rubber spatula. Beat in sugar and cornstarch until light and fluffy. Add bourbon and vanilla. At low speed, add eggs, one at a time, beating well after each addition; beat until mixture is completely smooth. Pour filling into prepared pan. Place springform pan in a large roasting pan. (Make sure there is at least 1 inch between springform and edges of roasting pan.) Place roasting pan on oven rack. Carefully pour enough hot tap water into roasting pan to come halfway up side of springform pan.

3. Bake 1 hour 30 minutes to 1 hour 40 minutes, until edge of cheesecake is firm and center is just set. Remove pan from water bath; transfer to wire rack and cool completely.

4. *Make ganache:* Meanwhile, combine chocolate and half-and-half in a medium saucepan. Cook over medium-low heat until chocolate is melted and smooth, stirring frequently. Remove from heat; cool at room temperature. Spread ganache on top of cheesecake. Cover pan with plastic wrap and refrigerate overnight. *(Can be made ahead. Refrigerate up to 2 days.)* Run a knife around inside edge of springform pan to loosen. Remove ring from pan. Makes 16 servings.

Per serving: 535 calories, 38 g total fat, 18.5 g saturated fat, 126 mg cholesterol, 229 mg sodium, 46 g carbohydrates, 8 g protein, 95 mg calcium, 2 g fiber

mini cheesecakes with pear compote *EASY* *LOW FAT*

Serve these individual-size lemon cheesecakes topped with a compote of canned pears and dried cranberries and watch for the smiles.

Prep time: 20 minutes plus standing and chilling
Baking time: 30 to 35 minutes

MINI CHEESECAKES:
- 1 **cup low-fat plain yogurt**
- 4 **ounces reduced-fat cream cheese (Neufchâtel), softened**
- ½ **cup sugar**
- 1 **large egg**
- 1 **large egg white**
- 1 **tablespoon flour**
- 1 **teaspoon grated lemon peel**
- 1 **teaspoon fresh lemon juice**

PEAR COMPOTE:
- 1 **can (15¼ oz.) pear halves in heavy syrup**
- ½ **cup dried cranberries**
- **Lemon zest, for garnish (optional)**

1. *Make mini cheesecakes:* Strain yogurt in a fine sieve set over a bowl 30 minutes.

2. Heat oven to 350°F. Lightly coat six 2-ounce ovenproof cups with vegetable cooking spray. Set aside. Process cream cheese and sugar in a food processor until smooth. Add egg, egg white, flour, lemon peel and lemon juice; pulse until combined. Transfer to a medium bowl and stir in yogurt. Pour evenly into prepared cups.

3. Place cups in a roasting pan. Place roasting pan on oven rack. Carefully pour enough hot tap water into roasting pan to come 1 inch up sides of cups. Bake 30 to 35 minutes, just until set. Turn oven off and let cheesecakes stand in oven 30 minutes. (Do not open oven door.) Transfer cups from water bath to wire rack; cool 15 minutes. Refrigerate 1 hour until cold. *(Can be made ahead. Cover and refrigerate overnight.)*

4. *Make pear compote:* Strain liquid from pears into a small saucepan; set pears aside. Add cranberries to pear liquid; bring to boil over medium heat. Reduce heat to medium-low; cook 5 to 8 minutes, until cranberries just soften. Transfer to a medium bowl; cool. Dice pears and stir into cranberry mixture. Makes 1½ cups.

5. Top each cheesecake with 2 tablespoons of the pear compote; garnish with lemon zest, if desired. (Reserve remaining compote for another use.) Makes 6 servings.

Per serving without garnish: 205 calories, 6 g total fat, 3.5 g saturated fat, 52 mg cholesterol, 126 mg sodium, 34 g carbohydrates, 6 g protein, 97 mg calcium, 1 g fiber

tiramisu

Many variations of this classic dessert exist today; only the real thing contains espresso and mascarpone cheese. Pictured on page 168.

Prep time: 35 minutes plus chilling
Baking time: 12 to 15 minutes

SPONGE CAKE:
- **4 large eggs, at room temperature**
- **¾ cup sugar**
- **1 teaspoon vanilla extract**
- **¾ cup all-purpose flour**
- **¼ teaspoon salt**

SYRUP:
- **½ cup brewed espresso**
- **¼ cup brandy**
- **2 tablespoons sugar**

FILLING:
- **1 pound mascarpone cheese**
- **¼ cup sugar**
- **1 cup heavy or whipping cream**
- **2 teaspoons unsweetened cocoa**
- **½ cup heavy or whipping cream, whipped**

1. *Make sponge cake:* Heat oven to 350°F. Grease a 15½×10½-inch jelly-roll pan. Line with waxed paper; grease and flour paper and tap out excess flour.

2. Beat eggs and sugar in a large mixer bowl on high speed 12 to 15 minutes, until pale and thick and mixture forms a ribbon when the beaters are lifted. Beat in vanilla. Combine flour and salt in a small bowl. Sift half of the flour mixture onto egg mixture, then gently fold in with a whisk; repeat with remaining flour mixture. Spread into prepared pan. Bake 12 to 15 minutes, until top springs back when lightly touched. Cool in pan on wire rack.

3. *Make syrup:* Meanwhile, combine hot espresso, brandy and sugar in a small bowl, stirring, until sugar is dissolved.

4. *Make filling:* Blend mascarpone with sugar in a large bowl. Beat heavy cream in a clean mixer bowl with clean beaters on high speed to stiff peaks; fold into mascarpone mixture with a rubber spatula.

5. *To assemble:* Unmold cake and peel off paper. Cut cake in half to form two 7½×10½-inch rectangles. Trim each half to fit a shallow 2-quart (11×7-inch) glass or ceramic dish. Place a cake layer on bottom of dish. Drizzle evenly with half of the syrup; spoon on half of the filling. Place remaining cake layer on top; drizzle with remaining syrup and spread top with remaining filling. Sift cocoa over filling. Cover and refrigerate overnight.

6. *To serve:* Pipe the whipped cream decoratively over tiramisu. Makes 16 servings.

Per serving: 305 calories, 22.5 g total fat, 13 g saturated fat, 120 mg cholesterol, 77 mg sodium, 21 g carbohydrates, 8 g protein, 24 mg calcium, 0 g fiber

apple galette

Bake this pretty, simple-to-assemble apple dessert year-round. Be careful to roll the pastry to an even ¼-inch thickness, especially at the edges. French in origin, this galette is free form. Ideal for get-togethers, it can be made up to 6 hours ahead.

Prep time: 30 minutes plus chilling and standing
Baking time: 40 to 45 minutes

> **Pâte Brisée (recipe, right)**
> 4 **large apples (Gala or Fuji), peeled, cored and cut in half**
> 4 **tablespoons sugar, divided**
> 1 **tablespoon cornstarch**
> 1 **egg yolk**
> **Water**
> 1 **tablespoon butter, cut into small pieces (no substitutes)**
> 4 **tablespoons apricot jam**
> 1 **tablespoon apple-flavored brandy or cognac (optional)**

1. Make Pâte Brisée. Roll out dough to a ¼-inch thickness, forming an 11×10½-inch oval. Place on a heavy-duty cookie sheet.

2. Heat oven to 400°F. Place each apple half, cut side down, on a cutting board and cut into ¼-inch-thick slices. Set aside the larger center slices of the same size and chop end slices coarsely to equal 1¼ cups. Sprinkle chopped apple over dough, leaving a 1½-inch border. Toss the slices with 3 tablespoons of the sugar and the cornstarch in a large bowl. Arrange large apple slices on dough over chopped apple, slightly overlapping with points facing center of pastry. Arrange smaller apple slices in the center of oval.

3. Bring up border of the dough and fold over apples. Galette should measure 10×9½ inches. Lightly beat egg yolk with 1 tablespoon water in a cup. Brush border with egg yolk mixture and sprinkle with remaining 1 tablespoon sugar. Dot apples with butter. Bake 40 to 45 minutes, until well browned and crusty. Place cookie sheet with galette on a wire rack; let stand 10 to 15 minutes.

4. Dilute apricot jam with apple-flavored brandy (if not using brandy and jam is thick, substitute 1 tablespoon water); spread on top of apples with the back of a spoon. If desired, spread some on top edge of crust. *(Can be made ahead. Cover loosely with foil and refrigerate up to 6 hours. Reheat in a 350°F. oven 20 minutes.)* Cut galette into wedges and serve warm. Makes 6 servings.

Per serving without brandy: 405 calories, 19.5 g total fat, 11.5 g saturated fat, 85 mg cholesterol, 126 mg sodium, 55 g carbohydrates, 4 g protein, 20 mg calcium, 3 g fiber

pâte brisée

The French pâte briseé *translated means "short pastry."*

Total prep time: 10 minutes plus chilling

> 1½ **cups all-purpose flour**
> ¼ **teaspoon salt**
> ½ **cup cold unsalted butter, cut up (no substitutes)**
> 4 **to 6 tablespoons cold water**

Combine flour and salt in a food processor; pulse to blend. Add butter and pulse until mixture forms pea-size pieces. Sprinkle 4 tablespoons of the cold water over top of flour. Pulse until dough is moistened and begins to come together. If still dry, add remaining water, 1 tablespoon at a time, pulsing after each addition until dough begins to come together. Shape dough into a ball and flatten into a thick disk. Wrap well in plastic wrap; refrigerate 30 minutes. Makes enough pastry for 1 single crust (6 servings).

Per serving: 255 calories, 16.5 g total fat, 10 g saturated fat, 44 mg cholesterol, 100 mg sodium, 24 g carbohydrates, 3 g protein, 10 mg calcium, 1 g fiber

blueberry-peach galette

This free-form fruit tart can be adapted to a 9-inch tart pan with a removable bottom. Just roll the pastry, fit it into the tart pan and fill as directed.

Prep time: 40 minutes
Baking time: 45 to 50 minutes

PASTRY:

- 1¼ cups all-purpose flour
- 2 teaspoons sugar
- ¾ teaspoon salt
- ½ cup cold butter, cut up (no substitutes)
- 3 to 4 tablespoons cold water

FILLING:

- 1½ pounds ripe peaches or nectarines (about 4), peeled and cut into eighths
- ⅓ cup plus 2 teaspoons sugar, divided
- 1½ tablespoons flour
- 2 teaspoons fresh lemon juice
- ¼ teaspoon cinnamon
- ½ cup fresh blueberries
- 1 large egg white, lightly beaten

1. Heat oven to 400°F.

2. *Make pastry:* Combine flour, sugar and salt in a medium bowl. With a pastry blender or 2 knives, cut in butter until mixture resembles coarse crumbs. Add cold water, 1 tablespoon at a time, tossing vigorously with a fork until pastry just begins to hold together. On a smooth surface, shape pastry into a ball, kneading lightly if necessary; set aside.

3. *Make filling:* Combine peaches, ⅓ cup of the sugar, the flour, lemon juice and cinnamon in a large bowl. Toss to coat well.

4. Line a large cookie sheet with foil. Turn up edges to form a 1-inch rim. On a lightly floured surface with a floured rolling pin, roll pastry into a 13-inch circle. Fold into quarters, then unfold onto prepared cookie sheet.

5. Spoon filling in center of pastry; spread into a single layer, leaving a 2-inch border. Sprinkle top evenly with blueberries. Fold border up over fruit to make a 2-inch-wide edge. Lightly brush pastry edge with egg white, then sprinkle with remaining 2 teaspoons sugar.

6. Bake galette 45 to 50 minutes, until center is bubbly. (If pastry browns too quickly, cover top loosely with foil.) Transfer galette on cookie sheet to wire rack and cool completely. Makes 10 servings.

Per serving: 210 calories, 10 g total fat, 6 g saturated fat, 26 mg cholesterol, 280 mg sodium, 29 g carbohydrates, 3 g protein, 10 mg calcium, 2 g fiber

---

test kitchen tip

peach perfect

Fortunately for peach connoisseurs, there are many varieties of this flavorful fruit to choose from. Its distinctive velvetlike skin ranges from pinkish to creamy white to red-yellow, while its juicy sweet flesh varies from yellow to pink-white.

SELECTING AND STORING: When purchasing peaches, look for very fragrant peaches that yield to palm pressure. Avoid those with bruises, soft spots or any signs of greening. Ripen peaches by placing them in a paper bag, poking holes in different spots on the bag and leaving it at room temperature for up to 2 days. Refrigerate ripe peaches in a plastic storage bag up to 5 days. Like many fruits, their flavor is best when brought to room temperature.

USES AND AVAILABILITY: Peaches are terrific eaten out of hand. They also often star in pies and cakes. For a quick dessert, try sautéing and spooning slices over ice cream. Peak season for peaches is usually May to October. (Look for ultrasweet fresh white peaches in July!) You can also find canned peaches, frozen peach slices and even dried peach halves.

TO PEEL A PEACH: Immerse in boiling water for 20 to 30 seconds. Remove with a slotted spoon and immediately plunge it into a bowl of cold water. If the peach is ripe, the skin will slide off easily.

northwest berry shortcake (EASY)

Sun-sweetened berries, a warm shortcake and chilled whipped cream come together in the ultimate summer dessert. Pictured on page 162.

Prep time: 30 minutes
Baking time: 23 to 25 minutes

- 4 cups assorted fresh berries (such as raspberries, blackberries, strawberries and blueberries)
- 3 to 4 tablespoons sugar
- 1 tablespoon raspberry-flavored liqueur or orange-flavored liqueur

SHORTCAKE:

- 1¾ cups all-purpose flour
- 2 teaspoons baking powder
- ¼ cup plus 1 tablespoon sugar, divided
- ¼ teaspoon salt
- 6 tablespoons cold butter, cut up (no substitutes)
- ½ cup toasted and skinned hazelnuts, chopped
- ¾ cup plus 1 tablespoon milk, divided

- 1 cup heavy or whipping cream
- 2 tablespoons sugar
  Assorted fresh berries, for garnish (optional)

1. Combine 4 cups berries, sugar and raspberry-flavored liqueur in a large bowl. Let stand 1 hour, until mixture is juicy.

2. *Make shortcake:* Meanwhile, heat oven to 375°F. Combine flour, baking powder, ¼ cup of the sugar and the salt in a large bowl. With a pastry blender or 2 knives, cut in butter until mixture resembles coarse crumbs. Toss in the hazelnuts. Gradually add ¾ cup of the milk to flour mixture, mixing lightly with a spoon until flour mixture is just moistened and dough begins to hold together.

3. On a lightly floured surface, gather dough into a ball; knead gently 2 to 3 times, just until smooth. Turn dough out onto an ungreased cookie sheet; pat into a 7×6-inch rectangle about ¾ inch thick. With a sharp knife, lightly score rectangle into 6 equal sections. (Do not cut all the way through.)

Brush top with remaining 1 tablespoon milk, then sprinkle with remaining 1 tablespoon sugar.

4. Bake shortcake 23 to 25 minutes, until golden brown and toothpick inserted in center comes out clean. Cool on a cookie sheet 5 minutes. Transfer shortcake to a wire rack. Let stand 10 minutes.

5. Meanwhile, beat cream and sugar in small mixer bowl on medium-high speed to stiff peaks. Separate shortcakes and split each in half horizontally with a knife. Transfer bottoms of shortcakes to 6 serving plates; divide and spoon berry mixture on top. Arrange shortcake tops over fruit. Serve warm with whipped cream. Garnish with additional fresh berries, if desired. Makes 6 servings.

Per serving without garnish: 595 calories, 34 g total fat, 17.5 g saturated fat, 90 mg cholesterol, 409 mg sodium, 67 g carbohydrates, 8 g protein, 200 mg calcium, 5 g fiber

fresh ginger cake with sautéed apples (EASY)

All dressed up with apples and whipped cream, this American favorite gets an added zing from freshly grated ginger. Pictured on page 163.

Prep time: 30 minutes
Baking time: 30 minutes

- 1 cup unsulfured molasses
- ½ cup buttermilk
- ¼ cup butter or margarine, melted
- 1 large egg
- 1 tablespoon freshly grated ginger
- 2 cups all-purpose flour
- 1 teaspoon baking soda
- ½ teaspoon salt

SAUTÉED APPLES:

- 3 tablespoons butter or margarine
- 3 tablespoons firmly packed brown sugar
- 2 tablespoons dark rum
- 4 Gala or Fuji apples, peeled and sliced

WHIPPED CREAM:

- 1 cup heavy or whipping cream
- 2 tablespoons packed brown sugar
- ½ teaspoon vanilla extract

1. Heat oven to 375°F. Butter a 9-inch square baking pan. Whisk together molasses, buttermilk, butter, egg and ginger in a large bowl until smooth. Add flour, baking soda and salt; whisk until smooth. Pour into prepared pan.

2. Bake 30 minutes, until a toothpick inserted in center comes out clean. Cool in pan on a wire rack about 15 minutes.

3. *Make sautéed apples:* Meanwhile, melt butter in a large skillet over medium-high heat. Stir in brown sugar and rum. Add apples and cook 8 minutes, until tender, stirring occasionally.

4. *Make whipped cream:* Beat together cream, brown sugar and vanilla in a large mixer bowl on medium-high speed 2 to 3 minutes, just until stiff.

5. *To serve:* Cut cake into squares and serve warm with sautéed apples and whipped cream. Makes 9 servings.

Per serving: 455 calories, 20.5 g total fat, 12.5 g saturated fat, 86 mg cholesterol, 414 mg sodium, 63 g carbohydrates, 5 g protein, 125 mg calcium, 2 g fiber

warm apple spice cake

Granny Smith apples offer a tart contrast to the sweet, spicy cake. For a super-satisfying touch, serve it warm with caramel sauce.

Prep time: 30 minutes plus cooling
Baking time: 1 hour 10 minutes
Microwave used

1 **pound Granny Smith apples (about 2 large), peeled and chopped (2½ cups)**
2 **cups all-purpose flour**
1½ **teaspoons baking powder**
½ **teaspoon baking soda**
¼ **teaspoon salt**
1 **teaspoon cinnamon**
½ **teaspoon ginger**
¼ **teaspoon cloves**
¼ **teaspoon nutmeg**
¾ **cup butter or margarine, softened**
½ **cup granulated sugar**
½ **cup firmly packed brown sugar**

3 **large eggs, at room temperature**
½ **cup milk**
½ **cup chopped walnuts**
½ **cup dark raisins**
1 **Granny Smith apple, peeled, cored and thinly sliced**
2 **tablespoons confectioners' sugar**
2 **tablespoons apple jelly, heated**
 Warm Caramel Sauce (recipe, page 187) (optional)

1. Heat oven to 350°F. Butter a 9-inch springform pan. Line bottom of the pan with waxed paper; butter paper.

2. Place chopped apples in a microwaveproof dish. Cover with plastic wrap, lifting back 1 corner to vent; microwave on High 3 to 4 minutes, until apples soften. Mash apples with the back of a spoon. Cool completely. Makes 1 cup.

3. Combine flour, baking powder, baking soda, salt, cinnamon, ginger, cloves and nutmeg in a bowl; set aside. Beat together butter, granulated sugar and brown sugar in a large mixer bowl on medium speed until light and fluffy. Add eggs, one at a time, beating well after each addition. At low speed, beat in flour mixture alternately with milk, beginning and ending with flour mixture. Fold in cooked apples, nuts and raisins. Spoon batter into prepared pan; spread evenly. Arrange apple slices in a circle along outside edge. Bake 1 hour 10 minutes, until toothpick inserted in center comes out clean. Cool 10 minutes on a wire rack.

4. *To unmold:* Run a knife around inside edge of springform pan to loosen. Remove ring from pan. Invert cake onto wire rack. Peel off waxed paper and invert again onto a serving plate. Sprinkle cake with confectioners' sugar, then brush apple slices with melted jelly. Serve warm with Warm Caramel Sauce, if desired. Makes 10 servings.

Per serving without caramel sauce: 435 calories, 20.5 g total fat, 10 g saturated fat, 104 mg cholesterol, 362 mg sodium, 59 g carbohydrates, 6 g protein, 91 mg calcium, 3 g fiber

fresh lemon cake

Think of this cake for your next special occasion. It's not too sweet and has a delicate lemon fragrance.

Prep time: 50 minutes plus standing and chilling
Baking time: 20 to 25 minutes
Microwave used

CAKE:

- 2 cups cake flour (not self-rising)
- 2 teaspoons baking powder
- ¼ teaspoon salt
- 1 cup milk, at room temperature
- ½ teaspoon vanilla extract
- ¾ cup unsalted butter, softened (no substitutes)
- 1¼ cups sugar
- 3 large eggs, at room temperature

GLAZE:

- ⅓ cup fresh lemon juice
- 3 tablespoons sugar

FILLING:

- 1 cup sugar
- ⅓ cup cornstarch
- ⅛ teaspoon salt
- 1½ cups water
- 1 tablespoon unsalted butter (no substitutes)
- 4 large egg yolks
- 2 teaspoons grated lemon peel
- ¼ cup fresh lemon juice

BUTTERCREAM:

- 1 cup plus 2 tablespoons sugar, divided
- ¼ cup water
- 5 large egg whites, at room temperature
- 1½ cups unsalted butter (no substitutes)
- 1½ teaspoons grated lemon peel
- 1 teaspoon vanilla extract

1. *Make cake:* Heat oven to 350°F. Grease and flour three 9-inch cake pans. Sift flour, baking powder and salt onto waxed paper. Combine milk and vanilla in a cup.

2. Beat butter and sugar in a large mixer bowl on medium speed until light and fluffy. Add eggs, one at a time, beating well after each addition. At low speed, beat in flour mixture alternately with milk, beginning and ending with flour mixture. Divide batter among prepared pans. Bake 20 to 25 minutes,

until a toothpick inserted in centers comes out clean. Cool in pans on wire racks 10 minutes. Invert on wire racks to cool completely.

3. *Make glaze:* Place lemon juice and sugar in a 1-cup glass measure; microwave on High 1 minute, until sugar is dissolved. Cool. Brush over tops of cake layers.

4. *Make filling:* Combine sugar, cornstarch and salt in a medium saucepan; stir in water until smooth. Gradually bring to boil over medium heat, stirring constantly. Cook 1 minute. Stir in butter. Whisk ⅓ cup of the cornstarch mixture into egg yolks in a small bowl; return to pan. Add lemon peel and juice; simmer 1 minute. Transfer to a clean bowl; place plastic wrap directly on surface of filling and refrigerate 2 hours.

5. *Make buttercream:* Combine 1 cup of the sugar and the water in a small saucepan. Bring to boil over medium heat. Cook until the syrup reaches soft-ball stage (240°F. to 245°F. on a candy thermometer), about 7 minutes. Meanwhile, beat egg whites in a large mixer bowl on high speed to soft peaks. Gradually add remaining 2 tablespoons sugar and beat to stiff peaks. Add hot syrup in a thin, steady stream, beating constantly. Beat on high speed 8 to 10 minutes more, until meringue is completely cool and forms soft peaks.

6. Beat butter in a large mixer bowl on medium speed until light and fluffy. Beat in meringue, ¼ cup at a time, blending well after each addition. Beat in lemon peel and vanilla. Makes 4 cups.

7. *To assemble:* Place one of the cake layers on a serving plate; spread with half of the filling. Add another layer and spread with remaining filling. Top with third layer; refrigerate 30 minutes. Reserve 1 cup of the buttercream. Spread top and side of cake with remaining buttercream. Fit pastry bag with a small star tube and fill with reserved buttercream. Pipe rosettes on top. (*Can be made ahead. Refrigerate cake, uncovered, 1 hour. Cover loosely with plastic wrap and refrigerate up to 24 hours. Let stand at room temperature 1 hour before serving.*) Makes 12 servings.

Per serving: 690 calories, 41 g total fat, 24.5 g saturated fat, 227 mg cholesterol, 197 mg sodium, 76 g carbohydrates, 7 g protein, 95 mg calcium, 0 g fiber

nectarine coffee cake

What's even better than coffee cake? Coffee cake with a sweet, creamy filling. Substitute fresh plums for the nectarines for a luscious variation.

Prep time: 20 minutes
Baking time: 30 minutes

DOUGH:

2	cups all-purpose flour
½	cup sugar
1	teaspoon salt
½	teaspoon baking powder
½	teaspoon cinnamon
½	cup butter or margarine
2	large eggs, lightly beaten
1	teaspoon vanilla extract

FILLING:

1	container (16 oz.) cottage cheese
⅓	cup sugar
2	large eggs
½	teaspoon vanilla extract
1	tablespoon flour
¼	teaspoon cinnamon

1¼	pounds nectarines (about 4 large)
2	tablespoons sugar
¼	teaspoon cinnamon

1. Heat oven to 425°F.

2. *Make dough:* Combine flour, sugar, salt, baking powder and cinnamon in a large bowl. With a pastry blender or 2 knives, cut in butter until mixture resembles coarse crumbs. Add eggs and vanilla; mix until smooth. Press into bottom and 1 inch up sides of a 13×9-inch baking pan.

3. *Make filling:* Puree cottage cheese in a blender or food processor 1 minute. Add sugar, eggs, vanilla, flour and cinnamon. Process until smooth. Pour into dough-lined pan and spread evenly.

4. Slice nectarines into quarters and arrange, skin sides up, in 4 rows over filling. Combine sugar and cinnamon and sprinkle over top. Bake 30 minutes, until golden brown. Cool on a wire rack. Serve warm or at room temperature. Makes 16 servings.

Per serving: 225 calories, 9 g total fat, 5 g saturated fat, 74 mg cholesterol, 351 mg sodium, 29 g carbohydrates, 7 g protein, 39 mg calcium, 1 g fiber

---

test kitchen tip

nectarine know-how

Similar in flavor and texture to peaches (without the fuzz), nectarines are one of the special treats of summer. They're usually at their peak between June and September. Here's how to enjoy them at their best.

CHOOSE nectarines that have a healthy golden yellow skin with no tinges of green. The pretty blush color of the fruit has to do with the variety of nectarine, not the ripeness. Healthy nectarines are firm and unblemished. Complete ripening them at room temperature in a loosely closed paper bag for several days.

USE the ripened fruit as soon as possible. Refrigerate ripe nectarines up to 5 days.

SERVE nectarines at room temperature for best flavor. As with peaches, whether or not you peel them is a personal choice.

cinnamon hints

One of the oldest long-standing spices, cinnamon comes from the bark of a small tropical evergreen tree. With its delicately sweet flavor and distinctive fragrance, cinnamon is commonly used in sweets such as cakes, puddings and cookies but also makes a savory contribution to stews, vegetables and curries.

CINNAMON TIPS: Buy cinnamon in rolled sticks or in ground form. Store it in airtight containers and leave in a cool, dark place. Use cinnamon sticks to flavor drinks such as hot chocolate, coffee and mulled wine.

dried plum kuchen

German desserts are famous for using a lot of fruits—fresh in summer and dried in winter. For this cake, we used humble dried plums, formerly known as prunes.

Prep time: 20 minutes
Baking time: 50 to 60 minutes

1¾	cups (12 oz.) pitted dried plums (prunes)
1	tablespoon fresh lemon juice
1	cup all-purpose flour
1	teaspoon baking powder
	Pinch salt
½	cup unsalted butter or margarine, softened
1	cup plus 1 tablespoon sugar, divided
2	large eggs
1½	teaspoons grated lemon peel
1	teaspoon vanilla
¼	teaspoon cinnamon

1. Heat the oven to 350°F. Grease a 9-inch cake pan with a removable bottom or a 9-inch springform pan.

2. Toss dried plums with lemon juice in a small bowl; set aside. Combine flour, baking powder and salt in a medium bowl; set aside.

3. Beat butter and 1 cup of the sugar in a medium mixer bowl on medium speed. Beat in eggs, one at a time, beating well after each addition. Beat in lemon peel and vanilla just until combined. Add flour mixture and beat on low speed just until combined. Spread batter evenly in bottom of prepared pan. Arrange dried plum and lemon mixture in concentric circles on top.

4. Combine remaining 1 tablespoon sugar and the cinnamon in a small bowl. Sprinkle over fruit.

5. Bake kuchen 50 to 60 minutes, until top is golden brown and toothpick inserted in center comes out clean. Transfer to a wire rack and cool 15 minutes. Remove side of pan. Serve warm. Makes 8 servings.

Per serving: 375 calories, 14 g total fat, 8 g saturated fat, 86 mg cholesterol, 88 mg sodium, 61 g carbohydrates, 4 g protein, 63 mg calcium, 3 g fiber

paris-brest

Guaranteed to impress, this legendary dessert pastry is shaped in a large ring, baked, filled with vanilla custard and sprinkled with almonds.

Prep time: 40 minutes plus standing and chilling
Baking time: 40 minutes

VANILLA CREAM FILLING:

1	cup milk
¼	cup cornstarch
½	cup granulated sugar
4	large egg yolks, at room temperature
1	tablespoon butter or margarine
2	teaspoons vanilla extract
▪	
	Cream-Puff Pastry (recipe, opposite page)
1	cup heavy or whipping cream
⅓	cup sliced almonds, toasted
	Confectioners' sugar

1. *Make vanilla cream filling:* Whisk together milk and cornstarch in a medium saucepan until completely dissolved. Heat over medium heat 2 to 4 minutes, just until warm. Whisk together sugar and egg yolks in a bowl until light and thick. Gradually whisk half of the milk mixture into yolks.

Return mixture to saucepan. Bring to boil, whisking constantly (mixture will be very thick). Cook 1 minute, stirring, over low heat. Stir in butter and vanilla. Transfer to a clean bowl; cover surface with plastic wrap and let stand until filling cools to room temperature.

2. Meanwhile, heat oven to 400°F. Line a cookie sheet with parchment paper. Using an 8-inch round cake pan as a guide, trace an 8-inch circle on the paper. Turn paper over.

3. Make Cream-Puff Pastry. Spoon into a pastry bag fitted with a ¾-inch plain or decorative tip. Pipe a 1½-inch-thick ring over circle on paper. Pipe second ring directly on top. Bake 40 minutes, until golden. Turn oven off; prick inside of ring with tip of knife in several places. Leave pastry in oven 15 minutes more with the door closed. Transfer to a wire rack and cool completely. Split in half horizontally with a serrated knife. Remove any soft dough from inside.

4. Beat heavy cream in a mixer bowl on medium-high speed to stiff peaks. Whisk cooled filling until smooth; whisk in one third of the whipped cream, then fold in remaining. Spoon into bottom pastry ring. Sprinkle with almonds; replace pastry top. Lightly dust with confectioners' sugar. Makes 8 servings.

Per serving: 400 calories, 28 g total fat, 14.5 g saturated fat, 254 mg cholesterol, 221 mg sodium, 30 g carbohydrates, 8 g protein, 95 mg calcium, 1 g fiber

cream-puff pastry

When baked, this rich dough, also known as choux paste, forms nearly hollow interiors perfect for filling with creamy custard to create a dazzling array of desserts.

Total prep time: 15 minutes

- ¾ **cup water**
- 5 **tablespoons butter or margarine, cut up**
- 1 **teaspoon sugar**
- ¼ **teaspoon salt**
- ¾ **cup all-purpose flour**
- 3 **large eggs, at room temperature**

1. Combine water, butter, sugar and salt in a medium saucepan. Bring to boil over medium-high heat. Remove from heat; stir in flour all at once. Return to heat; cook 30 seconds, until dough pulls away from side of pan, stirring constantly.

2. Remove from heat. Add eggs, one at a time, beating with a wooden spoon after each addition until smooth. Proceed with desired recipe. Makes 8 servings.

Per serving: 140 calories, 9.5 g total fat, 5.5 g saturated fat, 100 mg cholesterol, 175 mg sodium, 10 g carbohydrates, 4 g protein, 14 mg calcium, 0 g fiber

rhubarb fool

As easy as it is classic, this creamy dessert is a wonderful way to say good-bye to winter and ring in spring. It's truly an April fool's paradise! Pictured on page 164.

Prep time: 10 minutes plus chilling
Cooking time: 35 minutes

- 1 **package (16 oz.) frozen cut rhubarb**
- 2 **tablespoons water**
  Pinch salt
- ⅔ **cup sugar**
- 1 **cup heavy or whipping cream**
- ½ **teaspoon vanilla extract**
  Fresh raspberries and edible leaves, for garnish (optional)

1. Bring rhubarb, water and salt to boil in a medium saucepan. Boil 5 minutes; stir in sugar. Reduce heat to medium-low and simmer 30 minutes, until mixture reaches the consistency of jam, stirring occasionally. Cool to room temperature, about 15 minutes.

2. Beat heavy cream and vanilla in a small mixer bowl on medium-high speed to soft peaks. Spoon rhubarb mixture over whipped cream; run a knife or thin spatula through rhubarb and cream and swirl to marbleize. Pour into serving bowl or 8 dessert glasses. Cover and refrigerate at least 2 hours or up to 24 hours. Garnish with raspberries and edible leaves, if desired. Makes 8 servings.

Per serving without garnishes: 180 calories, 11.5 g total fat, 7 g saturated fat, 41 mg cholesterol, 48 mg sodium, 19 g carbohydrates, 1 g protein, 44 mg calcium, 1 g fiber

vanilla-apple bread pudding

How can anyone resist bread pudding? It's a true comfort food—sweet, creamy and warm. Use bread that is dense in texture, such as French country or day-old challah, for extra-rich flavor. Pictured on page 162.

Prep time: 30 minutes plus standing
Baking time: 65 to 70 minutes

APPLES:
- 3 tablespoons unsalted butter (no substitutes)
- 3 large Granny Smith apples, peeled, cored and diced
- ½ teaspoon cinnamon
- ⅛ teaspoon grated nutmeg

BREAD PUDDING:
- 5 large eggs
- 7 large egg yolks
- 1¼ cups sugar
- Pinch salt
- 1 quart half-and-half cream (4 cups)
- 1 vanilla bean, split, or 1 teaspoon vanilla extract
- 1 loaf (12 to 16 oz.) bread, diced (about 7 cups)

1. *Prepare apples:* Melt butter in a large skillet over medium-high heat. Add apples and cook 6 to 8 minutes, until golden and tender, stirring often. Transfer to a medium bowl and toss with cinnamon and nutmeg. Set aside.

2. *Make pudding:* Heat oven to 300°F. Lightly butter six 8-ounce baking dishes. Transfer to 2 roasting pans that are large enough to hold the dishes without touching. Set aside.

3. Whisk together the eggs, egg yolks, sugar and salt in a large bowl until combined. Bring the cream and vanilla bean to boil in a medium saucepan over medium heat. Slowly whisk 1 cup of the hot cream into the egg mixture. Whisk in remaining hot cream. With the tip of a small knife, scrape seeds from vanilla bean. Add seeds to custard mixture or add vanilla extract, if using. Save vanilla bean for another use, such as adding it to granulated sugar to flavor the sugar.

4. Layer half of the bread among the prepared baking dishes, then add half of the apples. Ladle enough of the custard over apples to cover. Let stand 5 minutes, pressing down bread several times to help bread absorb custard. Repeat with remaining bread, apples and custard. Fill the roasting pan with enough hot water to reach halfway up the sides of the baking dishes. Bake 65 to 70 minutes, until tops are golden brown and no liquid appears when centers are gently pressed. Cool in water bath 15 minutes. Remove puddings from water bath and cool on a wire rack 10 minutes. Serve warm. Makes 6 servings.

Per serving: 790 calories, 39 g total fat, 20 g saturated fat, 506 mg cholesterol, 507 mg sodium, 93 g carbohydrates, 19 g protein, 294 mg calcium, 3 g fiber

the perfect biscotti

"Biscotti" (bee-SKAWT-tee) are crisp cookies with textures ranging from crunchy to quite hard. They get their name from the Italian word for "bake twice." Sturdy enough for dunking into coffee, these biscotti remain tender thanks to the addition of butter. Pictured on page 167.

Prep time: 30 minutes plus cooling
Baking time: 49 to 52 minutes

- 1 cup whole nuts (natural almonds, shelled pistachio nuts, pecans or walnuts)
- 1 teaspoon anise seeds
- 3¼ cups all-purpose flour
- 2½ teaspoons baking powder
- ½ teaspoon salt
- 3 large eggs
- 1 cup sugar
- ½ cup butter or margarine, melted
- ¼ cup vegetable oil
- 1 teaspoon grated lemon peel
- 2 tablespoons fresh lemon juice

1. Arrange oven racks in center and one position directly below. Heat oven to 350°F.

2. Bake nuts and anise seeds on a cookie sheet 4 to 5 minutes, just until golden. Cool and chop together on a cutting board.

3. Whisk together flour, baking powder and salt in a large bowl. Whisk together the eggs, sugar, butter, oil, lemon peel and juice in another bowl until smooth. Stir egg mixture into flour mixture, then stir in nuts and anise seeds. Dough will be soft, but that's okay. *(Can be made ahead. Cover and refrigerate up to 24 hours.)*

4. Divide dough in half. Lightly grease and flour a large cookie sheet. With lightly floured hands, shape dough on prepared cookie sheet into two 14×2½-inch logs (logs should be slightly rounded in the center). Bake logs on center rack 30 to 32 minutes, until golden and firm to the touch. Cool logs on cookie sheet 20 minutes. Leave oven on.

5. Transfer logs to a cutting board. With a serrated knife gently cut on an angle into ½-inch-thick slices. Lay slices flat on 2 ungreased cookie sheets. Bake 15 minutes, until biscotti are lightly browned around edges. Transfer biscotti from the center oven rack to wire rack to cool. Switch biscotti from lower to center rack and bake 4 to 5 minutes more. Cool on another wire rack. *(Can be made ahead. Store in an airtight container at room temperature up to 1 week or freeze up to 2 months. Recrisp on a cookie sheet in a 350°F. oven 5 to 8 minutes.)* Makes 3½ dozen.

Per biscotti: 110 calories, 5.5 g total fat, 2 g saturated fat, 21 mg cholesterol, 84 mg sodium, 13 g carbohydrates, 2 g protein, 29 mg calcium, 1 g fiber

pavlova

Though Pavlova (pav-LOH-vuh) originated in Australia, it was named for the Russian ballerina Anna Pavlova. A simple dish, it consists of a crisp meringue shell topped with whipped cream and fruit. Pictured on page 165.

Prep time: 20 minutes plus standing
Baking time: 1 hour

MERINGUE:

- 1½ **cups superfine sugar, divided***
- 2 **teaspoons cornstarch**
- 4 **large egg whites, at room temperature**
- 1 **teaspoon vanilla extract**
- 1 **teaspoon white vinegar**

- 1 **quart fresh strawberries, quartered**
- 2 **kiwis, peeled and sliced**
- 2 **tablespoons orange-flavored liqueur**
- 1 **cup heavy or whipping cream**
- 1 **tablespoon confectioners' sugar**

1. Combine ½ cup of the superfine sugar and the cornstarch in a small bowl. Line a cookie sheet with parchment paper. Using a 9-inch round cake pan as a guide, trace a 9-inch circle on the middle of the paper. Turn paper over. Set both aside.

2. *Make meringue:* Heat oven to 250°F. Beat egg whites in large mixer bowl on medium speed just to stiff peaks. Gradually add remaining 1 cup superfine sugar, 1 tablespoon at a time. Beat in vanilla and vinegar. Sift half of the superfine sugar and cornstarch mixture over the beaten whites; gently fold in with a rubber spatula just until combined. Sift, then fold in the remaining superfine sugar and cornstarch mixture just until blended.

3. Spoon half of the egg white mixture onto the center of the circle on the paper on cookie sheet. Spread mixture with spatula, filling in the circle. Drop remaining batter by heaping spoonfuls along the edge, touching slightly, then spread lightly from center to form a rim. Bake 1 hour. Turn oven off. Let the meringue stand in oven 1 hour. (Do not open oven door.)

4. Transfer meringue to a wire rack. Cool completely. Carefully peel parchment paper from bottom. *(Can be made ahead. Transfer meringue to an airtight container. Cover and store at room temperature up to 1 week.)*

5. Gently stir together strawberries, kiwis and liqueur in a large bowl. Beat the cream and confectioners' sugar in a large mixer bowl on medium-high speed to stiff peaks.

6. Place meringue on a large serving plate. Spread whipped cream into center of meringue. Spoon fruit on top. Serve immediately. Makes 8 servings.

*To make superfine sugar: Process granulated sugar in food processor 1 to 2 minutes, until very fine.

Per serving: 310 calories, 11.5 g total fat, 7 g saturated fat, 41 mg cholesterol, 41 mg sodium, 50 g carbohydrates, 3 g protein, 37 mg calcium, 3 g fiber

ginger cookies

With these crunchy munchies, you'll please all the ginger fans in the crowd. We use three kinds: ground, crystallized and grated fresh. Cut into turkey shapes for Thanksgiving or use any 3-inch cookie cutter to serve anytime.

Prep time: 20 minutes plus chilling and decorating
Baking time: 7 to 8 minutes per batch

DOUGH:

¼	cup whole blanched almonds
1¾	cups all-purpose flour
1	teaspoon ground ginger
½	teaspoon baking soda
½	teaspoon freshly ground pepper
¼	teaspoon salt
½	cup butter or margarine, softened
⅔	cup firmly packed brown sugar
1	large egg
1	tablespoon crystallized ginger
1	teaspoon grated fresh ginger
1	teaspoon vanilla extract

ICING:

⅓	to ½ cup confectioners' sugar
2	teaspoons water

1. *Make dough:* Heat oven to 375°F. Spread almonds on a cookie sheet and bake 10 minutes, until golden. Cool completely. Process almonds in a food processor until finely ground; set aside.

2. Meanwhile, combine flour, ground ginger, baking soda, pepper and salt in a bowl.

3. Beat butter and sugar in a large mixer bowl on medium-high speed 5 minutes, until light and fluffy, scraping bowl with a rubber spatula if necessary. Beat in egg, then beat in crystallized ginger, grated fresh ginger and vanilla until blended. At low speed, gradually beat in flour mixture and ground almonds just until blended. Gather dough into a ball; flatten into a thick disk. Wrap and refrigerate at least 1 hour or overnight.

4. Heat oven to 375°F. Lightly grease 2 large cookie sheets. Divide dough in half. On a lightly floured surface, roll 1 piece of dough ⅛ inch thick. (Keep remaining dough refrigerated.) Cut out dough with a floured 3-inch turkey-shape cookie cutter.* Transfer cutouts 1 inch apart to prepared cookie sheets. Bake 7 to 8 minutes, until cookies are golden around edges. Transfer with a metal spatula to wire racks and cool completely. Repeat with remaining dough, rerolling and cutting scraps.

5. *Make icing:* Combine sugar and water in a small bowl. Spoon icing into a small plastic storage bag; snip a small hole in one corner of bag. Decoratively pipe icing over tops of cookies. Makes about 3 dozen cookies.

*Note: Can be found at kitchen specialty stores or ordered from Wilton Enterprises (800-794-5866).

Per cookie: 80 calories, 3.5 g total fat, 1.5 g saturated fat, 13 mg cholesterol, 63 mg sodium, 11 g carbohydrates, 1 g protein, 9 mg calcium, 0 g fiber

the perfect oatmeal cookie

For a slightly different (not to mention utterly delicious!) oatmeal cookie, we use dried tart cherries and toasted pecans. For optimum flavor and texture, refrigerate the dough overnight. Pictured on page 161.

Prep time: 40 minutes plus chilling and standing
Baking time: 15 to 16 minutes per batch

1	cup dried tart cherries
2	tablespoons brandy
2½	cups old-fashioned oats, divided
1¾	cups all-purpose flour
1	teaspoon baking soda
1	teaspoon cinnamon
½	teaspoon salt
2	large eggs
1	cup butter or margarine, melted
1½	cups firmly packed brown sugar
½	cup granulated sugar
¼	cup milk
1	teaspoon vanilla extract
1	cup pecans, toasted and coarsely chopped

1. Combine cherries and brandy in a small bowl. Set aside.

2. Process 1 cup of the oats in a food processor until finely ground; transfer oats to a large bowl. Whisk in remaining 1½ cups oats, the flour, baking soda, cinnamon and salt.

3. Beat eggs and butter in a large mixer bowl on medium speed until combined. Add brown and granulated sugars, beating until smooth. Beat in milk and vanilla. At low speed, beat in flour mixture, pecans and cherry-brandy mixture until combined.

4. Cover surface of dough with plastic wrap and refrigerate overnight.

5. Let the dough stand at room temperature 20 minutes before baking. Meanwhile, adjust oven racks to center and upper third of oven. Heat oven to 375°F. Line 2 large cookie sheets with parchment paper.

6. Using a 2-inch ice cream scoop or a ¼-cup dry measure, arrange 4 scoops of dough on each prepared sheet. With wet fingers, gently press each scoop into a 3-inch circle. Bake cookies 15 to 16 minutes, until edges begin to brown. Cool cookies on sheets 5 minutes. Peel off parchment paper and transfer cookies to wire racks to cool. Repeat with remaining dough. Makes 20 cookies.

Per cookie: 310 calories, 14 g total fat, 6.5 g saturated fat, 47 mg cholesterol, 230 mg sodium, 42 g carbohydrates, 4 g protein, 33 mg calcium, 2 g fiber

slice of lemon pie

For citrus lovers only, this custard pie of Shaker origin boasts an unusual sliced-lemon filling.

Prep time: 45 minutes plus chilling and cooling
Baking time: 35 to 40 minutes

    Old-Fashioned Vinegar Pastry (recipe, page 35)

6 **sugar cubes**

2 **small lemons, rinsed**

2 **cups sugar**

⅓ **cup all-purpose flour**

¼ **teaspoon salt**

⅔ **cup water**

2 **tablespoons butter or margarine, softened**

3 **large eggs**

1 **teaspoon grated orange peel**

1. Prepare Old-Fashioned Vinegar Pastry; set aside.

2. Heat oven to 400°F. Rub sugar cubes over lemons to extract oil from peel. Place cubes in a plastic bag and crush with a rolling pin; set aside. With a sharp knife, cut peel and white pith from lemons; discard. Cut lemons into ⅛-inch-thick slices and remove seeds.

3. On a lightly floured surface, roll larger piece of pastry into a 13-inch circle and fit into a 9-inch pie plate, letting pastry overhang edge. Roll remaining pastry into a 10-inch circle and cut vents in top pastry. Set aside.

4. Combine sugar, flour and salt in a large bowl. Whisk in water, butter, eggs and orange peel. Stir in lemon slices. Pour into pastry-lined pie plate. Top with remaining pastry circle and flute edge. Sprinkle with crushed sugar cubes. Bake 35 to 40 minutes, until filling is bubbly and crust is golden. Cool on a wire rack 2 hours before serving. Serve slightly warm. Store in refrigerator. *(Can be made ahead. Store in refrigerator up to 24 hours.)* Makes 8 servings.

Per serving: 530 calories, 22 g total fat, 11.5 g saturated fat, 121 mg cholesterol, 399 mg sodium, 79 g carbohydrates, 6 g protein, 24 mg calcium, 1 g fiber

cranberry pie

Top this autumn favorite with vanilla ice cream.

Prep time: 15 minutes
Baking time: 1 hour

> 3   cups fresh or frozen cranberries
> 1¾ cups sugar, divided
> ½   cup chopped walnuts
> 2   large eggs
> 1   cup all-purpose flour
> ½   cup butter or margarine, melted
>   Vanilla ice cream (optional)

1. Heat oven to 325°F. Spread cranberries over bottom of a well-greased 10-inch pie plate. Sprinkle with ¾ cup of the sugar and the nuts.

2. Beat eggs in a mixer bowl on medium-high speed 30 seconds, until well combined. Gradually add remaining 1 cup sugar and beat 1 minute, until thoroughly mixed. Beat in flour and butter until combined. Pour batter over top of cranberries. Bake 1 hour, until lightly golden. Invert onto serving plate. Serve warm with ice cream, if desired. Makes 8 servings.

Per serving without ice cream: 415 calories, 18.5 g total fat, 8.5 g saturated fat, 86 mg cholesterol, 141 mg sodium, 60 g carbohydrates, 5 g protein, 23 mg calcium, 3 g fiber

blackberry custard pie

While this creamy pie bakes, a custard forms on the bottom and the luscious berries float to the top.

Prep time: 20 minutes plus standing and chilling
Baking time: 70 to 80 minutes

> **Single Flaky Pastry (recipe, page 36)**
> ¾   cup plus 2 tablespoons sugar
> 2   tablespoons flour
> 2   large eggs, lightly beaten
> 1   cup milk
> 3   cups fresh blackberries (about 8 oz.)

1. Prepare Single Flaky Pastry.

2. Heat oven to 400°F. Line pastry shell with foil and fill with dried beans or pie weights. Bake

10 minutes. Remove foil and beans. Bake pastry 5 minutes more. Cool completely on a wire rack.

3. *Make filling:* Combine sugar and flour in a medium bowl. Whisk in eggs and milk. Arrange blackberries in baked pastry shell. Carefully pour egg filling over berries in pastry shell. Bake 10 minutes. Reduce oven temperature to 350°F. Bake 45 to 55 minutes more, until a small knife inserted in center of filling comes out clean. Cool pie completely on wire rack. Store in refrigerator. Makes 8 servings.

Per serving: 335 calories, 14.5 g total fat, 7.5 g saturated fat, 80 mg cholesterol, 197 mg sodium, 47 g carbohydrates, 5 g protein, 67 mg calcium, 3 g fiber

triple-berry pie

Taste summertime heaven: berries under a lattice crust.

Prep time: 20 minutes plus chilling
Baking time: 65 to 75 minutes

> **Old-Fashioned Vinegar Pastry (recipe, page 35)**
> **BERRY FILLING:**
> ¾   cup sugar
> ¼   cup all-purpose flour
> 3   cups fresh blueberries
> 1½ cups fresh raspberries
> 1½ cups fresh blackberries
>
> 1   tablespoon butter or margarine, cut up
> 1   tablespoon heavy cream or milk
> 1   tablespoon sugar

1. Prepare Old-Fashioned Vinegar Pastry; set aside.

2. Adjust oven rack to lowest position. Place a cookie sheet on rack. Heat oven to 425°F.

3. *Make berry filling:* Combine sugar and flour in a large bowl. Add blueberries, raspberries and blackberries, tossing to coat.

4. On a lightly floured surface with a floured rolling pin, roll the larger pastry disk into an 11-inch circle and fit into a 9-inch pie plate, leaving a 1-inch overhang. Spoon berry filling into pastry shell; dot with butter.

5. Roll remaining pastry into a 9-inch circle. Cut into ½-inch-wide strips using a fluted pastry cutter; arrange in a lattice pattern on top of filling. Trim lattice ends. Fold bottom pastry over lattice ends and flute edge of pastry. Brush pastry with heavy cream, then sprinkle with 1 tablespoon sugar.

6. Place pie in oven on cookie sheet and bake 15 minutes. Reduce oven temperature to 375°F.; bake 50 to 60 minutes more, until center is bubbly. Cool on a wire rack. Serve at room temperature. Makes 8 servings.

Per serving: 430 calories, 19.5 g total fat, 10 g saturated fat, 40 mg cholesterol, 290 mg sodium, 60 g carbohydrates, 5 g protein, 32 mg calcium, 5 g fiber

fig and pear tart

An exceptionally rich, flaky pastry makes a wonderful base for the unusually good combination of pears and fresh figs. Pictured on page 166.

Prep time: 30 minutes plus chilling
Baking time: 25 to 35 minutes

PASTRY:

- ½ cup cold butter, cut up (no substitutes)
- 1 cup all-purpose flour
- ¼ cup sour cream

- 6 tablespoons sugar, divided
- 2 Bosc pears, unpeeled, cut into 16 wedges each
- 4 fresh figs (5 to 6 oz.), cut into wedges
- ½ cup mascarpone cheese
- 1 tablespoon honey

1. *Make pastry:* With a pastry blender or 2 knives, cut butter into flour in a medium bowl until mixture resembles coarse crumbs. Stir in sour cream. Knead just to form a ball; flatten into a 5-inch square. Wrap well in plastic wrap and refrigerate at least 2 hours or overnight.

2. On a lightly floured surface, roll pastry to a 12×8-inch rectangle. Sprinkle evenly with 2 tablespoons of the sugar. Fold pastry into thirds, letter-style. Wrap and refrigerate 30 minutes.

3. Place pastry on a lightly floured surface with an open end facing you; roll to a 15-inch-long strip. Sprinkle evenly with 2 tablespoons of the sugar; fold up again, letter-style. Wrap in plastic wrap and refrigerate 30 minutes more.

4. Roll pastry to a 13-inch square. Transfer to a large ungreased cookie sheet. With a sharp knife, trim to a 13-inch circle. Refrigerate or freeze 10 minutes.

5. Heat oven to 375°F. Arrange pears, overlapping, with rounded side at outer edge of pastry circle. Layer figs in smaller circle in center. Sprinkle with remaining 2 tablespoons sugar. Bake 25 to 35 minutes, until pastry is golden and fruit is tender. Slide a long, flexible metal spatula under pastry to loosen. Cool on a cookie sheet on a wire rack.

6. *To serve:* Combine mascarpone and honey. Serve with tart. Makes 8 servings.

Per serving: 320 calories, 20.5 g total fat, 12 g saturated fat, 53 mg cholesterol, 136 mg sodium, 34 g carbohydrates, 5 g protein, 26 mg calcium, 2 g fiber

---

test kitchen tip

fig facts...

Fresh figs possess a soft flesh and a multitude of miniscule edible seeds. They can be oval or round and range from dark purple or black to almost white in color. Fresh figs are available from June through October. They are very perishable, so use them as soon as possible after purchase. Otherwise, store figs in the refrigerator up to 3 days. The most common types follow.

CALIMYRNA FIGS OR SMYRNA FIGS, from California and Turkey respectively, are large with green skin and white flesh.

ADRIATIC FIGS have a pear shape and violet to brown skin.

MISSION FIGS have purplish-black skin and extremely tiny seeds.

country-style sour cherry tart

If you can't find fresh sour cherries (available only a few weeks in the summer), substitute jarred or frozen ones and enjoy this country-style tart anytime of year.

Prep time: 20 minutes plus chilling
Baking time: 30 to 35 minutes

PASTRY:

- 1½   cups all-purpose flour
- 2   tablespoons sugar
- ¼   teaspoon salt
- ½   cup cold butter, cut up (no substitutes)
- 4   to 6 tablespoons ice water

FILLING:

- ¾   pound fresh sour cherries, pitted (2¼ cups)
- 3   tablespoons plus 2 teaspoons sugar, divided
- 2   tablespoons cornstarch
- 1   large egg yolk, lightly beaten
- 1   teaspoon water
- Sweetened whipped cream or vanilla ice cream (optional)

1. *Make pastry:* Combine flour, sugar and salt in a medium bowl. With a pastry blender or 2 knives, cut in butter until mixture resembles coarse crumbs. Sprinkle with the water, 1 tablespoon at a time, tossing with a fork until pastry just holds together. Shape the pastry into a ball and flatten into a thick disk; wrap well in plastic wrap and refrigerate 30 minutes.

2. Adjust oven rack to lowest position. Heat oven to 425°F. Roll pastry between 2 sheets of waxed paper into a 10-inch circle. Remove top sheet of waxed paper. Place a cookie sheet over pastry circle and invert onto cookie sheet. Remove second sheet of waxed paper.

3. *Make filling:* Drain cherries of excess juice, leaving only about 1 tablespoon juice. Toss cherries with 3 tablespoons of the sugar and the cornstarch in a large bowl. Place cherries on pastry circle, leaving a 1½-inch border. With a fork, whisk together egg yolk and water in a cup. Fold border up over cherries to make a 1-inch-wide edge. Brush pastry border with egg mixture and sprinkle with

remaining 2 teaspoons sugar. Bake 30 to 35 minutes, until golden and bubbly. Cool on cookie sheet on a wire rack. Serve warm or at room temperature with whipped cream or ice cream, if desired. Makes 6 servings.

Per serving without whipped cream or ice cream: 350 calories, 17.5 g total fat, 10.5 g saturated fat, 79 mg cholesterol, 266 mg sodium, 45 g carbohydrates, 4 g protein, 23 mg calcium, 2 g fiber

warm banana tart

This decadent tart boasts pecans, sliced bananas, a custard cream and, to top it off, caramel sauce.

Prep time: 45 minutes plus chilling and cooling
Baking time: 37 to 46 minutes

PASTRY:

- 1¼   cups all-purpose flour
- ½   cup confectioners' sugar
- Pinch salt
- 6   tablespoons cold butter, cut up (no substitutes)
- 1   large egg, lightly beaten

PECAN FILLING:

- 1¼   cups pecans, ground
- ⅓   cup butter, melted (no substitutes)
- ¼   cup sugar
- ¼   cup heavy or whipping cream
- 1   large egg

PASTRY CREAM:

- 1   cup milk
- 6   tablespoons sugar, divided
- ½   of a vanilla bean, split lengthwise, or 1½ teaspoons vanilla extract
- 2   large egg yolks
- 2   tablespoons all-purpose flour
- 1   large, ripe banana, thinly sliced
- 2   tablespoons sugar
- Warm Caramel Sauce (recipe, opposite page)

1. *Make pastry:* Pulse together flour, sugar and salt in a food processor to combine. Add butter; process until mixture resembles fine crumbs. With motor running, pour egg through feed tube, processing just until pastry forms a ball. Wrap and refrigerate 1 hour or overnight.

2. On lightly floured waxed paper, roll pastry into an 11-inch circle. Fit into a 9½-inch tart pan with removable bottom. Trim overhang to 1 inch and press in against sides. Prick bottom with fork. Refrigerate 1 hour or freeze 20 minutes.

3. Heat oven to 350°F. Bake pastry 22 to 26 minutes, until golden. Cool pastry completely on a wire rack.

4. *Make pecan filling:* Combine all ingredients in a medium bowl. Spread on bottom of cooled pastry shell. Bake in 350°F. oven 15 to 20 minutes, until filling is set. Cool completely on wire rack. *(Can be made ahead. Cover and refrigerate up to 24 hours.)*

5. *Make pastry cream:* Bring milk, 4 tablespoons of the sugar and the vanilla bean to boil in a medium saucepan over medium-high heat. Meanwhile, whisk yolks and remaining 2 tablespoons sugar in a medium bowl; whisk in flour. Gradually whisk hot milk mixture into yolk mixture; return to saucepan, whisking constantly. Bring to boil, whisking. Reduce heat and cook, stirring, 1 minute more. Remove from heat; discard vanilla bean. (Stir in vanilla extract, if using.) Transfer to a medium bowl and cover surface of pastry cream with plastic wrap. Cool, then refrigerate until ready to use. *(Can be made ahead. Cover and refrigerate up to 24 hours.)*

6. Heat broiler. Cover edge of tart with foil to prevent burning. Arrange banana slices on cooled tart. Spread an even layer of pastry cream over banana, leaving a ½-inch border. Sprinkle with 2 tablespoons sugar. Broil 3 minutes, until top is golden brown. Serve warm with Warm Caramel Sauce. Makes 12 servings.

Per serving without caramel sauce: 355 calories, 23.5 g total fat, 10 g saturated fat, 110 mg cholesterol, 165 mg sodium, 33 g carbohydrates, 5 g protein, 50 mg calcium, 2 g fiber

warm caramel
sauce EASY

Prep time: 5 minutes
Cooking time: 9 minutes

- ¼ cup butter (no substitutes)
- 1 cup sugar
- 1 cup heavy or whipping cream

Melt butter in a medium saucepan over medium-high heat. Add sugar and cook 6 to 8 minutes, until sugar melts and mixture is a deep amber color, stirring occasionally. Remove from heat. Gradually stir in heavy cream (mixture will bubble vigorously and be lumpy). Return to heat and cook 1 to 3 minutes, until smooth. Strain sauce through sieve into a small bowl. *(Can be made ahead. Cover and refrigerate up to 24 hours. Reheat before serving.)* Makes 1⅔ cups.

Per 2-tablespoon serving: 165 calories, 11.5 g total fat, 7 g saturated fat, 38 mg cholesterol, 49 mg sodium, 17 g carbohydrates, 0 g protein, 14 mg calcium, 0 g fiber

strawberry rhubarb tart

Fresh strawberries pair up with ruddy rhubarb for a sweet spring treat.

Prep time: 45 minutes plus chilling and standing
Baking time: 22 to 24 minutes

PASTRY:

1½   cups all-purpose flour
 2   tablespoons sugar
     Pinch salt
 ½   cup cold butter, cut up (no substitutes)
 1   large egg yolk
 2   to 3 tablespoons ice water

 4   cups fresh or frozen rhubarb (1 lb.), cut into ¼-inch-thick slices
 ½   cup sugar
1½   pints strawberries, sliced into thirds
 3   tablespoons red currant jelly, melted
     Sweetened whipped cream (optional)

1. *Make pastry:* Combine flour, sugar and salt in a bowl. With pastry blender or 2 knives, cut in butter until mixture resembles coarse crumbs. Combine egg yolk and water in a small bowl; stir into flour mixture until pastry just holds together. Shape pastry into a ball and flatten into a thick disk. Wrap well in plastic wrap and refrigerate at least 1 hour or overnight. On a lightly floured surface, roll to a 13-inch circle. Fit into a 10-inch tart pan with a removable bottom. Fold overhanging pastry into side of crust and gently press edge up to extend ¼ inch above side of tart pan. Prick bottom with a fork. Refrigerate 30 minutes.

2. Heat oven to 400°F. Line the pastry with foil and fill with dried beans or pie weights. Bake 10 minutes. Remove foil and beans. Bake 12 to 14 minutes more, until golden brown. Cool.

3. Meanwhile, combine rhubarb and ½ cup sugar in a medium saucepan. Let stand 30 minutes. Cover and bring to simmer. Cook 15 to 20 minutes, until rhubarb is tender and thickened. (If using frozen rhubarb, cook uncovered.) Transfer to a medium bowl; cool. Spread in pastry shell. Arrange strawberries, cut sides down, in a circular pattern,

pointed ends out, over rhubarb; brush with melted jelly. Refrigerate 1 hour. Serve with whipped cream, if desired. Makes 8 servings.

Per serving without whipped cream: 305 calories, 13.5 g total fat, 8 g saturated fat, 59 mg cholesterol, 167 mg sodium, 44 g carbohydrates, 4 g protein, 71 mg calcium, 3 g fiber

pear and apple tart tatin

The combination of pear and apple adds a new dimension of flavor to this classic upside-down French fruit tart.

Prep time: 30 minutes plus chilling
Baking time: 35 minutes

PASTRY:

 1   cup all-purpose flour
 2   teaspoons sugar
     Pinch salt
 ⅓   cup cold butter, cut up (no substitutes)
 3   to 4 tablespoons ice water

FILLING:

 6   tablespoons butter, softened (no substitutes), divided
 8   tablespoons sugar, divided
 3   ripe Anjou or Bartlett pears (1¼ lbs.), peeled, cored and quartered
 3   Golden Delicious apples (1¼ lbs.), peeled, cored and quartered

1. *Make pastry:* Combine flour, sugar and salt in a medium bowl. With a pastry blender or 2 knives, cut in cold butter until mixture resembles coarse crumbs. Add water, 1 tablespoon at a time, tossing with a fork until pastry comes together. Shape into a ball and flatten into a thick disk. Wrap well in plastic wrap and refrigerate 1 hour or overnight.

2. On a lightly floured surface, roll pastry ¼ inch thick and cut into a 9-inch circle. Freeze 1 hour on a cookie sheet lined with waxed paper.

3. Heat oven to 375°F.

4. *Make filling:* Spread 4 tablespoons of the softened butter over bottom and side of a 10-inch cast-iron skillet. Sprinkle bottom and side with 5 tablespoons of the sugar. Alternate apple and pear quarters, cored sides up and wide ends pointing out, in a tight concentric circle around outer edge of skillet. Arrange remaining apple and pear quarters in center. Dot with remaining 2 tablespoons softened butter and sprinkle with remaining 3 tablespoons sugar. Cook over medium-high heat 15 minutes, until sugar is caramelized and golden brown, shaking and swirling skillet frequently.

5. Place a cookie sheet on center oven rack. Invert frozen crust over fruit in skillet and remove waxed paper. Place skillet on cookie sheet and bake about 35 minutes, until crust is well browned.

6. Remove skillet from oven. Immediately invert tart onto serving dish. Serve warm or at room temperature. Makes 8 servings.

Per serving: 330 calories, 18 g total fat, 10.5 g saturated fat, 46 mg cholesterol, 212 mg sodium, 43 g carbohydrates, 2 g protein, 18 mg calcium, 3 g fiber

peach tarts with crème fraîche

These tarts top the charts with luscious peaches in season.

Prep time: 1½ hours plus standing and chilling
Baking time: 25 minutes
Microwave used

CRÈME FRAÎCHE:
- **1** cup sour cream
- **1** cup heavy or whipping cream

PASTRY:
- **3** cups all-purpose flour
- **1** tablespoon sugar
- **½** teaspoon salt
- **¾** cup cold unsalted butter, cut up (no substitutes)
- **¼** cup shortening
- **6** to 9 tablespoons ice water

    Water
- **6** firm ripe peaches
- **1** tablespoon fresh lemon juice
- **8** tablespoons sugar
- **8** teaspoons unsalted butter, cut up (no substitutes)
- **¼** cup peach or apricot preserves

1. *Make crème fraîche:* Place sour cream and heavy cream in a glass jar and stir until smooth. Cover and let stand at room temperature 2 to 5 hours, until it thickens. Stir again and refrigerate 24 hours. *(Can be made ahead. Refrigerate up to 1 week.)* Makes 2 cups.

2. *Make pastry:* Pulse together flour, sugar and salt in a food processor to blend. Add butter and shortening; process until mixture resembles coarse crumbs. With motor running, add water, 1 tablespoon at a time, through the feed tube, pulsing until mixture is moist enough to hold together. Shape into a ball and flatten into a disk. Cut into 8 equal wedges and shape each into a 3-inch disk. Place disks on a cookie sheet; cover with plastic wrap and refrigerate 1 hour or overnight.

3. Between 2 sheets of waxed paper, roll each disk into a 6½-inch circle. Using a saucer or saucepan lid as a guide, trim each into a 6-inch circle. Stack between sheets of waxed paper and refrigerate until ready to use. *(Can be made ahead. Wrap well in plastic wrap and freeze up to 2 weeks. Transfer to refrigerator to thaw 2 hours before using.)*

4. Heat oven to 425°F. Bring a small saucepan of water to boil. Add 1 of the peaches to boiling water and cook 20 to 40 seconds, until skin peels easily from fruit; repeat with remaining peaches. Peel peaches and slice into thin wedges. Toss with lemon juice in a large bowl.

5. Line each of 2 cookie sheets with foil, turning edges up to form a 1-inch-high rim. Place a pastry circle on a floured board. Brush edge with water and fold in edge to form ½-inch-wide rim; flute edge. Arrange ½ cup of the peaches on pastry circle. Sprinkle with 1 tablespoon of the sugar and dot with 1 teaspoon of the butter. Transfer to baking sheet. Repeat with remaining pastry, water, peaches, sugar and butter. Bake 25 minutes, until fruit is bubbly and pastry is golden, switching pans halfway through. Immediately transfer to wire racks to cool.

6. Place preserves in a small microwaveproof dish. Microwave on High 1 minute, until melted. Strain through sieve and brush over tarts. Serve with crème fraîche. Makes 8 tarts.

Per tart: 690 calories, 45 g total fat, 25.5 g saturated fat, 112 mg cholesterol, 177 mg sodium, 66 g carbohydrates, 7 g protein, 72 mg calcium, 3 g fiber

chèvre cheese

Made from goat's milk (chèvre is the French term for "goat"), chèvre cheeses have a distinctive tart flavor. A chèvre's texture varies from soft yet firm, like cream cheese, to dry and hard. They come in many shapes and sizes: rounds, logs, pyramids, loaves and cones. A few of the most popular chèvres include Montrachet cheese (at its best, young and fresh) and Bûcheron cheese—both have a mild tangy flavor and soft texture and are available in logs. Another well-known chèvre is Banon, which is cured in chestnut leaves. Its flavor is slightly lemony, and its texture is soft (look for Banon from late spring to the beginning of fall). Serve chèvre as a dessert cheese or prior to dinner drinks.

goat cheese-cherry tart

The mild tangy flavor of fresh goat cheese complements the sweet cherries and nutty liqueur in this unique tart.

Prep time: 40 minutes plus chilling and standing
Baking time: 30 to 35 minutes

PASTRY:
- 1¼ **cups all-purpose flour**
- 1 **teaspoon confectioners' sugar**
- ¼ **teaspoon salt**
- 7 **tablespoons cold butter, cut up (no substitutes)**
- 3 **to 4 tablespoons ice water**

FILLING:
- ½ **cup granulated sugar**
- ¼ **cup unsalted butter, softened (no substitutes)**
- 2 **packages (3 oz. each) cream cheese, softened**
- 4 **ounces fresh goat cheese (such as Montrachet)**
- 2 **large eggs**
- 2 **tablespoons amaretto liqueur**

GLAZE:
- ¼ **cup red currant jelly**
- 2 **tablespoons amaretto liqueur**
- ¾ **pound sweet cherries, pitted and halved (about 2 cups)**

1. *Make pastry:* Combine flour, confectioners' sugar and salt in a large bowl. With a pastry blender or 2 knives, cut in butter until mixture resembles coarse crumbs. Sprinkle with the water, 1 tablespoon at a time, tossing with a fork until pastry just holds together. Shape into a ball and flatten into a thick disk. Wrap well in plastic wrap and refrigerate 30 minutes.

2. Adjust oven rack to lowest position. Heat oven to 425°F. On a lightly floured surface, roll pastry into an 11-inch circle. Fit into a 9½-inch tart pan with a removable bottom. Gently press pastry with fingertips along bottom and up side of pan. Fold overhanging pastry to the inside of crust and gently press side up to top edge of pan. Freeze pastry shell 5 minutes. Prick bottom with a fork. Cover pastry with foil and fill with dried beans or pie weights. Bake 12 minutes. Remove foil and beans. Continue baking 12 minutes more, until golden. Transfer to a wire rack. Reduce oven temperature to 375°F.

3. *Make filling:* Beat sugar and butter in a clean mixer bowl on medium speed until light and fluffy. Beat in cheeses. Add eggs, one at a time, beating well after each addition. Beat in liqueur. Pour into prepared pastry. Bake 30 to 35 minutes, until set and edges are slightly browned. Cool on a wire rack.

4. *Make glaze:* Meanwhile, combine jelly and liqueur in a small saucepan. Cook over low heat, stirring, until jelly is melted; brush a thin layer on cooled tart. Place cherries, cut sides down on glaze. Brush cherries with remaining glaze. Cover loosely with foil, not touching cherries with foil; refrigerate overnight. Makes 8 to 10 servings.

Per serving: 475 calories, 29 g total fat, 17.5 g saturated fat, 128 mg cholesterol, 316 mg sodium, 43 g carbohydrates, 8 g protein, 57 mg calcium, 1 g fiber

frozen mango soufflé

When in season, buy ripe mangoes. If not, you can substitute frozen mango puree. Or for a change, substitute 1 pound fresh peaches.

Prep time: 45 minutes plus standing and freezing
Cooking time: 10 minutes
Microwave used

- 2 pounds (2 large) ripe mangoes or 1 package (14 oz.) frozen mango puree, thawed
- 1 cup heavy or whipping cream
- 6 large egg whites
- 1 cup sugar
- ⅓ cup plus 2 tablespoons water, divided
- 3 tablespoons light rum, divided
- 1 envelope unflavored gelatin
  Fresh strawberries, for garnish (optional)

1. Measure a piece of waxed paper long enough to wrap around a 1-quart soufflé dish. Fold in half and tape to create a "collar" around the dish that extends 3 inches above the rim.

2. Peel and remove pits from mangoes. Puree in a blender. Measure 2 cups into a bowl; set aside. (Save surplus for another use.)

3. Beat heavy cream in a mixer bowl on medium-high speed to soft peaks; refrigerate until ready to use.

4. Place egg whites in a large clean mixer bowl. Combine sugar and ⅓ cup of the water in a small saucepan over high heat. Boil until temperature registers 230°F. on a candy thermometer. Beat whites with clean beaters on medium speed to soft peaks. As soon as syrup registers 238°F. (soft-ball stage), slowly drizzle syrup in a fine stream into whites, beating constantly. Continue to beat on high speed 10 minutes, until the meringue cools to room temperature.

5. Meanwhile, combine remaining 2 tablespoons water with 2 tablespoons of the rum in a small microwaveproof bowl. Sprinkle gelatin on top and let stand 5 minutes. Microwave on High 30 to 45 seconds, until gelatin is completely dissolved.

Stir into the mango puree. Add remaining 1 tablespoon rum.

6. Gently fold mango mixture into meringue. Fold in whipped cream.

7. Pour the mango mixture into prepared dish. Cover and freeze until firm, 6 hours or overnight. *(Can be made ahead. Freeze up to 5 days.)* Place in refrigerator 30 minutes before serving. Garnish with strawberries, if desired. Makes 16 servings.

Per serving without berries: 155 calories, 5.5 g total fat, 3.5 g saturated fat, 21 mg cholesterol, 36 mg sodium, 24 g carbohydrates, 2 g protein, 15 mg calcium, 1 g fiber

---

test kitchen tip

food editors' quick desserts

Here are two of our food editors' favorite ways to satisfy a sweet tooth in a hurry.

HOT BERRY TOPPING: Heat 2 tablespoons butter and 2 tablespoons sugar in a medium saucepan over medium heat until smooth. Add 1 bag (10 or 12 oz.) frozen mixed berries, partially thawed. Bring to boil. Cook 2 minutes, just until berries are heated through. With a slotted spoon, transfer fruit to a serving bowl. Boil juices 1 minute, until thickened slightly. Stir into berries with 2 tablespoons almond-flavored liqueur. Serve with 1 pint vanilla ice cream. Makes 4 servings.

RICOTTA-CHIP FILLING: Process ¾ cup ricotta cheese, 1 package (3 oz.) cream cheese and 3 tablespoons confectioners' sugar in a food processor until smooth. Transfer to a medium bowl; stir in ¼ cup miniature chocolate chips. Assemble desserts using 12 Bordeaux cookies. For each serving, spread ¼ cup filling on 2 cookies; stack on top of each other and top with a plain cookie. Repeat with remaining filling and cookies. Dust tops with additional confectioners' sugar. Makes 4 servings.

triple nut caramel tart

This tart resembles pecan pie with a few surprises: caramelized sugar for flavor and color, and a tasty crunch from three kinds of nuts.

Prep time: 50 minutes plus chilling and standing
Baking time: 55 to 56 minutes

PASTRY:

- 1¼ **cups all-purpose flour**
- ⅛ **teaspoon salt**
- ¼ **cup cold butter, cut up (no substitutes)**
- 2 **tablespoons vegetable shortening**
- 3 **to 4 tablespoons ice water**

FILLING:

- ½ **cup sugar**
  Water
- ¾ **cup light corn syrup**
- 2 **large eggs, lightly beaten**
- 2 **tablespoons butter, melted (no substitutes)**
- 1 **tablespoon dark rum**
- ⅛ **teaspoon salt**
- ⅓ **cup walnuts, coarsely chopped**
- ⅓ **cup pecans, coarsely chopped**
- ⅓ **cup sliced almonds**

1. *Make pastry:* Combine flour and salt in a medium bowl. With a pastry blender or 2 knives, cut in butter and shortening until mixture resembles fine crumbs. Add water, 1 tablespoon at a time, tossing with a fork until pastry comes together. Shape into a ball and flatten into a thick disk. Wrap well in plastic wrap and refrigerate 30 minutes.

2. Adjust oven rack to lowest position. Place a cookie sheet on rack. Heat oven to 375°F. On a lightly floured surface, roll pastry into an 11-inch circle. Fit into a 9½-inch tart pan with a removable bottom or a 9-inch pie plate. Gently press pastry with fingertips along bottom and up side of pan. Fold overhanging pastry to inside of crust and gently press edge up to extend ¼ inch above side of tart pan; trim edge, or flute for pie plate. Freeze 10 minutes.

3. Line pastry with foil and fill with dried beans or pie weights. Place on cookie sheet. Bake 15 minutes.

Remove foil and beans; bake 15 to 16 minutes more, until pastry is golden brown. Cool on a wire rack.

4. *Make filling:* Combine sugar and 2 tablespoons water in a medium saucepan. Cook over medium heat just until sugar is dissolved. Continue cooking, without stirring, until syrup is a caramel color. Remove from heat. With a long-handled spoon, carefully add ⅓ cup water, stirring until smooth (mixture will bubble vigorously).

5. Reduce oven temperature to 350°F. Whisk together cooled caramel, corn syrup, eggs, melted butter, rum and salt in a medium bowl until smooth.

6. Spread nuts in an even layer in pastry crust; place on same cookie sheet. Pour in caramel mixture. Bake 25 minutes for 9½-inch tart or 45 minutes for 9-inch pie, until center is just set. Cool on a wire rack. Remove tart from pan before serving. Makes 8 servings.

Per serving: 430 calories, 23 g total fat, 7.5 g saturated fat, 78 mg cholesterol, 219 mg sodium, 52 g carbohydrates, 6 g protein, 38 mg calcium, 2 g fiber

pineapple rum sauce LOW FAT EASY

Get a taste of the tropics with each bite. Fresh pineapple in a rum and caramel glaze plays up the creaminess of ice cream. The syrup goes from clear to golden fairly quickly, so pay attention when it begins to color. To save time, purchase peeled fresh pineapple found in your supermarket's produce section.

Prep time: 10 minutes plus cooling
Cooking time: 10 minutes

- 1 **cup sugar**
- ½ **cup water**
- 1 **cup light rum**
- ½ **of a cinnamon stick**
- 3 **cups fresh pineapple chunks**
- 1 **tablespoon minced crystallized ginger**
- 1 **cup unsweetened coconut flakes**
  Assorted sorbets or vanilla ice cream
  Fresh mint sprigs, for garnish (optional)

1. Combine sugar and water in a medium saucepan; bring to boil. Boil 6 to 7 minutes, until syrup is an amber color. Carefully pour in the rum (mixture will bubble up); add cinnamon. Cook over medium heat until sauce is completely smooth and melted. Discard cinnamon stick. Stir in pineapple and ginger; cool.

2. Meanwhile, heat oven to 325°F. Toast coconut on a cookie sheet 3 to 4 minutes, just until golden, stirring once. *(Can be made ahead. Transfer sauce and coconut to 2 separate airtight containers; cover. Refrigerate sauce and store coconut at room temperature overnight.)* Scoop sorbets into 8 serving bowls. Top with pineapple sauce and coconut. Garnish with mint, if desired. Makes 8 servings.

Per serving without sorbet, ice cream or garnish: 250 calories, 5.5 g total fat, 4.5 g saturated fat, 0 mg cholesterol, 6 mg sodium, 36 g carbohydrates, 1 g protein, 9 mg calcium, 1 g fiber

tapioca pudding with caramelized pears EASY

Dessert doesn't get much better than creamy tapioca pudding with a hint of cinnamon. Except, of course, when you top it with caramelized pears. Pictured on page 161.

Prep time: 10 minutes plus chilling
Cooking time: 20 minutes

PUDDING:

- 3 **cups milk**
- ¼ **cup quick-cooking tapioca**
- 1 **cinnamon stick**
- 6 **tablespoons sugar, divided**
- 3 **large eggs, separated**
- ½ **teaspoon vanilla extract**
  Pinch salt

PEARS:

- 2 **tablespoons butter (no substitutes)**
- 2½ **pounds Bartlett pears, peeled, cored and cut into eighths**
- 2 **tablespoons sugar**
- ■
  Grated nutmeg

1. Bring the milk, tapioca and cinnamon stick to boil in a large saucepan over medium heat. Cook at a gentle boil, stirring, 9 to 10 minutes, until the mixture thickens.

2. Whisk together 4 tablespoons of the sugar and the egg yolks in a small bowl. Whisk a small amount of the tapioca mixture into yolk mixture; stir mixture into saucepan. Cook pudding 2 minutes, until temperature registers 160°F. on an instant-read thermometer. Remove from heat. Discard cinnamon stick; stir in vanilla and salt.

3. Beat egg whites in a medium mixer bowl on medium speed until whites are soft and foamy. With mixer running, gradually add remaining 2 tablespoons sugar. Beat egg whites on medium-high speed to stiff peaks. Fold beaten egg whites into saucepan. Cook tapioca mixture over low heat 3 to 5 minutes, until mixture registers 160°F. on an instant-read thermometer.

4. Transfer pudding to a large serving bowl. Cover and refrigerate until cold, 1 to 2 hours. *(Can be made ahead. Cover and refrigerate up to 2 days.)* Makes 4 cups.

5. *Make pears:* Meanwhile, melt butter in a 12-inch nonstick skillet over medium heat. Add pears and sugar; increase heat to medium-high and cook 15 to 20 minutes, until pears are golden brown, stirring often.

6. *To serve:* Spoon pudding into 6 individual bowls; divide pears evenly and sprinkle top of pudding with nutmeg. Makes 6 servings.

Per serving: 338 calories, 11 g total fat, 6 g saturated fat, 134 mg cholesterol, 184 mg sodium, 55 g carbohydrates, 8 g protein, 181 mg calcium, 4 g fiber

coffee semifreddo

When translated, the name of this Italian dessert means "somewhat cold." Our semifreddo gets its divine flavor from brewed espresso, coffee liqueur and a dusting of ground hazelnut praline. The praline also makes a great topping for ice cream, rice pudding or fruit.

Total prep time: 40 minutes plus freezing

- ⅔ cup brewed espresso, cooled, or ⅔ cup hot water plus 2 teaspoons instant espresso powder, divided
- 6 large egg yolks
- ½ cup sugar, divided
- 2 cups heavy or whipping cream
- 2 tablespoons coffee-flavored liqueur

HAZELNUT PRALINE:
- ½ cup sugar
- ¼ cup hazelnuts, toasted and skins removed*

1. Line a 6-cup ring mold or a 9×5-inch loaf pan with plastic wrap; set aside.

2. Whisk together ⅓ cup of the espresso, the egg yolks and ¼ cup of the sugar in the top of a double boiler. Set over, but not touching, simmering water. Whisk constantly 4 to 5 minutes, until thickened and smooth. Remove from heat. Place pan in a bowl half-filled with ice water. Continue whisking the mixture for 2 minutes to cool. Set aside.

3. Beat cream and the remaining ¼ cup sugar in a chilled large mixer bowl on medium speed to soft peaks. Add add remaining ⅓ cup espresso and the liqueur; beat to stiff peaks.

4. Gently fold egg yolk mixture into whipped cream mixture. Spoon into prepared pan. Cover with plastic wrap and freeze 6 hours or overnight. *(Can be made ahead. Freeze up to 1 week.)*

5. *Make hazelnut praline:* Grease a jelly-roll pan. Melt sugar in a large heavy skillet over medium-high heat until deep amber in color. Stir to dissolve any lumps. Stir in nuts. Immediately spread in prepared pan and cool completely. Break into chunks and process to a fine powder in a food processor. *(Can be made ahead. Store in an airtight container up to 1 week.)*

6. *To serve:* Unmold semifreddo onto chilled platter; unwrap. Sprinkle hazelnut praline over top. Save any leftover praline in an airtight container for another use. Cover and return to freezer until ready to eat. Cut into ½-inch-thick slices. Makes 16 servings.

Note: To remove skins, gently rub warm nuts with a clean kitchen towel.

Per serving: 190 calories, 14.5 g total fat, 7.5 g saturated fat, 121 mg cholesterol, 14 mg sodium, 14 g carbohydrates, 2 g protein, 31 mg calcium, 0 g fiber

walnut-almond brittle ice cream

This is the creamiest ice cream you ever tasted, and worth every calorie, too!

Prep time: 30 minutes plus chilling
Cooking time: 13 to 19 minutes

WALNUT-ALMOND BRITTLE:
- ½ cup sugar
- 3 tablespoons water
- Pinch cream of tartar
- ½ cup chopped walnuts
- ¼ cup blanched whole almonds

ICE CREAM:
- ½ cup sugar
- ¼ cup water
- 6 large egg yolks
- 2 tablespoons amber rum
- 2 teaspoons vanilla extract
- Pinch salt
- 2 cups heavy or whipping cream, whipped

1. *Make walnut-almond brittle:* Combine sugar, water and cream of tartar in a small saucepan. Cook, without stirring, over medium heat 10 to 15 minutes, until caramel-colored. Do not overcook. Stir nuts into caramel mixture. Immediately pour onto a cookie sheet; cool. Break into pieces and coarsely grind in a food processor.

2. *Make ice cream:* Combine sugar and water in a small saucepan. Bring to boil over high heat; continue to boil, stirring, 2 minutes. Beat yolks in a mixer bowl on high speed and add sugar syrup in a slow, steady stream. Continue beating on high speed 5 minutes, until mixture is the consistency of heavy cream and has cooled. Beat in rum, vanilla and salt. Fold in whipped cream. Cover and refrigerate until cold, 4 hours or overnight.

3. Freeze in ice-cream maker according to manufacturer's directions. Stir in walnut-almond brittle. Place in freezer until firm. Makes 1 quart.

Per ¼-cup serving: 215 calories, 16.5 g total fat, 8 g saturated fat, 121 mg cholesterol, 33 mg sodium, 14 g carbohydrates, 3 g protein, 37 mg calcium, 0 g fiber

mixed berry granita

Cool off this summer with a refreshing frozen granita. We use a combination of blueberries and raspberries, but just about any summer fruit will do.

Total prep time: 10 minutes plus standing and freezing

1½	cups water
¾	cup sugar
3	sprigs fresh mint
2	1-inch strips lemon peel
2	cups fresh blueberries
2	cups fresh raspberries
2	teaspoons fresh lemon juice

1. Bring water, sugar, mint and lemon peel to boil in a medium saucepan over medium heat. Reduce heat and simmer until sugar is completely dissolved. Remove from heat; cover and let stand 15 minutes. Transfer syrup to medium bowl; refrigerate until cool, 45 minutes. Discard mint leaves and lemon peel.

2. Meanwhile, place a 13×9-inch metal baking pan and a metal spoon in the freezer.

3. Puree blueberries and raspberries in a food processor until smooth. Strain berry puree through a fine sieve over the bowl of syrup. Add the lemon juice and stir until combined. Pour mixture into a chilled pan.

4. Freeze berry mixture until ice crystals form around edges of pan, 30 minutes. With the chilled spoon, scrape the ice crystals from edges and stir into the mixture. Freeze mixture 1 to 1½ hours more, until all of the liquid is frozen, stirring every 30 minutes. For a fluffy consistency, stir granita mixture with tines of fork just before serving. *(Can be made ahead. Line pan with plastic wrap, allowing a 1-inch excess to hang over side. Pour mixture into prepared pan. Freeze overnight. Lift granita out of pan by plastic overhang and transfer some of mixture to food processor. Pulse 2 or 3 times, until coarsely chopped. Do not overprocess or mixture will become too soft. Continue processing remaining mixture.)* Spoon granita into 8 small serving bowls. Makes 8 servings.

Per serving: 110 calories, 0.5 g total fat, 0 g saturated fat, 0 mg cholesterol, 2 mg sodium, 28 g carbohydrates, 0.5 g protein, 10 mg calcium, 2 g fiber

---

test kitchen tip

berry tidbits

STRAWBERRIES: Size doesn't affect sweetness. Just be sure to pick them when they're plump, and choose bright red fruit with fresh green caps.

RED RASPBERRIES: Choose fuchsia-colored fruit with a soft, slightly downy appearance.

BLACKBERRIES: Look for big, juicy, glossy purple-black berries.

BLUEBERRIES: The whitish "bloom" means they're fresh.

strawberries with black-pepper syrup and lemon-pepper wafers ᴇᴀsʏ

Black pepper in a dessert? It's the secret ingredient no one will ever suspect. This sugar syrup flavored with black peppercorns tastes fabulous poured over fresh berries. Our crunchy buttery wafers make the perfect accompaniment.

Prep time: 15 minutes plus standing and chilling
Baking time: 12 to 15 minutes per batch

LEMON-PEPPER WAFERS:
- 1½ cups all-purpose flour
- ¾ cup yellow cornmeal
- 2 teaspoons grated lemon peel
- 1 teaspoon freshly ground pepper
- ¼ teaspoon salt
- 1 cup butter, softened (no substitutes)
- 1 cup sugar
- 1 large egg
- 1 large egg yolk

BLACK-PEPPER SYRUP:
- ½ cup sugar
- ½ cup water
- 2 teaspoons black peppercorns, lightly crushed

- 1 quart fresh strawberries, quartered
  Vanilla ice cream (optional)

1. *Make lemon-pepper wafers:* Whisk together flour, cornmeal, lemon peel, pepper and salt in a medium bowl. Beat butter and sugar in a large mixer bowl on medium-high speed 3 to 5 minutes, until creamy. Beat in egg and egg yolk until well blended, scraping side of bowl with a rubber spatula. At low speed, beat in flour mixture just until combined.

2. Divide dough in half. Shape each piece into a 9×1-inch log. Wrap each log in waxed paper and refrigerate until firm, 3½ hours or overnight.

3. Adjust oven racks to middle and upper third of oven. Heat oven to 350°F. Working with 1 log at a time, unwrap log and cut into ¼-inch-thick slices. Place slices 1 inch apart on 2 large ungreased cookie

sheets. Bake 12 to 15 minutes, until edges are light golden. Cool on wire racks. Repeat with remaining dough. (*Can be made ahead. Freeze in airtight containers up to 1 month.*) Makes 5 dozen.

4. *Make black-pepper syrup:* Meanwhile, bring all ingredients to boil in a small saucepan over medium heat. Boil mixture 5 to 8 minutes, until sugar dissolves. Remove from heat. Cover and let stand 30 minutes. Pour syrup through a sieve over a medium bowl. Discard peppercorns. (*Can be made ahead. Refrigerate syrup in an airtight container up to 1 month.*) Makes ¾ cup.

5. Arrange strawberries in a large serving bowl. Spoon 2 tablespoons of the chilled black-pepper syrup over strawberries just before serving. Serve with lemon-pepper wafers and vanilla ice cream, if desired. Makes 4 to 6 servings.

Per serving without ice cream and lemon-pepper wafers:
135 calories, 0.5 g total fat, 0 g saturated fat, 0 mg cholesterol, 3 mg sodium, 34 g carbohydrates, 1 g protein, 23 mg calcium, 3 g fiber

Per lemon-pepper wafer: 60 calories, 3.5 g total fat, 2 g saturated fat, 16 mg cholesterol, 44 mg sodium, 7 g carbohydrates, 1 g protein, 3 mg calcium, 0 g fiber

raspberry blintzes ᴇᴀsʏ

Blintzes are nothing more than filled crêpes. We loaded these with an orange-spiked ricotta filling and topped with a tart berry sauce.

Prep time: 55 minutes
Cooking time: 2 to 4 minutes per batch

CRÊPES:
- 2 large eggs
- 1¾ cups water
- 1½ cups all-purpose flour
- 2 tablespoons plus 2 teaspoons butter, melted, divided (no substitutes)

RASPBERRY SAUCE:
- 1 bag (12 oz.) frozen whole raspberries, thawed
- 2 tablespoons sugar

FILLING:
- 1 package (8 oz.) cream cheese, at room temperature

¼ cup ricotta cheese

2 tablespoons sugar

2 teaspoons grated orange peel

1 large egg

■

1 pint fresh raspberries

2 tablespoons butter, divided (no substitutes)

3 oranges, peeled and sectioned

Fresh orange or mint leaves, for garnish
(optional)

1. ■ *Make crêpes:* Combine eggs, water, flour and 2 tablespoons of the melted butter in a blender; blend until smooth.

2. ■ Heat a 9-inch nonstick skillet over medium-high heat. Lightly brush with 1 teaspoon of the melted butter. Add a scant ¼ cup batter to skillet, tilting to evenly coat bottom of pan; cook 30 to 60 seconds, until bottom of crêpe is lightly browned. Transfer to a sheet of waxed paper. Repeat with remaining 1 teaspoon butter (as necessary) and batter, stacking with waxed paper between crêpes. *(Can be made ahead. Wrap well in plastic wrap and refrigerate up to 24 hours.)* Makes 12 crêpes.

3. ■ *Make raspberry sauce:* Puree raspberries with sugar in a blender until smooth. Strain through a fine sieve. Makes 2 cups.

4. ■ *Make filling:* Beat cream cheese, ricotta, sugar and orange peel in a large mixer bowl on medium speed until blended. Beat in egg.

5. ■ *To assemble:* Spoon 2 tablespoons of the filling in center of each crêpe; top each with 4 raspberries. Fold in all sides of crêpe over filling, envelope-style.

6. ■ Melt 1 tablespoon of the butter in a large skillet over medium-high heat. Cook blintzes in batches, seam sides down, 2 minutes per side, until golden, adding remaining 1 tablespoon butter as necessary (lower heat slightly if crêpes darken too quickly).

7. ■ *To serve:* Place 2 blintzes on each of 6 dessert plates. Top with raspberry sauce, oranges and remaining berries. Garnish with orange or mint leaves, if desired. Makes 6 servings.

Per serving: 490 calories, 27 g total fat, 16 g saturated fat, 178 mg cholesterol, 251 mg sodium, 51 g carbohydrates, 12 g protein, 109 mg calcium, 6 g fiber

flambéed bananas

Need dessert in a flash? Try these fancy bananas that are sure to impress your guests. Rum works especially well, but bourbon makes a good choice, too.

Prep time: 10 minutes
Baking time: 10 minutes

4 tablespoons butter, divided (no substitutes)

¾ cup firmly packed brown sugar, divided

6 well-ripened bananas

1 lemon

1 quart premium vanilla ice cream

⅓ cup dark rum or bourbon

1. ■ Grease the bottom of a large ovenproof platter with 2 tablespoons of the butter, then sprinkle with ¼ cup of the brown sugar. Peel bananas, split in half and arrange, flat sides down, on prepared platter.

2. ■ Heat oven to 450°F. Cut peel from lemon with a vegetable peeler, trimming off any bitter white pith. Stack peel into a pile and slice into very thin strips. Sprinkle strips over bananas. Squeeze 2 tablespoons fresh lemon juice; drizzle lemon juice over bananas. Sprinkle with remaining ½ cup brown sugar and dot with remaining 2 tablespoons butter. Place platter in oven and bake 10 minutes.

3. ■ *To serve:* Divide ice cream among 6 serving dishes. Remove hot platter from oven. Place the rum in a heatproof measuring cup; ignite and carefully pour over bananas (flame will be low). Using pot holders, bring platter of flaming bananas to serving table. Tilt platter slightly to gather juices, then spoon flaming juices back on top of the bananas. Keep basting bananas with juices until flame dies, then serve immediately over ice cream. Makes 6 servings.

Per serving: 550 calories, 24.5 g total fat, 15 g saturated fat, 82 mg cholesterol, 150 mg sodium, 77 g carbohydrates, 5 g protein, 150 mg calcium, 3 g fiber

caramel pears

This is a fantastically delicious way to serve fresh pears.

Prep time: 25 minutes
Baking time: 25 to 30 minutes

> 3 **medium, firm ripe Bosc or Bartlett pears, peeled, halved and cored**
> 3 **tablespoons sugar**
> 2 **tablespoons butter (no substitutes)**
> ½ **cup heavy or whipping cream**
> ¾ **teaspoon vanilla extract**

1. Adjust oven rack about 5 inches from heat source. Heat broiler. Grease a 9-inch square baking pan. Arrange pears in pan, cut sides down. Sprinkle on sugar and dot with butter. Broil 10 to 12 minutes, rotating pan (if necessary) to brown pears evenly. Remove from broiler.

2. Reduce oven temperature to 375°F. Combine cream and vanilla and pour over pears. Bake in lower third of oven 25 to 30 minutes, until sauce is golden and bubbly. Serve warm or at room temperature. Makes 6 servings.

Per serving: 170 calories, 12 g total fat, 7 g saturated fat, 38 mg cholesterol, 49 mg sodium, 17 g carbohydrates, 1 g protein, 22 mg calcium, 2 g fiber

peaches with sabayon sauce

Whether you say sabayon (French) or zabaglione (Italian), it's the same thing: a dessert made by whisking together egg yolks, wine or brandy and sugar.

Prep time: 20 minutes plus standing and chilling
Cooking time: 5 to 7 minutes

SABAYON SAUCE:
> 4 **large egg yolks**
> ¼ **cup sugar**
> ¼ **cup peach or apricot brandy**
> ½ **cup heavy or whipping cream**
>
> 6 **large fresh peaches (about 2 lbs.), peeled and sliced or nectarines, sliced**
> 1 **kiwi, peeled and sliced (optional)**

1. *Make sabayon sauce:* Combine egg yolks and sugar in top of a double boiler. Beat with a hand-held mixer until blended. Warm brandy in a small saucepan. Stir into egg yolk mixture. Set over, but not touching, simmering water and beat until thickened. Remove from heat and let stand until cooled to room temperature.

2. Whip cream to soft peaks; fold into sauce and refrigerate 1 hour. Makes 1¾ cups.

3. Place peaches and kiwi, if using, into 6 individual dishes or a large serving bowl. Spoon on sauce just before serving. Makes 6 servings.

Per serving without kiwi: 230 calories, 11 g total fat, 5.5 g saturated fat, 169 mg cholesterol, 13 mg sodium, 26 g carbohydrates, 3 g protein, 35 mg calcium, 3 g fiber

cardamom-ricotta pancakes

These pillow-light pancakes transcend the typical variety in two ways: spicy-sweet cardamom imparts its aromatic flavor, while ricotta cheese makes the pancakes moist and super tender. Enjoy these fluffy delights with maple or fruit-flavored syrup.

Prep time: 20 minutes
Cooking time: 3 to 4 minutes per batch

> 1 **cup all-purpose flour**
> 1 **teaspoon baking powder**
> 1 **teaspoon cardamom**
> ¼ **teaspoon salt**
> 1 **cup whole milk ricotta cheese**
> 3 **large eggs, separated**
> ¾ **cup milk**
> 1 **tablespoon butter or margarine, melted**
> 1 **tablespoon sugar**
> 4 **teaspoons butter or margarine, divided**
> **Warm maple syrup or fruit syrup (optional)**

1. Whisk together the flour, baking powder, cardamom and salt in a small bowl. Place ricotta in a medium bowl; stir in egg yolks, milk, melted butter and sugar. Stir in the flour mixture. Beat the egg whites in a mixer bowl on high speed just to stiff peaks. Fold half of the whites into the ricotta mixture just until blended; repeat with remaining beaten whites.

2. Heat a large nonstick griddle according to manufacturer's directions. (Or heat a 12-inch nonstick skillet over medium-high heat.) Melt 1 teaspoon of the butter on the griddle. Using a ladle or ⅓-cup dry measure, pour 3 spoonfuls of batter onto prepared griddle and spread each lightly to form three 4-inch-wide pancakes. Cook 2 minutes, until bubbles form around edges. Turn pancakes with a spatula and cook 1 to 2 minutes more, until golden. Repeat process with remaining butter and batter. Serve with maple or fruit syrup, if desired. Makes 12 pancakes.

Per pancake without syrup: 145 calories, 9.5 g total fat, 5.5 g saturated fat, 78 mg cholesterol, 174 mg sodium, 10 g carbohydrates, 5 g protein, 91 mg calcium, 0 g fiber

tropical tulipes

Brighten your table with these thin, flowery cookie cups filled with cashew-coconut ice cream and drizzled with a rum and pineapple sauce. The cookie cups and ice cream can be made ahead. Pictured on page 168.

Prep time: 1 hour plus chilling
Baking time: 8 to 10 minutes per batch

COCONUT TULIPES:
- 10 tablespoons unsalted butter, softened (no substitutes)
- ¾ cup granulated sugar
- ½ teaspoon vanilla extract
- 5 large egg whites
- 1⅓ cups all-purpose flour
- ½ cup shredded coconut

TROPICAL ICE CREAM:
- 2 quarts premium vanilla ice cream
- ¾ cup roasted cashews
- 1 tablespoon light corn syrup
- ¾ cup shredded coconut, toasted
- 3 ounces white chocolate squares, chopped

PINEAPPLE-TOFFEE SAUCE:
- ½ cup firmly packed brown sugar
- ¼ cup unsalted butter, cut up (no substitutes)
- 3 tablespoons heavy or whipping cream

- 1½ tablespoons dark rum
- ¼ teaspoon vanilla extract
- 1¼ cups chopped fresh pineapple

1. *Make coconut tulipes:* Beat butter and sugar in a large mixer bowl on medium speed until light and fluffy. Add vanilla. Add egg whites, one at a time, beating well after each addition. Stir in flour and coconut just until blended. Cover and let stand at room temperature 1 hour. (*Can be made ahead. Cover and refrigerate up to 24 hours. Bring to room temperature before using.*)

2. Heat oven to 375°F. Grease 2 large cookie sheets. Spoon scant ¼ cup of the batter onto cookie sheet; spread into a 6-inch circle. Repeat, making 2 circles per sheet. Bake 8 to 10 minutes, until edges are golden and centers begin to color. Working quickly, carefully remove each circle from cookie sheet with a metal spatula and *immediately* place between two 4-inch bowls, pressing gently to mold center, until firm (edges will be ruffled). Transfer to a wire rack and cool completely. Repeat with remaining batter. (*Can be made ahead. Store at room temperature in a resealable plastic storage bag up to 5 days.*) Makes 12 tulipes.

3. *Make tropical ice cream:* Heat oven to 325°F. Place ice cream in refrigerator 30 minutes to soften. Grease a cookie sheet. Combine cashews and corn syrup in a small bowl, tossing to coat well. Spread on prepared cookie sheet. Toast lightly 10 to 12 minutes. Cool completely on a wire rack; coarsely chop. Place softened ice cream in a large bowl; stir in nuts, coconut and white chocolate. Cover with plastic wrap and freeze at least 2 hours or overnight.

4. *Make pineapple-toffee sauce:* Meanwhile, combine brown sugar, butter, cream, rum and vanilla in a large saucepan. Bring to boil over medium-high heat; cook 5 minutes, until slightly thickened, stirring frequently. Remove from heat and stir in pineapple; keep warm. Makes 1½ cups.

5. *To serve:* Scoop ½ cup of the tropical ice cream into each prepared coconut tulipe and drizzle with 2 tablespoons of the warm pineapple-toffee sauce. Makes 12 servings.

Per serving: 545 calories, 34 g total fat, 21 g saturated fat, 84 mg cholesterol, 104 mg sodium, 58 g carbohydrates, 7 g protein, 105 mg calcium, 1 g fiber

banana oat muffins *EASY* *LOW FAT*

Not too dense or sweet, these tasty, heart-healthy muffins are a guilt-free treat. They freeze beautifully, so make extras and you'll always have a supply at the ready for the morning rush.

Prep time: 20 minutes
Baking time: 20 to 22 minutes

- 2¼ **cups old-fashioned oats, divided**
- ¾ **cup rye or whole wheat flour**
- ⅓ **cup plus 1 teaspoon sugar, divided**
- 1 **teaspoon baking powder**
- ½ **teaspoon baking soda**
- ½ **teaspoon salt**
- ¾ **teaspoon cinnamon, divided**
- ½ **teaspoon ginger, divided**
- 1 **cup buttermilk**
- 1 **large ripe banana, mashed (about ½ cup)**
- 2 **large eggs**
- 2 **tablespoons plus ½ teaspoon safflower or vegetable oil, divided**
- 1 **teaspoon vanilla extract**
-   **All-fruit preserves (optional)**

1. Heat oven to 350°F. Line twelve 2½-inch muffin pan cups with cupcake/muffin liners.

2. Process 2 cups of the oats in a food processor until finely ground. Transfer oats to a large bowl; stir in flour, ⅓ cup of the sugar, the baking powder, baking soda, salt, ½ teaspoon of the cinnamon and ¼ teaspoon of the ginger. Whisk together buttermilk, banana, eggs, 2 tablespoons of the oil and the vanilla in a medium bowl until well combined. With a rubber spatula, stir buttermilk mixture into flour mixture just until blended.

3. Combine remaining ¼ cup oats, 1 teaspoon sugar, ¼ teaspoon cinnamon, ¼ teaspoon ginger and ½ teaspoon oil in a cup.

4. Divide batter between prepared muffin-pan cups. Sprinkle tops with oat-sugar mixture. Bake 20 to 22 minutes, until a toothpick inserted in center of a muffin comes out clean. Remove from pans and cool completely. *(Can be made ahead. Wrap and freeze up to 1 month. Thaw at room temperature 2 hours.)* Serve with fruit preserves, if desired. Makes 12 muffins.

Per muffin without preserves: 160 calories, 4.5 g total fat, 1 g saturated fat, 36 mg cholesterol, 222 mg sodium, 25 g carbohydrates, 5 g protein, 62 mg calcium, 3 g fiber

baked ricotta

This dish relies on just one main ingredient—whole milk ricotta, simply drained and baked. Not only does it boast a good calcium profile, it can be served as a savory or a sweet. You'll be amazed at how delicious ricotta can be. Pictured on page 164.

Prep time: 5 minutes plus standing
Baking time: 45 to 50 minutes

- 2 **containers (15 oz. each) whole milk ricotta cheese**
-   **Pinch kosher salt (no substitutes)**
-   **Pinch freshly ground pepper**
-   **Honey or extra-virgin olive oil**
-   **Fresh berries (optional)**

1. Line a large sieve or colander with a double layer of cheesecloth, letting excess hang over side. Place over a bowl and spoon in ricotta. Let drain at room temperature 1 hour.

2. Heat oven to 400°F. Discard drained liquid. Turn cheese out onto paper towels; pat dry. Arrange the same cheesecloth in a 3-cup or 1-quart baking dish, letting cheesecloth overhang side. Spoon ricotta into prepared dish. Sprinkle top with salt and pepper. Fold overhanging cheesecloth over ricotta in dish. Bake 45 to 50 minutes, until top is browned. Cool completely on wire rack. *(Can be made ahead. Cover and refrigerate up to 48 hours. Bring to room temperature before serving.)*

3. Just before serving, peel off cheesecloth. Transfer to serving plate, drizzle top with honey or oil. Top with berries, if desired. Makes 10 servings.

Per serving: 150 calories, 11 g total fat, 7 g saturated fat, 43 mg cholesterol, 80 mg sodium, 3 g carbohydrates, 10 g protein, 176 mg calcium, 0 g fiber

DESSERT
CHIMICHANGAS
PG. 213

the year in chocolate

CHOCOLATE-PHYLLO
POCKETS
PG. 230

Oh, how we fall for chocolate. We'll swoon for chocolate with cream, with butter, fruit or nuts. There are those who go miles for a lick, a bite, a swirl of the best, be it milk or dark, light as air or dense and rich. You, too? Turn these pages and find your pleasure.

have a bite
for a **boost,**

BITTERSWEET
PECAN BROWNIES
PG. 239

CHOCOLATE-MINT
ICE CREAM
PG. 209

take a lick
for a luscious lift

CHOCOLATE
CRÊPES WITH
PEARS AND
CHOCOLATE
SAUCE
PG. 232

stir your senses
and your **soul**

BROWNIE BAKED
ALASKA
PG. 211

with chocolate, fruit and cream

FLOURLESS
CHOCOLATE
CAKE
PG. 220

this silky food
of the gods

CHOCOLATE-
PEANUT-BUTTER
LAYER CAKE
PG. 219

CHOCOLATE
BABKA
PG. 238

is our licit pleasure,
our decent vice

SOUTHERN
CHOCOLATE
LAYER CAKE
PG. 233

so how about some
more, or s'mores?

CHOCOLATE-
NUT TART
PG. 214

chocolate-mint ice cream *EASY*

For a pretty presentation, serve this delicacy in clear glass dishes, drizzle with melted chocolate (see tip, page 213) and garnish with a fresh mint sprig. Tip: Be sure to use fresh, blemish-free mint leaves. Pictured on page 203.

Prep time: 20 minutes plus standing, chilling and freezing
Cooking time: 10 minutes
Microwave used

- 2 **cups heavy or whipping cream**
- 2 **cups milk**
- 1½ **cups coarsely chopped fresh mint leaves**
- ½ **of a vanilla bean, split, or 1 teaspoon vanilla extract**
- 6 **large egg yolks, at room temperature**
- 1 **cup sugar**
  Pinch salt
- 4 **ounces semisweet chocolate squares**
- 3 **ounces unsweetened chocolate squares**

1. Bring cream, milk, mint and vanilla bean (if using) to boil over medium heat. Remove saucepan from heat. Cover and let stand 30 minutes. Strain liquid through a fine sieve into a bowl, pressing mint leaves with the back of a spoon. With the tip of a small knife, scrape seeds from vanilla bean; add seeds to cream mixture. (Reserve bean for another use.) Return cream mixture to saucepan.

2. Meanwhile, beat egg yolks, sugar and salt in a medium mixer bowl on medium-high speed 3 to 5 minutes, until mixture becomes thick and pale yellow.

3. Microwave chocolates in a large microwaveproof bowl on High 1½ minutes, until melted; stir until smooth. Set aside.

4. Whisk 1 cup of the hot cream mixture into yolk mixture until smooth. Stir yolk mixture into saucepan with remaining cream mixture. Cook over low heat 5 minutes, until custard is thick enough to coat the back of a spoon, stirring occasionally. Stir in vanilla extract, if using.

5. Strain custard through a sieve into the bowl of melted chocolate. Stir until well blended. Refrigerate 8 hours or overnight, until chocolate mixture is completely chilled. Transfer to a 2-quart ice cream maker and freeze according to manufacturer's directions. Makes about 4 cups.

Per ½ cup: 500 calories, 37 g total fat, 21.5 g saturated fat, 246 mg cholesterol, 77 mg sodium, 40 g carbohydrates, 8 g protein, 130 mg calcium, 3 g fiber

mexican hot chocolate *EASY*

True Mexican hot chocolate has cinnamon in it, so we've made this rich version with a cinnamon stick. The egg adds a silky quality as it slightly thickens the drink.

Total prep and cooking time: 15 minutes

- 4 **cups milk**
- 1 **cinnamon stick**
- 4 **ounces semisweet chocolate squares, chopped**
- 1 **large egg**
- 1 **teaspoon vanilla extract**
  Sweetened whipped cream, for garnish (optional)

Scald milk with the cinnamon stick in a 3-quart heavy saucepan over medium heat. Remove from heat; add chocolate and let stand 5 minutes, until chocolate is melted. With a hand-held mixer, beat until smooth. Lightly beat egg in a small bowl. Slowly beat 1 cup of the hot milk mixture into egg; return egg-milk mixture to saucepan with remaining hot milk and blend well. Cook over medium heat 5 to 6 minutes, stirring constantly, until mixture is thick and no longer separates and temperature registers 180°F. on an instant-read thermometer. Add vanilla. Beat on medium-high speed until frothy. Serve in mugs with a dollop of sweetened whipped cream, if desired. Makes 6 servings.

Per serving without whipped cream: 190 calories, 10 g total fat, 5.5 g saturated fat, 48 mg cholesterol, 92 mg sodium, 19 g carbohydrates, 8 g protein, 202 mg calcium, 1 g fiber

chocolate ice cream cake

Everyone loves ice cream, especially when it's accompanied by cake. Use one or two of your favorite flavors for the layers.

Prep time: 45 minutes plus standing and freezing
Baking time: 15 to 18 minutes
Microwave used

- **2**   ounces unsweetened chocolate squares, chopped
- **¾**   cup plus 3 tablespoons sugar, divided
-     Water
- **1**   teaspoon instant espresso or coffee powder
- **1**   cup all-purpose flour
- **1½** teaspoons baking powder
- **½**   teaspoon salt
- **⅓**   cup vegetable oil
- **4**   large eggs, separated, at room temperature
- **2**   teaspoons vanilla extract
- **¼**   teaspoon cream of tartar
- **2**   pints premium ice cream

GLAZE:

- **5**   ounces semisweet chocolate squares, chopped
- **6**   tablespoons unsalted butter, cut up (no substitutes)
- **2**   tablespoons water

-     Chocolate leaves, for garnish (recipe follows) (optional)

1. Heat oven to 375°F. Butter two 9-inch round cake pans. Line bottoms with waxed paper; grease and flour paper and sides of pans.

2. Place the chocolate, 3 tablespoons of the sugar, 3 tablespoons water and the espresso powder in a microwaveproof bowl; microwave on High 1 minute to 1 minute 15 seconds, until melted and smooth, stirring halfway through. Let stand 10 minutes.

3. Meanwhile, whisk together flour, remaining ¾ cup sugar, the baking powder and salt in a medium bowl; make a well in the center. Add oil, egg yolks, ¼ cup water and the vanilla to well; whisk until smooth. Whisk in melted chocolate mixture.

4. Beat egg whites in a clean mixer bowl with clean beaters until frothy. Add cream of tartar; beat to stiff, but not dry, peaks. Fold one quarter of the egg whites into batter, then fold in remaining whites. Divide batter between prepared pans.

5. Bake 15 to 18 minutes, until tops spring back when lightly touched and a toothpick inserted in centers comes out clean. Cool on wire racks 10 minutes. Invert cakes onto wire racks and remove pans. Peel off waxed paper and cool completely. Wrap each cake layer in plastic wrap and freeze overnight.

6. Place ice cream in refrigerator 30 minutes to soften. Line a 9-inch round cake pan with plastic wrap. Spoon 1 pint of the softened ice cream into pan and spread into an even layer; freeze 10 minutes. Layer with second pint of ice cream; spread into an even layer. Cover with plastic wrap and freeze at least 3 hours or overnight, until firm.

7. Place 1 cake layer on a serving platter. Remove plastic wrap from top of ice cream. Invert ice cream onto cake; remove remaining plastic wrap. Add second cake layer, top side down, over ice cream; even side of ice cream with a spatula. Freeze 1 hour or overnight, until firm.

8. *Make glaze:* Place the chocolate, butter and water in a small saucepan. Heat over low heat until smooth, stirring occasionally.

9. Quickly spread warm glaze over top and side of cake. Freeze 10 minutes to firm glaze. Garnish with chocolate leaves, if desired. Makes 16 servings.

Per serving without chocolate leaves: 320 calories, 21 g total fat, 10.5 g saturated fat, 88 mg cholesterol, 148 mg sodium, 31 g carbohydrates, 5 g protein, 77 mg calcium, 1 g fiber

For chocolate leaves: Chop 4 ounces semisweet chocolate squares. Place in a microwaveproof bowl. Microwave on High 1½ to 2 minutes, until melted, stirring halfway through; stir until smooth. Using a clean, flat brush about ½ inch wide, brush chocolate evenly over back side of 1 rose or other firm oval nontoxic leaf; turn leaf over and carefully wipe off any chocolate on front. Place, chocolate side up, on tray; repeat with 12 to 14 more leaves. Refrigerate 5 minutes to harden. Carefully peel off the chocolate leaves, starting from stem ends. Keep refrigerated until ready to garnish cake.

brownie baked alaska

How do you make this comeback classic better than ever? Add a layer of dark chocolate brownie! The brownie and ice cream layers can be completely assembled, frosted with meringue and frozen ahead, then baked just minutes before serving. Pictured on page 204.

Prep time: 30 minutes plus chilling and freezing
Baking time: 25 to 32 minutes
Microwave used

BROWNIE:

3	ounces unsweetened chocolate squares
½	cup butter or margarine, cut up
¾	cup sugar
2	large eggs
½	teaspoon vanilla extract
½	cup all-purpose flour
¼	teaspoon salt

ICE CREAM FILLING:

2	pints premium vanilla ice cream
2	pints premium chocolate ice cream
1	pint raspberry sorbet

MERINGUE:

1	tablespoon meringue powder*
¼	cup cold water
6	tablespoons plus 2 teaspoons sugar, divided

1. Heat oven to 325°F. Lightly grease bottom of a 9-inch round cake pan; line bottom with waxed paper. Grease and flour paper; tap out excess.

2. *Make brownie:* Place chocolate and butter in a large microwaveproof bowl. Microwave on High 1½ to 2 minutes, until melted; stir until smooth. Whisk in sugar, eggs and vanilla. Stir in flour and salt. Spread in prepared pan; bake 20 to 25 minutes, until a toothpick inserted in center comes out barely clean. Cool completely in pan on a wire rack. Invert brownie onto rack and remove pan. Peel off waxed paper.

3. *Make ice cream filling:* Meanwhile, place vanilla ice cream in refrigerator 15 minutes to soften. Line a 2½-quart bowl (8 inches wide at top) with plastic wrap, extending 2 inches above edge of bowl. Spread vanilla ice cream along side and bottom of

bowl, spreading slightly thicker on bottom. Freeze 15 to 20 minutes, until firm.

4. Meanwhile, place chocolate ice cream in refrigerator 15 minutes to soften. Spread chocolate ice cream along side and bottom of vanilla ice cream in bowl. Freeze 15 to 20 minutes, until firm.

5. Place raspberry sorbet in refrigerator 15 minutes to soften. Spoon sorbet into center of chocolate ice cream, packing to fill bowl. Invert brownie on top of bowl; trimming edge to fit. Cover with foil and freeze 4 hours or overnight, until firm. *(Can be made ahead. Cover and freeze up to 1 month.)*

6. *Make meringue:* In a large bowl combine meringue powder, water and 3 tablespoons plus 1 teaspoon of the sugar. Beat on high speed for 5 minutes. Gradually beat in remaining 3 tablespoons plus 1 teaspoon sugar; beat on high speed 5 minutes, until meringue is stiff and dry.

7. Peel foil from brownie; invert ice cream and brownie onto a a cookie sheet. Place a warm, damp cloth on outside of bowl. Holding onto excess plastic wrap, lift off bowl. Remove plastic wrap.

8. Spread meringue evenly over ice cream, swirling with back of spoon to form peaks. Freeze Alaska on cookie sheet, uncovered, 24 hours. (Cover loosely with foil for longer storage.)

9. Adjust rack to center of oven. Heat oven to 450°F. Bake 5 to 7 minutes, until peaks turn light golden brown. Transfer to a cutting board; let stand a few minutes before slicing to serve, if necessary. Makes 12 to 16 servings.

Note: Can be found at kitchen specialty stores and the baking section of most supermarkets, or order it from Wilton Enterprises (800-794-5866).

Per serving: 525 calories, 31.5 g total fat, 19 g saturated fat, 183 mg cholesterol, 214 mg sodium, 54 g carbohydrates, 8 g protein, 194 mg calcium, 2 g fiber

frozen chocolate mousse

This rich, frozen mousse tastes like premium chocolate ice cream. For a more traditional mousse, move the dessert from the freezer to the refrigerator 3 hours before serving. If you don't have a soufflé dish, use a 1½-quart bowl.

Total prep time: 30 minutes plus freezing
Microwave used

> 6 ounces unsweetened chocolate squares
> 2 ounces semisweet chocolate squares
> 1½ cups heavy or whipping cream, divided
> 2 tablespoons brandy
> 1¼ cups sugar, divided
> ½ cup water
> 4 large egg whites, at room temperature
> 1 cup whipped cream, for garnish (optional)
> Semisweet chocolate, shaved, for garnish (optional)

1. *Make collar for a 4-cup soufflé dish:* Fold a piece of waxed paper, long enough to fit around the soufflé dish, lengthwise into thirds. Wrap around dish so that waxed paper extends 2 inches above rim. Secure with tape and set aside.

2. Combine chocolates, ½ cup of the heavy cream and the brandy in a medium microwaveproof bowl. Microwave on High 3 minutes, until chocolate is melted, stirring halfway through; stir until smooth.

3. Combine 1 cup of the sugar and the water in a small saucepan. Bring to boil over medium-high heat. Boil 3 minutes.

4. Beat egg whites in a large mixer bowl on medium-high speed to soft peaks. Add sugar syrup in a thin steady stream, beating constantly. Beat 4 minutes, until meringue forms soft peaks and is cooled to room temperature. Fold in one quarter of the chocolate mixture until smooth. Fold in remaining chocolate mixture.

5. Beat remaining 1 cup heavy cream and ¼ cup sugar in a small mixer bowl on medium-high speed to soft peaks. Fold into chocolate-meringue mixture; spread into prepared soufflé dish. Cover with plastic wrap and freeze at least 4 hours. *(Can be made ahead. Freeze up to 2 days. Transfer to*

refrigerator 1 hour before serving.) Garnish with whipped cream and shaved chocolate, if desired. Makes 8 servings.

Per serving without garnishes: 435 calories, 30.5 g total fat, 18.5 g saturated fat, 62 mg cholesterol, 48 mg sodium, 41 g carbohydrates, 5 g protein, 46 mg calcium, 4 g fiber

chocolate bark with praline EASY

Surprise! This impressive candy is simple to make. We melted bittersweet chocolate, then topped it with a praline mixture. Superb!

Prep time: 10 minutes plus standing
Cooking time: 5 minutes
Microwave used

> ⅓ cup sugar
> 1 tablespoon light corn syrup
> 1 teaspoon water
> ¼ cup shelled pistachios, lightly toasted
> ¼ cup whole blanched almonds, lightly toasted
> 9 ounces bittersweet chocolate, cut up

1. Lightly coat a cookie sheet with vegetable cooking spray.

2. Stir sugar, corn syrup and water together in a small saucepan (mixture will be very thick). Cook mixture over medium-high heat 3 to 5 minutes, until sugar melts to a honey color. Stir in nuts over heat until combined. Immediately pour praline onto prepared cookie sheet. Cool completely.

3. Finely chop one-third of the praline and coarsely chop the remaining praline; combine and set aside.

4. Melt chocolate in a medium microwaveproof bowl on High 1½ to 2 minutes; let stand 3 minutes. Stir until smooth. Pour onto the same cookie sheet, spreading out to ¼-inch thickness. Immediately sprinkle chopped praline over chocolate, covering top; press lightly. Cool completely. Break into large pieces. Makes ¾ pound or fifty-four 1-inch pieces.

Per 1-inch piece: 35 calories, 2.5 g total fat, 1 g saturated fat, 0 mg cholesterol, 1 mg sodium, 4 g carbohydrates, 1 g protein, 4 mg calcium, 0.5 g fiber

chocolate mocha cream

Guests will say yes to this yummy no-bake coffee-flavored chocolate dessert.

Total prep time: 10 minutes

- 1   package (3 oz.) ladyfingers, split
- 1   cup heavy or whipping cream
- ¾   cup part-skim ricotta cheese
- 3   tablespoons granulated sugar
- 1   ounce semisweet chocolate square, melted
- 1   teaspoon instant espresso powder dissolved in 1 teaspoon very hot water
- ½   teaspoon vanilla extract
- 2   tablespoons miniature chocolate chips

TOPPING:
- 2   teaspoons confectioners' sugar
- 2   teaspoons unsweetened cocoa

1. Line six 6-ounce soufflé dishes or custard cups with the ladyfingers.

2. Combine cream, ricotta, granulated sugar, melted chocolate, espresso and vanilla in a blender; blend 1 minute, until smooth and thickened. Stir in chocolate chips and spoon into prepared cups. Refrigerate until ready to serve.

3. *Make topping:* Using a fine sieve, lightly dust tops with confectioners' sugar, then with cocoa. Makes 6 servings.

Per serving: 315 calories, 21.5 g total fat, 13 g saturated fat, 116 mg cholesterol, 74 mg sodium, 24 g carbohydrates, 7 g protein, 123 mg calcium, 0.5 g fiber

dessert chimichangas

Who would guess that this fabulous dessert from Pedro's Mexican Restaurante in Wisconsin Dells, Wisconsin, is made with such few ingredients? Pictured on page 201.

Prep time: 10 minutes plus chilling
Baking time: 20 minutes

- 7   peanut-caramel chocolate-coated candy bars (2 oz. each), divided
- 4   burrito-size (12-inch) tortillas
- 2   tablespoons butter or margarine, melted
     Vanilla ice cream (optional)
     Whipped cream, chocolate sauce and maraschino cherries (optional)

1. Cut each of 6 of the candy bars crosswise into 4 equal pieces. Arrange 6 pieces in the center of each tortilla. Fold up burrito style; seal ends with a toothpick. Transfer to a small cookie sheet. Brush all sides of each burrito with the melted butter, then cover with plastic wrap. Refrigerate 1 hour. *(Can be made ahead. Refrigerate up to 24 hours.)*

2. Heat oven to 400°F. Uncover and bake burritos 20 minutes, until golden brown and crisp.

3. Coarsely chop remaining candy bar. Place each chimichanga in a shallow dessert bowl. Top with ice cream, whipped cream, chocolate sauce, chopped candy bar and maraschino cherries, if desired. Makes 4 servings.

Per serving without ice cream, whipped cream, chocolate sauce, cherries and chopped candy bar: 780 calories, 35.5 g total fat, 13 g saturated fat, 28 mg cholesterol, 699 mg sodium, 103 g carbohydrates, 15 g protein, 193 mg calcium, 5 g fiber

---

test kitchen tip
melting chocolate

TO MELT IN THE MICROWAVE: Coarsely chop chocolate and place in a microwaveproof bowl or cup. Microwave on High 1 minute; stir. Repeat in 30-second increments until melted. Keep in mind that chocolate pieces won't appear melted until they are stirred.

TO MELT ON THE STOVETOP: Coarsely chop the chocolate. Make sure all utensils are dry. Place chocolate in the top of a double boiler over hot, not boiling, water. Stir the chocolate frequently until it is completely melted.

chocolate-nut tart

Filled with hazelnuts and almonds and topped with whipped cream and chocolate scrolls, this luscious tart becomes the talk of any special occasion. Pictured on page 208 and on cover Ω.

Prep time: 1 hour plus chilling
Baking time: 20 to 25 minutes

> **Ultimate Tart Pastry Shell (recipe follows)**
> 2 ounces semisweet or bittersweet chocolate squares, melted

FILLING:

> 1⅓ cups sugar
> ⅓ cup water
> 1 cup heavy or whipping cream
> ¼ cup butter, cut up (no substitutes)
> 1 large egg, lightly beaten
> ½ cup hazelnuts, toasted and coarsely chopped
> ½ cup whole blanched almonds, toasted and coarsely chopped

CHOCOLATE SCROLLS:

> 2 to 3 ounces semisweet chocolate squares, melted
>
> ¾ cup heavy or whipping cream

1. Prepare and bake Ultimate Tart Pastry Shell as directed. Increase oven temperature to 400°F. Brush the bottom of cooled pastry shell with melted chocolate. Place the tart pan with pastry shell on a cookie sheet.

2. *Make filling:* Combine sugar and water in a medium, heavy saucepan. Bring to boil over medium heat; boil 15 minutes, until amber-colored and sugar is dissolved. (Do not stir.) Remove from heat and gradually whisk in cream until smooth. Add butter and whisk until melted; let stand 10 minutes, then whisk in egg. Stir in nuts.

3. Carefully pour filling into prepared pastry shell. Bake 10 minutes. Reduce oven temperature to 350°F. Bake 10 to 15 minutes more, until filling is bubbly in the center. Cool completely on a wire rack. *(Can be made ahead. Cover and refrigerate up to 24 hours.)*

4. *Make chocolate scrolls:* On a sheet of waxed paper, draw 2 sets of parallel lines, 2½ inches apart.

Turn paper over so lines are on bottom. Place waxed paper on a cookie sheet. Spoon chocolate into a small plastic storage bag and cut a small hole in 1 corner. Using lines as a guide, pipe a V-shape between lines, 2½ inches long and 1 inch wide at the top of V. Make a diagonal zigzag over the V, starting at the top (using more pressure while squeezing chocolate will produce thicker lines). Repeat, making 4 scrolls between each set of lines. Transfer scrolls on cookie sheet to refrigerator and chill 10 to 15 minutes, until set.

5. *To serve:* Beat the ¾ cup cream to stiff peaks. Carefully peel chocolate scrolls off waxed paper. Top tart with dollops of whipped cream and chocolate scrolls. Makes 8 servings.

Per serving: 715 calories, 52.5 g total fat, 27 g saturated fat, 148 mg cholesterol, 131 mg sodium, 59 g carbohydrates, 8 g protein, 75 mg calcium, 3 g fiber

ultimate tart pastry shell ⊛EASY⊛

Use this tender, buttery pastry for Chocolate-Nut Tart or other recipes that call for a 10-inch tart pastry.

Prep time: 10 minutes plus chilling
Baking time: 26 to 28 minutes

> 1¼ cups all-purpose flour
> ⅛ teaspoon salt
> ½ cup unsalted butter, cut up (no substitutes)
> 3 to 4 tablespoons ice water

1. Combine flour and salt in a medium bowl. Gradually add butter, tossing gently until all pieces are coated with flour. With a pastry blender or 2 knives, cut in butter until mixture resembles fine crumbs. Add the ice water, 1 tablespoon at a time, tossing with a fork until pastry just begins to hold together.

2. On a smooth surface, shape pastry into a ball, kneading lightly if necessary. Flatten into a thick disk. Tightly wrap pastry in plastic wrap and refrigerate 1 hour or overnight.

3. On a lightly floured surface, use a floured rolling pin to roll the pastry into a 14-inch circle about

⅛ inch thick. Fold pastry in half. Carefully transfer pastry to a 10-inch tart pan with a removable bottom. Gently press pastry with fingertips along the bottom and up the side of the pan. With scissors, trim pastry to 1 inch above the edge of the pan. Fold overhanging pastry to the inside of crust and gently press edge up to extend ¼ inch above side of pan. Freeze pastry shell 20 minutes.

4. Meanwhile, adjust oven rack to lowest position. Place a cookie sheet on rack. Heat oven to 375°F.

5. Line frozen pastry shell with foil; fill with dried beans or pie weights. Bake 12 minutes. Remove foil and beans. Bake pastry 14 to 16 minutes more, until deep golden. Cool completely on a wire rack. Continue as directed in specific recipe, or remove side of pan, transfer pastry to a serving plate and fill as desired. Makes 8 servings.

Per serving: 175 calories, 12.5 g total fat, 7.5 g saturated fat, 33 mg cholesterol, 38 mg sodium, 14 g carbohydrates, 2 g protein, 6 mg calcium, 0 g fiber

chocolate cookie pie

This yummy pie, filled with a fluffy mousse and chocolate sandwich cookies, creates big smiles at kids' parties.

Prep time: 35 minutes plus chilling
Baking time: 10 minutes

CRUST:
- 1½ cups finely crushed chocolate wafers (about 30)
- ½ cup finely chopped pecans (optional)
- 1 tablespoon sugar
- ⅓ cup butter or margarine, melted

FILLING:
- ¾ cup water
- 1 envelope unflavored gelatin
- 2 tablespoons sugar, divided
- ⅛ teaspoon salt
- 3 large egg yolks
- 6 ounces semisweet chocolate squares, chopped, or 1 cup semisweet chocolate chips
- ½ teaspoon vanilla extract

- 1½ cups heavy or whipping cream
- 1½ cups broken chocolate sandwich cookies
- 10 chocolate sandwich cookies, for garnish (optional)

1. *Make crust:* Heat oven to 400°F. Combine wafers, pecans (if using) and sugar in a bowl. Add melted butter; stir until evenly moistened. Press against bottom and side of a 9-inch pie plate. Bake 10 minutes. Cool on a wire rack.

2. *Make filling:* Place water in a 1½-quart saucepan. Sprinkle gelatin over top. Let stand 1 minute. Add sugar, salt and egg yolks. Whisk until well blended. Stir constantly over low heat until gelatin is completely dissolved and mixture is hot and the consistency of thin syrup. (Do not boil.) Remove from heat. Add chopped chocolate, stirring until completely melted.

3. Let mixture cool slightly. Stir in vanilla. Chill until mixture thickens to consistency of unbeaten egg whites, stirring occasionally (about 30 minutes).

4. Whisk gelatin mixture until smooth; set aside.

5. In a large mixer bowl, beat cream on medium-high speed to soft peaks. Fold into chocolate mixture; fold in broken cookies.

6. Spoon filling into prepared crust, mounding center. Garnish with chocolate sandwich cookies around outer edge of pie in a circle, spacing evenly and pushing halfway into pie, if desired. Chill 5 hours, until set. *(Can be made ahead. Cover loosely with plastic wrap and refrigerate up to 24 hours.)* Makes 10 servings.

Per serving: 485 calories, 33.5 g total fat, 16.5 g saturated fat, 133 mg cholesterol, 371 mg sodium, 42 g carbohydrates, 6 g protein, 38 mg calcium, 2 g fiber

chocolate marble cheesecake ⊙

Chocolate and cheesecake, what could be better? Bake it in a water bath for an extra-creamy cake.

Prep time: 25 minutes plus standing and chilling
Baking time: 1 hour

CRUST:

1¼	cups graham-cracker crumbs
¼	cup sugar
3	tablespoons whole blanched almonds, toasted and finely ground
5	tablespoons butter or margarine, melted

FILLING:

¾	cup sugar
2	tablespoons flour
⅛	teaspoon salt
3	packages (8 oz. each) cream cheese, at room temperature
2	large eggs, at room temperature
1	cup heavy or whipping cream
1	tablespoon vanilla extract
3	ounces semisweet chocolate squares, melted

1. Heat oven to 350°F.

2. *Make crust:* Combine graham-cracker crumbs, sugar and almonds in a small bowl; stir in butter until crumbs are evenly moistened. Press mixture into bottom of a 9-inch springform pan. Bake 10 minutes, until golden brown. Cool on a wire rack. Wrap bottom and side of pan with heavy-duty foil. Set aside.

3. *Make filling:* Reduce oven temperature to 325°F. Combine sugar, flour and salt in a large mixer bowl. Beat in cream cheese on high speed until smooth and well blended. Reduce speed to low. Add eggs, one at a time, beating just until blended after each addition. Beat in cream and vanilla just until combined. Set aside 2 cups of the filling. Pour remaining filling over crust. Stir chocolate into reserved filling until well combined. Drop chocolate mixture by tablespoonfuls onto cream cheese filling, forming 6 pools. Swirl filling with a knife

2 or 3 times to marbleize. Place springform pan in a large baking pan. Place on the oven rack. *(Make sure there is at least 1 inch between springform and baking pan.)* Carefully add enough very hot tap water into the baking pan to reach 1 inch up side of springform pan.

4. Bake 1 hour, until center is only slightly jiggly (it will firm as it cools). Turn oven off. Let cheesecake stand in oven 1 hour (do not open door). Remove cheesecake from water bath and remove foil. Cool on a wire rack 1 hour; cover and refrigerate 4 to 5 hours before cutting. *(Can be made ahead. Cover and refrigerate up to 2 days.)* Makes 12 servings.

Per serving: 480 calories, 37 g total fat, 22 g saturated fat, 139 mg cholesterol, 310 mg sodium, 31 g carbohydrates, 8 g protein, 74 mg calcium, 1 g fiber

dacquoise au chocolat

Dacquoise is a French baked meringue made with ground nuts. We use it to make this elegant layer cake filled with chocolate buttercream.

Prep time: 1 hour plus chilling
Baking time: 1½ hours
Microwave used

MERINGUE LAYERS:

1	cup pecans, toasted
¾	cup granulated sugar, divided
3	large egg whites, at room temperature
⅛	teaspoon cream of tartar

CHOCOLATE BUTTERCREAM:

2	ounces unsweetened chocolate squares
1	ounce semisweet chocolate square
⅓	cup granulated sugar
¼	cup water
3	large egg yolks, at room temperature
1	cup unsalted butter, softened (no substitutes)
	■
1½	cups heavy or whipping cream
4	tablespoons confectioners' sugar, divided
1	teaspoon crème de cacao or dark rum

1. Heat oven to 225°F. Line 2 large cookie sheets with foil. Using a 9-inch round cake pan as a guide, trace a 9-inch circle on each; set aside.

2. *Make meringue layers:* Combine nuts and ¼ cup of the granulated sugar in a food processor. Process 20 seconds, just until nuts are finely chopped. Transfer to a large bowl. Combine egg whites and cream of tartar in a small mixer bowl. Beat on medium-high speed until foamy. Gradually beat in remaining ½ cup sugar; beat to stiff peaks, 3 minutes. Transfer to bowl with nuts; fold in nuts just until combined (do not overmix). Divide mixture in half and spoon 1 half onto each outlined circle; spread evenly into 9-inch rounds. Bake 1½ hours, until meringues feel completely dry and are very lightly golden at edges. Transfer meringues on cookie sheets to wire racks and cool completely.

3. *Make chocolate buttercream:* Meanwhile, place chocolates in a small microwaveproof bowl. Microwave on High 1 minute to 1 minute 15 seconds, until melted, stirring halfway through; stir until smooth. Let cool slightly. Combine granulated sugar and water in a small saucepan. Bring to boil over medium heat; boil 2 minutes. Lightly beat egg yolks in a small mixer bowl on medium speed. While still beating, add syrup in a fine, steady stream. Increase speed to high; beat 5 minutes, until thick and lemon colored and mixture forms soft peaks. Reduce speed to low and beat in butter, 2 tablespoons at a time, beating just until blended after each addition; beat until smooth. Beat in melted chocolate until smooth. Set aside.

4. *To assemble:* Beat heavy cream in a large mixer bowl on medium-low speed 5 minutes, until thickened. Add 2 tablespoons of the confectioners' sugar and the crème de cacao; continue to beat on medium speed 30 seconds, until mixture holds its shape when dropped from a spoon. Set aside. Carefully peel foil from meringues. Place 1 layer on a serving plate. Spread ½ cup of the chocolate buttercream evenly on meringue, leaving a 1-inch border around outside edge. Spoon remaining chocolate buttercream into a pastry bag fitted with a ½-inch star tip. Pipe rosettes about 1¼ inches high around edge of meringue, reserving 2 to 3 tablespoons of the chocolate buttercream. Spoon whipped cream inside ring of rosettes. Sprinkle top of second meringue with remaining 2 tablespoons confectioners' sugar. Place over cream layer. Pipe small rosettes around top edge of cake with reserved chocolate buttercream. Refrigerate 1 to 2 hours before serving. Makes 16 servings.

Per serving: 330 calories, 29 g total fat, 15 g saturated fat, 104 mg cholesterol, 22 mg sodium, 18 g carbohydrates, 3 g protein, 30 mg calcium, 1 g fiber

test kitchen tip
chocolate chips

Sure, semisweet chocolate chips are at their traditional best in the chocolate chip cookie, but true chocolate fans are always on the lookout for ways to sprinkle them into something good. Here are a few of our favorite ideas.

INSTANT FROSTING
Sprinkle ½ cup semisweet chocolate chips over hot cake or brownies. Let stand 5 minutes, until melted; spread over cake or brownies.

DARK BARK
Melt 1⅓ cups semisweet chocolate chips. Stir in ½ cup each raisins and peanuts. Pour into a foil-lined 8-inch square pan; refrigerate 30 minutes. Cut into squares.

CHOCOLATE PIZZA
Place one 9-inch unbaked refrigerated prepared piecrust on a cookie sheet. Sprinkle top with ¼ cup each miniature chocolate chips and chopped walnuts (or your favorite nut); cut into 8 wedges and bake at 375°F. for 9 to 12 minutes.

blooming chocolate

Ever unwrap a square of chocolate only to find a grayish layer on the surface? Don't throw it out! Though the gray color, called bloom, may not look appetizing, it will disappear when heated, and it doesn't hurt the quality of the chocolate. The bloom is caused by storing the chocolate in conditions that are humid or warm.

chocolate mud torte

Our version of this favorite childhood dessert features melt-in-your-mouth layers of malted and light chocolate mousses atop a cashew-cookie crumb crust.

Prep time: 1 hour plus chilling • Baking time: 10 minutes

CRUST:

1½ cups chocolate sandwich-cookie crumbs
      (16 cookies)
 ½ cup roasted cashews, finely chopped
 ¼ cup butter, melted (no substitutes)

CHOCOLATE-MALTED MOUSSE:

 11 ounces semisweet chocolate squares,
      coarsely chopped
1½ cup heavy or whipping cream
 ½ cup butter (no substitutes)
 ⅓ cup malted milk powder
 ¼ cup sugar

MILK CHOCOLATE MOUSSE:

1½ cup heavy or whipping cream
  4 ounces semisweet chocolate squares,
      coarsely chopped
 ⅓ cup sugar
  3 tablespoons butter (no substitutes)

      Roasted cashews, for garnish (optional)

1. *Make crust:* Heat oven to 350°F. Combine cookie crumbs, cashews and butter in a large bowl. Press into bottom of a 9-inch springform pan. Bake 10 minutes. Cool on a wire rack. Refrigerate until ready to use.

2. *Make chocolate-malted mousse:* Combine chocolate, heavy cream, butter, malted milk powder and sugar in a medium, heavy saucepan. Cook, stirring constantly, over low heat until chocolate is melted; whisk until mixture is smooth. Transfer to a large mixer bowl. Cover and chill in refrigerator 1 to 2 hours, until mixture is completely chilled, stirring often. Beat on medium speed 1 minute, until slightly thickened, being careful not to overbeat. Spoon over crust; refrigerate.

3. *Make milk chocolate mousse:* Combine heavy cream, chocolate, sugar and butter in a small, heavy saucepan. Cook, stirring constantly, over low heat until chocolate is melted; whisk until mixture is smooth. Transfer to a medium mixer bowl. Cover and chill in refrigerator for 1½ to 2 hours, until mixture is completely chilled, stirring often. Beat on medium speed 1 minute, until mixture is fluffy and mounds, being careful not to overbeat. Spoon evenly over chocolate-malted mousse. Cover and refrigerate overnight. *(Can be made ahead. Cover and refrigerate up to 2 days.)*

4. *To serve:* Run a sharp knife around edge of pan; remove side of pan. Garnish with additional roasted cashews around top edge of cake, if desired. Makes 16 servings.

Per serving without garnish: 515 calories, 41 g total fat, 23.5 g saturated fat, 94 mg cholesterol, 228 mg sodium, 37 g carbohydrates, 5 g protein, 58 mg calcium, 2 g fiber

chocolate-peanut-butter layer cake

As rich as a candy bar, but not as sweet, these dark cocoa layers spread with peanut-butter filling are enrobed with chocolate glaze and topped with chunks of golden peanut-praline brittle. Perfect for any celebration, the cake can be made up to 2 days ahead. Pictured on page 206.

Prep time: 1 hour plus standing and chilling
Baking time: 18 to 20 minutes

- 1 **cup all-purpose flour**
- ¼ **cup plus 2 tablespoons unsweetened cocoa**
- ½ **teaspoon salt**
- ¼ **teaspoon baking soda**
- ¼ **teaspoon baking powder**
- 10 **tablespoons unsalted butter, softened (no substitutes)**
- 1¼ **cups granulated sugar**
- 1 **teaspoon vanilla extract**
- 2 **large eggs**
- ½ **cup light sour cream or plain yogurt**

GLAZE:
- 6 **ounces semisweet chocolate squares, chopped**
- ½ **cup unsalted butter, cut up (no substitutes)**
- 1 **tablespoon light corn syrup**

PEANUT BUTTER FILLING:
- 1 **cup natural or reduced-sodium creamy peanut butter**
- ½ **cup confectioners' sugar, sifted**
- 6 **tablespoons unsalted butter, softened (no substitutes)**
- ¼ **teaspoon vanilla extract**

PEANUT-PRALINE BRITTLE:
- ½ **cup granulated sugar**
- ¼ **cup water**
- ⅛ **teaspoon cream of tartar**
- ½ **cup lightly salted dry-roasted peanuts, coarsely chopped**

1. Heat oven to 350°F. Adjust oven rack to lower third of oven. Grease two 9-inch round cake pans; line bottoms with waxed paper and grease paper.

2. Combine flour, cocoa, salt, baking soda and baking powder in a bowl; set aside. Beat butter in a medium mixer bowl on medium speed until creamy. Gradually add granulated sugar and vanilla. Add eggs, one at a time, beating well after each addition; beat 2 minutes. At medium speed, beat in flour mixture alternately with sour cream just until blended, beginning and ending with flour mixture. Spoon batter evenly into prepared pans.

3. Bake 18 to 20 minutes, until a toothpick inserted in centers comes out clean. Cool cakes in pans on wire racks 5 minutes. Invert and remove pans; peel off waxed paper. Invert cakes on racks again and cool completely.

4. *Make glaze:* Meanwhile, place chocolate, butter and corn syrup in a small bowl. Set bowl in a skillet of barely simmering water. Stir frequently until mixture is nearly melted and smooth. Remove bowl from heat; stir until smooth. Set aside.

5. *Make peanut butter filling:* Beat all ingredients in a small mixer bowl until blended. Set aside.

6. *Make peanut-praline brittle:* Place a sheet of foil on a cookie sheet and grease lightly; set aside. Combine sugar, water and cream of tartar in a small saucepan. Bring to simmer over medium heat (do not stir). Cover and simmer 3 minutes. Cook 10 minutes, until syrup is pale amber in color. Gently stir in peanuts. Cook just until syrup is deep amber, being careful not to burn. Immediately pour mixture onto prepared cookie sheet, spreading brittle as thin as possible. Cool completely. Break into pieces.

7. *To assemble:* Place 1 cake layer on a serving plate; spread ¾ cup of the peanut butter filling over top. Add second cake layer. Spread remaining filling over top and side of cake. Refrigerate 10 minutes, until filling is set.

8. If glaze has thickened, set bowl in pan of simmering water to thin slightly *(glaze should be the consistency of heavy cream)*. Tuck 4 strips of waxed paper under side of cake. Pour all of the glaze on top of cake. Spread with a metal spatula to cover top and side of cake.

9. Garnish top with peanut-praline brittle. Let stand until glaze sets; carefully remove waxed paper strips. Makes 12 servings.

Per serving: 650 calories, 45 g total fat, 21 g saturated fat, 104 mg cholesterol, 208 mg sodium, 56 g carbohydrates, 11 g protein, 79 mg calcium, 3 g fiber

one-bowl chocolate cake

This cake exemplifies the idea that sometimes simple is best. Pour the liquid ingredients into the dry ones and bake—what could be simpler? The frosting design may sound complicated, but it's not. Tip: Immediately after spreading warm frosting on the cake, pipe on the melted chocolate and pull a knife through it. Doing so creates a chevron design, which gives the appearance of arrow points running into each other.

Prep time: 30 minutes plus standing
Baking time: 30 to 35 minutes
Microwave used

- 1¾ **cups all-purpose flour**
- 1⅓ **cups sugar**
- ½ **cup unsweetened cocoa**
- 1 **teaspoon baking powder**
- ½ **teaspoon baking soda**
- ¼ **teaspoon salt**
- ¾ **cup butter or margarine, softened, cut up**
- 1½ **cups milk, at room temperature**
- 2 **large eggs, at room temperature**
- 1 **teaspoon vanilla extract**
- 2 **ounces semisweet chocolate squares, chopped**

FLUFFY WHITE FROSTING:

- 1 **large egg white**
- ½ **cup sugar**
- 2 **tablespoons water**
- 1 **tablespoon light corn syrup**
- ⅛ **teaspoon cream of tartar**
- ½ **teaspoon vanilla extract**

1. Heat oven to 350°F. Grease a 13×9-inch baking pan. Line bottom with waxed paper; grease and flour paper and sides.

2. Combine flour, sugar, cocoa, baking powder, baking soda and salt in a large mixer bowl. Add butter and beat on low speed until mixture is crumbly. Add milk, eggs and vanilla; beat 3 minutes on medium speed. Pour into prepared pan. Bake 30 to 35 minutes, until top springs back when lightly touched and a toothpick inserted in center comes out clean. Cool in pan on a wire rack 10 minutes. Invert cake onto wire rack; remove waxed paper and

cool completely. Place a serving platter over cake and invert, holding rack and platter.

3. Place chocolate in a microwaveproof bowl and microwave on High 1 to 1½ minutes, until melted; stir until smooth. Place in a small plastic storage bag; cut a small hole in 1 corner of the bag.

4. *Make fluffy white frosting:* Place egg white, sugar, water, corn syrup and cream of tartar in the top of a double boiler over rapidly boiling water. Beat constantly with a hand-held mixer 3 to 5 minutes, until thick and fluffy and temperature registers 160°F. on an instant-read thermometer. Remove from heat and beat over boiling water 1 minute more. Remove top pan from water; add vanilla and beat until meringue is thick and shiny. Immediately spread warm frosting over top and sides of cake. Pipe thin strips of melted chocolate, 1 inch apart, crosswise on frosting. Gently drag the tip of a knife lengthwise through chocolate and frosting, reversing direction for alternating rows and spacing rows 1 inch apart. Makes 12 servings.

Per serving: 355 calories, 15.5 g total fat, 9 g saturated fat, 71 mg cholesterol, 291 mg sodium, 49 g carbohydrates, 5 g protein, 108 mg calcium, 1 g fiber

flourless chocolate cake

Even with just six ingredients, this cake is decadent. Tip: Use the best-quality chocolate available. Pictured on page 205.

Prep time: 15 minutes plus standing
Baking time: 30 minutes

- 5 **large eggs, at room temperature**
- 1 **cup sugar**
- ⅓ **cup coffee-flavored liqueur**
- 1 **cup unsalted butter, softened and cut up (no substitutes)**
- 6 **ounces high-quality bittersweet chocolate, melted**
- 1 **teaspoon vanilla extract**
   Unsweetened whipped cream (optional)
   Fresh raspberries and fresh mint sprigs, for garnish (optional)

1. Heat oven to 350°F. Grease a 9-inch springform pan. Wrap the outside of the pan with foil. Set aside.

2. Beat eggs and sugar in a large mixer bowl on medium-high speed 8 to 10 minutes, until thick and fluffy. Reduce speed to medium; beat in liqueur and butter until blended. (It's normal for batter to look curdled.) Beat in chocolate and vanilla until combined. Pour batter into prepared pan. Bake 30 minutes, just until set.

3. Cool on a wire rack 30 minutes. Remove side of pan and serve warm or at room temperature with whipped cream, if desired; garnish with berries and mint, if desired. Makes 12 servings.

Per serving without whipped cream and garnish: 310 calories, 22.5 g total fat, 13 g saturated fat, 130 mg cholesterol, 29 mg sodium, 27 g carbohydrates, 4 g protein, 22 mg calcium, 0 g fiber

white chocolate mousse cake

This decadent dessert features a fluffy white chocolate mousse complemented by a chocolate-wafer crust and a dark chocolate mousse. Look for dried egg whites in the baking section of your supermarket.

Prep time: 1 hour plus standing and freezing
Baking time: 10 minutes

CHOCOLATE-WAFER CRUST:
- 2 tablespoons butter (no substitutes)
- ¾ cup chocolate-wafer crumbs

WHITE CHOCOLATE MOUSSE:
- 12 ounces white chocolate squares, chopped
- ½ cup water
- 4 egg yolks, beaten
- ¼ cup white crème de cacao
- 2½ cups heavy or whipping cream
- Dried egg whites and water to equal 4 egg whites
- ⅛ teaspoon cream of tartar
- Pinch salt
- 2 tablespoons sugar

DARK CHOCOLATE MOUSSE:
- 2 ounces unsweetened chocolate squares, chopped
- ½ cup heavy or whipping cream

- White and dark chocolate curls or grated chocolate, for garnish (optional)

1. *Make chocolate-wafer crust:* Heat oven to 350°F. Melt butter in a small saucepan. Stir in wafer crumbs. Pat evenly in bottom of a 9-inch springform pan. Bake 10 minutes. Transfer to a wire rack; cool while preparing filling.

2. *Make white chocolate mousse:* Combine white chocolate and water in a heavy, medium saucepan. Heat and stir over low heat until chocolate is melted; stir until smooth. Gradually stir hot mixture into egg yolks; return mixture to saucepan. Cook over medium-low heat just until mixture bubbles on edge. Quickly transfer to medium bowl; place the bowl in a sink or larger bowl filled with ice water. Stir in crème de cacao. Let stand in ice water bath for 12 minutes, stirring occasionally.

3. Beat heavy cream in a very large mixer bowl on medium-high speed just to stiff peaks; set aside. Prepare dried egg whites according to package directions in a clean mixer bowl; add cream of tartar and salt. Beat with clean beaters on medium-high speed until frothy. Gradually add sugar, beating constantly, until stiff (but not dry) peaks form. Fold one-third of the meringue into white chocolate mixture to lighten; fold white chocolate mixture into remaining meringue. Fold into whipped cream. Set aside.

4. *Make dark chocolate mousse:* Place chocolate and heavy cream in a medium saucepan. Heat and stir over low heat until chocolate is melted; stir until smooth. Cool just to room temperature. Fold ½ cup of the white chocolate mousse into dark chocolate mixture to lighten; fold in another 2½ cups of the white chocolate mousse.

5. *To assemble:* Pour half of the white chocolate mousse into prepared pan; gently spread evenly with a spatula. Carefully pour dark chocolate mousse over; spread evenly. Pour remaining white chocolate mousse over dark chocolate mousse; smooth top. Place in freezer 1 hour, until top begins to set. Garnish top with chocolate curls, if desired. Cover loosely with foil and freeze 24 hours. *(Can be made ahead. After freezing 24 hours, wrap well with plastic wrap, then foil and freeze up to 1 week.)* Makes 14 servings.

Per serving without garnish: 410 calories, 33 g total fat, 20 g saturated fat, 145 mg cholesterol, 122 mg sodium, 23 g carbohydrates, 5 g protein, 72 mg calcium, 1 g fiber

chocolate pound cake EASY

Serve this super-moist pound cake plain or dress it up with a chocolate glaze.

Prep time: 20 minutes plus standing
Baking time: 50 to 55 minutes

- 1½ **cups all-purpose flour**
- ¾ **cup unsweetened cocoa**
- 1½ **teaspoons baking powder**
- ¼ **teaspoon salt**
- 1 **cup butter, softened (no substitutes)**
- 1 **cup granulated sugar**
- ⅔ **cup firmly packed brown sugar**
- 2 **teaspoons vanilla extract**
- 4 **large eggs, at room temperature**
- ¾ **cup milk, at room temperature**
  Chocolate Glaze (recipe follows) (optional)

1. Heat oven to 325°F. Grease and flour one 12-cup Bundt pan.

2. Whisk flour, cocoa, baking powder and salt in a medium bowl. Beat butter in a large mixer bowl on medium-high speed until light. Add sugars and vanilla; beat until light and fluffy. Add eggs, one at a time, beating well after each addition. Reduce speed to low; gradually beat in flour mixture alternately with milk, beginning and ending with flour mixture. Beat 1 minute on medium speed until combined, scraping side of bowl with a rubber spatula. Pour into prepared pan.

3. Bake 50 to 55 minutes, until toothpick inserted in center comes out clean. Cool in pan on a wire rack 10 minutes. Invert cake onto wire rack; remove pan and cool completely. Decorate with chocolate glaze, if desired. Makes 10 servings.

Per serving without glaze: 440 calories, 23 g total fat, 13 g saturated fat, 139 mg cholesterol, 357 mg sodium, 52 g carbohydrates, 7 g protein, 160 mg calcium, 1 g fiber

For chocolate glaze: Place *2 ounces white chocolate squares* in the top of a double boiler over simmering water (with bottom of chocolate bowl at least 2 inches above simmering water); heat just until melted. Stir in *½ teaspoon vegetable oil* until smooth. Heat *3 ounces semisweet chocolate squares*

and *1 ounce unsweetened chocolate square* in another bowl over simmering water just until melted; stir until smooth. Using a tablespoon, spoon enough of the dark chocolate mixture over cake to cover the top, allowing the excess to drip down side of cake. Then, using a teaspoon, drop small dollops of the white chocolate mixture over the dark chocolate on top of the cake; spread to a 1-inch-wide strip around top of cake. Immediately drag a fork lightly through the chocolates to create a marbleized pattern. Let stand until chocolate is set or refrigerate 10 to 15 minutes, just until chocolate is set.

glazed fudge cake EASY

This incredibly light cake simply melts in your mouth.

Prep time: 25 minutes plus standing and chilling
Baking time: 43 to 46 minutes

- ¾ **cup plus 2 tablespoons cake flour (not self-rising)**
- 1 **teaspoon baking powder**
- 1 **teaspoon baking soda**
- ½ **teaspoon salt**
- 1¼ **cups granulated sugar, divided**
- 2 **ounces unsweetened chocolate squares, chopped**
- 1 **tablespoon unsweetened cocoa**
- ⅓ **cup boiling water**
- 2 **large eggs**
- ¾ **cup unsalted butter, at room temperature and cut up (no substitutes)**
- ½ **cup sour cream**
- 1 **tablespoon rum**

CHOCOLATE-RUM GLAZE:

- 3 **ounces semisweet chocolate squares**
- 4 **tablespoons confectioners' sugar, sifted**
- 2 **tablespoons water**
- 2 **tablespoons unsalted butter (no substitutes)**
  Pinch salt
- 1 **teaspoon rum**

  Whole blanched almonds, for garnish (optional)

1. Adjust rack to center of oven. Heat oven to 325°F. Cut a circle of waxed paper to fit bottom of a 9-inch springform pan. Place in pan and butter paper and side of pan. Wrap outside of pan with foil.

2. Process flour, baking powder, baking soda and salt in a food processor 5 seconds to blend; set aside. Process 1 cup of the granulated sugar, the 2 ounces chocolate and the cocoa 1 minute, until chocolate is finely chopped. With motor running, pour boiling water through feed tube. Process until chocolate is melted. Add eggs; process 1 minute. Add remaining ¼ cup granulated sugar; process 1 minute, stopping once to scrape down bowl. Add the ¾ cup butter; process 1 minute more. Add sour cream and rum; process 5 seconds. Add flour mixture; pulse 3 or 4 times, just until flour disappears. (Do not overprocess.)

3. Transfer batter to prepared pan; spread evenly with a spatula. Bake 43 to 46 minutes, until cake begins to pull slightly from side of pan. Cool in pan on a wire rack. (It's normal for cake to fall in center as it cools.)

4. *Make chocolate-rum glaze:* Meanwhile, combine chocolate, confectioners' sugar, water, butter and salt in the top of a double boiler. Cook slowly, stirring, over simmering water until heated through and chocolate is melted. Stir in rum. Refrigerate 15 minutes, until glaze thickens to the consistency of maple syrup.

5. *Make garnish (optional):* Dip half of each almond in chocolate-rum glaze; refrigerate 5 minutes, just until set.

6. When cake has cooled, remove side of pan. Invert onto a cake platter; remove bottom of pan and the waxed paper. Spread glaze over top and side with a rubber spatula. Garnish with almonds around edge of cake, if desired. *(Can be made ahead. Freeze, unwrapped, 1 hour. Wrap well in plastic wrap and freeze up to 2 weeks. Thaw at room temperature, uncovered, 3 hours.)* Makes 12 to 16 servings.

Per serving without garnish: 290 calories, 18.5 g total fat, 11 g saturated fat, 66 mg cholesterol, 227 mg sodium, 29 g carbohydrates, 3 g protein, 41 mg calcium, 1 g fiber

mocha-chip chiffon cake

Appearing here, the legendary combo of coffee and chocolate.

Prep time: 20 minutes plus standing
Baking time: 1 hour 17 to 20 minutes

2	tablespoons instant espresso powder
¾	cup boiling water
2	cups cake flour (not self-rising)
1¾	cups sugar, divided
1	tablespoon baking powder
¼	teaspoon salt
½	cup vegetable oil
7	large eggs, separated
1	teaspoon vanilla extract
¾	cup miniature semisweet chocolate chips, divided
½	teaspoon cream of tartar

1. Heat oven to 325°F. Dissolve instant espresso in boiling water; set aside to cool.

2. Meanwhile, combine flour, 1 cup of the sugar, the baking powder and salt in a large bowl. Make a well in center; add oil, egg yolks, vanilla and cooled espresso. With a wire whisk, beat until smooth. Stir in ½ cup of the chocolate chips.

3. Beat egg whites in a large mixer bowl on high speed until foamy. Gradually add remaining ¾ cup sugar and the cream of tartar. Continue beating to soft peaks. Fold one third of the beaten whites into chocolate chip mixture; fold in remaining whites until well blended. Spoon batter into an ungreased 10-inch tube pan. Sprinkle with remaining ¼ cup chocolate chips. Bake 1 hour 17 to 20 minutes, until cake springs back when lightly touched. Immediately invert pan onto neck of funnel or bottle; let hang 3 hours, until completely cool.

4. *To loosen:* Run a metal spatula or thin knife around side of pan and tube. Lift cake from pan by pulling up on center tube. Invert pan and run a knife along bottom of cake to loosen and remove from center tube. Turn cake upright onto serving plate. Makes 12 servings.

Per serving: 380 calories, 16.5 g total fat, 5 g saturated fat, 124 mg cholesterol, 187 mg sodium, 53 g carbohydrates, 6 g protein, 85 mg calcium, 0 g fiber

chocolate and walnut praline layer cake

Want to end your get-together with a grand finale? This tender cake, filled with luscious chocolate buttercream and mouth-watering praline, does the trick.

Prep time: 45 minutes plus standing
Baking time: 28 to 30 minutes
Microwave used

WALNUT PRALINE:

- 1   **cup granulated sugar**
- ½   **cup walnut pieces**

CHOCOLATE-PRALINE SHARDS (OPTIONAL):

- 2   **ounces semisweet chocolate squares**

CAKE:

- ¾   **cup milk**
- 1   **tablespoon instant espresso powder**
- 1½   **cups all-purpose flour**
- ⅔   **cup unsweetened cocoa**
- 1½   **teaspoons baking powder**
- ½   **teaspoon salt**
- 1   **cup unsalted butter, softened (no substitutes)**
- 1¼   **cups granulated sugar**
- ½   **cup firmly packed brown sugar**
- 4   **large eggs, at room temperature**

BUTTERCREAM:

- 5   **ounces semisweet chocolate squares**
- 2   **ounces unsweetened chocolate squares**
- 4   **large eggs, at room temperature**
- ⅔   **cup granulated sugar**
- 12   **tablespoons unsalted butter, softened (no substitutes)**
- 2   **tablespoons walnut-flavored liqueur**

   Edible gold leaves,* for garnish (optional)

1. *Make walnut praline:* Heat sugar in a large skillet over medium heat until several melted amber pools appear. Gently swirl pan to allow caramelized sugar to run into areas not yet melted (you can gently stir the unmelted sugar into the amber pools) until mixture is a smooth caramel. Stir in walnuts and immediately pour out onto a cookie sheet. Cool completely. Break into pieces and process in food processor until finely ground; set aside.

2. *Make chocolate-praline shards (optional):* Place chocolate in a small microwaveproof bowl. Microwave on High 1 to 1½ minutes, until melted; stir until smooth. Spread evenly, about ⅛ inch thick, on waxed paper with a spatula. Sprinkle melted chocolate with 2 tablespoons of the walnut praline; cool completely. Break into large and small shards; set aside.

3. *Make cake:* Heat oven to 325°F. Lightly grease bottom of a 15½×10½-inch jelly-roll pan; line bottom with waxed paper. Grease and flour paper and sides of pan. Heat milk in a microwaveproof measuring cup on High 30 seconds, until very warm. Stir in espresso until dissolved; cool. Meanwhile, whisk together flour, cocoa, baking powder and salt in a medium bowl. Beat butter and sugars in a large mixer bowl on high speed 4 to 5 minutes, until light and fluffy. Add eggs, one at a time, to butter mixture, beating well after each addition. Reduce speed to medium-low. Beat in flour mixture alternately with milk mixture, beginning and ending with flour mixture; beat 30 seconds after last flour addition (do not overmix). Spread in prepared pan; bake 28 to 30 minutes, until center puffs slightly and a toothpick inserted in center comes out clean. Cool cake in pan on a wire rack. Run a sharp knife around edges of cake and invert onto wire rack; remove pan. Peel off waxed paper.

4. *Make buttercream:* Place chocolates in a bowl suspended over (but not touching) simmering water and heat until melted; stir until smooth. Whisk eggs and sugar constantly in top of double boiler (or bowl) over simmering water until temperature of egg mixture registers 140°F. on an instant-read thermometer. Continue whisking and cooking for 3 minutes, being sure to maintain temperature (electric range heat can be shut off—lower gas to very low if temperature goes above 140°F.). Remove mixture from heat and beat with a hand-held mixer on high speed 10 to 15 minutes, until cool. Add melted chocolate; beat 5 minutes. Reduce speed to medium; add butter, 1 tablespoonful at a time, beating well after each addition. Increase speed to high; beat 5 minutes, until frosting is thick and lighter in color. Beat in liqueur just until blended.

5. *To assemble:* Trim edges of cake. Cut cake crosswise into 3 equal rectangles. Place 1 cake rectangle on a serving platter. Spread buttercream evenly to a generous ¼-inch thickness over entire surface. Sprinkle evenly with ¼ cup of the walnut praline. Repeat with the second cake rectangle, buttercream and walnut praline. Top with remaining cake rectangle; spread remaining buttercream over top and sides of cake. Sprinkle sides of cake evenly with remaining walnut praline. Arrange chocolate-praline shards with gold leaves around top edge of cake, if desired. Makes 12 to 14 servings.

Note: Can be found at baking specialty stores or ordered from the New York Cake and Baking Distributors (800-942-2539).

Per serving without garnish: 685 calories, 40.5 g total fat, 22 g saturated fat, 203 mg cholesterol, 190 mg sodium, 76 g carbohydrates, 9 g protein, 135 mg calcium, 2 g fiber

chocolate cupcakes

These unfrosted mini cakes are perfect for picnics.

Total prep and baking time: 30 minutes plus standing

- ½ **cup unsweetened cocoa**
- ¾ **cup warm water**
- 2 **large eggs**
- ½ **cup vegetable oil**
- 1 **teaspoon vanilla extract**
- 1¾ **cups all-purpose flour**
- 1⅓ **cups sugar**
- ¾ **teaspoon baking powder**
- ¾ **teaspoon salt**
- ¼ **teaspoon baking soda**
  Sugar, for garnish (optional)

1. Heat oven to 400°F. Line twelve 2¾-inch muffin-pan cups with cupcake/muffin liners. Whisk together the cocoa and water in a medium bowl until smooth. Beat in eggs, oil and vanilla.

2. Whisk together flour, the 1⅓ cups sugar, baking powder, salt and baking soda in a large bowl. Stir in cocoa mixture with a rubber spatula just until combined.

3. Transfer batter to a large glass measure; pour batter into prepared muffin-pan cups. Bake 17 to 19 minutes, until toothpick inserted in centers of cupcakes comes out clean. Sprinkle a small amount of sugar over cupcake tops, if desired. Remove from pans; cool on wire racks. Makes 12 cupcakes.

Per cupcake without sugar: 255 calories, 10.5 g total fat, 1.5 g saturated fat, 35 mg cholesterol, 213 mg sodium, 38 g carbohydrates, 4 g protein, 29 mg calcium, 2 g fiber

best-ever brownies

Prep time: 20 minutes plus standing
Baking time: 20 to 25 minutes

- 4 **ounces unsweetened chocolate squares, coarsely chopped**
- ⅓ **cup butter or margarine**
- 1 **cup all-purpose flour**
- ¼ **teaspoon salt**
- 4 **large eggs**
- 1½ **cups sugar**
- 1 **teaspoon vanilla extract**
- 1 **cup semisweet chocolate chips**
- 1 **cup chopped walnuts**

1. Heat oven to 350°F. Line a 13×9-inch baking pan with foil; lightly coat with vegetable cooking spray. Set aside.

2. Melt chocolate and butter in a small bowl set over hot, not boiling, water. Remove from heat and cool slightly. Combine flour and salt in a medium bowl. Set aside.

3. Beat together eggs and sugar in a large mixer bowl on medium-high speed until thick and light. Beat in chocolate mixture and vanilla. Beat in flour mixture just until combined. Fold in chocolate chips and nuts. Pour batter into prepared pan. Bake 20 to 25 minutes, until a toothpick inserted in center comes out barely clean. Cool completely in pan on a wire rack. Cut into 2¼×2⅛-inch bars. Makes 2 dozen brownies.

Per brownie: 195 calories, 11.5 g total fat, 5 g saturated fat, 43 mg cholesterol, 64 mg sodium, 23 g carbohydrates, 3 g protein, 17 mg calcium, 2 g fiber

chocolate sandwich cookies

These impressive cookies are surprisingly easy to make—minimal effort, maximal results!

Prep time: 30 minutes plus standing
Baking time: 10 to 12 minutes per batch
Microwave used

- **2 cups all-purpose flour**
- **¼ cup unsweetened cocoa**
- **½ teaspoon salt**
- **¼ teaspoon baking powder**
- **1 cup butter, softened (no substitutes)**
- **⅔ cup sugar**
- **1 large egg**
- **1 teaspoon vanilla extract**

FILLING:
- **4 ounces white chocolate squares, melted**
- **1 tablespoon butter**

- **3 ounces semisweet chocolate squares, melted (optional)**

1. Heat oven to 350°F.

2. Combine flour, cocoa, salt and baking powder in a bowl; set aside. Beat butter and sugar in a large mixer bowl on medium-high speed 1 minute, until light and fluffy. Beat in egg and vanilla until well combined. Reduce speed to low; beat in flour mixture just until combined.

3. Insert desired disk into cookie press. Spoon one third of the dough into press. Pipe cookies, ½ inch apart, onto 2 ungreased cookie sheets. Bake 10 to 12 minutes, until cookies are just firm to the touch. Cool completely on a wire rack. Repeat with remaining dough.

4. *Make filling:* Place white chocolate and butter in a microwaveproof bowl. Microwave on Medium 3 minutes, stirring every minute until melted; stir until smooth.

5. Working with 12 cookies at a time, frost flat sides of half of the cooled cookies with melted white chocolate; top with remaining unfrosted cookies to make sandwiches. Dip half of each sandwich cookie into melted semisweet chocolate,

if desired. Place on cookie sheet lined with waxed paper; let stand 30 minutes, until set. Makes 36 cookies.

Per undipped sandwich cookie: 110 calories, 7 g total fat, 4.5 g saturated fat, 23 mg cholesterol, 99 mg sodium, 11 g carbohydrates, 1 g protein, 15 mg calcium, 0 g fiber

giant chocolate chip cookies

The secret to making giant cookies: Shape the dough with an ice cream scoop and flatten with a floured hand.

Prep time: 15 minutes plus standing
Baking time: 12 to 15 minutes per batch

- **½ cup butter, softened (no substitutes)**
- **½ cup vegetable shortening**
- **1 cup firmly packed light brown sugar**
- **¾ cup granulated sugar**
- **2 large eggs**
- **1 teaspoon vanilla extract**
- **2 cups all-purpose flour**
- **1 teaspoon baking soda**
- **1 teaspoon salt**
- **1½ cups semisweet chocolate chips**

1. Heat oven to 325°F. Grease 2 large cookie sheets. Beat together butter, shortening and sugars in a large mixer bowl on medium-high speed 4 to 5 minutes, until light and fluffy. Add eggs and vanilla; beat until combined. Add flour, baking soda and salt; beat just until combined. Stir in chocolate chips. Using a spring-loaded ice cream scoop or a ¼-cup dry measure, drop 3 or 4 scoops of batter, 6 inches apart, onto cookie sheets. With a floured hand, flatten each scoop into a 4-inch round.

2. Bake 12 to 15 minutes, until edges are set but centers are slightly soft. Cool cookies on cookie sheets on wire racks 5 minutes; carefully transfer cookies with a metal spatula to wire racks and cool completely. Makes about 16 cookies.

Per cookie: 340 calories, 17.5 g total fat, 8.5 g saturated fat, 43 mg cholesterol, 301 mg sodium, 45 g carbohydrates, 3 g protein, 29 mg calcium, 1 g fiber

almond and hazelnut chocolate crescents

Teatime with these impressive and not-too-sweet cookies is good anytime.

Prep time: 25 minutes plus chilling and standing
Baking time: 15 to 17 minutes per batch

- 1¾ **cups all-purpose flour**
- 1¼ **cups ground almonds**
- ½ **cup toasted skinned ground hazelnuts**
- ½ **cup unsweetened cocoa**
- 1¼ **cups butter, softened (no substitutes)**
- 1 **cup confectioners' sugar**
- 1 **teaspoon vanilla extract**
- 8 **ounces semisweet chocolate squares, melted and slightly cooled**
- 3 **tablespoons confectioners' sugar**

1. ■ Combine flour, nuts and cocoa in a medium bowl. Beat butter in a large mixer bowl on medium-high speed until light. Gradually add the 1 cup confectioners' sugar; beat until light and fluffy. Beat in vanilla. Reduce speed to medium-low; gradually beat in flour mixture until well combined. Cover and refrigerate at least 1 hour or overnight.

2. ■ Heat oven to 350°F. Pinch off walnut-size pieces of dough and shape into crescents. Place on 2 large ungreased cookie sheets. Bake 15 to 17 minutes, until cookies are just firm to the touch. Transfer cookies with a metal spatula to wire racks and cool completely. Dip half of each cookie into melted chocolate and place on a cookie sheet lined with waxed paper. Let chocolate set at least 1 hour (or refrigerate 10 to 15 minutes, just until chocolate sets). Sprinkle undipped halves of crescents with the 3 tablespoons confectioners' sugar. Makes about 54 crescents.

Per crescent: 115 calories, 8.5 g total fat, 3.5 g saturated fat, 12 mg cholesterol, 46 mg sodium, 9 g carbohydrates, 2 g protein, 20 mg calcium, 1 g fiber

tropical blondies

In the world of brownies, brunettes reign. But for those who prefer blondes, chocolate chips and macadamia nuts flavor these chewy brown sugar brownies.

Prep time: 20 minutes plus standing
Baking time: 45 minutes

- 1½ **cups all-purpose flour**
- 1 **teaspoon baking powder**
- ¼ **teaspoon salt**
- ½ **cup butter or margarine, at room temperature**
- 1¼ **cups firmly packed brown sugar**
- 2 **large eggs**
- 2 **teaspoons vanilla extract**
- ½ **cup chopped toasted macadamia nuts, divided**
- 4 **ounces semisweet chocolate squares, chopped**

1. ■ Heat oven to 350°F. Line a 9-inch square baking pan with foil; grease foil. Set aside.

2. ■ Combine flour, baking powder and salt in a medium bowl. Beat butter and sugar in a large mixer bowl on medium-high speed 5 minutes, until well blended. Beat in eggs, one at a time, beating well after each addition, scraping side of bowl with rubber spatula. Beat in vanilla. Reduce speed to low; beat in flour mixture until combined. Stir in ⅓ cup of the macadamia nuts and the chocolate. Spread batter evenly into prepared pan. Sprinkle remaining nuts over top of batter. Bake 45 minutes, until top is golden brown and toothpick inserted in center comes out clean. Cool on wire rack. Cut into 3×2¼-inch bars. *(Can be made ahead. Store in airtight container 2 days or freeze up to 1 month.)* Makes 12 bars.

Per bar: 315 calories, 16 g total fat, 7.5 g saturated fat, 56 mg cholesterol, 188 mg sodium, 41 g carbohydrates, 4 g protein, 58 mg calcium, 1 g fiber

tropical crunch bars

A mix of nuts, chocolate and homemade toffee renders these buttery cookies addictive. Don't say we didn't warn you.

Prep time: 35 minutes plus standing
Baking time: 37 to 40 minutes

TOFFEE:
- ½ cup butter (no substitutes)
- ½ cup granulated sugar
- 1 tablespoon water
- 1 tablespoon light corn syrup

CRUST:
- ½ cup butter or margarine, cut up
- ¼ cup firmly packed brown sugar
- 1 cup all-purpose flour

- 2 large eggs
- 1 cup firmly packed brown sugar
- 1 teaspoon vanilla extract
- 2 tablespoons flour
- 1 teaspoon baking powder
- ½ teaspoon salt
- 8 ounces bittersweet chocolate, cut into chunks
- 1 cup flaked coconut
- 1 cup coarsely chopped, toasted unsalted cashews
- ½ cup coarsely chopped Brazil or macadamia nuts

1. Heat oven to 350°F. Line a 13×9-inch baking pan with foil; lightly grease foil. Set aside.

2. *Make toffee:* Lightly grease a cookie sheet. Melt butter in a small, heavy saucepan over medium heat. Stir in sugar, water and corn syrup. Cook 7 to 10 minutes, until mixture is deep golden amber in color and registers 290°F. on a candy thermometer, stirring occasionally. Pour onto prepared cookie sheet; cool completely, about 20 minutes. Chop toffee; measure ½ cup chopped toffee and set aside. (Reserve remaining toffee for another use.)

3. *Make crust:* Meanwhile, beat together butter and brown sugar in a large mixer bowl on medium speed 1 minute, until smooth and creamy. Beat in flour until crumbly. Press evenly into prepared pan. Bake 12 to 15 minutes, until golden. Cool on a wire rack.

4. Meanwhile, beat eggs with the 1 cup brown sugar and the vanilla in a large mixer bowl on medium speed until blended. Reduce speed to low; beat in flour, baking powder and salt just until combined. Stir in chocolate chunks, coconut, nuts and the ½ cup chopped toffee. Spread over baked crust. Bake 25 minutes, until golden brown. Cool completely in pan on a wire rack. Remove from pan and loosen foil from sides. Cut into 2¼×1⅝-inch bars. Makes 32 bars.

Per bar: 205 calories, 13 g total fat, 6.5 g saturated fat, 30 mg cholesterol, 120 mg sodium, 22 g carbohydrates, 2 g protein, 25 mg calcium, 1 g fiber

congo bars

These rich, slightly cakey bars feature peanut butter and milk chocolate morsels in place of the typical semisweet chocolate chips. Tip: If you can't find the bag with a combination of the two, buy individual bags of peanut butter and milk chocolate chips and use 1 cup of each.

Prep time: 20 minutes plus standing
Baking time: 28 to 30 minutes

- 2 cups all-purpose flour
- 1½ teaspoons baking powder
- ½ teaspoon salt
- ½ cup butter or margarine, softened
- ½ cup vegetable shortening
- 1¼ cups firmly packed brown sugar
- 3 large eggs
- 1½ teaspoons vanilla extract
- 1 cup chopped pecans
- 1 package (11 oz.) peanut butter and milk chocolate morsels

1. Heat oven to 350°F. Line a 13×9-inch baking pan with foil; lightly coat with vegetable cooking spray. Set aside.

2. Combine flour, baking powder and salt in a medium bowl; set aside. Beat butter and shortening in a large mixer bowl on medium-high speed until light. Gradually add sugar and beat until light and fluffy. Add eggs, one at a time, beating well after each addition. Add vanilla. Reduce speed to low; beat in flour mixture just until combined. Stir in pecans and half of the peanut butter and chocolate morsels. Spread evenly into prepared pan. Sprinkle remaining morsels over top. Bake 28 to 30 minutes, until a toothpick inserted in center comes out barely clean. Cool in pan on a wire rack 10 minutes. Remove from pan and cool completely on wire rack. Cut into 1⅝×1½-inch bars. Makes 48 bars.

Per bar: 135 calories, 8 g total fat, 3.5 g saturated fat, 19 mg cholesterol, 75 mg sodium, 14 g carbohydrates, 1 g protein, 19 mg calcium, 0 g fiber

chocolate-peanut butter bars EASY

If you like chocolate-covered peanut-butter cups, you're sure to fall in love with these bars.

Prep time: 25 minutes plus standing
Baking time: 12 to 15 minutes

FILLING:

1¼	cups confectioners' sugar
¾	cup finely chopped pecans
1½	cups creamy peanut butter
¼	cup butter or margarine, melted
1	teaspoon vanilla extract

CRUST:

1½	cups all-purpose flour
⅔	cup firmly packed brown sugar
½	teaspoon baking powder
½	teaspoon salt
¼	teaspoon baking soda
⅔	cup butter or margarine, softened
2	large egg yolks, lightly beaten
1	teaspoon vanilla extract

1	package (12 oz.) semisweet or 1 package (11½ oz.) milk chocolate chips

1. *Make filling:* Toss together confectioners' sugar and pecans in a medium bowl. Add remaining ingredients and stir until well blended. Set aside.

2. *Make crust:* Heat oven to 350°F. Line a 13×9-inch baking pan with foil, extending foil 2 inches past long sides of pan. Lightly coat with vegetable cooking spray. Combine flour, sugar, baking powder, salt and baking soda in a large mixer bowl; add butter, egg yolks and vanilla. Beat on low speed until crumbly. Press crumbs into bottom of prepared pan. Bake 12 to 15 minutes, until golden brown. Remove from oven; turn oven off.

3. Let crust cool 2 to 3 minutes. While still warm, spread filling evenly over crust. Sprinkle chocolate chips over filling and return pan to warm oven for 2 minutes, until chocolate has softened. Remove from oven and spread chocolate evenly. Cool completely on a wire rack. Lift out in 1 piece. Remove foil and cut vertically and horizontally into 6 rows. Makes 36 bars.

Per bar: 220 calories, 15 g total fat, 6 g saturated fat, 25 mg cholesterol, 150 mg sodium, 20 g carbohydrates, 4 g protein, 19 mg calcium, 2 g fiber

test kitchen tip

long live chocolate

As long as basic conditions are met, solid chocolate stores well for up to 1 year. Keep it well wrapped and in a cool (55°F. to 65°F.), dry place. See the tip on page 218 for information on bloom, which is the pale gray discoloration that sometimes develops on the surface of chocolate.

rich marbled wonders ⓔⓐⓢⓨ

Two batters—a dark chocolate and a light blondie—are marbled in the pan to make a brownie that's as attractive as it is delicious. Espresso coffee powder adds a touch of sophistication to the flavor. Tip: Let the brownie stand until it sets for easier cutting.

Prep time: 20 minutes plus standing
Baking time: 30 to 35 minutes

- 1   cup butter or margarine, softened
- 2   cups sugar
- 4   large eggs
- 2   tablespoons instant espresso powder
- 1   tablespoon orange-flavored liqueur
- ¼   teaspoon salt
- 2¼ cups chopped pecans
- 1¼ cups all-purpose flour
- 3   ounces unsweetened chocolate squares, melted

1. Heat oven to 350°F. Line a 13×9-inch baking pan with foil; lightly coat with vegetable cooking spray. Set aside.

2. Beat butter in a large mixer bowl on medium-high speed until light. Gradually add sugar and beat until light and fluffy. Add eggs, one at a time, beating well after each addition. Beat in espresso powder, liqueur 3and salt. Stir in pecans and flour.

3. Divide batter in half. Stir melted chocolate into half of the batter. Drop into prepared pan by teaspoonfuls, alternating the batters to form a checkerboard. With a knife, pull through batters to marbleize. Bake 30 to 35 minutes, until a toothpick inserted in center comes out barely clean. Cool on a wire rack; let stand at least 4 hours before cutting. Cut into 1⅝×1½-inch bars. Makes 48 bars.

Per bar: 130 calories, 9 g total fat, 3.5 g saturated fat, 29 mg cholesterol, 59 mg sodium, 12 g carbohydrates, 2 g protein, 9 mg calcium, 1 g fiber

chocolate-almond slices ⓔⓐⓢⓨ

If you grew up on chocolate-almond candy bars, as we did, you'll flip over these.

Total prep time: 20 minutes plus standing and chilling

- 3   packages (6 oz. each) semisweet chocolate chips
- 1   can (14 oz.) sweetened condensed milk
      Dash salt
- 1   teaspoon vanilla extract
- 2   cups toasted slivered almonds

1. Combine chips, sweetened condensed milk and salt in a heavy saucepan. Cook over low heat until chocolate is melted and smooth, stirring frequently. Remove from heat; stir in vanilla. Let stand until cooled to room temperature.

2. Divide chocolate mixture into quarters. Place each quarter on a 15-inch sheet of waxed paper. Shape into 12-inch logs. Pat almonds onto logs to coat, using about ½ cup of the almonds per log. Wrap tightly in waxed paper; refrigerate 2 hours, until firm. *(Can be made ahead. When firm, wrap each log well in plastic wrap and store in refrigerator up to 2 weeks.)* Remove from waxed paper; cut into ¼-inch-thick slices. Makes about 200 slices.

Per slice: 25 calories, 1.5 g total fat, 0.5 g saturated fat, 1 mg cholesterol, 4 mg sodium, 3 g carbohydrates, 1 g protein, 10 mg calcium, 0 g fiber

chocolate-phyllo pockets ⓔⓐⓢⓨ

Wrapped in crisp phyllo dough, a dollop of gooey hazelnut fudge and marble cake bake together for a simple yet elegant dessert. Pictured on page 201.

Total prep and baking time: 30 minutes
Microwave used

- 5   ounces semisweet chocolate squares
- ½   cup chocolate-hazelnut spread (Nutella)
- 6   slices ½-inch-thick prepared marble or vanilla pound cake

4 sheets phyllo dough

6 tablespoons butter, melted (no substitutes)

2 tablespoons confectioners' sugar

Fresh raspberries, for garnish (optional)

1. Heat oven to 400°F. Chop 2 ounces of the chocolate; combine with hazelnut spread in a medium bowl. Cover and refrigerate.

2. Using a 2½-inch-wide biscuit cutter or drinking glass, cut out 1 circle from each slice of pound cake. (Reserve scraps for another use.) Set aside.

3. Place 1 sheet of the phyllo on the work surface. Brush lightly with butter. Arrange another sheet on top; brush with butter. Cut phyllo stack into three 12×5-inch pieces. Arrange 1 circle of the pound cake in the center of 1 piece of phyllo. Spoon 1 rounded tablespoon of the chocolate-hazelnut mixture on top of cake. Fold up 2 long phyllo sides to enclose chocolate, then fold up short ends to form a pocket; pinch top to seal. Brush pocket with butter; transfer to an ungreased jelly-roll pan. Repeat process with remaining phyllo, butter, cake and chocolate-hazelnut mixture. Sprinkle confectioners' sugar over each pocket. *(Can be made ahead. Cover with plastic wrap and refrigerate overnight.)* Bake 12 to 15 minutes, until golden brown (17 to 19 minutes, if pockets have been refrigerated).

4. Meanwhile, microwave remaining 3 ounces chocolate in a small microwaveproof bowl on High 1½ minutes, until melted; stir until smooth. Cool slightly and transfer to a small, heavy-duty plastic storage bag. Snip a small hole in 1 corner of the bag. Decoratively pipe chocolate on the bottom of 6 dessert plates. Arrange phyllo pocket on each plate. Serve immediately with raspberries, if desired. Makes 6 servings.

Per serving: 420 calories, 27.5 g total fat, 12 g saturated fat, 31 mg cholesterol, 236 mg sodium, 43 g carbohydrates, 4 g protein, 47 mg calcium, 1 g fiber

double-chocolate cherry-chip cookies EASY

Studded with dried cherries and white chocolate, these extra-large cookies won't stick around for long!

Prep time: 10 minutes plus freezing and standing
Baking time: 12 to 13 minutes
Microwave used

4 ounces unsweetened chocolate squares

5 tablespoons butter or margarine

1 cup plus 2 tablespoons sugar

2 large eggs

1 teaspoon vanilla extract

½ cup all-purpose flour

¼ teaspoon baking powder

¼ teaspoon salt

½ cup dried cherries, chopped

½ cup white chocolate chips

1. Microwave chocolate and butter in a large microwaveproof bowl on High 1½ to 2 minutes, until melted; stir until smooth. Stir in sugar, then eggs and vanilla until smooth. Stir in flour, baking powder and salt just until blended; stir in cherries and chips. Freeze dough 5 minutes. Scrape cold dough around edge of bowl into center; freeze 5 to 10 minutes more, until slightly firm.

2. Meanwhile, heat oven to 350°F. Line a large cookie sheet with foil.

3. Drop 8 rounded tablespoonfuls of the dough onto prepared cookie sheet. Bake 12 to 13 minutes, until puffed. Cool the cookies on cookie sheet on a wire rack 5 minutes; transfer cookies with a metal spatula to wire rack and cool completely. Repeat with remaining dough. Makes about 24 cookies.

Per cookie: 135 calories, 7 g total fat, 4.5 g saturated fat, 25 mg cholesterol, 67 mg sodium, 17 g carbohydrates, 1 g protein, 9 mg calcium, 1 g fiber

chocolate crêpes with pears and chocolate sauce EASY

Crêpes never go out of style. And this version, with pears and chocolate sauce, can be made ahead. Pictured on page 203.

Prep time: 25 minutes plus chilling
Cooking time: 30 minutes

POACHED PEARS:

- 5 **cups water**
- 4 **large Bartlett or Anjou pears (about 2½ lbs.), peeled and halved lengthwise**
- ½ **cup sugar**
- ⅓ **cup honey**
- 3 **3×1-inch strips lemon peel**
- 2 **tablespoons lemon juice**
- 2 **teaspoons vanilla extract**
- 2 **cinnamon sticks**
- 4 **whole cloves**

BATTER:

- 2 **large eggs, at room temperature**
- ¾ **cup milk**
- ½ **cup heavy or whipping cream**
- 3 **tablespoons butter or margarine, melted**
- ½ **teaspoon vanilla extract**
- 1 **cup all-purpose flour**
- ¼ **cup sugar**
- 2 **tablespoons unsweetened cocoa**
- ¼ **teaspoon salt**

CHOCOLATE SAUCE:

- 1 **cup water**
- ½ **cup sugar**
- ½ **cup heavy or whipping cream**
- 4 **ounces semisweet chocolate squares, chopped**
- 2 **ounces unsweetened chocolate squares, chopped**

  Vegetable oil
- 1 **cup crème fraîche or whipped cream**
  Unsweetened cocoa, for dusting
  Fresh mint sprigs and raspberries, for garnish (optional)

1. *Make poached pears:* Combine all ingredients in a large saucepan. Bring to boil over high heat; reduce heat to medium-low and simmer 20 minutes, until pears are tender. Remove from heat; cool pears in liquid to room temperature. *(Can be made ahead. Transfer pears and liquid to a bowl. Cover and refrigerate overnight. Remove from refrigerator 1 hour before serving.)*

2. *Make batter:* Meanwhile, combine all ingredients in blender container. Blend until completely smooth, scraping down side with a rubber spatula a few times. Transfer batter to a large glass measure. Cover with plastic wrap; refrigerate 1 hour.

3. *Make chocolate sauce:* Meanwhile, combine all ingredients in a 2-quart saucepan. Bring to boil over medium heat. Reduce heat to medium-low; simmer 10 minutes, until sauce thickens. *(Can be made ahead. Transfer sauce to a microwaveproof bowl and cool. Cover and refrigerate up to 5 days. To serve: Microwave on High 1½ to 2 minutes, until warm, stirring halfway through.)* Makes 2 cups.

4. Stir batter and let stand 10 minutes at room temperature. Heat oven to 325°F.

5. Lightly brush a 6-inch nonstick skillet with oil. Heat skillet over medium heat 1 minute. Pour a scant ¼ cup of the batter into skillet, swirling to evenly coat bottom of pan. Cook 1 to 2 minutes, until bottom is golden brown; turn over crêpe with a small off-set spatula and cook other side 1 minute. Transfer crêpe to a large piece of foil. Repeat with remaining batter, stacking crêpes with parchment paper between. *(Can be made ahead. Cool crêpes. Seal foil and refrigerate overnight. Remove from refrigerator 1 hour before serving.)* Seal foil and reheat in oven 5 to 10 minutes.

6. *To assemble:* Drain pears well (discard poaching liquid). Pour ¼ cup of the chocolate sauce on bottom of each of 8 dessert plates. Working with 2 crêpes at a time, place 1 tablespoon crème fraîche in center of each crêpe; fold into quarters. Arrange 2 crêpes on each plate. Arrange a pear half on each plate. Lightly dust with cocoa; garnish with mint and berries, if desired. Makes 8 servings.

Per serving without garnish: 535 calories, 34.5 g total fat, 20.5 g saturated fat, 135 mg cholesterol, 177 mg sodium, 54 g carbohydrates, 7 g protein, 108 mg calcium, 4 g fiber

southern chocolate layer cake

The brown sugar in the fluffy frosting gives this cake a Southern flair. For a special touch, garnish the top with delicate chocolate curls. Pictured on page 207.

Prep time: 45 minutes plus standing
Baking time: 25 to 27 minutes
Microwave used

CAKE:

5	ounces unsweetened chocolate squares, coarsely chopped
8	tablespoons butter, softened, divided (no substitutes)
1	tablespoon instant espresso powder (optional)
2	cups sifted cake flour (not self-rising)
1	teaspoon baking soda
¾	teaspoon salt
1¾	cups granulated sugar
3	large eggs, at room temperature
1	teaspoon vanilla extract
1¼	cups milk

SOUTHERN FROSTING:

1½	cups firmly packed brown sugar
½	cup water
¼	teaspoon cream of tartar
4	large egg whites, at room temperature
⅛	teaspoon salt
1	teaspoon vanilla extract
	Chocolate curls, for garnish (optional)

1. Heat oven to 350°F. Lightly grease bottom of two 9-inch round cake pans. Line bottoms with waxed paper; grease and flour paper and pans. Set aside.

2. *Make cake:* Microwave chocolate with 2 tablespoons of the butter in a microwaveproof bowl on High 1 to 1½ minutes, until melted; stir until smooth. Stir espresso powder (if using) into warm chocolate until dissolved and mixture is smooth. Set aside.

3. Whisk together flour, baking soda and salt in a medium bowl. Beat the remaining 6 tablespoons butter with the granulated sugar in a large mixer bowl on high speed 4 minutes, until light and fluffy. Add eggs, one at a time, beating well after each addition. Beat in vanilla. Reduce speed to medium-low. Gradually beat in flour mixture alternately with milk, beginning and ending with flour mixture; beat about 30 seconds after the last flour addition, scraping side of bowl with a rubber spatula. Spread batter evenly in prepared pans. Bake 25 to 27 minutes, until a toothpick inserted in centers comes out clean. Cool cakes in pans on wire racks 5 minutes. Run a sharp knife around edges of cakes and unmold onto rack; remove waxed paper and cool completely.

4. *Make Southern frosting:* Combine sugar, water and cream of tartar in a small saucepan; cook over medium heat, stirring, until sugar is dissolved. Increase heat to high and cook until syrup registers 234°F. on a candy thermometer. Meanwhile, beat egg whites and salt in a clean large mixer bowl with clean beaters on medium-high speed just until stiff. Gradually add syrup in a thin, steady stream, away from the beaters. Beat in vanilla. Continue beating 10 minutes, until icing comes to room temperature and holds stiff peaks.

5. Place 1 cake layer on a cake platter. Spread top with one third of the Southern frosting. Top with second cake layer; spread entire cake evenly with remaining Southern frosting, swirling with a spatula. Garnish top with chocolate curls, if desired. Makes 16 servings.

Per serving without garnish: 310 calories, 12.5 g total fat, 7 g saturated fat, 58 mg cholesterol, 313 mg sodium, 49 g carbohydrates, 5 g protein, 57 mg calcium, 2 g fiber

french chocolate roll

This is one of the most elegant desserts we know, yet it's relatively low in calories.

Prep time: 25 minutes plus chilling
Baking time: 15 minutes

- 1 teaspoon vegetable oil
- 6 ounces semisweet chocolate squares
- ¼ cup strong-brewed coffee
- 6 large eggs, separated
- ¾ cup granulated sugar
- ½ teaspoon vanilla extract
- ⅛ teaspoon salt
- 1 tablespoon unsweetened cocoa
- 1 cup heavy or whipping cream
- 4 teaspoons almond liqueur or 2 drops almond extract (optional)
- 2 tablespoons confectioners' sugar

1. Adjust oven rack to highest position. Heat oven to 350°F.

2. Spread oil on a 15½×10½-inch jelly-roll pan. Line bottom and sides with waxed paper, then flip paper over (oiled side up); set pan aside.

3. Combine chocolate and coffee in a small saucepan. Stir over low heat until chocolate is melted; keep warm.

4. Beat egg yolks in a large mixer bowl on high speed 5 to 10 minutes, until very thick and lemon colored. Beat in granulated sugar, then chocolate mixture, vanilla and salt until combined. In another clean large mixer bowl with clean beaters, beat egg whites to stiff (but not dry) peaks. Fold into chocolate mixture. Pour into prepared pan and spread evenly to edges. Bake 15 minutes. Cover with a slightly damp dish towel and refrigerate 15 minutes. Remove towel and sift cocoa over top of cake. Top cake with waxed paper, then a cookie sheet. Flip cake over onto cookie sheet. Carefully peel off waxed paper.

5. Beat cream with almond liqueur (if using) to stiff peaks. Spread over chocolate sponge cake, leaving a ½-inch border around edges. Roll cake up from a long side, using waxed paper to help lift.

(Don't worry if roll cracks; that's characteristic of this roll.) Trim off ends diagonally. Transfer to serving tray or board. Cover top of cake and around edge of tray with plastic wrap; chill at least 2 hours or overnight. Sprinkle with confectioners' sugar just before serving. Makes 12 servings.

Per serving: 235 calories, 15 g total fat, 8 g saturated fat, 134 mg cholesterol, 63 mg sodium, 22 g carbohydrates, 5 g protein, 31 mg calcium, 1 g fiber

chocolate-rum bread pudding

Bread pudding is comfort food at its best. But chocolate bread pudding—now, that's the ultimate!

Prep time: 15 minutes plus chilling and standing
Baking time: 28 to 30 minutes

RUM-CUSTARD SAUCE:
- 3 large egg yolks
- 5 tablespoons sugar
- 1 cup half-and-half cream, scalded
- 1 to 2 tablespoons dark rum

- ½ cup sugar
- 2 tablespoons unsweetened cocoa
- ⅛ teaspoon salt
- 1 cup milk
- 1 cup heavy or whipping cream
- 6 ounces semisweet chocolate squares
- 3 tablespoons unsalted butter (no substitutes)
- 3 large eggs, lightly beaten
- ¼ cup dark rum
- 5 cups cubed crustless day-old bread (about 12 slices)

1. *Make rum-custard sauce:* Whisk egg yolks with sugar in a bowl. Slowly beat ½ cup of the hot half-and-half into yolk mixture. Pour yolk mixture into remaining ½ cup hot half-and-half in saucepan; cook over low heat, stirring, 5 minutes, until mixture coats the back of a spoon. Stir in rum. Place plastic wrap directly on surface of custard. Refrigerate at least 1 hour, until cool. Makes about 1½ cups.

2. Meanwhile, combine sugar, cocoa and salt in a medium saucepan. Stir in milk, heavy cream, chocolate and butter. Cook over low heat until chocolate is melted, stirring constantly. Gradually beat in eggs; heat through. Remove from heat; stir in the ¼ cup rum.

3. Toss bread with chocolate mixture in a large bowl; let stand 30 minutes.

4. Heat oven to 350°F. Grease a 2-quart shallow baking dish. Place baking dish in a large roasting pan, making sure there is at least 1 inch between baking dish and pan. Transfer bread mixture to prepared dish. Carefully pour enough very hot water into roasting pan to come halfway up sides of baking dish. Bake 28 to 30 minutes, until a knife inserted in center comes out clean. Let stand 30 minutes before serving. Serve warm with rum-custard sauce. Makes 8 servings.

Per serving with 3 tablespoons sauce: 515 calories, 31.5 g total fat, 17.5 g saturated fat, 226 mg cholesterol, 220 mg sodium, 47 g carbohydrates, 10 g protein, 146 mg calcium, 2 g fiber

do-ahead chocolate soufflés _easy_

Yes, you can make soufflés ahead. We learned this trick from a New York pastry chef: Make them in the morning and bake them in the evening.

Total prep and baking time: 30 minutes
Microwave used

   3 **tablespoons plus 1 teaspoon butter or margarine, divided**
   ½ **cup plus 1 tablespoon sugar, divided**
   4 **ounces bittersweet or semisweet chocolate squares, chopped**
   4 **large eggs, at room temperature, separated**
   1 **tablespoon coffee-flavored liqueur**
      Whipped cream (optional)

1. Grease eight 4-ounce ramekins or baking cups with 1 teaspoon of the butter; sprinkle 1 tablespoon of the sugar evenly among ramekins, tapping out excess. Transfer ramekins to a jelly-roll pan.

2. Microwave chocolate and remaining 3 tablespoons butter in a large microwaveproof bowl on High 1½ minutes, until melted; stir until smooth. Stir in egg yolks and liqueur until combined.

3. Beat egg whites in a medium bowl on medium speed until foamy. Gradually add remaining ½ cup sugar, beating on medium-high speed to stiff peaks. With a rubber spatula, fold one-third of the beaten whites into chocolate just until blended; fold in remaining whites. Spoon batter evenly into prepared cups. *(Can be made ahead. Cover and refrigerate up to 6 hours.)*

4. Heat oven to 400°F. Bake soufflés 12 minutes, until tops are puffed and barely set (15 minutes, if soufflés have been refrigerated). Serve immediately with whipped cream, if desired. Makes 8 servings.

Per serving without whipped cream: 210 calories, 12 g total fat, 6.5 g saturated fat, 119 mg cholesterol, 80 mg sodium, 23 g carbohydrates, 4 g protein, 20 mg calcium, 0 g fiber

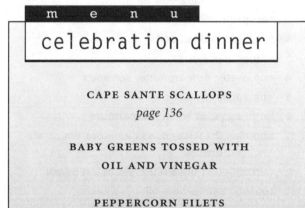

m e n u

celebration dinner

CAPE SANTE SCALLOPS
page 136

**BABY GREENS TOSSED WITH
OIL AND VINEGAR**

PEPPERCORN FILETS
page 140

CABERNET SAUVIGNON

DO-AHEAD CHOCOLATE SOUFFLÉS
left

peanut butter-chip loaf ⊕ EASY

This quick bread is dotted with mini chips and topped with chocolate and chopped peanuts. Like most sweet breads, the flavor improves if made a day ahead.

Prep time: 15 minutes plus standing
Baking time: 60 to 63 minutes
Microwave used

TOPPING:

- ¼ cup miniature chocolate chips
- 1 tablespoon flour
- 1 tablespoon sugar

- ⅔ cup buttermilk, at room temperature
- 2 teaspoons vanilla extract
- 2 cups all-purpose flour
- ¾ teaspoon baking powder
- ¾ teaspoon salt
- ½ teaspoon baking soda
- ½ cup peanut butter
- ¼ cup butter or margarine, softened
- 1 cup sugar
- 3 large eggs, at room temperature
- ¾ cup plus 2 tablespoons miniature chocolate chips, divided
- ¼ cup chopped unsalted dry-roasted peanuts
- ½ teaspoon vegetable oil

1. Heat oven to 350°F. Line long sides and bottom of a 9×5-inch loaf pan with a 16×8-inch piece of foil, allowing the long ends to extend past the edges of the pan. Grease and flour foil and pan.

2. *Make topping:* Microwave chocolate chips in a microwaveproof bowl on High 1½ to 2 minutes, until melted; let stand 2 minutes. Stir until smooth; cool completely. Add flour, stirring with the side of a spoon until crumbly. Repeat with the sugar. Set aside.

3. Combine buttermilk and vanilla in a bowl. Whisk together the 2 cups flour, the baking powder, salt and baking soda in another bowl.

4. Beat peanut butter and butter in a large mixer bowl on medium speed until smooth. Add the 1 cup sugar; beat 5 minutes, until well combined.

Add eggs, one at a time, beating well after each addition; beat until light and fluffy. Reduce speed to low; add flour mixture alternately with buttermilk mixture, beating just until combined, beginning and ending with flour mixture. Stir in ¾ cup of the chocolate chips. Scrape batter into prepared pan. Sprinkle top with nuts; with fingertips, break topping mixture into crumb-size pieces and sprinkle over top of loaf. Bake 60 to 63 minutes, until center has risen with a slight crack and is golden brown. Cool loaf 5 minutes in pan on a wire rack. Remove loaf by lifting with foil ends. Remove foil and cool loaf completely on wire rack.

5. Microwave remaining 2 tablespoons chocolate chips and the oil in a microwaveproof cup on High 1 minute, until melted; stir until smooth. Drizzle over top of loaf. Makes 12 servings.

Per serving: 360 calories, 17.5 g total fat, 6.5 g saturated fat, 65 mg cholesterol, 345 mg sodium, 41 g carbohydrates, 8 g protein, 46 mg calcium, 3 g fiber

chocolate-pecan scones ⊕ EASY

This sweet biscuit enhanced with chocolate and pecans is a perfect mid-afternoon pick-me-up.

Prep time: 15 minutes plus standing
Baking time: 15 to 18 minutes

- 2½ cups all-purpose flour
- 1 tablespoon baking powder
- ¼ teaspoon salt
- ½ cup butter or margarine, softened
- ½ cup sugar
- ½ cup milk
- 1 teaspoon vanilla extract
- ½ cup pecans, toasted and coarsely chopped
- 4 ounces semisweet chocolate squares, chopped

1. Adjust oven racks to middle and lower third of oven. Heat oven to 400°F.

2. Whisk flour, baking powder and salt together in a medium bowl. Beat butter and sugar in a large mixer bowl on medium-high speed 5 minutes, until creamy. Combine milk and vanilla in a cup. Reduce speed to low; add flour mixture alternately with milk mixture, beating just until combined, beginning and ending with flour mixture. Stir in pecans and chocolate. Using a 2-inch-wide ice cream scoop or ⅓-cup dry measure, arrange 6 scoops of dough ½ inch apart on a large ungreased cookie sheet. Repeat with remaining dough and another cookie sheet. Bake 15 to 18 minutes, until a toothpick inserted in center of 1 scone comes out clean. Cool scones on cookie sheets on a wire rack 5 minutes. Serve warm. Makes 12 scones.

Per scone: 280 calories, 15 g total fat, 7 g saturated fat, 23 mg cholesterol, 237 mg sodium, 34 g carbohydrates, 4 g protein, 82 mg calcium, 2 g fiber

mocha panna cotta

The secret to a silky panna cotta is in the stirring. Place it over an ice-water bath and stir until it cools down and is the consistency of unbeaten egg whites. The result? A smooth custard without a dark line around the top.

Total prep time: 30 minutes plus chilling
Microwave used

1	cup heavy or whipping cream, divided
2	ounces semisweet chocolate squares, broken into pieces
1½	cups milk, divided
3	tablespoons sugar
1	tablespoon instant espresso powder
¼	teaspoon vanilla extract
1	envelope unflavored gelatin

1. Combine 3 tablespoons of the heavy cream and the chocolate in a medium microwaveproof bowl. Microwave on High 30 to 60 seconds; let stand 1 minute, then stir until smooth.

2. Combine 1 cup of the milk, the remaining cream and the sugar in a small saucepan. Cook over medium-high heat, stirring, until small bubbles appear around edge of pan; stir in espresso powder and vanilla until dissolved. Gradually whisk mixture into the melted chocolate.

3. Sprinkle gelatin over remaining ½ cup milk in a microwaveproof cup; let stand 5 minutes. Microwave on High 40 to 60 seconds, just until hot; stir until dissolved. Gently whisk into cream mixture. Place bowl in a larger bowl halfway filled with ice and water. Stir mixture frequently until thickened (should be the consistency of unbeaten egg whites). Evenly pour mixture into six 6-ounce custard cups, filling each three quarters full. Refrigerate panna cotta at least 4 hours, until set. *(Can be made ahead. Cover and refrigerate up to 2 days.)* Makes 6 servings.

Per serving: 245 calories, 19 g total fat, 11.5 g saturated fat, 59 mg cholesterol, 48 mg sodium, 16 g carbohydrates, 5 g protein, 102 mg calcium, 1 g fiber

---

test kitchen tip
magical treats

Transform melted semisweet chocolate into these quick-fix treats and garnishes. See the tip on page 213 about how to melt chocolate.

SWEET STIRRINGS
Dip the tips of 8 metal or plastic teaspoons into 2 ounces melted semisweet chocolate squares; refrigerate 5 minutes, just until set. Serve with coffee.

CHOCOLATE BANANA ROCKETS
Cut 2 bananas in half crosswise; insert a wooden stick into each half. Freeze until firm. Peel bananas. Dip bananas completely into 2 ounces melted semisweet chocolate squares. Freeze 15 minutes, until chocolate is firm.

CHOCOLATE RIMS
Place a 1 ounce semisweet chocolate square on a small microwaveproof plate. Microwave on High 1 minute, until melted. Place a wineglass upside down in chocolate on plate and rotate clockwise to coat ⅛ inch around rim; repeat to coat 7 more glasses. Turn upright; let set before filling. Use for serving puddings, ice cream, cordials and other drinks.

chocolate babka

Unlike the standard breakfast coffee cake, this one is appropriate anytime of the day. Pictured on page 207.

Prep time: 30 minutes plus chilling, rising and standing
Baking time: 1 hour
Microwave used

DOUGH:

- **1 package plus 1 teaspoon active dry yeast (do not use rapid rise yeast)**
- **Pinch sugar**
- **¼ cup warm water (110°F. to 115°F.)**
- **½ cup warm milk (110°F. to 115°F.)**
- **4 large eggs, at room temperature**
- **4¾ cups all-purpose flour plus additional flour for kneading**
- **½ cup sugar**
- **½ teaspoon salt**
- **¼ teaspoon nutmeg**
- **⅛ teaspoon cardamom**
- **1 cup butter or margarine, cut up**

CHOCOLATE FILLING:

- **1 package (9 oz.) chocolate wafer cookies**
- **¼ cup sugar**
- **½ teaspoon cinnamon**
- **½ cup walnuts, toasted and finely chopped**
- **¼ cup butter or margarine, melted**
- **3 ounces semisweet chocolate squares, chopped**

- **1 large egg beaten with 1 tablespoon water, for brushing dough**

CHOCOLATE DRIZZLE:

- **2 ounces semisweet chocolate squares**
- **1 ounce unsweetened chocolate square**

1. *Make dough:* Sprinkle yeast and a pinch of sugar over warm water in a medium bowl. Let mixture stand 5 minutes, until foamy. Whisk in warm milk and eggs.

2. Pulse 4¾ cups flour, sugar, salt, nutmeg and cardamom in a food processor until combined. Add butter; pulse several times until mixture resembles coarse crumbs. Pour yeast mixture over flour; pulse until a soft dough forms.

3. Transfer dough to a large bowl. Cover with plastic wrap and refrigerate overnight.

4. Remove dough from refrigerator and let stand 1 hour.

5. *Make chocolate filling:* Meanwhile, process cookies, sugar and cinnamon in food processor until finely ground. Transfer to a medium bowl; stir in walnuts, butter and chopped chocolate. Transfer ¼ cup of the chocolate filling to a small bowl. Grease a 10-cup tube or Bundt pan. Set aside.

6. On a floured surface, knead dough 5 to 8 minutes, until smooth and no longer sticky, adding just enough additional flour (if necessary) to prevent dough from sticking. Divide dough in half. Roll 1 piece into a 13×11-inch rectangle, ⅛ inch thick. Sprinkle half of the chocolate filling over the rectangle. Starting with the long side, roll up dough, jelly-roll style. Transfer, seam side down, to prepared pan. Repeat process with remaining dough and filling, arranging second roll of dough in prepared pan so both rolls fit snugly together in bottom of pan. (Try not to have the rolls overlap too much.) Cover pan with a damp kitchen towel. Let rise in a warm draft-free place until doubled in bulk, about 1 hour.

7. Heat oven to 350°F. Brush top of dough with beaten egg mixture and sprinkle with reserved chocolate filling.

8. Bake bread 1 hour, until top is golden brown and toothpick inserted in center comes out clean. Cool bread in pan on a wire rack 15 minutes. Remove bread from pan; cool completely on wire rack.

9. *Make chocolate drizzle:* Microwave chocolates in a medium microwaveproof bowl on High 1½ minutes, until melted; stir until smooth. With a fork, drizzle chocolate over cooled bread. Makes 10 servings.

Per serving: 770 calories, 41.5 g total fat, 20 g saturated fat, 176 mg cholesterol, 602 mg sodium, 87 g carbohydrates, 14 g protein, 54 mg calcium, 4 g fiber

bittersweet pecan brownies

These rich and decadent brownies are for the chocolate lovers of the world. Pictured on page 202.

Prep time: 25 minutes plus standing and chilling
Baking time: 25 minutes
Microwave used

BROWNIES:

- 3 ounces unsweetened chocolate squares
- ½ cup butter (no substitutes)
- 2 large eggs
- ¾ cup sugar
- ¾ cup all-purpose flour
- 1 teaspoon vanilla extract
- ¾ cup coarsely chopped pecans, toasted

GLAZE:

- 2 ounces semisweet or bittersweet chocolate squares
- 2 teaspoons vegetable shortening, divided
- 2 ounces white chocolate squares
- ½ cup pistachio or macadamia nuts, coarsely chopped

1. Heat oven to 325°F. Line a 9-inch round baking pan with foil; grease foil and side of pan. Set aside.

2. *Make brownies:* Place unsweetened chocolate and butter in a microwaveproof bowl and microwave on High 1 to 2 minutes, until melted; stir until smooth. Remove from heat and let stand until cooled to room temperature.

3. Beat eggs in a mixer bowl on high speed 1 minute, until frothy. Add sugar and beat 2 minutes, until thick and lemon colored. Beat in melted chocolate. Stir in flour and vanilla. Pour into prepared pan. Sprinkle evenly with nuts; press lightly into batter. Bake 25 minutes. Cool completely in pan on a wire rack. Remove brownie from pan. Cut into quarters; cut each quarter into 4 wedges. Wrap well in plastic wrap and refrigerate 30 minutes.

4. *Make glaze:* Place semisweet chocolate and 1 teaspoon of the shortening in a microwaveproof bowl and microwave on High 1½ minutes, until melted; stir until smooth. Place white chocolate and remaining 1 teaspoon shortening in another microwaveproof bowl and microwave on High 1½ minutes, until melted; stir until smooth. Dip outer edge of 8 brownie wedges, 1 at a time, into semisweet chocolate, then dip into pistachio or macadamia nuts. Dip outer edge of remaining 8 brownie wedges, 1 at a time, in white chocolate, then in nuts. Let stand 30 to 60 minutes before serving, until chocolate is set. *(Can be made ahead. Place in a heavy-duty plastic storage bag and freeze up to 1 month.)* Makes 16 brownies.

Per brownie: 245 calories, 18 g total fat, 8 g saturated fat, 44 mg cholesterol, 75 mg sodium, 21 g carbohydrates, 4 g protein, 23 mg calcium, 2 g fiber

s'mores bars

We could have called them "nostalgia bars" because their taste takes us back to nights around the campfire. These S'mores feature chocolate graham crackers layered with a heavenly butter-and-brown-sugar mix.

Prep time: 5 minutes plus standing
Baking time: 8 to 10 minutes
Microwave used

- 12 whole chocolate or regular graham crackers (5×2½ inches)
- 2 cups miniature marshmallows
- 1 package (11½ oz.) milk chocolate chips
- ¾ cup butter or margarine
- ¾ cup firmly packed brown sugar

1. Heat oven to 350°F. Arrange graham crackers evenly in a 15½×10½-inch jelly-roll pan. Sprinkle marshmallows evenly over graham crackers; top with chocolate chips.

2. Combine butter and sugar in a medium microwaveproof bowl. Microwave on High 1½ to 2 minutes, until butter is melted. Whisk until well blended and butter no longer separates. Spoon evenly over marshmallows and chips. Bake 8 to 10 minutes, until barely golden. Cool completely in pan on a wire rack. Cut into squares. Makes 24 squares.

Per square: 195 calories, 10.5 g total fat, 6 g saturated fat, 16 mg cholesterol, 122 mg sodium, 25 g carbohydrates, 2 g protein, 28 mg calcium, 0 g fiber

chocolate pancakes with cherry sauce *(EASY)*

For a lovely change of pace, try these gently sweetened chocolate pancakes—great for special-occasion breakfasts or brunches. Look for high-quality cherry toppings in the specialty section of your market or gourmet store. The purer the ingredients (avoid those with gums or artificial colors and flavors), the better the flavor and consistency.

Prep time: 25 minutes
Cooking time: 2½ to 4 minutes per batch
Microwave used

- ¼ **cup butter or margarine**
- 1½ **cups milk, at room temperature**
- 2 **large eggs, at room temperature, separated**
- 1 **teaspoon vanilla extract**
- 1⅔ **cups all-purpose flour**
- 4 **teaspoons unsweetened cocoa**
- 1¾ **teaspoons baking powder**
- ¾ **teaspoon baking soda**
- ¼ **teaspoon salt**
- ⅓ **cup sugar**
- 3 **ounces semisweet chocolate, coarsely grated, divided**
- ¼ **to ⅓ cup butter, divided**
- 1 **jar (12 to 16 oz.) high-quality cherry topping***
- ½ **cup sliced natural almonds, lightly toasted**

1. Heat oven to 200°F. Microwave the ¼ cup butter in a large microwaveproof bowl on High 30 to 60 seconds, just until melted. Whisk in milk, egg yolks and vanilla. Set aside.

2. Sift the flour, cocoa, baking powder, baking soda and salt on a large piece of waxed paper. Set aside.

3. Beat the egg whites in a small mixer bowl on high speed until soft peaks begin to form; gradually add sugar, beating to stiff peaks.

4. Whisk the flour mixture into the milk mixture just until blended. Fold in the beaten whites and ½ cup of the grated chocolate.

5. Heat a large nonstick or seasoned cast-iron skillet or pancake griddle over medium heat; add

1 teaspoon of the butter. Using a ¼-cup dry measure, pour batter into skillet (2 or 3 cupfuls at a time, as will fit). Cook 1½ to 2 minutes, until small bubbles appear around edges and on surfaces of pancakes. Turn and cook 1 to 2 minutes more, until bottom is golden. Transfer to a 9-inch glass pie plate. Dot each pancake with 1 teaspoon of the butter and grated chocolate. Repeat with remaining batter, butter and grated chocolate. Cover loosely with foil and keep warm in oven. Place 2 to 3 pancakes on each serving plate; top with 2 tablespoons of the cherry topping and lightly sprinkle with almonds. Makes fourteen 4-inch pancakes.

*Note: Can be found in gourmet stores or upscale supermarkets, or order by mail from American Spoon Foods (888-735-6700).

Per 2 pancakes with cherry topping and almonds: 485 calories, 26.5 g total fat, 13 g saturated fat, 105 mg cholesterol, 554 mg sodium, 55 g carbohydrates, 10 g protein, 183 mg calcium, 3 g fiber

---

m e n u

brunch bonanza

**CHOCOLATE PANCAKES
WITH CHERRY SAUCE**
left

HAM AND CHEESE OMELET
page 55

BACON OR SAUSAGE LINKS

MIMOSAS

COFFEE OR HOT TEA

BISCOCHITOS
PG. 278

BERLINERKRANZE
PG. 272

HOLIDAY MINCEMEAT
COOKIES WITH COFFEE
FROSTING
PG. 280

holiday happenings

Delight in the warmth and cheer that come from the magical combination of good food and company at holiday time. Need more ideas to keep that magic alive? You'll find them here ... fresh takes on favorites and new dishes to please those you love.

...mix, melt, shape, layer, **bake** and frost

CHOCOLATE MINT
MELT-AWAYS
PG. 275

TRIPLE TREAT CRÈME
DE MENTHE BARS
PG. 274

NANNY'S FILLED
RAISIN COOKIES
PG. 274

whip up a confection
collection

KIFLI
PG. 278

Give thanks, give love,

BUTTER FUDGE
FINGERS
PG. 279

RASPBERRY
SHORTBREAD
PG. 276

RUSTIC APPLE PIE
PG. 271

have fun in the
kitchen and give it away

CITRUS-ROSEMARY
WAFERS
PG. 273

waves of **savory**
scent fill the house

TURKEY WITH
HERB GRAVY
PG. 254

WALNUT-
RAISIN BREAD
STUFFING
PG. 262

OYSTER
STUFFING
PG. 262

come to the table;

it's time to eat

CORN BREAD
STUFFING
PG. 263

WEST INDIAN
PUMPKIN SOUP
PG. 252

bring a bowl of
tradition
or something new to
repeat next year

HORNO DI
TORO SAUCE
PG. 251

PARSLEY AÏOLI
PG. 251

OYSTER SOUP
PG. 252

champagne punch

EASY · LOW FAT

Berries, apricot-flavored liqueur, brandy, citrus slices plus a chunk of cucumber combine with your favorite champagne for this outstanding punch. If you prefer something lighter, add a 16-ounce can of ginger ale.

Total prep time: 15 minutes

- 3 thin slices lemon
- 4 thin slices orange
- 1 1-inch chunk cucumber
- 1 cup sliced fresh strawberries or raspberries
- ¼ cup apricot-flavored liqueur
- 2 tablespoons brandy
- 1 bottle chilled champagne
- 2 cups chilled ginger ale (optional)
   Ice
   Sugar cubes

Combine all ingredients *except* ice and sugar cubes in a large bowl. Pour over a block of ice in a punch bowl. Drop 1 sugar cube into each champagne glass. Stir punch and ladle into glasses. Makes 5 cups.

Per ½-cup serving without ginger ale: 100 calories, 0 g total fat, 0 g saturated fat, 0 mg cholesterol, 0 mg sodium, 9 g carbohydrates, 0 g protein, 2 mg calcium, 0 g fiber

spiked eggnog

EASY

There's nothing more delicious than this holiday classic.

Prep time: 15 minutes plus chilling
Cooking time: 6 to 7 minutes

- 1 pint half-and-half cream
- 2 cups whole milk (no substitutes)
- 1 cinnamon stick
- 5 large egg yolks
- ¼ cup sugar
- ⅔ cup bourbon
- ¼ cup orange-flavored liqueur
- ½ cup heavy or whipping cream
   Freshly ground nutmeg, for garnish (optional)

1. Heat half-and-half, milk and cinnamon stick in a medium saucepan over medium heat until small bubbles appear around the edge.

2. Meanwhile, beat egg yolks and sugar in a large mixer bowl on medium speed until light and fluffy. Gradually beat half of the hot milk mixture into the egg yolk mixture. Return to saucepan; cook over medium heat, stirring, 3 to 5 minutes, just until mixture begins to thicken (coats the back of a spoon) and registers 165°F. on an instant-read thermometer. Transfer to a 1½-quart glass punch bowl. Cool to lukewarm; discard cinnamon stick. Whisk in bourbon and orange-flavored liqueur. Cover and refrigerate about 1 hour, until cold.

3. Beat heavy cream in a small mixer bowl on medium-high speed to soft peaks. *(Can be made ahead. Cover and refrigerate up to 1 hour before using.)* Lightly whisk the whipped cream into the cold eggnog mixture. Ladle into short glasses and lightly dust tops with nutmeg, if desired. Makes 5 cups.

Per ½-cup serving: 235 calories, 14 g total fat, 8 g saturated fat, 147 mg cholesterol, 52 mg sodium, 11 g carbohydrates, 5 g protein, 128 mg calcium, 0 g fiber

hot spiced cider

EASY · LOW FAT

Some brands of cider contain more apple particles than others; simply strain through a double layer of cheesecloth into the punch bowl with the rum just before serving.

Prep time: 10 minutes · Cooking time: 30 minutes

- 2 quarts natural unfiltered apple cider
- ¼ cup firmly packed brown sugar
   Peel from ½ of a lemon
   Peel from 1 orange
- 3 cinnamon sticks
- 1 teaspoon allspice berries
- 1½ to 2 cups spiced rum

Combine all ingredients *except* rum in a 4-quart saucepan. Bring to simmer over medium heat. Reduce heat and cook at low simmer 30 minutes. Pour rum into a punch bowl; strain in hot apple cider mixture. Stir until combined. Makes 8 cups.

Per ½-cup serving: 120 calories, 0 g total fat, 0 g saturated fat, 0 mg cholesterol, 5 mg sodium, 18 g carbohydrates, 0 g protein, 12 mg calcium, 0 g fiber

duck terrine with caramelized apples

EASY   LOW FAT

Specialty stores carry duck mousse terrine, a cold preparation sold in slices and best when used immediately. Ask for it where gourmet cheeses are sold.

Prep time: 10 minutes • Cooking time: 15 to 18 minutes

2 tablespoons butter (no substitutes)

⅓ cup minced shallots

3 Gala or Fuji apples, peeled, cored and cut into ¼-inch-thick wedges

2 teaspoons brown sugar

½ cup granulated sugar

3 tablespoons water

5 tablespoons apple brandy, divided

¼ teaspoon salt

2 ½-inch-thick slices duck mousse terrine (4 oz. total)

1. Heat butter in a large nonstick skillet over medium-high heat. Add shallots and cook 30 seconds; add apples and brown sugar. Cook 15 to 18 minutes, until apples are browned and tender, turning occasionally.

2. Meanwhile, shake the granulated sugar to an even layer in a medium skillet; sprinkle the water over the top. Cook over medium heat until pools of caramelized sugar appear; gently stir the undissolved sugar into the melted caramel and cook until all the sugar is dissolved and caramel is medium amber in color. Carefully add 3 tablespoons of the apple brandy and stir over low heat until completely combined.

3. Pour caramel over warm apples; add remaining 2 tablespoons apple brandy and salt and gently turn with a rubber spatula to combine.

4. Cut each slice of mousse crosswise to form 4 rectangles, each approximately 2½×2 inches. Place 1 rectangle on each of 4 small serving plates. Divide caramelized apples among plates, arranging them alongside mousse. Makes 4 servings.

Per 1-ounce serving duck terrine with apples: 350 calories, 11 g total fat, 5.5 g saturated fat, 102 mg cholesterol, 319 mg sodium, 51 g carbohydrates, 5 g protein, 22 mg calcium, 3 g fiber

spiced meat phyllo triangles

Guests will adore these crisp phyllo packages filled with ground lamb or beef, spices and feta cheese.

Prep time: 50 minutes • Baking time: 20 to 25 minutes

MEAT FILLING:

½ pound ground lamb or beef

2 garlic cloves, minced

1 can (14½ oz.) stewed tomatoes

⅓ cup water

¼ cup long-grain rice

1½ teaspoons red wine vinegar

½ teaspoon salt

⅛ teaspoon dried oregano

⅛ teaspoon cinnamon

⅛ teaspoon ground red pepper

½ cup crumbled feta cheese

2 tablespoons chopped fresh cilantro

10 sheets phyllo dough

¼ cup unsalted butter, melted (no substitutes)

1 tablespoon plain dry bread crumbs

1. *Make meat filling:* Heat a large skillet 1 minute over medium-high heat. Add lamb and cook until brown. Add the garlic and cook, stirring, 1 minute. Reduce heat to medium. Add tomatoes, water, rice, vinegar, salt, oregano, cinnamon and red pepper. Cook 20 to 22 minutes, until rice is almost cooked, stirring occasionally. Cool to room temperature. Stir in feta and cilantro.

2. Place phyllo sheets in 1 stack on the work surface. With a sharp knife, cut phyllo crosswise into 3-inch-wide strips. Remove 2 strips; cover remaining phyllo with plastic wrap. Place the 2 strips one on top of the other; place 1 tablespoon of the lamb filling about 1 inch from one end. Fold corner of phyllo up around filling, flag-style, to form a triangle. Continue to fold flag-style the length of the strip. Lightly brush all sides of triangle with butter. Trim end if necessary. Transfer, seam side down, to an ungreased cookie sheet. Lightly sprinkle with bread crumbs. Repeat with remaining phyllo, meat filling, butter and crumbs. (*Can be made ahead. Place unbaked triangles* on a cookie sheet. Freeze 1 hour. Transfer to an airtight container and freeze up to 1 month.)

3. Heat oven to 375°F. Bake triangles (unthawed if frozen) 20 to 25 minutes, until golden brown and puffed in center. Makes 30 triangles.

Per triangle: 65 calories, 3.5 g total fat, 2 g saturated fat, 11 mg cholesterol, 124 mg sodium, 6 g carbohydrates, 2 g protein, 17 mg calcium, 0 g fiber

horno di toro sauce

"I love the name of this sauce, Horn of the Bull," says Roxsand Scocos, the chef and owner of RoxSand Restaurant and Bar, Phoenix, Arizona. "The sauce is Spanish in origin although recipes such as this one seem to be associated with the Southwest. I always associate red with the holidays and think this roasted red pepper sauce makes for a delicious and festive accompaniment." Pictured on page 248.

Prep time: 20 minutes plus standing
Cooking time: 15 to 18 minutes

1½	**pounds red bell peppers, halved and seeded**
6	**tablespoons olive oil, divided**
2	**tablespoons chopped shallots**
2	**tablespoons chopped garlic**
¾	**teaspoon cumin**
¼	**teaspoon salt**
¼	**teaspoon ground red pepper**
½	**teaspoon grated lemon peel**
2	**tablespoons fresh lemon juice**
2	**tablespoons good-quality balsamic vinegar**
1½	**tablespoons chopped fresh cilantro**

1. Heat broiler. Line a broiler pan with foil. Place bell peppers, cut sides down, on prepared pan. Broil 12 to 15 minutes, until skins are evenly charred. Wrap in foil; cool 20 minutes. Peel and discard skins. (Can be made ahead. Cover and refrigerate up to 2 days.)

2. Heat 2 tablespoons of the oil in a large skillet over medium heat. Add shallots, garlic, cumin, salt and ground red pepper; cook 5 to 8 minutes, until vegetables soften. Stir in bell peppers and cook 10 minutes, until peppers are heated through and well flavored with spice mixture.

3. Transfer bell pepper mixture to a food processor or blender and puree until smooth. (Can be made ahead. Cover and refrigerate overnight.)

4. Bring pepper mixture to room temperature. Stir in lemon peel, juice, vinegar, cilantro and remaining 4 tablespoons oil. Serve with assorted vegetables and crackers. Makes 1¾ cups sauce.

Per 1-tablespoon serving: 30 calories, 3 g total fat, 0.5 g saturated fat, 0 mg cholesterol, 22 mg sodium, 1 g carbohydrates, 0 g protein, 3 mg calcium, 0 g fiber

parsley aïoli

This herby homemade mayonnaise with a hint of lemon is lovely served with crackers or crudités. It can be made up to 24 hours ahead of time. Pictured on page 248.

Total prep time: 10 minutes

2	**tablespoons refrigerated egg product**
1	**tablespoon fresh lemon juice**
1	**tablespoon Dijon mustard**
1½	**tablespoons chopped garlic**
1	**tablespoon red wine vinegar**
1	**cup olive oil**
1	**tablespoon finely chopped fresh flat-leaf parsley**
½	**teaspoon finely chopped fresh sage**
½	**teaspoon chopped fresh rosemary**
½	**teaspoon chopped fresh thyme**
¼	**teaspoon salt**
⅛	**teaspoon freshly ground pepper**
	Milk (optional)

Process egg product, lemon juice, mustard, garlic and vinegar in a blender or food processor until combined. With motor running, slowly add oil through feed tube. Blend or process until smooth and the consistency of mayonnaise. Add parsley, sage, rosemary, thyme, salt and pepper and blend or process until just combined. If a thinner consistency is desired, stir in 1 to 2 tablespoons milk. (Can be made ahead. Cover and refrigerate up to 24 hours.) Serve with assorted vegetables and crackers. Makes 1¼ cups.

Per 1-tablespoon serving: 100 calories, 11 g total fat, 1.5 g saturated fat, 0 mg cholesterol, 36 mg sodium, 1 g carbohydrates, 0 g protein, 5 mg calcium, 0 g fiber

1. Drain oysters through a large fine strainer over a 1-quart glass measure. Rinse oysters under cold running water to remove any sand or shell particles; transfer to a bowl. Line strainer with cheesecloth; set over another bowl. Strain oyster liquid into bowl.

2. Puree half of the oysters in a food processor until smooth. Set aside both pureed and whole oysters.

3. Melt butter in a 2-quart saucepan over medium heat. Add onions, garlic, salt and red pepper. Cook 5 minutes, until onions soften. Stir in flour; cook 3 minutes, until onion mixture begins to turn golden, stirring often. Slowly pour in milk, whisking until well combined. Reduce heat to medium-low and cook mixture 3 to 5 minutes, stirring often. Stir in reserved oyster liquid, oyster puree, whole oysters and the 1 tablespoon parsley. *(Can be made ahead. Cover and refrigerate up to 4 hours.)* Cook over low heat 8 minutes, just until heated through. Garnish with additional parsley, if desired. Makes 4 cups.

Per 1-cup serving: 310 calories, 16.5 g total fat, 8 g saturated fat, 169 mg cholesterol, 684 mg sodium, 19 g carbohydrates, 20 g protein, 182 mg calcium, 1 g fiber

test kitchen tip
oysters

OYSTER CONNOISSEURS are truly passionate about these little shellfish gems. The oysters' hard gray shells hold flavorful meat, at its best when they are not spawning (a condition that results in soft and fatty oysters). Since they spawn during the summer, it's best to consume oysters during the fall and winter months.

CONSUME ONLY LIVE, FRESH OYSTERS in the shell. If a shell is open and doesn't quickly close when handled, throw it away. Discard oysters with broken shells, too. Fresh-shucked oysters also are available. Look for those that are uniform in size, plump, fresh-smelling and packaged in clear oyster "liquor" (liquid).

LIVE OR SHUCKED, oysters are at their best when consumed as soon as possible. To store, cover live oysters with a damp towel and keep in the refrigerator up to 3 days. Shucked oysters also need to be kept in the refrigerator; use within 2 days.

oyster soup

During the 1920s, it was common to serve oyster soup or oyster stuffing at Thanksgiving dinner, and thanks to our delicious cream soup, you will be enticed to revive the tradition. Some of the oysters are pureed, giving the soup an intense seafood flavor, so serve it in small portions. Tip: Reheat the soup gently over low heat just until hot. Do not boil, or the mixture will curdle. Pictured on page 248.

Prep time: 30 minutes • Cooking time: 19 to 21 minutes

- 1 quart fresh shucked oysters in liquid
- 3 tablespoons butter or margarine
- 1 cup finely chopped onions
- 1 teaspoon chopped garlic
- ½ teaspoon salt
- ¼ teaspoon ground red pepper
- 2 tablespoons flour

west indian pumpkin soup

"The original celebrants of Thanksgiving were, of course, the Indians and the pilgrims, but it was down in the West Indies and the Caribbean that Columbus 'discovered' America," says Norman Van Aken, chef and owner of Norman's in Miami, Florida. "The 'pumpkin' that the Indians would have fed the Italian explorer would have been new to him but still delicious. It would have been the West Indian pumpkin which he called 'calabaza' from the Spanish word he could most closely associate the gourd with." Pictured on page 247.

Prep time: 1 hour 30 minutes plus standing
Cooking time: 40 minutes

- 2 pounds calabaza squash (West Indian pumpkin), kabocha squash or acorn squash, peeled and cut into 1-inch pieces

1   pound sweet potatoes, peeled and cut into
    1-inch pieces
½   cup sugar
¼   cup butter, melted (no substitutes)
1   teaspoon kosher salt or ½ teaspoon
    regular salt
1   teaspoon freshly ground pepper
2   tablespoons olive oil
1   large Spanish onion, chopped
½   of a Scotch bonnet chile, seeded and minced,
    or 1 jalapeño chile, seeded and minced (see
    tip, page 92)
1   tablespoon chopped garlic
1   tablespoon grated fresh ginger
¼   cup curry powder
2   tablespoons chopped fresh thyme or
    2 teaspoons dried thyme
2   teaspoons grated orange peel
¼   teaspoon nutmeg
2   small bay leaves
1   cinnamon stick
6   cups chicken broth
¼   cup heavy or whipping cream
¼   cup coconut milk
2   Granny Smith apples, cored and diced
½   cup toasted pumpkin seeds

1. Heat oven to 350°F. Gently toss together the
squash, sweet potatoes, sugar, butter, salt and
pepper in a large roasting pan. Roast 1 hour
15 minutes, until tender, stirring occasionally.
Set aside.

2. Meanwhile, heat oil in a large Dutch oven over
medium heat. Add onion and cook 5 minutes, until
softened. Stir in chile, garlic and ginger; cook
1 minute. Add curry, thyme, orange peel, nutmeg,
bay leaves and cinnamon stick. Cook 1 minute,
stirring to coat vegetables. (The mixture will
resemble a paste and begin to stick to the bottom of
the Dutch oven; that's okay.) Add the roasted
vegetables and any accumulated liquid; stir until
well combined.

3. Pour in broth and bring to boil. Reduce heat and
simmer 30 minutes, stirring occasionally. Remove
from heat; cool 10 minutes. Discard bay leaves and
cinnamon. Working in batches, puree soup in a
blender or food processor until smooth. Return
soup to Dutch oven. Stir in cream and coconut

milk. *(Can be made ahead. Cover and refrigerate
up to 24 hours. Reheat over medium heat until
heated through.)*

4. Serve soup in shallow bowls and sprinkle top of
soup with apples and pumpkin seeds. Makes
10 cups.

Per 1-cup serving: 300 calories, 17.5 g total fat, 7 g saturated fat,
21 mg cholesterol, 854 mg sodium, 33 g carbohydrates,
7 g protein, 58 mg calcium, 4 g fiber

turkey with herb gravy

Prior to roasting, our holiday turkey is placed over onions, shallots, garlic and a plethora of fresh thyme and sage, which later help flavor the luscious gravy. If desired, a little apple brandy adds a special touch to the gravy. Stuff the turkey with one of our stuffings (see recipes, pages 262–263) or your favorite stuffing. Pictured on page 246.

Prep time: 20 minutes plus standing
Baking time: 3¾ to 4½ hours

- **1 whole turkey (10 to 18 lbs.), thawed if frozen**
- **2 medium onions, quartered**
- **4 shallots, quartered**
- **1 head garlic, peeled**
- **1 bunch fresh thyme**
- **1 bunch fresh sage**
- **1 cup white wine**
- **2 tablespoons melted butter (no substitutes)**
- **2½ teaspoons kosher salt**
- **½ teaspoon freshly ground pepper**

HERB GRAVY:
- **¼ cup all-purpose flour**
- **1 cup chicken broth**
- **2 tablespoons apple brandy (optional)**
- **½ teaspoon salt**
- **½ teaspoon freshly ground pepper**

1. Prepare desired stuffing as directed.

2. Heat oven to 325°F. Remove neck and giblets from body and neck cavities of turkey. Rinse turkey and drain; pat dry with paper towels. Loosely fill neck and body cavities with stuffing. Fold neck skin over back of turkey and fasten with skewers or toothpicks.

3. Arrange onions, shallots, garlic, thyme and sage on bottom of a shallow roasting pan; pour wine over vegetables. Place stuffed turkey, breast side up, on top of vegetables and herbs. Brush skin with butter and sprinkle with salt and pepper. Cover stuffing in cavity with a small piece of foil.

4. Roast turkey 3¾ to 4½ hours, until done (see step 5). When turkey skin is golden brown, about two-thirds done (2 to 2¾ hours), shield breast loosely with foil to prevent overbrowning.

5. *Start testing for doneness ½ hour before end times:* Insert the metal section of an instant-read meat thermometer at least 2 inches into the inner thigh of the turkey. Let stand 15 to 20 seconds, until thermometer registers 180°F. To test the stuffing doneness, insert thermometer into the center part of stuffing and let stand 15 to 20 seconds, until the thermometer registers between 160°F and 165°F. (If turkey needs more roasting, remove the thermometer before returning turkey to the oven; thoroughly wash the stem section of thermometer in hot soapy water after each use. Even if your turkey has a pop-up temperature device, the USDA recommends double-checking with another thermometer to be sure the turkey registers 180°F. for safety and doneness.)

6. Transfer turkey to a serving platter; cover loosely with foil and let stand 20 minutes.

7. *Make herb gravy:* Meanwhile, place a large strainer or sieve over a large glass measuring cup. Scrape vegetables, herbs and drippings from roasting pan into strainer. With the back of a spoon, press vegetables against side of strainer, extracting as much liquid as possible. Let stand 5 minutes, until fat rises to the top. Skim off fat, reserving ¼ cup (reserve remaining fat for another use, if desired). Return reserved fat to roasting pan and heat over medium heat. Whisk in flour and cook 2 minutes, until golden brown. Whisk in broth, brandy (if using) and reserved drippings, whisking 2 to 3 minutes, until gravy thickens slightly. Season with salt and pepper. Makes 2¾ cups.

8. Carve turkey. Serve with stuffing and herb gravy. Makes 10 to 14 servings.

Per 3-ounce serving of turkey with ¼ cup gravy (no stuffing): 245 calories, 13 g total fat, 4.5 g saturated fat, 79 mg cholesterol, 584 mg sodium, 3 g carbohydrates, 25 g protein, 26 mg calcium, 0 g fiber

roasted goose with chestnut stuffing

Do not remove the fat from the pan when it is time to brush the goose with the glaze. When you return the goose to the oven, the fat will keep the browned drippings used for the gravy from burning. Goose fat is very flavorful and can be used for sautéing. Just strain it through a double layer of cheesecloth into an airtight container and refrigerate for up to 1 week or freeze for up to 3 months.

Prep time: 40 minutes • Baking time: 2 hours 50 minutes

STUFFING:

- ¼ **pound sliced bacon, diced**
- 1 **goose heart and liver, minced**
- 1 **cup chopped onions**
- 1 **cup chopped celery**
- ¼ **cup butter or margarine, cut up**
- 1½ **teaspoons minced garlic**
- 1 **package (8 oz.) herb stuffing mix**
- 1 **jar (7.4 oz.) chestnuts, coarsely chopped**
- ½ **cup chopped apples**
- ¾ **teaspoon salt**
- ½ **teaspoon freshly ground pepper**
- 2 **large eggs, beaten**

- 1 **goose (15 lbs.), thawed if frozen**
- 1 **tablespoon salt**
- 1 **cup water**
- 1 **cup white wine**
- 2 **tablespoons honey**
- 2 **tablespoons fresh lemon juice**
- 2½ **cups chicken broth**
- 1 **goose gizzard, coarsely chopped**

PAN GRAVY:

- 3 **tablespoons flour**
- ¾ **cup red wine**

1. *Make stuffing:* Cook bacon in a large skillet over medium heat 4 minutes, just until crisp. Add goose heart and liver, onions and celery; cook 6 minutes, until onions are softened. Stir in butter and garlic.

Remove from heat; stir in stuffing mix, chestnuts, apples, salt and pepper. Cool completely. *(Can be made ahead. Cover and refrigerate overnight.)* Stir in eggs. Makes 6 cups.

2. Heat oven to 450°F. Remove all excess fat from goose; rinse goose and pat dry with paper towels. Rub inside cavity and outside of goose with the 1 tablespoon salt. Loosely fill neck and body cavities with stuffing. Fold neck skin over back of goose and fasten with skewer or toothpick. Tie legs together with string. Prick goose all over with a fork.

3. Place goose, breast side up, on a rack in a large, heavy roasting pan. Pour water and white wine into pan. Roast 30 minutes. Reduce oven temperature to 350°F. Roast 2 hours more. Combine honey and lemon juice; brush over goose. Roast 20 minutes more, until an instant-read meat thermometer inserted into the thickest part of the thigh registers 180°F.

4. Meanwhile, bring chicken broth and gizzard to boil in a small saucepan. Reduce heat and simmer 15 minutes; strain broth for gravy. Set aside. Discard gizzard.

5. Transfer goose to a carving board or platter and let stand 15 minutes before carving.

6. *Make pan gravy:* Pour off all but 2 tablespoons of the drippings from roasting pan (reserve remaining goose fat for another use, if desired). Stir flour into pan and cook, stirring, over medium heat 1 minute. Add strained broth and the red wine. Bring to boil and cook 3 minutes more, until thickened, stirring and scraping up any browned bits. Strain into a gravy pitcher. Makes 2¼ cups.

7. Serve sliced goose with pan gravy. Makes 8 to 10 servings.

Per 4-ounce serving of goose with ½ cup stuffing and 2 tablespoons gravy: 610 calories, 39 g total fat, 13.5 g saturated fat, 208 mg cholesterol, 994 mg sodium, 24 g carbohydrates, 36 g protein, 97 mg calcium, 2 g fiber

roast filet of beef

Try this neat trick for a more controlled way to cook meat to an even doneness. If you like the meat medium to medium-well with just a hint of pink, roast the beef to 140°F., then wrap the individual beef tenderloins tightly in heavy-duty foil and let them stand 15 to 30 minutes (depending on your preferred level of doneness). Unwrap and serve. By wrapping the hot, cooked meat tightly in foil, the internal heat continues to cook the meat without making it tough.

Prep time: 10 minutes plus marinating
Baking time: 25 to 30 minutes

- 2 whole beef tenderloin roasts (about 4 lbs. each after trimming)
- 2 tablespoons chopped garlic
- 2 teaspoons salt
- ¼ cup olive oil
- 1 teaspoon freshly ground pepper
   French bread (optional)
   Sauce Verte (see recipe, at right)

1. Place beef in a large roasting pan. With the flat side of a knife, mash garlic with salt into a paste. Rub evenly over all sides of roasts. Drizzle with oil, coating all sides. Marinate at room temperature 15 minutes.

2. Heat oven to 450°F. Sprinkle meat with pepper. Roast 25 to 30 minutes, until an instant-read meat thermometer inserted in center registers 140°F. for medium-rare. Remove from oven. Let stand 5 minutes before serving. Cut into thin slices. Serve warm with French bread, if desired, and Sauce Verte. Makes about 24 servings.

Per serving without bread or sauce: 245 calories, 12 g total fat, 3.5 g saturated fat, 75 mg cholesterol, 263 mg sodium, 1 g carbohydrates, 32 g protein, 11 mg calcium, 0 g fiber

sauce verte

This elegant sauce flavored with fresh cilantro is perfect with any beef, pork or chicken dish. If cilantro is unavailable, substitute fresh flat-leaf parsley.

Total prep time: 10 minutes

- 3 cups fresh cilantro leaves, divided
- 1½ cups olive oil, divided
- ¼ cup mayonnaise
- ¼ cup cider vinegar
- 2 teaspoons sugar
- 2 teaspoons salt
- 2 teaspoons dry mustard
- ½ teaspoon ground white pepper
- 1 cup sour cream
- 2 medium tomatoes, skinned, seeded and finely chopped (1½ cups)

Combine 1 cup of the cilantro and ½ cup of the oil in a blender. Cover and blend until cilantro is minced. Add mayonnaise, vinegar, sugar, salt, dry mustard and white pepper. Cover and blend 1 to 2 seconds. With blender at high speed, add remaining 1 cup oil in a fine, steady stream. Blend until smooth and thickened. If necessary, stop blender and scrape side with a rubber spatula; continue blending until smooth. Transfer to a small bowl. Whisk in sour cream. Mince remaining 2 cups cilantro; stir into sauce. Stir in tomatoes. *(Can be made ahead. Cover and refrigerate up to 24 hours.)* Makes 2 cups.

Per 1-tablespoon serving: 120 calories, 13 g total fat, 2.5 g saturated fat, 4 mg cholesterol, 163 mg sodium, 1 g carbohydrates, 0 g protein, 13 mg calcium, 0 g fiber

tournedos with cognac and herb sauce

There's no classier way to impress your guests than with these beef tenderloin steaks.

Prep time: 20 minutes plus standing
Cooking time: 14 minutes

4	beef filet mignon steaks (6 to 8 oz. each), 1½ inches thick
¼	teaspoon salt
¼	teaspoon freshly ground pepper
1	tablespoon olive oil
1	tablespoon butter (no substitutes)
⅓	cup chopped shallots
⅓	cup cognac
⅓	cup chicken broth
⅓	cup heavy or whipping cream
2	teaspoons chopped fresh tarragon

1. Let the steaks stand at room temperature 30 minutes.

2. Sprinkle salt and pepper on both sides of steaks.

3. Heat oil in a large skillet over medium heat. Add steaks and butter; cook 5 minutes per side for medium. Transfer steaks to an ovenproof pan and keep warm in a 200°F. oven. Increase heat to medium-high and add shallots, then cognac to same skillet; cook 1 minute. Stir in broth and cook 3 minutes. Add cream and cook 2 minutes more, until thickened. Stir in tarragon. Remove from heat.

4. Arrange steaks on a serving platter. Spoon sauce over steaks. Makes 4 servings.

Per serving: 435 calories, 24.5 g total fat, 11 g saturated fat, 120 mg cholesterol, 346 mg sodium, 3 g carbohydrates, 36 g protein, 29 mg calcium, 0 g fiber

holiday ham

Southern-influenced and always elegant, our version of this classic is studded with cloves and marinated overnight in a spice-vinegar mixture. The ham is then slow-baked and topped with a peach glaze, making it memorably moist and tender. There are many varieties of ham, so read the labels carefully and purchase one that's "fully cooked."

Prep time: 20 minutes plus chilling and standing
Baking time: 2 to 2½ hours

1	fully cooked bone-in smoked ham (7 to 9 lbs.), shank or butt portion
20	whole cloves
¾	cup firmly packed brown sugar
¼	cup cider vinegar
9	bay leaves, stems removed and ground
9	garlic cloves, crushed through a press
1	tablespoon red pepper flakes
1½	teaspoons paprika
½	cup peach preserves

1. Line a 17×11-inch roasting pan with foil.

2. Score top and sides of ham in a small crisscross pattern. Stud ham with cloves. Combine brown sugar, vinegar, bay leaves, garlic, red pepper flakes and paprika in a small bowl. Rub two-thirds of the spice mixture over ham. Place ham in prepared pan; cover and refrigerate overnight.

3. Heat oven to 325°F. Bake ham 2 to 2½ hours (after 1 hour, cover ham loosely with foil to prevent overbrowning), until an instant-read meat thermometer inserted in center (not touching bone) registers 140°F.

4. Meanwhile, combine preserves and remaining spice mixture in a small bowl. Uncover ham and brush with spice mixture during the last 30 minutes of baking.

5. Cover and let stand 15 minutes before carving. Makes 8 to 12 servings.

Per serving: 555 calories, 22.5 g total fat, 8 g saturated fat, 147 mg cholesterol, 3,755 mg sodium, 29 g carbohydrates, 57 g protein, 43 mg calcium, 0 g fiber

the crowning glory

A CUT ABOVE THE REST, crown roast of pork is special in that it's formed from the rib section and tied into a circle with its ribs up. The loin—considered an especially tender cut—is taken from the area on both sides of the backbone, which extends from shoulder to leg.

THOUGH WE don't call for the tips of the bones to be decorated, they are often trimmed with paper frills—socks made of fluted paper that are then pulled over the bones. The hollow center of the roast is commonly filled with some type of vegetable or stuffing (our recipe below calls for an unforgettable sausage-vegetable stuffing flavored with fennel).

crown roast of pork with savory stuffing EASY

A crown roast of pork is spectacular anytime, for any occasion, especially during the holidays. In this recipe the stuffing is made with potatoes instead of bread and flavored with crushed fennel seeds. To save time, order the tied crown roast from your butcher.

Prep time: 35 minutes • Baking time: 2½ to 2¾ hours

- 1 **16-rib crown roast of pork (about 9 lbs.)**
- 1 **tablespoon olive oil**
- ¼ **teaspoon salt**
- ¼ **teaspoon freshly ground pepper**

STUFFING:

- 1 **pound sweet Italian sausage (about 6 links)**
  Water
- 2 **tablespoons olive oil**
- 4 **cups finely chopped onions**
- 2 **cups finely chopped carrots**
- 2 **cups finely chopped celery**
- 2 **garlic cloves, crushed through a press**
- 4 **large potatoes (about 2 lbs.), peeled and diced**

- 1¼ **teaspoons salt, divided**
- ½ **cup chopped fresh flat-leaf parsley**
- 1 **teaspoon fennel seed, crushed**
- ½ **teaspoon freshly ground pepper**

GRAVY:

- ¼ **cup water**
- ¼ **cup all-purpose flour**
- 1 **can (14½ oz.) chicken broth**
- ¼ **cup white wine**
- ¼ **teaspoon salt**
- ⅛ **teaspoon freshly ground pepper**

1. Remove crown roast from refrigerator and place in a shallow roasting pan; let stand at room temperature 35 minutes.

2. Heat oven to 475°F. Brush roast with oil; sprinkle with salt and pepper. Cover exposed bone tips with strips of foil to prevent overbrowning. Roast 15 minutes; reduce oven temperature to 325°F. and roast 1½ hours more, until an instant-read meat thermometer inserted in thickest part of roast (not touching the bone) registers 135°F.

3. *Make stuffing:* Meanwhile, cut sausage links in half lengthwise; remove from casings. Cook sausage with ½ cup water in a heavy skillet over medium heat 10 minutes, until water has evaporated and sausage is brown, breaking up sausage with a wooden spoon. With a slotted spoon, transfer sausage to a plate lined with paper towels. Chop into fine pieces. Add oil to drippings in skillet. Sauté onions, carrots, celery and garlic over medium heat 15 minutes, until carrots are tender.

4. Bring potatoes, enough water to cover and ½ teaspoon of the salt to boil in a medium saucepan over high heat; boil 7 to 10 minutes, until tender. Drain. Place sausage, sautéed vegetables, potatoes, parsley, fennel, remaining ¾ teaspoon salt and the pepper in a large bowl; gently stir until combined. Makes 11 cups.

5. Remove roast from oven. Fill the center with stuffing, mounding it slightly. (Wrap extra stuffing in heavy-duty foil and bake with the roast.) Roast 45 minutes to 1 hour more, until an instant-read meat thermometer inserted in thickest part of roast (not touching the bone) registers 155°F. Transfer roast to a serving platter; remove foil and let stand 15 minutes before serving.

6. *Make gravy:* Meanwhile, pour drippings from roasting pan into a 2-cup glass measure; set aside. Pour water into roasting pan and bring to simmer over medium heat, scraping up any browned bits; add to drippings. Place 4 tablespoons of the fat from drippings in a medium saucepan (discard remaining fat from the surface of drippings). Stir in flour and cook over medium heat 2 to 3 minutes, until golden. Add chicken broth, wine, salt, pepper and reserved defatted drippings. Bring to simmer and cook 3 minutes more, until thickened. Transfer to gravy boat and serve with roast and stuffing. Makes 16 servings.

Per serving pork and gravy with ½ cup stuffing: 375 calories, 18 g total fat, 6.5 g saturated fat, 96 mg cholesterol, 448 mg sodium, 12 g carbohydrates, 37 g protein, 52 mg calcium, 2 g fiber

chanukkah brisket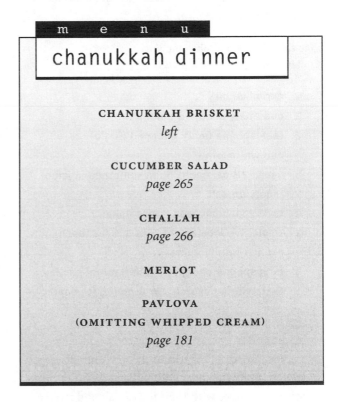

A Jewish holiday favorite, the flavor of this hearty dish improves if you refrigerate the cooked brisket overnight.

Prep time: 15 minutes • Baking time: 3½ hours

- 1 **beef brisket (5 lbs.), trimmed**
- 1 **teaspoon minced garlic**
- 1 **teaspoon salt**
- ½ **teaspoon freshly ground pepper**
- ½ **teaspoon paprika**
- 2 **tablespoons vegetable oil**
- 8 **carrots, cut into 3-inch pieces**
- 5 **celery ribs, cut into 3-inch pieces**
- 3 **large onions, thinly sliced**
- 3½ **cups beef broth**
- ½ **cup red wine**
- 5 **garlic cloves, crushed**
- 1½ **teaspoons dried thyme**

1. Heat oven to 350°F. Rinse beef under cold water and pat dry. Rub all over with minced garlic. Sprinkle with salt, pepper and paprika.

2. Heat oil in a large Dutch oven over high heat. Add beef and brown well on all sides, about 10 minutes. Add remaining ingredients and bring to boil. Transfer to oven. Bake, covered, 3 hours;

uncover and bake 30 minutes more. Transfer beef to serving platter; cover and keep warm. Strain cooking broth from vegetables; skim off fat. *(Can be made ahead. Cool. Cover beef, broth and vegetables separately; refrigerate overnight. Skim fat from top of broth; return to Dutch oven and heat to boil. Add meat and vegetables and reheat in 350°F. oven 30 minutes.)* Slice beef and serve with broth and vegetables. Makes 8 servings.

Per serving: 500 calories, 20.5 g total fat, 6 g saturated fat, 171 mg cholesterol, 852 mg sodium, 13 g carbohydrates, 63 g protein, 64 mg calcium, 3 g fiber

m e n u

chanukkah dinner

CHANUKKAH BRISKET
left

CUCUMBER SALAD
page 265

CHALLAH
page 266

MERLOT

PAVLOVA
(OMITTING WHIPPED CREAM)
page 181

linguine with lobster sauce

EASY **LOW FAT**

This delicious Italian specialty provides an opulent alternative for any special holiday gathering. If you like your sauce really spicy, use more red pepper flakes. To master the removal of the lobster meat, use kitchen shears to cut vertically up the underside of the tail. Pull the tail meat out with a fork. Also, the claws and joints to the claws have good meat. Use a nutcracker and picks to loosen and remove the meat.

Prep time: 35 minutes plus standing
Cooking time: 1 hour 30 minutes

¼	cup olive oil
1	cup finely chopped onions
2	tablespoons finely chopped garlic
½	cup white wine
3	cans (28 oz. each) plum tomatoes in juice
1	teaspoon salt
½	to ¾ teaspoon red pepper flakes
2	whole live lobsters (1¼ to 1½ lbs. each)
1½	pounds thin linguine
3	tablespoons chopped fresh flat-leaf parsley
	Extra-virgin olive oil, for drizzling (optional)

1. Heat the ¼ cup oil in a Dutch oven over medium heat. Add onions and cook 5 minutes, until softened. Add garlic and cook 1 minute, until golden. Add wine; bring to boil and boil 2 minutes. Stir in tomatoes with their juices, salt and red pepper flakes. Then coarsely cut tomatoes in Dutch oven with kitchen shears. Simmer, uncovered, 1 hour, stirring occasionally. Place lobsters in simmering sauce head first; cover and simmer 20 minutes more, stirring occasionally. Remove from heat.

2. Immediately remove lobsters from sauce with tongs and place on cutting board. Let stand 5 minutes, until cool enough to handle. Meanwhile, start cooking pasta according to package directions.

3. Use a nutcracker to break lobsters' claws and joints; remove meat. To remove tail meat, use kitchen shears to make a vertical slit down underside of tail. Using a kitchen towel, grasp both sides of tail and pull back to expose meat; pull out meat with a fork and coarsely chop. Reserve tomalley (liver) and coral (roe), if any. *(Can be made ahead. Cover sauce and lobster separately; refrigerate up to 24 hours. Reheat sauce, stirring, over low heat about 15 minutes.)* Bring sauce to boil and stir in lobster, tomalley, coral and any juices.

4. Toss pasta with 6 cups of the sauce in a serving bowl. Sprinkle with parsley. Serve with remaining sauce and drizzle with additional olive oil, if desired. Makes 6 servings.

Per serving without additional oil: 655 calories, 11.5 g total fat, 1.5 g saturated fat, 34 mg cholesterol, 1,162 mg sodium, 107 g carbohydrates, 29 g protein, 188 mg calcium, 7 g fiber

spinach cannelloni with fontina

Melt-in-your-mouth cannelloni rolls make an elegant vegetarian main dish for a buffet. Tender homemade crêpes replace the dried cannelloni pasta shells.

Prep time: 1 hour plus standing
Baking time: 25 to 30 minutes

TOMATO SAUCE:

1	teaspoon olive oil
2	tablespoons minced shallots
1	can (28 or 32 oz.) whole tomatoes in puree, chopped
⅔	cup water
2	tablespoons chopped fresh flat-leaf parsley
½	teaspoon dried rosemary
¼	teaspoon salt

CRÊPES:

¾	cup water
¾	cup milk
3	large eggs

¼ teaspoon salt
⅛ teaspoon nutmeg
1½ cups all-purpose flour
1 teaspoon vegetable oil

BÉCHAMEL SAUCE:
2 tablespoons butter or margarine
3 tablespoons minced shallots
3 tablespoons flour
1 cup milk
½ cup heavy or whipping cream
¼ teaspoon salt
2 ounces fontina cheese, cut up

FILLING:
1 tablespoon olive oil
1 cup chopped fennel
1 teaspoon chopped garlic
2 bags (10 oz. each) fresh spinach
1 container (32 oz.) ricotta cheese
1 large egg yolk
½ cup freshly grated Parmesan cheese
½ teaspoon salt
¼ teaspoon freshly ground pepper

1. *Make tomato sauce:* Heat oil in a medium saucepan over medium-high heat. Add shallots; cook 1 minute. Add remaining ingredients; bring to boil. Reduce heat and simmer 25 minutes; set aside.

2. *Make crêpes:* Meanwhile, blend all ingredients *except* flour and oil on low speed in a blender. Add flour and blend until smooth. Lightly coat a 6-inch nonstick skillet with oil; heat over medium-high heat 1 minute. Pour 2 tablespoons of the batter into skillet, tilting to coat bottom. Cook 1 minute, until crêpe sets on top and begins to brown on bottom. Invert onto plate. Repeat with remaining batter, stacking crêpes. Cover lightly with plastic wrap. *(Can be made ahead. Wrap crêpes well in plastic wrap and transfer tomato sauce to an airtight container. Refrigerate both up to 5 days.)*

3. *Make béchamel sauce:* Melt butter in a small saucepan over medium-high heat. Add shallots; cook 1 minute. Stir in flour; cook 1 minute. While stirring constantly, gradually add milk, cream and

salt. Bring to boil; reduce heat to medium-low and simmer 1 minute. Stir in cheese until melted. Cover and set aside.

4. *Make filling:* Heat oil in a 12-inch skillet over medium heat. Add fennel and garlic; cook 2 to 3 minutes, until tender. Add spinach; cover and cook until wilted. Transfer spinach to sieve, pressing out excess liquid. Coarsely chop and combine with remaining ingredients in a large bowl.

5. *To assemble:* Heat oven to 375°F. Cover bottom of a shallow 4-quart rectangular baking dish with 1 cup of the tomato sauce. Working in batches, arrange crêpes on work surface. Spoon ⅓ cup of the filling along center of each crêpe; roll up. Arrange cannelloni in 3 rows in prepared dish. Spoon 1 cup of the tomato sauce down center of dish; spoon remaining sauce around edge. Spoon béchamel sauce between rows of tomato sauce to cover cannelloni. *(Can be made ahead. Cover cannelloni with plastic wrap. Refrigerate up to 24 hours.)* Bake cannelloni 25 to 30 minutes, until tomato sauce is bubbly around edges. Let stand 10 minutes before serving. Makes 8 to 10 servings.

Per serving: 500 calories, 30.5 g total fat, 17 g saturated fat, 186 mg cholesterol, 998 mg sodium, 33 g carbohydrates, 26 g protein, 475 mg calcium, 6 g fiber

walnut-raisin bread stuffing

Gale Gand, pastry chef and owner of Tru, Chicago, Illinois, loves this stuffing because it appeals to her passion for combining savory and sweet. Pictured on page 247.

Prep time: 30 minutes • Baking time: 35 minutes

- **1** **1-pound loaf walnut-raisin bread, cut into ½-inch cubes**
- **8** **ounces sourdough bread, cut into ½-inch cubes**
- **½** **cup butter or margarine, melted**
- **2** **cups chopped onions**
- **2** **cups chopped celery**
- **½** **cup chopped fresh flat-leaf parsley**
- **1** **teaspoon dried sage, ground**
- **¾** **teaspoon salt**
- **½** **teaspoon freshly ground pepper**
- **1½** **cups chicken broth**
- **2** **large eggs, lightly beaten**

1. Heat oven to 400°F. Arrange bread cubes on 2 large cookie sheets. Bake 10 to 12 minutes, until dry and lightly colored, stirring twice. Transfer bread to a large bowl. Set aside.

2. Melt butter in a large skillet over medium heat. Add onions and celery; cook 8 to 10 minutes, until vegetables soften. Stir in parsley, sage, salt and pepper; cook 2 minutes. Transfer vegetables to bowl with bread. Add broth and eggs and stir until well combined.

3. *To stuff turkey:* Proceed as directed starting with step 2 of Turkey with Herb Gravy (see recipe, page 254). *To bake stuffing separately:* Heat oven to 325°F. Spoon stuffing into a well-buttered 13×9-inch baking dish. Cover with foil and bake 25 minutes. Uncover and bake 10 minutes more, until an instant-read thermometer inserted in center registers 160°F. Makes 12 cups.

Per ½-cup serving: 135 calories, 7 g total fat, 3 g saturated fat, 29 mg cholesterol, 304 mg sodium, 15 g carbohydrates, 3 g protein, 29 mg calcium, 1 g fiber

oyster stuffing

Sandy Shea, owner and executive chef of Chez Shea Restaurant & Lounge, in Seattle, Washington, says this recipe brings back fond memories of her childhood. Be sure to use the freshest oysters you can find. Pictured on page 247.

Prep time: 20 minutes • Baking time: 30 minutes

- **¼** **cup butter or margarine**
- **1** **cup chopped onions**
- **1** **cup chopped celery**
- **12** **ounces (8 cups) day-old bread, cut into ½-inch cubes**
- **1** **teaspoon salt**
- **½** **teaspoon freshly ground pepper**
- **½** **teaspoon dried sage, ground**
- **1** **pint fresh shucked oysters in liquid (see tip, page 252)**
- **¼** **cup milk**
- **1** **large egg, lightly beaten**

1. Melt butter in a large skillet over medium heat. Add onions and celery; cook 3 to 5 minutes, until vegetables soften. Transfer to a large bowl; stir in bread, salt, pepper and sage.

2. Drain oysters through a large fine strainer over a 1-quart glass measure. Rinse oysters under cold running water to remove any sand or shells; transfer oysters to a bowl. Strain oyster liquid into a separate bowl; set aside. Coarsely chop oysters. Add oysters to bowl with bread mixture.

3. Gently stir in oyster liquid, milk and egg, stirring just until all ingredients are combined.

4. *To stuff turkey:* Proceed as directed starting with step 2 of Turkey with Herb Gravy (see recipe, page 254). *To bake stuffing separately:* Heat oven to 325°F. Spoon stuffing into a well-buttered 13×9-inch baking dish. Cover with foil and bake 30 minutes, until an instant-read thermometer inserted in center registers 160°F. Makes 7½ cups.

Per ½-cup serving: 115 calories, 5 g total fat, 2.5 g saturated fat, 35 mg cholesterol, 348 mg sodium, 14 g carbohydrates, 4 g protein, 48 mg calcium, 1 g fiber

corn bread stuffing

Chef David Page co-owns Home Restaurant, in New York City, with his wife, Barbara Shinn. In their cookbook Recipes from Home *(Artisan 2001), they say, "The Thanksgiving stuffing has to be memorable. We know 'stuffing' refers to the bird, but when the stuffing is delectable, what really happens is that everyone at the table ends up stuffing themselves. This is the recipe we use every Thanksgiving at our home and at Home Restaurant."* Tip: Use a gentle touch when mixing the bread with the other ingredients. Pictured on page 247.

Prep time: 35 minutes plus corn bread baking
Baking time: 40 to 45 minutes

CORN BREAD:

- 2 cups all-purpose flour
- 1½ cups yellow cornmeal
- 2 tablespoons sugar
- 2 tablespoons baking powder
- 1 teaspoon kosher salt or ½ teaspoon regular salt
- 2 tablespoons minced fresh sage or 1 teaspoon dried sage
- 2 cups milk
- 2 large eggs
- ¼ cup unsalted butter or margarine, melted
- 2 tablespoons unsalted butter or margarine, softened, divided

STUFFING:

- 3 tablespoons unsalted butter or margarine
- 2 cups chopped onions
- 2 cups chopped celery
- 2 tablespoons chopped garlic
- 1 bay leaf
- 2 teaspoons kosher salt or 1 teaspoon regular salt
- ½ teaspoon freshly ground pepper
- 3 tart green apples, peeled, cored and diced into ½-inch pieces
- ½ pound smoked ham, diced into ¼-inch pieces (optional)
- 3 cups chicken broth
- 2 large eggs
- ½ cup heavy or whipping cream
- 3 tablespoons chopped fresh flat-leaf parsley
- 2 tablespoons minced fresh sage or 2 teaspoons dried sage, crumbled

1. *Make corn bread:* Heat oven to 425°F. Grease two 8×4-inch loaf pans. Set aside.

2. Whisk together the flour, cornmeal, sugar, baking powder and salt in a large bowl. Stir in sage until evenly distributed. Whisk together the milk, eggs and melted butter in a small bowl; pour into cornmeal mixture, stirring just until combined.

3. Spoon batter evenly into prepared pans. Bake 15 minutes; spread 1 tablespoon of the softened butter on top of each bread. Bake 10 minutes more, until tops are golden brown and toothpick inserted in centers comes out clean. Cool in pans on wire racks 20 minutes. Invert breads onto 2 cookie sheets; cool completely. Coarsely crumble into large pieces.

4. *Make stuffing:* Melt butter in a large saucepan over medium heat. Add onions, celery, garlic, bay leaf, salt and pepper; cook 5 minutes, until vegetables soften. Stir in apples and ham (if using); cook 1 minute. Transfer vegetable mixture to a medium bowl; discard bay leaf.

5. Whisk together the broth, eggs, cream, parsley and sage in a large bowl. Add the corn bread and vegetables and gently stir just until combined.

6. *To stuff turkey:* Proceed as directed starting with step 2 of Turkey with Herb Gravy (see recipe, page 254). *To bake stuffing separately:* Heat oven to 325°F. Spoon stuffing into 2 well-buttered 13×9-inch baking dishes. Cover with foil; bake 30 minutes. Uncover and bake 10 to 15 minutes more, until crisped and an instant-read thermometer inserted in center registers 160°F. Makes 15 cups stuffing.

Per ½-cup serving without ham: 140 calories, 6.5 g total fat, 3.5 g saturated fat, 45 mg cholesterol, 399 mg sodium, 17 g carbohydrates, 3 g protein, 87 mg calcium, 1 g fiber

brussels sprouts with bacon

Tom Colicchio, chef-owner of two restaurants, Gramercy Tavern and Craft, New York City, New York, and author of Think Like a Chef, *notes, "This side dish is the only one I've added to the traditional Thanksgiving meal I had growing up. I like to get the Brussels sprouts from the local farmer's market because they don't remove them from the stalks. This way I know they will be fresh. If you buy them at the grocery store, make sure the stems aren't dried out."*

Prep time: 30 minutes • Cooking time: 11 to 15 minutes

- 2 containers (10 oz. each) Brussels sprouts, trimmed and discolored outer leaves removed
  Water
- 1¼ teaspoons kosher salt, divided
- 4 ounces slab bacon or thick-cut bacon, diced
- 1½ teaspoons fresh thyme leaves
- ¼ teaspoon freshly ground pepper

1. With a paring knife, remove and discard cores from Brussels sprouts.

2. Bring 2 quarts water and 1 teaspoon of the salt to boil in a medium saucepan. Add Brussels sprouts and cook 3 minutes, until leaves begin to open slightly. With a slotted spoon, transfer Brussels sprouts to a colander; discard water. Rinse sprouts under cold running water; drain. Meanwhile, bring another 2 quarts water to boil. Separate the Brussels sprouts leaves and add to the boiling water. Cook the leaves 3 to 5 minutes, until almost tender. Drain in colander and rinse leaves under cold running water. Blot dry with paper towels. Set aside.

3. Cook bacon over medium heat in a large skillet 3 to 5 minutes, just until cooked through but not crisp. Reduce heat to medium-low; add Brussels sprouts leaves, thyme, remaining ¼ teaspoon salt and the pepper. Cook 2 minutes, until leaves are heated through. Transfer to a serving bowl. *(Can be made ahead. Cover and store at room temperature up to 2 hours. Microwave on High 2 minutes, until heated through.)* Makes 8 servings.

Per serving: 105 calories, 8.5 g total fat, 3 g saturated fat, 9 mg cholesterol, 209 mg sodium, 6 g carbohydrates, 3 g protein, 27 mg calcium, 2 g fiber

molasses mashed sweet potatoes

Ben and Karen Barker, owners of Magnolia Grill in Durham, North Carolina, and authors of Not Afraid of Flavor, *say, "These are not your usual 'sweet' sweet potatoes. Perfect for the holiday table, they are a great accompaniment to turkey or duck."*

Prep time: 15 minutes • Cooking time: 23 minutes

- 1½ pounds sweet potatoes, peeled and cut into 1-inch pieces
- 1½ pounds russet potatoes, peeled and cut into 1-inch pieces
- 1½ teaspoons salt, divided
  Water
- ¾ cup half-and-half cream, divided
- 6 tablespoons unsalted butter or margarine, divided
- 6 tablespoons sour cream
- 6 tablespoons molasses
- ½ teaspoon freshly ground pepper
  Chopped fresh flat-leaf parsley, for garnish (optional)

1. Bring potatoes, ½ teaspoon of the salt and enough water to cover to boil in a large saucepan. Reduce heat and simmer 20 minutes, until tender. Drain potatoes. Return to saucepan and cook over low heat 3 to 5 minutes to dry.

2. Mash the potatoes with a potato masher or large wooden spoon. Stir in ½ cup of the half-and-half cream, 4 tablespoons of the butter, the sour cream, molasses, remaining 1 teaspoon salt and the pepper. *(Can be made ahead. Transfer potatoes to a large microwaveproof bowl; cover with plastic wrap and refrigerate overnight. Stir in remaining ¼ cup half-and-half cream. Microwave on High 4 to 5 minutes, until heated through.)* Stir in remaining ¼ cup half-and-half cream.

3. Transfer potatoes to a large serving bowl. Dot top with remaining 2 tablespoons butter and the chopped parsley, if desired. Makes 8 servings.

Per serving: 300 calories, 14 g total fat, 8.5 g saturated fat, 37 mg cholesterol, 342 mg sodium, 42 g carbohydrates, 3 g protein, 89 mg calcium, 3 g fiber

cucumber salad

Put cucumbers to good use in this refreshing salad.

Total prep time: 15 minutes plus standing

- **3** large cucumbers, peeled and thinly sliced
- **1** teaspoon salt
- **2** tablespoons mayonnaise or salad dressing
- **1** teaspoon Dijon mustard
- **1** garlic clove, crushed with flat side of knife
  Pinch ground white pepper
- **1** tablespoon chopped fresh dill or 1 teaspoon dried dillweed

Toss cucumbers and salt in a colander; let stand over a shallow bowl 30 minutes. Rinse under cold water; drain well and pat cucumbers dry. Combine mayonnaise, mustard, garlic and white pepper in a large bowl. Add cucumbers; toss to coat. Sprinkle with dill. *(Can be made ahead. Cover and refrigerate up to 2 hours.)* Remove garlic before serving. Makes 8 servings.

Per serving: 40 calories, 3 g total fat, 0.5 g saturated fat, 2 mg cholesterol, 98 mg sodium, 3 g carbohydrates, 1 g protein, 17 mg calcium, 1 g fiber

sweet and sour cabbage

Tom Douglas. the chef-owner of Dahlia Lounge, Etta's Seafood and Palace Kitchen, in Seattle, Washington, and author of Tom Douglas' Seattle Kitchen, *says, "Sweet and Sour Cabbage is a family favorite, handed down from great-grandma Duchess."*

Prep time: 10 minutes • Cooking time: 55 minutes

- **¼** cup unsalted butter or margarine
- **1** head (2 lbs.) red cabbage, cored and thinly sliced (about 6 cups)
- **¾** cup cider vinegar
- **½** cup sugar
- **1½** teaspoons caraway seeds
- **½** teaspoon salt
- **¼** teaspoon freshly ground pepper

1. Melt butter in a large, deep nonreactive skillet over medium-low heat. Add cabbage, vinegar, sugar and caraway seeds. Cover and cook 45 minutes, until cabbage softens, stirring often.

2. With a slotted spoon, remove cabbage from skillet, letting excess liquid drip into skillet. Transfer cabbage to a large bowl. Cook liquid over medium-high heat 10 minutes, until reduced to ½ cup. Add reduced liquid, salt and pepper to cabbage in bowl, stirring well to coat. *(Can be made ahead. Cool completely. Cover and refrigerate up to 6 hours. Microwave on High 2 to 3 minutes, just until heated through.)* Makes 6 cups.

Per ½-cup serving: 80 calories, 4 g total fat, 2.5 g saturated fat, 11 mg cholesterol, 102 mg sodium, 11 g carbohydrates, 1 g protein, 22 mg calcium, 1 g fiber

cranberry jam

Tom Douglas explains, "Often times my daughter will request 'Thanksgiving dinner' for her birthday dinner in March. This jam is a spectacular way to enhance the flavor of a charcoal-roasted turkey."

Total prep time: 10 minutes plus standing

- **1** tablespoon unsalted butter (no substitutes)
- **1** tablespoon grated fresh ginger
- **1** bag (12 oz.) fresh or frozen cranberries
- **1½** to 1¾ cups sugar
- **½** cup water
- **¼** cup port wine
- **1** teaspoon grated orange peel
- **1** tablespoon fresh orange juice
- **1** teaspoon grated lemon peel
- **1** tablespoon fresh lemon juice
- **¼** teaspoon cinnamon

Melt butter in a medium saucepan over medium heat. Add ginger and cook 1 minute. Stir in remaining ingredients. Reduce heat to medium-low and bring to simmer; cook 5 to 7 minutes, until the cranberries begin to pop. Transfer to a serving bowl. Cool completely. *(Can be made ahead. Cover and refrigerate up to 5 days.)* Makes 2½ cups.

Per 1-tablespoon serving: 40 calories, 0.5 g total fat, 0 g saturated fat, 1 mg cholesterol, 0 mg sodium, 9 g carbohydrates, 0 g protein, 1 mg calcium, 0 g fiber

challah

This lightly sweetened, braided loaf is traditionally made for Jewish holidays but also makes terrific French toast. Be sure to allow the dough to double during each standing time for a light-textured bread.

Prep time: 40 minutes plus rising and standing
Baking time: 24 to 27 minutes

3	packages active dry yeast
1¼	cups warm water (105°F. to 115°F.)
½	cup sugar
4⅔	to 5¼ cups bread flour, divided
2	teaspoons salt
3	large eggs
¼	cup vegetable shortening
2	tablespoons cornmeal
1	large egg yolk
1	tablespoon water
1	tablespoon sesame or poppy seeds

1. Combine yeast with the 1¼ cups warm water and sugar in a small bowl. Let stand 10 minutes. Combine 4 cups of the flour and the salt in a large bowl. With a wooden spoon, beat in yeast mixture, then whole eggs and shortening 1 minute, until blended. Knead dough on a floured surface 8 minutes, until smooth and elastic, gradually adding enough of the remaining ⅔ cup to 1¼ cups flour as needed to make a soft dough. Place in a large oiled bowl, turning dough to oil top. Cover and let rise in a warm, draft-free place until doubled in bulk, 1 to 1¼ hours.

2. Adjust oven racks in top and bottom thirds of oven. Heat oven to 375°F. Sprinkle a large cookie sheet with cornmeal. Punch down dough and knead briefly on a lightly floured surface. Divide dough into 6 equal pieces. Roll each piece into a 12-inch-long rope. Place 3 ropes side by side on prepared cookie sheet and braid together, tucking ends underneath. Repeat, braiding remaining 3 ropes. With a fork, whisk together egg yolk and the 1 tablespoon water in a cup; brush over tops of loaves. Immediately sprinkle with seeds. Cover; let rise until doubled in bulk, 35 to 45 minutes.

3. Bake loaves 24 to 27 minutes, until golden, switching pans between racks and rotating front to back halfway through baking time for even browning. Cool on cookie sheet on a wire rack 10 minutes. Transfer breads to wire rack and cool completely. Makes 2 loaves, twenty four ½-inch-thick slices each.

Per slice: 75 calories, 2 g total fat, 0.5 g saturated fat, 18 mg cholesterol, 102 mg sodium, 12 g carbohydrates, 2 g protein, 6 mg calcium, 0 g fiber

cornmeal rolls

Fill your bread basket with golden rolls on Thanksgiving Day! As delicate as classic dinner rolls, these also are slightly nutty and crunchy, thanks to the cornmeal. They freeze beautifully, so bake them before the hectic holiday season begins.

Prep time: 30 minutes plus rising
Baking time: 14 to 15 minutes

1	cup boiling water
1¼	cups yellow cornmeal (not stone-ground)
1	package active dry yeast
¼	cup warm water (105°F. to 115°F.)
	Sugar
1	cup milk
¼	cup butter or margarine, at room temperature, cut up
2	large egg yolks
2	teaspoons salt
6	to 6½ cups all-purpose flour, divided

1. Pour boiling water over cornmeal in a large mixer bowl; let stand 10 minutes.

2. Sprinkle yeast over warm water in a 1-cup glass measure; add a pinch of sugar and let stand 5 minutes, until mixture is foamy.

3. Meanwhile, heat milk in a medium saucepan over medium-high heat until small bubbles appear around edge; remove from heat, add butter and let stand until butter is melted.

4. Beat milk mixture into cornmeal mixture on medium speed until smooth. Beat in egg yolks, ⅓ cup sugar and the salt. Add the yeast mixture and beat until smooth.

5. Reduce speed to low; gradually beat in 3 cups of the flour (mixture should start to leave side of bowl). Gather dough into a ball and transfer to a work surface sprinkled with ½ cup of the flour. Press dough into flour, then fold dough in half to incorporate flour. Repeat process with another ½ cup of the flour. Knead dough for 12 minutes, until smooth and elastic, adding the remaining 2 to 2½ cups flour as needed (dough will be sticky). Transfer dough to a large oiled bowl, turning to oil top. Cover and let rise in a warm, draft-free place until doubled in bulk, 1 hour. Lightly press down on dough with palm of hand to deflate; cover and let rise until doubled in bulk, 20 to 30 minutes.

6. Lightly coat 2 large cookie sheets with vegetable cooking spray. Shape dough by ¼ cupfuls and roll into balls; arrange balls 2 inches apart on prepared cookie sheets. Cover and let rise until balls have puffed slightly, 45 to 55 minutes.

7. Meanwhile, adjust oven racks in middle and lower third of oven. Heat oven to 400°F.

8. Uncover rolls and bake 7 minutes. Switch pan positions and bake 7 to 8 minutes more, until rolls are deep golden brown and sound hollow when tapped on bottoms. Serve warm. *(Can be made ahead. Cool completely. Transfer to airtight containers and freeze up to 2 weeks. Thaw at room temperature 1 to 1½ hours. Wrap rolls in foil. Reheat in 325°F. oven 20 to 25 minutes.)* Makes 26 rolls.

Per roll: 160 calories, 3 g total fat, 1.5 g saturated fat, 22 mg cholesterol, 203 mg sodium, 29 g carbohydrates, 4 g protein, 19 mg calcium, 1 g fiber

hot cross buns

Traditionally served at Easter, these pleasantly spiced rolls are a delicious addition to any holiday meal.

Prep time: 45 minutes plus rising and standing
Baking time: 20 to 25 minutes

1	cup plus 2 teaspoons milk, divided
¼	cup plus 2 tablespoons granulated sugar, divided
½	teaspoon salt
1	package active dry yeast
¼	cup warm water (105°F. to 115°F.)
4½	to 5 cups all-purpose flour, divided
3	tablespoons butter, melted (no substitutes)
2	large eggs, beaten
½	cup raisins
¼	cup finely diced candied citron
½	teaspoon cinnamon
½	teaspoon nutmeg
2	tablespoons heavy or whipping cream
½	cup confectioners' sugar

1. Combine 1 cup of the milk, ¼ cup of the granulated sugar and the salt in a small saucepan. Heat over medium-high heat 2 to 4 minutes, until sugar dissolves, stirring occasionally. Pour milk mixture into a large heatproof bowl and cool to lukewarm. Add yeast to warm water and stir until dissolved; stir into lukewarm milk. With a wooden spoon, stir 2 cups of the flour into the yeast mixture. Cover with plastic wrap and let rise in a warm, draft-free place until spongy, 1½ hours.

2. Stir in butter, eggs, raisins, citron and spices. Stir in 2½ cups of the flour, ½ cup at a time. Knead dough 3 minutes, until dough is smooth and elastic, adding as much of the remaining ½ cup flour as needed. Place in a large greased bowl; cover and let rise in a warm, draft-free place until doubled in bulk, 1 hour.

3. Heat oven to 350°F. Butter 2 large cookie sheets. Divide dough into 24 pieces; shape into balls. Place on prepared cookie sheets; cover with plastic wrap and let rise again until doubled in bulk, 30 minutes. Cut an X on top of each bun. Bake 20 to 25 minutes, switching position of pans halfway through baking.

4. Mix heavy cream with the remaining 2 tablespoons granulated sugar in a small bowl; brush on buns. Cool on a wire rack.

5. Blend together the confectioners' sugar and the remaining 2 teaspoons milk in a small bowl until smooth; transfer to a small resealable plastic storage bag. Snip a small hole in 1 corner of bag and pipe an X on each bun. Makes 24 buns.

Per bun: 150 calories, 3 g total fat, 1.5 g saturated fat, 24 mg cholesterol, 78 mg sodium, 28 g carbohydrates, 4 g protein, 22 mg calcium, 1 g fiber

stollen

For those who enjoy a bread chockful of fruit, use the greater amount of citron and candied cherries suggested. The secret to a tender dough is to use only as much flour as necessary to prevent sticking while you knead. Keep your hands and your work surface lightly floured as you knead, instead of adding flour directly to the dough. The finished dough should feel very soft and pliable, not stiff.

Prep time: 25 minutes plus rising and standing
Baking time: 28 to 30 minutes

- ¾ **cup milk**
- ¾ **cup butter, divided (no substitutes)**
- ½ **cup granulated sugar**
- 1 **teaspoon salt**
- 1 **package active dry yeast**
- ½ **cup warm water (105°F. to 115°F.)**
- 2 **large eggs, at room temperature**
- 5 **to 5¼ cups all-purpose flour, divided**
- 1 **cup seedless raisins**
- ½ **cup blanched chopped almonds**
- ¼ **to ½ cup chopped citron**
- ¼ **to ½ cup candied cherries, chopped**
- 1 **tablespoon grated lemon peel**

ICING:
- 1 **cup confectioners' sugar**
- 2 **tablespoons orange-flavored liqueur**
- 1 **teaspoon water**

   Red and green candied cherries, for garnish (optional)

1. Combine milk, ½ cup of the butter, granulated sugar and the salt in a small saucepan. Heat until bubbles appear around edge of pan. Remove mixture from heat and cool to lukewarm.

2. Dissolve yeast in warm water in a cup and let stand 5 minutes. Pour lukewarm milk mixture into a large bowl; whisk in yeast mixture and eggs until combined. Add 4 cups of the flour and stir with a wooden spoon until smooth. With a wooden spoon or your fingers, gradually stir in enough of the remaining 1 to 1¼ cups flour to make a soft dough.

3. Turn out dough onto a lightly floured surface and knead 5 to 8 minutes. Place dough in a well-greased bowl, turning to grease top. Cover with a clean, damp kitchen towel. Allow dough to rise in a warm, draft-free place until doubled in bulk, 1 to 1½ hours.

4. Punch dough down. Add raisins, almonds, citron, candied cherries and lemon peel by turning and folding dough until incorporated. Form into a round ball and return to bowl, turning to grease top. Cover and let dough rise until doubled in bulk, about 45 minutes.

5. Grease 2 large cookie sheets. Turn out dough onto a lightly floured surface. Divide dough in half. Shape each half into a 12×5-inch oval. Fold the long side of each three fourths of the way across the top. Place on prepared cookie sheets; cover with a clean, damp kitchen towel. Let dough rise until doubled in bulk, 45 minutes to 1 hour.

6. Heat oven to 375°F. Melt remaining ¼ cup butter. Bake 28 to 30 minutes, switching pans between racks and rotating front to back halfway through for even browning; brush breads with melted butter 2 to 3 times throughout baking time. Cool on cookie sheets on wire racks 10 minutes. Transfer breads to wire racks and cool completely.

7. *Make icing:* Beat all ingredients in a small bowl with a wooden spoon until smooth. Spoon icing into a small resealable plastic storage bag; snip a very small hole in 1 corner and drizzle over top of breads. Garnish with red and green cherries, if desired. Let stand until icing is set. Makes 2 loaves, about 12 slices per loaf.

Per slice: 245 calories, 8.5 g total fat, 4 g saturated fat, 35 mg cholesterol, 174 mg sodium, 38 g carbohydrates, 5 g protein, 28 mg calcium, 1 g fiber

ruby
cheesecake

If you try just one new recipe this year, make it this irresistible cranberry cheesecake. We mixed the cottage-cheese and cream-cheese filling in the food processor for a texture that's ultralight and creamy. Tip: Let the cheesecake cool undisturbed in the oven 1 hour after baking to prevent the top from cracking. Don't open the oven door!

Prep time: 20 minutes plus chilling
Baking time: 45 minutes plus standing

CRUST:
- 1 cup finely ground zwieback toast
     or graham-cracker crumbs
- ¼ cup butter or margarine, melted
- 2 tablespoons sugar
     Pinch cinnamon

FILLING:
- 1 cup (4% milk fat) cottage cheese
- 1 package (8 oz.) cream cheese, softened
- 1 cup sugar
- 2 tablespoons flour
- 1 cup heavy or whipping cream
- 1 teaspoon grated lemon peel
- 2 tablespoons fresh lemon juice
- 4 large eggs

CRANBERRY TOPPING:
- ½ cup sugar
- 8 tablespoons water, divided
- 2 cups fresh or frozen cranberries, divided
- 4 teaspoons cornstarch

1. *Make crust:* Heat oven to 350°F. Lightly coat a 9-inch springform pan with vegetable cooking spray. Combine zwieback crumbs, butter, sugar and cinnamon in a medium bowl until crumbs are evenly moistened. Press mixture into bottom of prepared pan. Bake 10 minutes. Cool on a wire rack.

2. *Make filling:* Meanwhile, reduce oven temperature to 325°F. Puree cottage cheese in a food processor until smooth. Add cream cheese, sugar and flour and process until smooth, scraping side of bowl with a rubber spatula. Add cream, lemon peel and juice; process until smooth. Add eggs and pulse just until blended.

3. Pour filling over crust. Bake 45 minutes. Turn off oven. Let cheesecake stand in oven 1 hour. (Do not open oven door.) Transfer cheesecake to a wire rack. Cool to room temperature. Cover top loosely with foil. Refrigerate overnight. *(Can be made ahead. Remove springform-pan ring. Wrap well in plastic wrap and freeze up to 1 month. Thaw in refrigerator 4 hours.)*

4. *Make cranberry topping:* Bring sugar and 6 tablespoons of the water to boil over high heat in a medium saucepan; reduce heat to medium-high and simmer until sugar is dissolved. Add 1 cup of the cranberries and simmer 5 minutes. Dissolve cornstarch in remaining 2 tablespoons water in a cup; stir into cranberry mixture. Bring to boil; reduce heat and simmer, stirring, 2 minutes. Stir in remaining 1 cup cranberries. Cool completely. *(Can be made ahead. Cover and refrigerate up to 2 days.)*

5. Remove springform-pan ring and transfer cake to serving platter. Spoon cranberry topping over top. Makes 10 servings.

Per serving: 450 calories, 25.5 g total fat, 15 g saturated fat, 160 mg cholesterol, 260 mg sodium, 48 g carbohydrates, 9 g protein, 62 mg calcium, 1 g fiber

ginger roll with frozen maple mousse

This superstar spice roll, filled with a frozen mousse made with real maple sugar, can remain in the freezer until it's time to take the spotlight. Let the roll stand at room temperature 10 to 15 minutes before serving; doing so returns the cake to a fork-tender texture.

Prep time: 40 minutes plus chilling
Baking time: 17 to 18 minutes

GINGER ROLL:

- ¼ **cup all-purpose flour**
- ¼ **cup cornstarch**
- ½ **teaspoon cinnamon**
- ½ **teaspoon ginger**
  Pinch cloves
- 4 **large eggs, at room temperature, separated**
- ¾ **cup granulated sugar, divided**
  Pinch salt
- ⅛ **teaspoon cream of tartar**
  Confectioners' sugar

MAPLE MOUSSE:

- ¾ **cup pure maple syrup (no substitutes)**
- 2 **large egg whites, at room temperature**
  Pinch salt
- 1 **cup heavy or whipping cream**
  ▪
- 1 **tablespoon unsweetened cocoa**
  Additional pure maple syrup (optional)

1. ▪ *Make ginger roll:* Heat oven to 350°F. Grease a 15×10½-inch jelly-roll pan. Line with waxed paper; grease paper. Sift together flour, cornstarch, cinnamon, ginger and cloves into a bowl; set aside.

2. ▪ Beat egg yolks and ¼ cup of the granulated sugar in a large mixer bowl on high speed 3 minutes, until a ribbon forms when beaters are lifted. Beat egg whites and salt in a clean mixer bowl with clean beaters on medium speed until foamy. Add cream of tartar; beat to soft peaks. Gradually increasing speed to high, beat in remaining ½ cup sugar, 1 tablespoon at a time, to form stiff peaks.

3. ▪ Fold one fourth of meringue into egg yolk mixture with a rubber spatula. Fold in dry ingredients alternately with remaining meringue just until blended. Spread batter evenly into prepared pan. Bake 17 to 18 minutes, until cake springs back when lightly touched in center.

4. ▪ Meanwhile, place a clean kitchen towel on work surface and sift confectioners' sugar over towel. Invert cake onto towel; remove jelly-roll pan and carefully peel off paper. Roll up cake from 1 long side with towel. Cool completely in towel.

5. ▪ *Make maple mousse:* Meanwhile, bring maple syrup to boil in a small saucepan over medium-low heat. Heat until syrup registers 225°F. to 230°F. (thread stage) on a candy thermometer.

6. ▪ Meanwhile, beat egg whites and salt in a clean, small mixer bowl with clean beaters on medium speed to stiff peaks. With mixer running, slowly add hot maple syrup in a thin, steady stream. Increase speed to high and beat 5 minutes more, until mixture is cool. In another mixer bowl, beat cream just to stiff peaks; fold into maple mixture just until combined.

7. ▪ *To assemble:* Line a large cookie sheet with waxed paper. Unroll cake and carefully transfer to prepared cookie sheet. Spread with an even layer of maple mousse. Freeze flat 1 hour, until filling is semifirm. Reroll cake into a log and place, seam side down, onto a cookie sheet. Trim ends at a slight angle. Sift cocoa evenly over roll. Freeze 2 hours. *(Can be made ahead. Wrap well in plastic wrap and freeze up to 2 days.)*

8. ▪ *To serve:* Let roll stand at room temperature 10 to 15 minutes before serving. Cut cake into sixteen ½-inch-thick slices. Arrange 2 slices on each plate and drizzle with additional maple syrup, if desired. Makes 8 servings.

Per serving without additional maple syrup: 330 calories, 14 g total fat, 7.5 g saturated fat, 147 mg cholesterol, 96 mg sodium, 47 g carbohydrates, 5 g protein, 63 mg calcium, 0 g fiber

rustic apple pie

David Page is chef and co-owner, with his wife Barbara Shinn, of Home Restaurant in New York City, New York. This recipe, from their cookbook Recipes from Home *(Artisan 2001), is the ultimate apple pie. "We pile our pies high with fruit and roll out a thick dough for the crust," says David. "At first you may think the dough is too thick, but once the pie is baked, the crust is light, crumbly and the perfect match for all those luscious apples. Using spices as light accents in the pie filling lets the wonderful flavor of the apples predominate. Think of the spices as enhancements, not stars." Pictured on page 244.*

Prep time: 45 minutes plus chilling and standing
Baking time: 1 hour to 1 hour 10 minutes

PASTRY:

3	cups all-purpose flour
3	tablespoons granulated sugar
1½	teaspoons salt
1	cup cold unsalted butter, cut up (no substitutes)
5	to 6 tablespoons water

APPLE FILLING:

¾	cup firmly packed brown sugar
3	tablespoons flour
½	teaspoon cinnamon
½	teaspoon cardamom
¼	teaspoon nutmeg
	Pinch salt
2½	pounds Granny Smith apples, peeled, cored and cut into ¼-inch-thick slices (about 6 cups)
1	tablespoon fresh lemon juice

EGG WASH:

1	large egg yolk
1	tablespoon water
▪	
1	tablespoon unsalted butter, melted (no substitutes)
1	tablespoon granulated sugar

1. ▪ *Make pastry:* Whisk together the flour, sugar and salt in a large bowl. With a pastry blender or 2 knives, cut in butter until mixture resembles coarse crumbs. With a fork, gradually stir in enough of the water, 1 tablespoon at a time, until dough begins to come together. Turn dough out onto surface and gently press into a disk. Remove one-fourth of the dough; shape into a thick disk, wrap in plastic wrap and set aside for decorative pastry leaf cutouts. Cut remaining dough in half and shape into 2 thick disks. Wrap each disk well in plastic wrap and refrigerate all disks 1 hour. *(Can be made ahead. Refrigerate up to 2 days.)*

2. ▪ *Make filling:* Toss together all ingredients in a large bowl. Set aside.

3. ▪ *Make egg wash:* Combine all ingredients in a small cup. Set aside.

4. ▪ Adjust oven rack in lower third of oven. Heat oven to 400°F. On a lightly floured surface with a floured rolling pin, roll 1 pastry disk out to a 14-inch circle. Fit into a 9-inch pie plate, leaving a 1-inch overhang. Spoon filling into prepared pie shell. Brush edge with egg wash. Roll remaining pastry disk into a 12-inch square. Using a pastry wheel or sharp knife, trim edges of pastry and cut into 10 even strips. Weave strips over apples to make a lattice crust. Trim ends and flute edge. Brush strips and edge with melted butter and sprinkle with the 1 tablespoon granulated sugar. If desired, using reserved dough, cut out 30 leaf shapes with a sharp paring knife or a 1½-inch leaf-shape cookie cutter. Brush 1 side of a pastry leaf with egg wash and gently press this side down on edge of pie. Repeat with remaining leaves, slightly overlapping around edge of pie. Brush tops of pastry leaves with egg wash.

5. ▪ Place pie on a cookie sheet in the oven. Bake 30 minutes, then cover pie loosely with foil to avoid overbrowning. Bake 30 to 40 minutes more, until juices are bubbly. Cool on a wire rack 1 hour. Serve warm. Makes 8 servings.

Per serving: 590 calories, 27.5 g total fat, 16.5 g saturated fat, 96 mg cholesterol, 469 mg sodium, 83 g carbohydrates, 6 g protein, 45 mg calcium, 5 g fiber

hazelnut and dried cranberry tart

Ben and Karen Baker, owners of the Magnolia Grill in Durham, North Carolina, and authors of Not Afraid of Flavor, *say, "This is a terrific autumnal dessert. Based on dried fruit and nuts, it represents traditional and historical ingredients used in a modern new way. Any nut can be substituted for the hazelnuts. Walnuts and pecans, or a mixture of different nuts, work well. Lightly toasting the nuts always accentuates their flavor."*

Prep time: 1 hour 20 minutes plus chilling and standing
Baking time: 45 minutes

PASTRY:

1	large egg, separated
1	tablespoon milk
1¼	cups plus 2 tablespoons all-purpose flour
1	tablespoon plus 1 teaspoon sugar
⅛	teaspoon salt
½	cup unsalted butter, cut up (no substitutes)

FILLING:

¾	cup light corn syrup
6	tablespoons unsalted butter, melted (no substitutes)
3	large eggs
⅓	cup sugar
1	tablespoon flour
2	tablespoons orange-flavored liqueur
2	tablespoons grated orange peel
1	tablespoon frozen orange juice concentrate, thawed
1	teaspoon vanilla extract
1½	cups dried cranberries
1¼	cups toasted chopped hazelnuts
■	
	Whipped cream (optional)

1. *Make pastry:* Whisk together egg yolk and milk in a small bowl. In another small bowl, whisk egg white until foamy. Set both aside. Pulse together the flour, sugar and salt in a food processor. Add butter and pulse until the mixture resembles coarse crumbs. Add egg yolk mixture and pulse just until dough begins to come together. Shape pastry into a ball and flatten into a thick disk. Wrap well in plastic wrap and refrigerate 1 hour or overnight.

(Can be made ahead. Wrap well in plastic wrap and freeze up to 2 weeks. Thaw dough in refrigerator overnight. Allow dough to soften slightly at room temperature before rolling.)

2. Heat oven to 350°F. On a lightly floured surface, roll pastry into a 13-inch circle. Fit dough into a 10½-inch tart pan with a removable bottom. Trim edge of pastry. Freeze tart shell 15 minutes. Line pastry with foil and fill with dried beans or pie weights. Bake 20 minutes, until set. Remove foil and beans. Bake 15 minutes more, until golden brown. Transfer to a wire rack and brush the pastry bottom with reserved egg white.

3. *Make filling:* Whisk together all ingredients *except* cranberries and nuts in a large bowl. Stir in cranberries and nuts; pour into crust. Place tart pan on a cookie sheet; bake 45 minutes, until filling is set and golden brown. Cool on a wire rack. *(Can be made ahead. Cover and store at room temperature overnight.)* Serve warm or at room temperature with whipped cream, if desired. Makes 10 servings.

Per serving without whipped cream: 520 calories, 29.5 g total fat, 12 g saturated fat, 131 mg cholesterol, 89 mg sodium, 60 g carbohydrates, 7 g protein, 44 mg calcium, 3 g fiber

berlinerkranze

Breakfast in Cairo, Dinner in Rome • Community cookbook from the International School of Minnesota Foundation • Eden Prairie, MN
More than a century old, this recipe was brought over from Norway by a contributor's great-great grandmother. In her honor, her family includes these sugar-coated cookies on the holiday table. Traditional German bakers shape Berlinerkranze into wreaths. Tip: Shaping the dough is easier with floured fingers. Pictured on page 241.

Prep time: 15 minutes plus chilling and standing
Baking time: 20 to 25 minutes per batch

4	large hard-cooked egg yolks, pressed through a fine sieve
4	large raw egg yolks
1	cup butter, softened (no substitutes)
1	cup granulated sugar
2	cups all-purpose flour
1	large egg white, lightly beaten
¼	cup pearl or granulated sugar

1. Mix hard-cooked egg yolks and raw egg yolks in a small bowl just until combined. Line 2 large cookie sheets with parchment paper.

2. Beat butter and granulated sugar in a large mixer bowl on high speed 3 to 5 minutes, until light and fluffy. Add egg yolk mixture and beat 2 minutes, until well combined. Reduce speed to low; beat in flour just until combined. Chill dough in refrigerator 15 minutes.

3. Heat oven to 300°F. Fill a measuring tablespoon with dough. Roll the piece of dough into a 4-inch-long log, then shape into a knot. Repeat with remaining dough. Arrange knots on prepared cookie sheets, placing them about 1 inch apart. Brush tops with egg white and sprinkle with pearl sugar. Chill in refrigerator 20 minutes.

4. Bake cookies 20 to 25 minutes, until lightly golden. Cool on cookie sheets on wire racks 10 minutes. Transfer cookies to wire racks. Cool completely. Makes 5 dozen cookies.

Per cookie: 65 calories, 4 g total fat, 2 g saturated fat, 37 mg cholesterol, 35 mg sodium, 6 g carbohydrates, 1 g protein, 5 mg calcium, 0 g fiber

citrus-rosemary wafers

Variations and Improvisations • Community cookbook from the Friends of KEDM Public Radio • Monroe, LA

One of the Friends of KEDM's most requested recipes, this is a great slice-and-bake cookie that's not too sweet. The addition of rosemary is unexpected and makes these cookies a delightfully unique gift. Pictured on page 245.

Prep time: 20 minutes plus chilling and standing
Baking time: 12 to 15 minutes per batch

- ½ **cup butter, softened (no substitutes)**
- ½ **cup sugar**
- 1 **large egg white, lightly beaten**
- 2 **tablespoons chopped fresh rosemary**
  or 1 teaspoon dried rosemary
- 2 **tablespoons grated lemon or orange peel**
- ½ **teaspoon vanilla extract**
- 1 **cup all-purpose flour**

1. Beat butter and sugar in a large mixer bowl on medium high speed until light and creamy. Beat in egg white, rosemary, lemon peel and vanilla. Reduce speed to low; beat in flour just until combined.

2. With lightly floured hands, shape dough into a 10-inch log. Wrap well in plastic wrap and refrigerate 4 hours or overnight.

3. Heat oven to 350°F. Unwrap log; cut into ¼-inch-thick slices. Place slices ½ inch apart on 2 large ungreased cookie sheets. Bake 12 to 15 minutes, until edges are lightly golden. Transfer cookies to wire racks. Cool completely. Makes 3½ dozen wafers.

Per wafer: 40 calories, 2.5 g total fat, 1.5 g saturated fat, 6 mg cholesterol, 25 mg sodium, 4 g carbohydrates, 0 g protein, 2 mg calcium, 0 g fiber

test kitchen tip
decorative icing

Use this versatile icing to decorate a variety of cookies, cakes and breads:

Combine 1 box (1 lb.) confectioners' sugar, 3 tablespoons meringue powder* and 6 tablespoons cold water in a large mixer bowl. Beat on medium speed until smooth. Increase speed to high and beat 5 minutes, until thick and smooth; add up to 1 tablespoon additional cold water for piping consistency, if necessary.

To tint: Dab paste food coloring* into icing with a toothpick. (Paste food colorings provide the most vibrant hues, and because they are concentrated, you won't need to use much.) Mix with a spoon until well blended, gradually adding dabs of paste food coloring, if necessary, to achieve desired color.

*Note: You can find meringue powder and paste food colorings in the baking section of supermarkets or specialty baking stores, or order them from Wilton Enterprises (800-794-5866).

triple treat crème de menthe bars

Cooks of the Green Door • Community cookbook from the League of Catholic Women • Minneapolis, MN
These no-bake bars are a consistent hit at functions sponsored by the League of Catholic Women. They are sure to be one of your new holiday favorites as well. If you like, top each bar with a candy heart. Pictured on page 242.

Total prep time: 30 minutes plus chilling

CRUST:

2	cups graham-cracker crumbs
1½	cups finely chopped walnuts, toasted
1	cup shredded coconut
½	cup confectioners' sugar
¼	cup unsweetened cocoa
¾	cup butter or margarine, melted
1	large egg, beaten
1	teaspoon vanilla extract

CRÈME DE MENTHE LAYER:

2	cups confectioners' sugar
½	cup butter, softened (no substitutes)
3	tablespoons crème de menthe
½	teaspoon vanilla extract

CHOCOLATE LAYER:

1	package (12 oz.) semisweet chocolate chips, melted
½	cup butter, melted (no substitutes)

1. *Make crust:* Line a 13×9-inch baking pan with foil, extending foil 1 inch past edges. Stir together all ingredients in a large bowl until well combined. Press into prepared pan. Chill in refrigerator 1 hour, until firm.

2. *Make crème de menthe layer:* Beat together all ingredients in a large mixer bowl on medium speed until smooth. Spread evenly over crust. Chill in refrigerator 30 minutes, until firm.

3. *Make chocolate layer:* Combine the chocolate and butter in a small bowl. Spread evenly over the crème de menthe layer. Chill in refrigerator 1 hour, until chocolate sets. Lift out of pan. Peel off foil and cut into squares. Makes 4½ dozen bars.

Per bar: 155 calories, 11 g total fat, 5.5 g saturated fat, 21 mg cholesterol, 83 mg sodium, 10 g carbohydrates, 1 g protein, 12 mg calcium, 1 g fiber

nanny's filled raisin cookies

Nice Homespun Recipes • Community cookbook from New Horizons Resources, Inc. • Poughkeepsie, NY
Donna Seelbach's grandmother made these for her when she was a child, and now she makes them for her kids. These very homey yet tasty sandwich cookies are filled with a cranberry-raisin filling. Pictured on page 243.

Prep time: 15 minutes plus chilling and standing
Baking time: 13 to 15 minutes per batch

FILLING:

1	can (8 oz.) whole cranberry sauce
½	cup raisins
¼	cup sugar
¼	cup water
½	teaspoon flour
½	teaspoon vanilla extract

DOUGH:

3½	cups all-purpose flour
2	teaspoons cream of tartar
1	teaspoon baking soda
¼	teaspoon salt
½	cup butter or margarine, softened
½	cup vegetable shortening
1	cup sugar
1	large egg
1	teaspoon vanilla extract
½	cup milk

Decorative Icing (see tip, page 273)

1. *Make filling:* Combine all ingredients in a small saucepan. Bring to boil over medium heat; cook 5 to 7 minutes, until mixture thickens. Transfer to a bowl. Cover and refrigerate 1 hour or overnight.

2. *Make dough:* Whisk together the flour, cream of tartar, baking soda and salt in a large bowl. Set aside.

3. Beat butter, shortening and sugar in a large mixer bowl on medium-high speed 3 minutes, until light and fluffy. Beat in egg and vanilla. Reduce speed to low; beat in flour mixture alternately with the milk, beginning and ending with flour mixture. Divide dough into 4 equal pieces.

4. Heat oven to 350°F. On a lightly floured surface, roll each piece of dough ¼ inch thick. Cut out cookies with a 2- or 2½-inch round fluted cookie cutter. With a ½-inch round pastry tip, cut out 1 circle from center of each of half of the unbaked cookies. Remove circles of dough; reserve scraps.

5. Spread ½ measuring teaspoonful of the filling on top of each circle of dough without a hole; top each with a circle of dough with a hole. Gently press edges together to seal. Transfer cookies with a spatula to a large ungreased cookie sheet. Refrigerate 10 minutes. Repeat with remaining dough, rerolling and cutting scraps. (Reserve remaining filling for another use.) Bake 13 to 15 minutes, until golden brown. Transfer to wire racks. Cool completely. Decorate as desired with Decorative Icing. Makes 3 dozen cookies.

Per cookie: 135 calories, 6 g total fat, 2.5 g saturated fat, 13 mg cholesterol, 83 mg sodium, 19 g carbohydrates, 1 g protein, 8 mg calcium, 0 g fiber

chocolate mint melt-aways

Savor the Moment • Community cookbook from the Junior League of Boca Raton • Boca Raton, FL

These tasty nuggets are made with a cookie press, then spread with a layer of white chocolate and topped with dark chocolate. The perfect package for holiday giving. Pictured on page 242.

Prep time: 45 minutes plus chilling
Baking time: 15 to 17 minutes per batch
Microwave used

DOUGH:

- 1   cup butter, softened (no substitutes)
- 2   teaspoons vanilla extract
- ½   teaspoon peppermint extract
- ½   cup plus 2 tablespoons confectioners' sugar
- 2   cups all-purpose flour

WHITE CHOCOLATE LAYER:

- ¼   cup plus 2 tablespoons heavy or whipping cream
- 2   tablespoons unsalted butter (no substitutes)
- 9   ounces imported white chocolate squares, chopped
- ¼   teaspoon peppermint extract

DARK CHOCOLATE COATING:

- 9   ounces semisweet or bittersweet chocolate squares, chopped
- 1   tablespoon vegetable shortening
    ▪
    Decorative Icing (see tip, page 273)
    Red dot candies (optional)

1. *Make dough:* Heat oven to 350°F. Line 2 large cookie sheets with parchment paper. Beat butter, vanilla and peppermint extract in a large mixer bowl on medium-high speed 2 minutes, until creamy. Reduce speed to low; beat in confectioners' sugar until smooth. Gradually beat in flour just until combined.

2. Spoon dough into a cookie press fitted with desired stencil. Press cookies onto prepared cookie sheets, placing them 1 inch apart. Bake 15 to 17 minutes, until edges are golden brown. Cool on cookie sheets 10 minutes. Transfer cookies to wire racks. Cool completely.

3. *Make white chocolate layer:* Meanwhile, bring cream and butter to simmer in a medium saucepan over medium heat. Add white chocolate and stir until smooth. Stir in peppermint extract. Transfer to a small bowl. Refrigerate 30 minutes, until firm enough to spread. Spread a measuring teaspoonful of the white chocolate mixture on flat side of each cooled cookie. Arrange cookies, white chocolate sides up, on a large foil-lined cookie sheet. Refrigerate 30 minutes, until white chocolate is firm.

4. *Make dark chocolate coating:* Place chocolate and shortening in a medium microwaveproof bowl; microwave on High 2 minutes, until melted and smooth. Spread 1 measuring teaspoonful on top of white chocolate on each cookie. Arrange cookies, chocolate sides down, on foil-lined cookie sheet. Chill 30 minutes, until dark chocolate sets. Decorate with Decorative Icing and red dot candies, if desired. Makes 3½ dozen cookies.

Per cookie: 190 calories, 10.5 g total fat, 6 g saturated fat, 19 mg cholesterol, 55 mg sodium, 23 g carbohydrates, 2 g protein, 11 mg calcium, 1 g fiber

raspberry shortbread

In Good Company • Community cookbook from the Junior League of Lynchburg, VA • Lynchburg, VA

A layer of jam hidden between a shortbread crust and a pecan topping gives these bars a richness and depth of flavor unlike any other. Pictured on page 244.

Prep time: 25 minutes plus standing
Baking time: 45 to 47 minutes

SHORTBREAD CRUST:
- 1½ cups all-purpose flour
- ½ cup granulated sugar
- ½ cup butter (no substitutes)

FILLING:
- 3 tablespoons flour
- ¼ teaspoon salt
- ¼ teaspoon baking soda
- 2 large eggs
- ½ cup firmly packed brown sugar
- 1 teaspoon vanilla extract
- ⅓ cup seedless raspberry jam
- 1 cup chopped pecans, toasted
- Confectioners' sugar (optional)

1. Heat oven to 350°F. Line a 9-inch square baking pan with foil, extending foil 1 inch past edges.

2. *Make shortbread crust:* Whisk together flour and granulated sugar in a medium bowl. With a pastry blender or 2 knives, cut in butter until mixture resembles coarse crumbs. Press evenly into the bottom of the prepared pan. Bake 20 to 22 minutes, until edges are lightly browned. Cool on a wire rack.

3. *Make filling:* Meanwhile, whisk together the flour, salt and baking soda in a small bowl. Set aside. Beat eggs, brown sugar and vanilla in a medium mixer bowl on medium-high speed until well combined. Reduce speed to low; beat in flour mixture just until blended.

4. Spread jam evenly over cooled shortbread crust. Pour filling on top of jam layer, then sprinkle pecans over top. Bake 25 minutes, until center is completely set and top is golden brown. Cool in pan on a wire rack. Lift shortbread from the pan.

Peel off foil and cut into 16 squares, then halve each diagonally. Sprinkle with confectioners' sugar, if desired. Makes 32 triangles.

Per triangle: 110 calories, 6 g total fat, 2 g saturated fat, 21 mg cholesterol, 65 mg sodium, 14 g carbohydrates, 1 g protein, 9 mg calcium, 1 g fiber

lemon sandwich cookies with poppy seeds

Oh My Stars, Recipes That Shine • Community cookbook from the Junior League of Roanoke Valley • Roanoke, VA

Poppy seeds and lemon partner to create these exquisite sandwich cookies that are sweet enough for dessert, yet perfect for a Christmas coffee with friends and family.

Prep time: 30 minutes plus chilling and standing
Baking time: 12 to 14 minutes per batch

DOUGH:
- 2¾ cups all-purpose flour
- ½ teaspoon baking powder
- ½ teaspoon salt
- 1 cup butter, softened (no substitutes)
- 1¼ cups granulated sugar
- 1 large egg
- 2 tablespoons poppy seeds
- 2½ teaspoons grated lemon peel
- 1 teaspoon vanilla extract
- ½ teaspoon lemon extract

FILLING:
- 1 package (8 oz.) cream cheese, softened
- ⅓ cup confectioners' sugar
- 1 teaspoon lemon extract
- ¼ teaspoon vanilla extract

1. *Make dough:* Whisk together the flour, baking powder and salt in a medium bowl. Beat butter and sugar in a large mixer bowl on medium-high speed until light and fluffy. Beat in egg, poppy seeds, lemon peel, vanilla and lemon extract. Reduce speed to low; gradually add flour mixture, beating just until combined. Divide dough into 3 equal pieces and flatten into thick disks. Wrap well in plastic wrap and refrigerate 2 hours or overnight.

2. Heat oven to 325°F. Working with 1 piece of dough at a time (keep remaining dough refrigerated), on a lightly floured surface, roll dough ⅛ inch thick. Cut out with a 2¾-inch star-shape cookie cutter. With a spatula, transfer cookies to a large ungreased cookie sheet, placing them ½ inch apart. With a ¾-inch round cutter, cut out centers of half of the unbaked cookies. Bake cookies 12 to 14 minutes, just until edges begin to brown. Cool on cookie sheet on a wire rack 3 to 5 minutes. Transfer cookies to wire racks and cool completely. Repeat with remaining dough, rerolling and cutting scraps.

3. *Make filling:* Beat cream cheese, confectioners' sugar, lemon and vanilla extracts in a mixer bowl on medium-high speed until smooth.

4. Spread 1 rounded measuring teaspoonful of the filling on each cookie without a hole; top each with a cookie with a hole. Decorate as desired. Makes 3 dozen sandwich cookies.

Per sandwich cookie: 135 calories, 8 g total fat, 5 g saturated fat, 27 mg cholesterol, 114 mg sodium, 15 g carbohydrates, 2 g protein, 19 mg calcium, 0 g fiber

cardamom
cookies

Concert in the Kitchen • Community cookbook from the Friends of the Portland Symphony Orchestra • Cape Elizabeth, ME
Want to add a different but tasty flavor to the holiday cookie offering? You can use any kind of cutter for these spicy rolled-out cookies.

Prep time: 20 minutes plus chilling and standing
Baking time: 7 to 8 minutes per batch

2½	**cups all-purpose flour**
1	**tablespoon cardamom**
2	**teaspoons cinnamon**
1	**teaspoon baking soda**
1	**teaspoon ginger**
1	**teaspoon cloves**
1	**teaspoon nutmeg**
1	**teaspoon allspice**
½	**teaspoon salt**

1	**cup butter or margarine, softened**
1½	**cups sugar**
1	**large egg**
1	**teaspoon molasses**
	Decorative icing (see tip, page 273) (optional)

1. Whisk together the flour, cardamom, cinnamon, baking soda, ginger, cloves, nutmeg, allspice and salt in a large bowl; set aside.

2. Beat the butter and sugar in a large mixer bowl on medium-high speed 3 minutes, until light and fluffy. Beat in egg and molasses. Reduce speed to low; beat in flour mixture just until combined. Divide dough into 4 equal pieces. Shape each piece into a thick disk; wrap well in plastic wrap and refrigerate 2 hours or overnight, until firm enough to roll out.

3. Heat oven to 400°F. Working with 1 piece of the dough at a time (keep remaining dough refrigerated), on a lightly floured surface, roll dough ⅛ inch thick. If dough is soft, freeze on cookie sheet 10 minutes. Cut out with a floured 3-inch star-shape cookie cutter. With a spatula, transfer cookies to a large, ungreased cookie sheet, placing them ½ inch apart. (If using margarine, the dough may be very soft. Freeze 10 minutes before baking.)

4. Bake 7 to 8 minutes, until edges just begin to darken. Cool cookies on cookie sheet on a wire rack 2 minutes. Transfer cookies to a wire rack and cool completely. Repeat with remaining dough, rerolling and cutting scraps. Decorate with Decorative Icing, if desired. Makes about 5 dozen cookies.

Per cookie: 65 calories, 3.5 g total fat, 2 g saturated fat, 12 mg cholesterol, 75 mg sodium, 9 g carbohydrates, 1 g protein, 3 mg calcium, 0 g fiber

kifli

Good Food Served Right • Community cookbook from Traditional Arts of Upstate New York • Canton, NY
This recipe comes from Magda Breg, who remembers serving these treats to Christmas carolers in her Hungarian town. Pictured on page 243.

Prep time: 1 hour plus chilling and standing
Baking time: 17 minutes per batch

DOUGH:

- 1 package active dry yeast
- ¼ cup warm water (105°F. to 115°F.)
- 6 large eggs, at room temperature, lightly beaten
- ⅔ cup (half of a 14-oz. can) sweetened condensed milk
- 1 teaspoon salt
- 2 tablespoons grated lemon peel
- 1 tablespoon fresh lemon juice
- 2 teaspoons almond extract
- 1½ pounds (3 cups) cold butter (no substitutes)
- 1 cup vegetable shortening
- 9 cups all-purpose flour

NUT FILLING:

- ⅔ cup (half of a 14-oz. can) sweetened condensed milk
- ½ cup butter, melted (no substitutes)
- ½ teaspoon vanilla extract
- 2 pounds toasted walnuts, coarsely chopped
- 1 cup sugar
- 2 large egg whites, lightly beaten

  ■
  Decorative Icing (see tip, page 273) (optional)
  Pearl or granulated sugar (optional)

1. ■ *Make dough:* Sprinkle yeast over warm water in a large bowl; let stand 5 minutes, until yeast is bubbly. Stir in eggs, condensed milk, salt, lemon peel, juice and almond extract until well combined.

2. ■ Meanwhile, with a pastry blender or 2 knives, cut butter and shortening into flour in a very large bowl until mixture resembles coarse crumbs. With a wooden spoon or your hands, stir in yeast mixture until well combined. Divide dough into 8 equal pieces. Shape each into a thick disk. Wrap well in plastic wrap and refrigerate overnight.

3. ■ *Make nut filling:* Combine condensed milk, butter and vanilla in a large bowl. Process half of the nuts and ½ cup of the sugar in a food processor until finely ground. Repeat with remaining nuts and ½ cup sugar. Stir nuts into butter mixture. Beat egg whites in a small mixer bowl on medium-high speed to stiff peaks. Fold egg whites into nut mixture just until blended.

4. ■ Heat oven to 350°F. Working with 1 piece of dough at a time (keep remaining dough refrigerated), roll disk between 2 sheets of floured waxed paper into a 12-inch circle. Remove top sheet of waxed paper. Cut circle into 12 equal pie-shape wedges. Spread 2 slightly rounded teaspoonfuls of the nut filling over the rounded third of each wedge. Roll wedges up from the rounded edges toward the points. Transfer to a large ungreased cookie sheet, placing them ½ inch apart and curving into crescent shapes. Repeat with remaining dough and nut filling. Bake 17 minutes, until lightly browned. Transfer to wire racks. Cool completely. Decorate as desired with Decorative Icing and pearl sugar, if desired. Makes 8 dozen.

Per kifli: 205 calories, 16 g total fat, 5.5 g saturated fat, 33 mg cholesterol, 104 mg sodium, 14 g carbohydrates, 3 g protein, 27 mg calcium, 1 g fiber

biscochitos

Seasons of Santa Fe • Community cookbook from the Kitchen Angels • Santa Fe, NM
Anise-scented Biscochitos (biz-co-cheetos) are traditional New Mexican cookies that were introduced by early Spanish settlers. Pictured on page 241.

Prep time: 15 minutes plus standing
Baking time: 10 minutes per batch

DOUGH:

- 6 cups all-purpose flour
- 1 tablespoon baking powder
- 1 teaspoon salt
- 2 cups vegetable shortening
- 1½ cups sugar
- 2 large eggs
- 1 tablespoon anise seeds
- ½ cup white wine

SUGAR TOPPING:

- **1 cup sugar**
- **2 teaspoons cinnamon**

1. ■ Heat oven to 400°F. Line 2 large cookie sheets with parchment paper.

2. ■ *Make dough:* Whisk together the flour, baking powder and salt. Beat shortening and sugar in a large mixer bowl on medium speed 2 minutes, until fluffy. Add eggs and anise seeds; beat 2 minutes, until combined. Reduce speed to low; beat in flour mixture and wine just until combined. (The dough will be stiff. That's okay.) Divide dough into quarters.

3. ■ *Make sugar topping:* Combine both ingredients in a medium shallow bowl or pie plate. Set aside.

4. ■ On a floured surface, roll one piece of the dough ¼ inch thick. Cut dough with 3-inch cookie cutters. With a small spatula, transfer cut-outs to prepared cookie sheets, placing them 1 inch apart. Using the tip of a small spoon, press indentations along outer edge of each cookie. Repeat with remaining dough, rerolling and cutting scraps. Bake 10 minutes, until lightly golden. Cool on cookie sheets on wire racks 5 minutes.

5. ■ Dredge the warm cookies in sugar topping. Cool the cookies completely on wire racks. Makes 7 dozen cookies.

Per cookie: 100 calories, 5 g total fat, 1.5 g saturated fat, 5 mg cholesterol, 44 mg sodium, 12 g carbohydrates, 1 g protein, 12 mg calcium, 0 g fiber

butter fudge fingers 🄴🄰🅂🅈

Twice Treasured Recipes • Community cookbook from The Bargain Box of Hilton Head Island • Hilton Head, SC
These bars have been baked by John Jakes' family for over 50 years. Pictured on page 244.

Prep time: 30 minutes plus standing
Baking time: 22 to 26 minutes

CHOCOLATE LAYER:

- **¾ cup all-purpose flour**
- **½ teaspoon baking powder**
- **½ teaspoon salt**
- **⅓ cup butter or margarine, melted**
- **2 ounces unsweetened chocolate squares, melted**
- **1 cup granulated sugar**
- **2 large eggs**
- **½ cup chopped pecans, toasted**

BUTTERCREAM TOPPING:

- **¼ cup butter or margarine, melted**
- **2 cups sifted confectioners' sugar**
- **2 tablespoons heavy or whipping cream**
- **1 tablespoon vanilla extract**

CHOCOLATE DRIZZLE:

- **1 ounce unsweetened chocolate square, melted**
- **1 tablespoon butter or margarine, melted**
- ■ **Assorted dot candies (optional)**

1. ■ *Make chocolate layer:* Heat oven to 350°F. Line an 8-inch square baking pan with foil. Grease foil. Whisk together the flour, baking powder and salt in a medium bowl. Set both aside.

2. ■ Place butter and chocolate in a large microwaveproof bowl; microwave on High 1½ to 2 minutes, until melted. Transfer to a large mixer bowl; beat in granulated sugar and eggs on medium-high speed 2 to 3 minutes, until well combined. Reduce speed to low; beat in flour mixture just until combined. Fold in pecans. Pour batter into prepared pan. Bake 22 to 26 minutes, just until edges begin to pull away from the side of pan and mixture is just set in middle. Cool completely on a wire rack.

3. ■ *Make buttercream topping:* Beat all ingredients together in a large mixer bowl on medium speed 1 minute, until smooth. Reduce speed to low; beat 1 to 2 minutes more, until fluffy and smooth.

4. ■ *Make chocolate drizzle:* Stir chocolate and butter together in a small bowl until smooth. Cool slightly and transfer to a small resealable plastic storage bag.

5. ■ Lift chocolate layer out of pan. Peel off foil. Transfer to a flat surface lined with waxed paper. Spread buttercream evenly over top of chocolate layer. Snip a tiny hole in 1 corner of bag; drizzle chocolate drizzle over top. Let stand 30 minutes to 1 hour, until chocolate is set. Cut into 4×1-inch bars. Decorate with dot candies, if desired. Makes 16 bars.

Per bar: 255 calories, 14.5 g total fat, 7.5 g saturated fat, 50 mg cholesterol, 175 mg sodium, 31 g carbohydrates, 2 g protein, 22 mg calcium, 1 g fiber

holiday mincemeat cookies with coffee frosting EASY

A Thyme to Remember • Community cookbook from The Dallas County Medical Society Alliance • Dallas, TX

Sarah Jo Hardin, contributor of this recipe, says, "This recipe was handed down to me from my great grandmother who homesteaded in Billings, Oklahoma, after the Oklahoma Land Run in 1889. She used simple farm ingredients that included making her own mincemeat. I made a simple coffee frosting to update the recipe, giving it an elegant touch for holiday entertaining." Pictured on page 241.

Prep time: 20 minutes plus standing
Baking time: 10 to 12 minutes per batch

DOUGH:

- 3 **cups all-purpose flour**
- 1 **teaspoon baking soda**
- ½ **teaspoon salt**
- 1 **cup vegetable shortening**
- 1½ **cups granulated sugar**
- 3 **large eggs**
- 1⅓ **cups mincemeat**

COFFEE FROSTING:

- 1 **box (1 lb.) confectioners' sugar**
- ½ **cup butter or margarine, melted**
- 2 **tablespoons cold brewed coffee**
- 96 **toasted pecan halves**

1. *Make dough:* Heat oven to 375°F. Line 2 large cookie sheets with parchment paper. Whisk together flour, baking soda and salt in a medium bowl. Beat shortening and granulated sugar in a large mixer bowl on medium-high speed 2 minutes, until light and fluffy. Beat in eggs, one at time, beating well after each addition. Reduce speed to low; gradually add flour mixture, beating just until combined. Stir in mincemeat until well combined.

2. Arrange measuring tablespoonfuls of the dough on prepared cookie sheets, placing them 2 inches apart. Bake 10 to 12 minutes, until golden brown. Cool cookies on cookie sheets on wire racks 1 minute. Transfer cookies to wire racks and cool completely.

3. *Make coffee frosting:* Meanwhile, beat all ingredients in a large bowl on medium speed until smooth.

4. Spread a rounded measuring teaspoonful of the coffee frosting on top of each cooled cookie. Top each cookie with 1 pecan half. Makes about 8 dozen cookies.

Per cookie: 95 calories, 4.5 g total fat, 1.5 g saturated fat, 9 mg cholesterol, 49 mg sodium, 13 g carbohydrates, 1 g protein, 4 mg calcium, 0 g fiber

test kitchen tip

mad for mincemeat

For those who have never had the pleasure of consuming or cooking with this underrated culinary delight, mincemeat is a spicy preserves made of a variety of fruit including chopped cherries, apples or pears, dried apricots, raisins, candied citrus peel, nuts, beef suet, spices and brandy or rum. Like many preserves, after it's made it matures for a month or so, allowing the flavors to blend. Mincemeat comes in jars and is found in local supermarkets. Besides being used in the dough of our tasty holiday cookies, mincemeat also can be used in tarts, pies and puddings.

nutrition information

To help you plan well-balanced meals, calorie and nutrient analyses appear at the end of each of our recipes.

how we analyze

- When a recipe gives a choice of ingredients, such as butter or margarine, we use the first ingredient mentioned when figuring the analysis.

- When the recipe gives a range in the amount of an ingredient, we average the two amounts. For example, if a recipe calls for ½ to 1 lb. of boneless beef top loin steak, we use ¾ pound when figuring the analysis.

- The analysis docs not include optional ingredients.

- When there is a range in the amount of servings a recipe yields, the nutrition analysis is based on the average of the two numbers. For example, if a recipe serves 4 to 6, the analysis is based on 5 servings.

- When milk is a recipe ingredient, the analysis is calculated using whole milk.

- Nutrition values are rounded to the nearest whole number, with the exception of calories, which are rounded to the nearest 5 calories, and total fat and saturated fat, which are rounded to the nearest .5 grams.

daily goal

The dietary guidelines below are nutrient levels suggested for moderately active adults. While there's no harm in occasionally going over or under these guidelines, maintaining a balanced diet can help you maintain good health.

	WOMEN	MEN
Calories	2,000	2,500
Total fat	60 g or less	70 g or less
Saturated fat	20 g or less	23 g or less
Cholesterol	300 mg or less	300 mg or less
Sodium	2,400 mg or less	2,400 mg or less
Carbohydrates	250 g or more	250 g or more
Protein	55 g to 90 g	55 g to 90 g
Calcium	1,000 mg	1,000 mg
Fiber	20 g to 35 g	20 g to 35 g

low-fat recipes

In planning a healthy diet, it's a good idea to try to keep the percentage of calories from fat to no more than 30 percent. To help you choose recipes that are low in fat, some of our recipes have been flagged with a low-fat symbol. This means that one serving of the recipe contains less than 3 grams of fat per 100 calories.

substitutions in a pinch

It's always best to use the exact ingredients a recipe calls for. But for those times when that's not possible, here are a few substitution ideas. Because they may affect the success of the recipe, use them only in a pinch.

BAKING POWDER
For 1 teaspoon: Use ½ teaspoon cream of tartar plus ¼ teaspoon baking soda.

BOK CHOY
Use equal amount spinach, broccolini, or napa cabbage.

BREADCRUMBS, PLAIN DRY
For 1 cup: Use ¾ cup cracker crumbs.

BROTH, BEEF OR CHICKEN
For 1 cup: Use 1 bouillon cube or 1 teaspoon granules mixed with 1 cup boiling water.

BUTTERMILK
For 1 cup: Use 1 tablespoon lemon juice or vinegar plus enough milk to make 1 cup (let stand 5 minutes before using); or 1 cup plain yogurt.

CAKE FLOUR
For 1 cup: Use 1 cup minus 2 tablespoons all-purpose flour.

CANADIAN BACON
Use equal amount smoked lean ham slices.

CAPERS
Use equal amount chopped pitted green olives.

CATFISH
Use equal amount of red snapper or sea trout.

CHOCOLATE CHIPS
For 1 cup: Use 1 cup chopped semisweet chocolate squares.

CORNSTARCH
For 1 tablespoon: Use 2 tablespoons all-purpose flour.

CORN SYRUP
For 1 cup: Use 1 cup granulated sugar plus ¼ cup water.

CURRANTS (DRIED)
Use equal amount dark seedless raisins.

EGGS
For each whole egg, use 2 egg whites; 2 egg yolks; or ¼ cup frozen egg product, thawed.

ESPRESSO POWDER
Use equal amount instant coffee crystals.

FIVE-SPICE POWDER
Combine 4 teaspoons black peppercorns (preferably Szechuan), 1 tablespoon cinnamon, 2 teaspoons fennel seeds, 2 teaspoons anise or 6 star anise and ½ teaspoon cloves. Blend in a spice or coffee grinder until powdery. Measure amount needed.

FRUIT-FLAVORED LIQUEUR
Use equal amount fruit juice that has the same flavor of the liqueur called for.

HERBS
To substitute dried herbs for fresh: For 1 tablespoon snipped fresh herb, use ½ to 1 teaspoon dried herb, crushed.
To substitute fresh herbs for dried herbs: Generally, triple the amount of dried herb called for. Add fresh herbs toward the end of cooking time; the exception is rosemary, which can withstand a long cooking time.

GARLIC
For 1 small clove: Use ⅛ teaspoon garlic powder.

substitutions in a pinch

FRESH GINGER (GINGERROOT)
For 1 teaspoon grated fresh ginger (gingerroot): Use ¼ teaspoon ground ginger.

GRAHAM CRACKER CRUMBS
Use equal amount vanilla wafer crumbs.

GRUYÈRE CHEESE
Use equal amount Swiss cheese.

HALF-AND-HALF OR LIGHT CREAM
For 1 cup: Use 1 tablespoon melted butter or margarine plus enough whole milk to make 1 cup.

HAZELNUTS
Use equal amount blanched almonds.

KALAMATA OLIVES
Use equal amount other brine-cured olives.

LEMON JUICE
For 1 teaspoon: Use ½ teaspoon vinegar.

LEMON OR ORANGE PEEL, GRATED
Use a few drops lemon or orange extract.

LENTILS
Use equal amount green split peas; cook longer.

MASCARPONE CHEESE
Use equal amount whipped cream cheese.

NUTMEG
Use equal amount mace.

ROMANO CHEESE
Use equal amount Parmesan cheese.

SEMISWEET CHOCOLATE SQUARES
For each ounce: Use 3 tablespoons semisweet chocolate chips. Or use 1 ounce unsweetened chocolate plus 1 tablespoon sugar.

SWEET BAKING CHOCOLATE SQUARES
(Also known as German chocolate) For 4 ounces: Use ¼ cup unsweetened cocoa plus ⅓ cup sugar and 3 tablespoons shortening.

SUGAR (CONFECTIONERS')
For 1 cup: Whirl 1 cup granulated sugar and 1 tablespoon cornstarch in a food processor until powdery.

SUGAR (GRANULATED)
For 1 cup: Use one cup of firmly packed brown sugar or 2 cups confectioners' sugar.

TERIYAKI SAUCE
For ¼ cup: Use ¼ cup soy sauce plus 1 tablespoon brown sugar.

TOMATO SAUCE
For 2 cups: Use ¾ cup tomato paste plus 1 cup water.

WATERCRESS
Use equal amount arugula or chicory.

WORCESTERSHIRE SAUCE
Use equal amount steak sauce.

YELLOW SUMMER SQUASH
Use equal amount zucchini.

index

EASY RECIPES
indicated with a 🖐

LOW-FAT AND NO-FAT RECIPES
indicated with a 💛

PHOTOGRAPHS
indicated in **bold italics**